Teaching for Quality Learning at University

SRHE and Open University Press Imprint

Current titles include:

Teaching for Quality Learning at University

What the Student Does

3rd edition

John Biggs and Catherine Tang

Society for Research into Higher Education
& Open University Press

Open University Press
McGraw-Hill Education
McGraw-Hill House
Shoppenhangers Road
Maidenhead
Berkshire
England
SL6 2QL

email: enquiries@openup.co.uk
world wide web: www.openup.co.uk

and Two Penn Plaza, New York, NY 10121–2289, USA

First edition published 1999
Second edition published 2003
This third edition published 2007
Reprinted 2009

A catalogue record of this book is available from the British Library

ISBN-10 0 335 22126 2 (pb)   0 335 22127 0 (hb)
ISBN-13: 978 0 335 22126 4 (pb)   978 0 335 22127 1 (hb)

Library of Congress Cataloging-in-Publication Data
CIP data has been applied for

Typeset by RefineCatch Limited, Bungay, Suffolk
Printed in Great Britain by Ashford Colour Press Ltd, Gosport, Hants.
www.ashford-colour-press.co.uk

The McGraw·Hill Companies

Learning takes place through the active behavior of the student: it is what *he* does that he learns, not what the teacher does.

Ralph W. Tyler (1949)

If students are to learn desired outcomes in a reasonably effective manner, then the teacher's fundamental task is to get students to engage in learning activities that are likely to result in their achieving those outcomes. . . . It is helpful to remember that what the student does is actually more important in determining what is learned than what the teacher does.

Thomas J. Shuell (1986)

Contents

List of boxes

List of figures

List of tables

List of tasks

Foreword to original edition

The book is an exceptional introduction to some difficult ideas. It is full of downright good advice for every academic who wants to do something practical to improve his or her students' learning. So much of what we read on this subject is either a recycling of sensible advice topped by a thin layer of second-hand theory, or a dense treatise suitable for graduate students with a taste for the tougher courses. Not many writers are able to take the reader along the middle road, where theory applied with a delicate touch enables us to transform our practice. What is unique about Biggs is his way with words, his outspoken fluency, his precision, his depth of knowledge, his inventiveness, or rather how he blends all these things together. Like all good teachers, he engages us from the start, and he never talks down to us. He achieves unity between his objectives, his teaching methods and his assessment; and thus, to adapt his own phrase, he entraps the reader in a web of consistency that optimizes his or her own learning.

Perhaps not everyone will agree with Biggs's treatment of the academic differences between phenomenography and constructivism. I'm not sure I do myself. But does it matter? The author himself takes a pragmatic approach. In the daunting task that faces lecturers in responding to the pressures of mass higher education, reduced public funding, and students who are paying more for their education, the bottom line of engineering better learning outcomes matters more than nice theoretical distinctions.

Readers of the present book will especially enjoy its marvellous treatment of student assessment (particularly Chapters 3, 8 and 9).* Biggs's most outstanding single contribution to education has been the creation of the Structure of the Observed Learning Outcome (SOLO) taxonomy. Rather than read about the extraordinary practical utility of this device in secondary sources, get it from the original here. From assessing clinical decision

---

* This material is covered in Chapters 5, 9, 10 and 11 in the present edition.

making by medical students to classifying the outcomes of essays in history, SOLO remains the assessment apparatus of choice.

There are very few writers on the subject of university teaching who can engage a reader so personally, express doubts so clearly, relate research findings so eloquently to personal experience and open our eyes to the wonder around us. John Biggs is a rare thing: an author who has the humility born of generosity and intelligence to show us how he is still learning himself.

Paul Ramsden
Brisbane

Preface to third edition

It is very gratifying to discover that, since the second edition of this book, the concept of 'constructive alignment' has become part of the working theory not only of individual teachers, researchers and teaching developers, but has been implemented in many institutions and is now part of the language of quality assurance on a systemic basis. Google 'constructive alignment' and you now get over 24,000 references.

This upsurge of interest in constructive alignment is paralleled by that in outcomes-based education (OBE): this is not surprising, given that constructive alignment is itself one form of OBE. Unfortunately, there are other forms of OBE that have received a less than favourable press. To make sure we keep constructively aligned OBE quite separate from the others, we refer to ours as one instance of outcomes-based teaching and learning (OBTL). Our concern is *exclusively* with enhancing learning through quality teaching, not with managerialism, on the one hand, or with politically controversial school-based curricula, on the other. These tangled skeins are unravelled in Chapter 1.

However, this edition is not intended only for those interested in outcomes-based education. The major intention is as it has always been: to enhance teaching and learning through reflective practice using constructive alignment as the framework for reflection.

An important feature of this edition is that whereas in previous editions Catherine Tang was acknowledged as 'a continuing source of inspiration' to JB, she is now on board as co-author. While Catherine was head of staff development at the Hong Kong Polytechnic University (PolyU), she initiated an inter-institutional project implementing constructive alignment, funded by the University Grants Committee (UGC) of Hong Kong, resulting eventually in the PolyU adopting constructive alignment throughout the university. Then both of us were invited as consultants to the institution-wide implementation of OBTL, in the form of constructive alignment, at the City University of Hong Kong. This experience has taught us a great deal, not only about implementing constructive alignment in different disciplines in individual classrooms, but also about the strategies – and the politics – of implementation on an institution-wide basis. The UGC is currently committed to bring outcomes-based education, of which constructive alignment is one example, to all eight Hong Kong tertiary institutions in due course.

The language of OBE has become widespread and for that reason, this edition uses that language consistently: for example, we now speak of 'intended learning outcomes' (ILOs), not 'curriculum objectives' as before. In fact, we are grateful for the reminder, because 'curriculum objectives' wasn't quite the right term anyway, as we discuss in Chapter 5.

Our recent experience has also resulted in several changes from previous editions, apart from terminology. One is that we are concerned with implementation at the institutional level as well as in the classroom. What were in the previous edition special topics – large class teaching, using educational technology, teaching international students – are now dealt with as all part of designing and implementing constructively aligned teaching and assessment. Educational technology is now so much an integral part of university teaching that it should be treated as such, not as a special topic. And while international students undoubtedly have specials needs with regard to provision for language and social support, when teaching is focused on students' learning activities that are aligned to the intended outcomes of learning, the need to teach to presumed differences between students on the grounds of ethnicity disappears, as was made clear in the previous edition.

Another change is that, following our own hands-on experience with implementing constructive alignment, this edition is even more practically oriented than the last, aimed directly at practising teachers, staff developers and administrators. Readers looking for a comprehensive update of research into student learning will not find it here. We do, however, provide two or three tasks in every chapter, making some 28 tasks in all. Doing those tasks as you, the reader, progress will without doubt enhance your understanding of constructive alignment, but you may prefer to tackle those tasks if and when you are seriously attempting to implement constructive alignment in your own teaching. In that case, the tasks are virtually a 'how-to' manual. To emphasize that practical orientation, and to show that implementation is possible under a variety of conditions, the final chapter gives concrete examples of implementing constructive alignment on a faculty-wide basis and of recently constructively aligned curricula in various subjects. We also provide URLs for some excellent material that is 'up there' waiting to be accessed.

Finally, a further note on terminology. Many different terms are used to refer to degree programmes and the unit courses making up those programmes. Bachelor's degree programmes we refer to as 'programmes', which some refer to as 'courses'. The units of study that make up programmes we call 'courses', which others refer to as 'units', modules' or 'subjects'.

John Biggs, Catherine Tang
Hobart, Tasmania

Acknowledgements

As was stated in the acknowledgements in the first and second editions, there are many ideas in this book that came about through interacting with friends and colleagues over the years. These are not repeated here.

For this edition, we must mention Professor Richard Ho, for bringing us on board at the City University of Hong Kong, and Aman Shah, Tracy Lo, Roger Fung and Helen Mak, for expediting our work there. Others who have been directly helpful in providing stimulation, ideas and content for this edition are: Denise Chalmers, Catherine Chiu, Melanie Collier, Alan Dunnett, Mark Endean, Ron Kwok, David Johnston, Olivia Leung, Lawrence Li, Peter Looker, Janice McKay, Elaine Payne, Paul Ramsden, Paul Shin, Rosanne Taylor, Agnes Tiwari, Patrick Wong and Sandy Wong.

Finally, we must thank Katy Hamilton, Louise Caswell, Shona Mullen and Catriona Watson of McGraw-Hill/Open University Press who have seen us through this edition, patiently and helpfully.

John Biggs, Catherine Tang
Hobart, Tasmania

When you have read this book

When you have read this book you should be able to:

1 Explain to a colleague what 'constructive alignment' is and where it fits into other models of outcomes-based education.
2 Write a set of no more than five or six *intended learning outcomes*, each containing a key 'learning verb', for a semester-long course you are teaching.
3 Reflect on your current teaching using the constructive alignment framework and devise:

   - *teaching/learning activities* that address your intended learning outcomes and that activate those key verbs
   - *assessment tasks* that likewise address those key verbs
   - *rubrics* or criteria for assessment that enable judgments to be made as to how well your outcomes have been addressed.

4 Develop quality enhancement processes for your own teaching.
5 Identify quality assurance and enhancement processes within your institution that support the implementation of constructively aligned teaching.

1

The changing scene in university teaching

In the days when university classes contained highly selected students, the lecture and tutorial seemed to work well enough. However, the increasingly drastic changes in the tertiary sector have redrawn the university scene – not entirely disadvantageously for teaching quality. With student fees now a high proportion of funding, universities have had to improve the quality of their teaching. Many are using constructive alignment – what this book is about – as the means of doing so. We see how it may do that by looking at two very different students, Susan and Robert, who we are likely to meet in today's classrooms.

The nature of the change

The university sector in most western and some eastern countries continues to change at an increasingly hectic rate. A major difference in the period separating this edition from the last, published in 2003, is that there is now an increasing recognition that teaching and learning have been neglected in favour of leaner and meaner universities – and that something needs to be done about it, particularly given that teaching now has a higher priority in most of today's universities. How this came about is rather paradoxical.

Twenty years ago, public funding paid for virtually 100% of costs of the tertiary sector, but today that is very far from being the case. Australia, for example, is now heading towards 30% of university funding from the public purse. The bulk of the missing funding comes from student fees. That is having profound effects on both students and on university teaching.

However, the reason for the enormous cuts in public funding was not only to save money and keep taxes low, although that was the rhetoric; it was ideological. It stems from the neo-conservative belief that education is a private good and therefore one should pay for it, like one does for any other goods. That changed the nature of universities and the university mission: they became corporatized and competitive for markets.

First, let us look at what happened to teaching and learning.

Teaching and learning

Now that students have to pay higher fees, they will be likely to demand high-profile programmes that are well taught and will enhance their employment prospects. Those who can, will shop around to find the right one for them. Some, using the logic that education is a commodity to be bought, feel that having paid for a degree they are entitled to be awarded one. The pressures on staff are complex: to teach in a student-friendly manner, but that may encourage them to lower standards. Such downward pressures, in some celebrated cases, have also emanated from administration, because of the funding implications of failing students.

Universities in many Asian countries have improved their teaching considerably, so that the cost benefits of Asian students leaving their countries to complete a degree are, for Hong Kong, Singaporean, Malaysian, Korean and increasingly PRC students, not so apparent as they once were. There'll always be linguistic and cultural reasons for moving to another country to study, but the *educational* case for international students to study abroad is not nearly as strong as it once was. Universities will need to provide teaching of a quality well above that which these students would receive in their home countries, not to mention making special provision for them in providing a supportive extracurricular environment and services.

Despite the financial disincentives, a greater proportion of school leavers is now in higher education. Ten years ago the proportion was around 15%; now it is over 40% in many countries, and some politicians are signalling a target of up to 60%. The brightest and most committed students still go to university, as they have in the past, but they sit alongside students of rather different academic bent. The *range* of ability within classes is now considerable, which presents teaching-related problems to staff.

Cramming students into large lecture halls is no longer good enough. Many universities, accepting that teaching is no longer the poor cousin of research, have responded positively with an increasingly teaching-friendly environment. It is increasingly being recognized that good teaching is as much a function of an institution-wide infrastructure as it is a gift with which some lucky academics are born. Many universities are funding on a larger scale than previously staff development centres and centres for teaching and learning, giving recognition of research into teaching one's content area as legitimate research, and accepting an institution-wide responsibility for teaching-related issues, with policies and procedures that encourage good teaching and assessment.

In sum, under the new financial arrangements in universities, both teaching quality and maintenance of standards are under greater pressure than ever. However, as argued in previous editions of this book, maintaining standards when the quality of students is so diverse is indeed possible. This is the 'Robert and Susan' problem, to which we return later in this chapter. The solution to the problem, briefly, is a matter of immersing students in a teaching environment that requires them to use learning activities that are likely to lead to the intended outcomes – and we use constructive alignment to achieve this.

If a focus on improving teaching at the classroom level is one consequence of the rigorous new financial regime on universities, it had quite a different effect on the management of institutions.

Managerial concerns

The new agenda for universities, to sell education and to provide for market needs, makes them like any other corporation that sells a product. Vice-chancellors become CEOs of a firm; the administration, top heavy with managers, dictates policy and such matters as what courses are to be taught and what are to be cut. This has enormous implications for both research and teaching, but we concentrate only on the latter here.

The managerial climate demands a new modularized credit-based curriculum, accountability and quality assurance. If a degree is a commodity to be sold, then the 'customer' will demand assurance as to the quality of the product, and that a degree commenced in one university can be completed in another. As students move between university and workforce and back to university, or start their degree at one institution and finish at another, they can trade in credit transfers. Hence the appearance of benchmarking institutions, in a more formalized attempt to standardize the outcomes of education than the previous external examiner system and of the modularization of degree programmes.

One version of outcomes-based education (OBE) made its appearance as a means of benchmarking and increasing accountability – but the outcomes are at institutional rather than the course level. This application and theory of OBE is quite different from that in outcomes-based teaching and learning, and constructive alignment in particular, which is concerned with more effective teaching and assessment at the course and programme level. We discuss these differences between different types of outcomes-based education later.

A danger of benchmarking and the credit transfer curriculum is that one of the important characteristics of the university, the pursuit of excellence, is endangered. Ideally, departments should build on their strengths so that they became renowned for their research and teaching in a specific area of the discipline. Credit transfers, however, may work on the equivalence not only of standards but of curriculum, so the net effect is likely not to differentiate but to homogenize the offerings between universities. Care must be taken that credit transfers do not 'dumb down' institutions to the standards of the weakest. Many stakeholders are aware of this problem, claiming that market forces will force universities to continue to offer better quality, and/or different, programmes than the opposition.

Universities have attempted to meet these demands relating to quality and differentiation with 'graduate attributes'. These are outcome statements at institutional level to the effect that graduates of any of university X's degree programmes will display certain attributes that employers would find attractive, and that hopefully might distinguish them from graduates from other universities. Such attributes would include 'creativity', 'independent problem solving', 'professional skills', 'communications skills', 'teamwork', 'lifelong learning', and so on.

Graduate attributes are conceived in mainly two different ways: as *generic*, comprising context-free qualities of individuals, as if graduates are simply 'creative' whatever they do; or as *embedded*, that is, as abilities or ways of handling issues that are context dependent, so that creativity is only guaranteed, as it were, in a graduate's content area. We take the embedded view here, as developed in Chapter 5. The generic view of graduate attributes often comes close to personality change. One university we know states categorically that 'a university X graduate *is* culturally sensitive' (our emphasis) – in which case, a university X graduate arrested for inciting a race riot would seem to have an excellent case for suing university X for failing to deliver. These 'hard', context-free claims, reifying the attribute, are hard to sustain as anything else but spin, and an inappropriate use of outcomes-based education. As Hussey and Smith (2002) put it, outcomes 'have been misappropriated and adopted widely . . . to facilitate the managerial process'.

We need to carefully distinguish between outcomes-based approaches that are used managerially and those that are used to enhance teaching and learning. An anonymous review that appeared on the Amazon UK site of the last edition of this book didn't make that distinction. It read in part:

> The book (*Teaching for Quality Learning at University*) as a whole is an apology for the fraudulent way in which higher education is currently managed at an institutional level.

Either the reviewer hadn't read the book or the previous edition wasn't clear enough that the very last thing this book is meant to be is an apology for managerialism (see also Biggs and Davis 2001). It is not meant to be an attack either, except in so far as managerial concerns override educational concerns, to the detriment of the latter – which can be a danger, as we examine in Chapter 12.

So let us be absolutely clear about where we stand on outcomes-based education in the present edition. As we explain here, outcomes-based education refers to very different kinds of animal, some with bad names.

What then is outcomes-based education?

Since the previous edition of this book, the principles of constructive alignment have become widely used, under the more general label of 'outcomes-based education' (OBE) or 'outcomes-based teaching and learning' (OBTL). Outcomes-based teaching and learning is a convenient and practical way of maintaining standards and of improving teaching. Standards are stated up front and teaching is tuned to best meet them, assessment being the means of checking how well they have been met.

Outcomes-based education (OBE) has been used in quite different ways: for enhancing teaching and learning, and for furthering a managerial agenda. Outcomes-based education is sometimes identified with competency-based education. This is a mistake: competency-based education is just one example of outcomes-based education. Where it differs from other forms of OBE is in the definition of the outcomes, which in competency-based education are narrow competencies such as skills. For this reason, competency-based education is common in vocational and technical education. Constructive alignment might be called 'competency-based' if we restricted our intended learning outcomes to competencies and skills – but as we don't so restrict the level of our intended learning outcomes, but extend them to as high a cognitive level a university teacher wants, constructive alignment cannot be identified with competency-based education.

Yet another version of OBE has in the last decade become headline news, damned as 'the Nazi model' (Kjos no date), 'left wing propaganda' (Donnelly 2004), an 'infection in the Australian education system' (Brendan Nelson, one-time Australian Federal Minister of Education).

The fact that the same term, outcomes-based, has been used in these different ways has created immense confusion, not to say mischief – as indeed we have seen in the case of our anonymous Amazon reviewer. Because of the confusions, and the emotion that OBE has aroused, we must clarify what we are talking about, and forthwith.

OBE version one

William Spady (1994) proposed an individualized programme for disadvantaged school students that he called 'outcome-based education'. Instead of teaching the standard disciplines, he set up targets for each student to reach so that all could achieve some sort of success. What attracted most ire was that his targets included a values component of a general humanistic kind that Christian fundamentalists thought were not the school system's business. The Spady model, less some of the values outcomes, was picked up and adapted by several Australian state education departments. However, they made the bad mistakes, so some thought, of designing cross-disciplinary targets – no more 'basics', you see – and of using a sort of postmodern management-speak that many parents and teachers didn't understand and that conservative politicians took for left-wing propaganda.

OBE version two

This version comes from the accountability movement in the USA (Ewell 1984; Miller and Ewell 2005). Here the 'outcomes' are at the institutional level, comprising averaged student performances and other kinds of institutional outcomes, in order to meet accreditation requirements and the requests of external stakeholders like employers and policymakers. Most US institutions now have a set of outcomes statements in place, constructed with the aid of an enormous 'template' comprising four dimensions and 12 sub-dimensions, each containing its own outcomes (Ewell 1984): knowledge outcomes (two sub-dimensions), skills outcomes (two sub-dimensions), attitude/value outcomes (four sub-dimensions), and relationships with society and with particular constituency outcomes (four sub-dimensions). The possible total of outcomes amounts to 48 in all.

Unfortunately, the term 'assessment' in the USA can mean assessing individual students, as it does in most other English-speaking countries, but it can also mean assessing at the institutional level, as in quality assurance. This double meaning causes a great deal of confusion, suggesting to teachers that they should be teaching and assessing students on all or most outcome dimensions and sub-dimensions. Benchmarking exercises require teachers to stipulate how the courses they teach meet these outcome statements, using them as a template, but in our experience many teachers see each dimension and its sub-dimensions not just for benchmarking but as mandatory in their teaching and assessment of students, creating a procrustean monster to which they are to fit their own course outcome statements. As we see in Chapter 5, programme and course outcomes alike should rarely exceed five or six in number, otherwise it is practically impossible to align teaching/learning activities and assessment tasks to them all.

OBE version three

The final version we distinguish is outcomes-based teaching and learning (OBTL), which had its seeds in the Dearing Report (1997), where outcomes are defined specifically to enhance teaching and assessment, not to serve any other purpose*.

The essential features of OBTL are that, first, we state what we intend the outcomes of our teaching a particular course or programme to be. An

---

* Hong Kong's University Grants Committee has just adopted the very appropriate 'Outcomes-based Approaches to Student Learning' (OBASL)

outcome statement is a statement of how we would recognize if or how well students have learned what is intended they should learn, not a prompt list of topics for teachers to 'cover' in a curriculum. Such an outcome statement tells us what, and how well, students are able to do something that they were unable, or only partially able, to do before teaching. Good teachers have always had some idea of that – that is one reason why they are good teachers. In outcomes-based teaching and learning, we are simply making that as explicit as we can – always allowing for unintended but desirable outcomes. Teachers and critics often overlook this last point; that students may also learn outcomes that hadn't been foreseen, but which are eminently desirable. Of course, we should allow for these in our assessment strategies! The issue of unexpected or unintended outcomes is discussed in Chapter 9.

The second essential feature of outcomes-based teaching and learning is that teaching should be done in such a way as to increase the likelihood of most students achieving those outcomes. Talking about the topic, as in traditional teaching, is probably not the best way of doing that. We need to engage the students in learning activities that directly link to achieving the intended outcomes. The Susan and Robert story in the next section expands on this point.

The third essential feature is that we need to assess how well the outcomes have been achieved. Usually this means using an assessment task that requires the student to perform the intended outcome itself. This, in many cases, is not best achieved by giving students questions to which they write answers in an invigilated exam room.

Constructive alignment, the theme of this book and its previous editions, differs from other forms of outcomes-based teaching and learning in that in constructive alignment we systematically align the teaching/learning activities, and the assessment tasks to the intended learning outcomes, according to the *learning activities* required in the outcomes.

All this might sound difficult, time consuming and way too idealistic. That is not what an increasingly large number of university teachers are finding. This book will explain the background and lead you through all the stages of implementing constructive alignment, but using the outcomes-based terminology that is now current.

In order to clarify the distinctions made in this section, and in the hope of standardizing usage that to date has been all over the place, we propose Box 1.1. Previously, there has been little consistency about hyphenation and the use of outcome- or outcomes-: both sometimes appear in the same article.

So, let outcome-(singular)-based education (OBE) refer to version one, the Spady model; outcomes-(plural)-based education (OBE) refer to version two, the Ewell and like managerial models; and outcomes-based teaching and learning (OBTL) refer to version three. In this book, the form of OBTL we are using is where constructive alignment is the means of enhancing teaching and learning.

Box 1.1   Outcomes-based education, outcomes based education, outcome-based education and outcome based education: Which do we use?

To hyphen or not to hyphen?

Google produces identical results with or without the hyphen. Usage suggests the hyphen so let's keep it.

Outcomes-based education or outcome-based education?

Outcomes-based education: 155,000 Google hits. These mostly refer to OBE at the tertiary level.

Outcome-based education: 51,000 Google hits. These refer to school, primary and secondary levels, and to the tertiary level. However, William Spady first used the term *outcome*-based at school level, so let's keep it at that.

Solution

Outcomes-based education for tertiary. Outcome-based education for school level.

Problem

But in that case how do we distinguish the top-down managerialist OBE, which is mainly concerned with institutional-level outcomes from our OBE, which is concerned with excellent classroom teaching?

Solution

Top-down managerialist OBE can stay as it is and welcome.

Classroom-level OBE addresses teaching and learning: hence OBTL.

Constructive alignment (22,900 Google results at time of writing) is OBTL that aligns teaching and assessment to the intended learning outcomes (see Chapter 4).

Now let us return to the changing scene in university education and its effects on teaching and learning by looking at the 'Robert and Susan' problem.

Making Robert learn like Susan

Let us look at two students attending a lecture. Susan is academically committed; she is bright, interested in her studies and wants to do well. She has clear academic or career plans and what she learns is important to her. When she learns, she goes about it in an 'academic' way. She comes to the lecture with sound, relevant background knowledge, possibly some questions she wants answering. In the lecture, she finds an answer to a preformed question; it forms the keystone for a particular arch of knowledge she is constructing. Or it may not be the answer she is looking for and she speculates, wondering why it isn't. In either event, she reflects on the personal significance of what she is learning. Students like Susan virtually teach themselves; they typically do not need much help from us.

Now take Robert. He is at university not out of a driving curiosity about a particular subject or a burning ambition to excel in a particular profession, but to obtain a qualification for a decent job. A few years ago, he would never have considered going to university. He is less committed than Susan, possibly not as bright, academically speaking. He has little background of relevant knowledge. He comes to lectures with few questions. He wants only to put in sufficient effort to pass. Robert hears the lecturer say the same words as Susan is hearing but he doesn't see a keystone, just another brick to be recorded in his lecture notes. He believes that if he can record enough of these bricks and can remember them on cue, he'll keep out of trouble come exam time.

Students like Robert are in higher proportions in today's classes. They do need help if they are to achieve the acceptable levels of understanding. To say that Robert is 'unmotivated' may be true but it is unhelpful. All it means is that he is not responding to the methods that work for Susan, the likes of whom were sufficiently visible in most classes in the good old days to satisfy us that our teaching *did* work. But, of course, it was the students who were doing the work and getting the results, not our teaching.

The challenge we face as teachers is to teach so that Robert learns more in the manner of Susan. Figure 1.1 suggests that the present differences between Robert and Susan (point A) may be lessened by appropriate teaching (point B). Three factors are operating:

- The students' levels of engagement in relation to the level of learning activity required to achieve the intended learning outcomes in relation to a particular content and context (ranging from 'describing' to 'theorizing', as between the dashed lines in Figure 1.1, p. 10).
- The degree of learning-related activity that a teaching method is likely to stimulate.
- The academic orientation of the students.

Point A is towards the 'passive' end of the teaching method continuum, where there is a large gap between Susan's and Robert's levels of engagement. A lecture would be an example of such passive teaching and we get the picture just described. Susan is working at a high level of engagement within the target range of learning activities – relating, applying and theorizing from time to time – while Robert is taking notes and memorizing and is not within the target range of activities. If you compare this with

High-level engagement

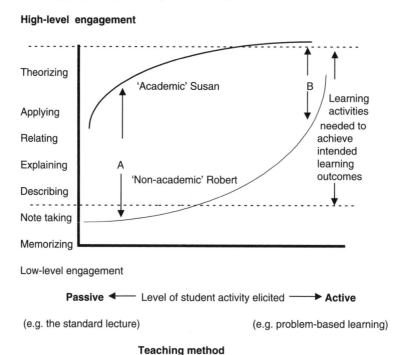

Figure 1.1 includes labels: Theorizing, Applying, Relating, Explaining, Describing, Note taking, Memorizing; 'Academic' Susan, 'Non-academic' Robert, A, B, Learning activities needed to achieve intended learning outcomes.

Low-level engagement

Passive ◄——— Level of student activity elicited ———► **Active**

(e.g. the standard lecture)   (e.g. problem-based learning)

Teaching method

Figure 1.1   Student orientation, teaching method and level of engagement

Figure 2.1 (on page 27), you will see that Susan is using a 'deep' approach, comprising outcomes-appropriate learning activities, while Robert is operating below what is required using a 'surface' approach.

At point B, towards the 'active' end of the teaching method continuum, the gap between Susan and Robert is not so wide; he is actually using many of the learning activities needed to achieve the intended learning outcomes. Problem-based learning would be an example of an active teaching method, because it requires students to question, to speculate, to generate solutions, so that Robert is now using the higher order cognitive activities that Susan uses spontaneously. The teaching has narrowed the gap between their levels of active engagement in learning. This is because the teaching environment requires the students to go through learning activities that are aligned to the intended outcomes. Problem-based learning is an example of such aligned teaching: the intended outcome is that the student solve professional problems and the teaching requires the student to go through solving such problems. The assessment is how well the problems are solved. This is one example of constructive alignment in teaching.

Of course, there are limits to what students can do that are beyond the teacher's control – a student's ability is one – but there are other things that are within our control and capitalizing on them is what good teaching is all about. Although Figure 1.1 is a hypothetical graph, it helps us to define good teaching, as follows:

> *Good teaching is getting most students to use the level of cognitive processes needed to achieve the intended outcomes that the more academic students use spontaneously.*

Good teaching narrows the gap between the Susans and the Roberts of this world.

Design of this book

This book is addressed to teachers, to staff developers and to administrators. Individual teachers experience the problems, and will need to generate the solutions. Those solutions will not be found in learning a whole new bag of teaching tricks, any one of which may or may not be useful for your particular circumstances. Solutions are likely to be found in reflecting on your teaching problems, and deriving your own ways of handling them within your departmental context (see Chapters 3 and 12). But before you can do that, you need a framework with which to structure your reflections. Constructive alignment provides such a framework, anchoring teaching decisions all the time to achieving or assessing the intended learning outcomes.

Staff developers, for their part, need to continue to work with individuals, but not so much in generic standalone workshops, but within the context of their department. More generally, staff developers need to work with departments themselves on their teaching programmes and with administration to get the institutional policies and procedures right on teaching-related matters. If this book is to address quality teaching, we need to go beyond the individual and examine the institution. How the institution may be reflective is addressed in Chapter 12, together with the closely related theme of quality enhancement, not just quality assurance.

All three – teachers, staff developers and administrators – need to immerse themselves in the 'scholarship of teaching' (Boyer 1990). Academics have always been teachers, but the first priority of the majority is to keep up with developments in their content discipline and to contribute to them through research. Developing teaching expertise usually takes second place: a set of priorities dictated as much by institutional structures and reward systems as by individual choice. But there is another body of knowledge, apart from their content areas, that academics also have a responsibility to address. This is the body of knowledge that underwrites good teaching, much of which is addressed in this book.

In Chapter 2, we look at some of the research on student learning with a view to using that knowledge in designing more effective teaching. Students can use effective (deep) and ineffective (surface) approaches to their learning and, in turn, effective teaching maximizes the former and minimizes the latter. Chapter 3 sets the stage for effective teaching by looking at what 'motivating' students might mean and what the climate for teaching might be like: this requires that teachers reflect on what they are doing and why.

The rest of the book is concerned with implementing constructive alignment in our version of outcomes-based teaching and learning, as explained in Chapter 4. Following chapters focus on crucial points in the teaching process: what constitutes a good teaching/learning environment, designing intended learning outcomes, teaching/learning activities and assessment tasks that are appropriately aligned to the outcomes and grading based on those tasks.

Chapter 12 discusses questions of how best to implement constructive alignment, both by individual teachers, and by whole departments, faculties or schools, and what lessons this has for enhancing the quality of teaching and learning in the institution as a whole. Chapter 13 presents several examples of implementing constructive alignment in one whole faculty, and in several courses drawn from different content areas. Perhaps this will convince any readers, who might have lingering doubts, that constructive alignment is not pie in the sky but eminently manageable, workable and effective.

Summary and conclusions

The nature of the change

The changing face of universities has several aspects. Financially, public funding is much decreased. The shortfall has been picked up by charging higher and higher student fees, on the neo-conservative assumption that education is a personal benefit, a commodity that should, therefore, be paid for by the individual. At the same time, proportionally more students are at university than ever before, pursuing professionally and vocationally oriented rather than the traditional academic programmes. Classrooms are thus full of a diverse range of students, all demanding the quality teaching they believe they have paid for and should be receiving. Universities are now responding to this demand for better teaching, increasingly with 'outcomes-based education'.

What is outcomes-based education?

Outcomes-based education is, however, a thoroughly confused concept. This is because there are three quite different versions, with overlapping terminology. One version arose in a scheme for disadvantaged school students, which, for various reasons, drew criticisms from the far right of politics.

Another version is used as a tool in managerialism's new role in universities for benchmarking institutions, for accountability and credit transfers, which many academics find practically and ideologically uncomfortable. The third version we refer to as outcomes-based teaching and learning (OBTL), which is solely concerned with enhancing teaching and learning. OBTL is ideally implemented using our old friend constructive alignment, introduced in the first edition of this book in 1999. Its relevance in the present context can be seen in reference to teaching Robert and Susan.

Making Robert learn like Susan

Susan is the sort of 'academic' student teachers dream about. She hardly needs teaching: she is motivated, knowledgeable and actively learning even in lectures. Robert is unsure of his goals, is doing subjects that don't really interest him and sits passively in class. There is a large gap between Susan's performance and Robert's. In a class that requires students to engage in learning activities that directly address the intended learning outcomes – where the teaching is constructively aligned, in other words – Robert is more likely to engage in the sort of learning that Susan does spontaneously. This book is designed to explain how this works and how it can be put into practice in most teaching situations.

Further reading

On trends in higher education

Beach, C., Broadway R. and McInnes, M. (eds) (2005) Higher education in Canada. www.jdi.econ.queensu.ca/

One of the major problems in Canada is underfunding, the cost being borne by rising tuition fees. Overcrowded classes, teaching quality has declined. Students seek out good-quality academic programmes.

Dearing, R. (1997) *National Committee of Inquiry into Higher Education (Dearing Report)*. Higher Education in the Learning Society, Report of the National Committee. Norwich: HMSO.

The first major thrust towards outcomes-based education in the UK. Now most universities explicitly describe course and programme outcomes in terms of the outcomes students are intended to attain, although how far these filter through into outcomes-based teaching and learning varies between institutions.

Wittenberg, H. (2006) *Current and Future Trends in Higher Education*. Commissioned by the Austrian Federal Ministry for Education, Science and Culture.

The shape of things to come in Europe: the Bologna process, involving standard-izing modular and tiered programmes across countries with credit systems 'to make educational achievements transparent'; effects of increased participation rates, performance assessment of teaching–learning processes resulting in new forms of quality assurance.

On Susan and Robert

Buckridge, M. and Guest, R. (2007) A conversation about pedagogical responses to increased diversity in university classrooms, *Higher Education Research and Development*, 26, 133–146.

Margaret, a staff developer, and Ross, an economics teacher, hold a dialogue about dealing with the increasingly large number of Roberts sitting alongside the Susans in our classes. Is it fair to Susan to divert resources from her in order to deal with Robert? Is it fair to Robert if you don't? Is it really possible to obtain the optimum from each student in the same overcrowded class? Read, and draw your own conclusions.

2
Teaching according to how students learn

How effectively we teach depends, first, on what we think teaching is. Three levels of thinking about teaching are distinguished. The first two are 'blame' models, the first blaming the learner, the second the teacher. The third model integrates learning and teaching, seeing effective teaching as encouraging students to use the learning activities most likely to achieve the outcomes intended. To do this requires some knowledge of how students learn. Students may use inappropriate or low level activities, resulting in a *surface* approach to learning, or high-level activities appropriate to achieving the intended outcomes, resulting in a *deep* approach to learning. Good teaching supports those appropriate learning activities and discourages inappropriate ones.

Levels of thinking about teaching

All teachers have some theory of what teaching is when they are doing it, even if they are not explicitly aware of that theory and their theories deeply affect the kind of learning environment they create in their classrooms (Gow and Kember 1993). Three common theories of teaching exist, which teachers tend to hold at different points in their teaching career. In fact, these levels describe a sequence in the development of teachers' thinking and practice: a routemap towards reflective teaching, if you like, where the level at which a teacher operates depends on what is focused on as most important.

But before discussing different theories of teaching and learning, what are yours (Task 2.1 p. 16)?

> **Task 2.1**   What are your theories of teaching and learning?
>
> Learning is _____
> _____
> _____
> _____
>
> Teaching is _____
> _____
> _____
> _____
>
> When you have finished this chapter, come back to these statements
> and see how they check out against the transmission and student learn-
> ing models, and the theories of teaching outlined in the chapter.
> Where do your own views lie? Now that you have seen these other views,
> have you changed your theory of teaching? _____
> _____
> _____
>
> Comments _____
> _____

Now let's see what others think.

Level 1. Focus: What the student is

Teachers at Level 1 focus on the differences between students, as most
beginning teachers do: there are good students, like Susan, and poor students, like Robert. Level 1 teachers see their responsibility as knowing the
content well, and expounding it clearly. Thereafter, it's up to the student to
attend lectures, to listen carefully, to take notes, to read the recommended
readings, and to make sure it's taken on board and unloaded on cue. Susan
does – good student; Robert doesn't – poor student.

At Level 1, teaching is in effect held constant – it is transmitting information, usually by lecturing – so differences in learning are due to differences
between students in ability, motivation, what sort of school they went to, A
level results, ethnicity and so on. Ability is usually seen as the most important
factor, an interesting consequence of which is that teaching becomes not so
much an educative activity as a *selective* one, assessment being the instrument
for sorting the good students from the bad after teaching is over. Many
common but counterproductive practices spring from this belief, as we discuss when dealing with teaching and assessment methods. The curriculum is
a list of items of content that, once expounded from the podium, have been
'covered'. How the students receive that content and what their depth of
understanding of it might be are not specifically addressed.

Level 1 is founded on a *quantitative* way of thinking about learning and teaching (Cole 1990), which manifests itself most obviously in assessment practices, such as 'marking', that is, counting up points. We examine this model, its manifestations and its consequences, in Chapter 9.

The view of university teaching as transmitting information is so widely accepted that teaching and assessment the world over are based on it. Teaching rooms and media are specifically designed for one-way delivery. A teacher is the knowledgeable expert, the sage on the stage, who expounds the information the students are to absorb and to report back accurately. How well students do these things depends, in this view, on their ability, their motivation – even their ethnicity, Asian students frequently being unfairly and inaccurately stereotyped as 'rote-learners' (Biggs 1996).

Explaining the variability in student learning on students' characteristics is a *blame-the-student* theory of teaching. When students don't learn (that is, when teaching breaks down), it is due to something the students are lacking, as exemplified in the following comments:

> *How can I be expected to teach that lot with those A level results? They wouldn't even have been admitted 10 years ago.*

> *They lack any motivation at all.*

> *These students lack suitable study skills. But that's not my problem, they'll have to go to the counselling service.*

In themselves, these statements may well be true: school leaving results might be poor, students nowadays may be less academically oriented. That is exactly the challenge for teachers, not their excuse for poor teaching.

Blame-the-student is a comfortable theory of teaching. If students don't learn, it's not that there is anything wrong with the teaching, but that they are incapable, unmotivated, foreign or they possess some other non-academic defect, which is not the teacher's responsibility to correct. Level 1 teaching is totally unreflective. It doesn't occur to the teacher to ask the key generative question: 'What else could I be doing?' And until they do ask that, their teaching is unlikely to change.

Level 2. Focus: What the teacher does

Teachers at Level 2 focus on what teachers do. This view of teaching is still based on transmission, but transmitting concepts and understandings, not just information (Prosser and Trigwell 1998). The responsibility for 'getting it across' now rests to a significant extent on what the teacher does. The possibility is entertained that there may be more effective ways of teaching than what one is currently doing, which is a major advance. Learning is seen as more a function of what the teacher is doing, than of what sort of student one has to deal with.

The teacher who operates at Level 2 works at obtaining an armoury of teaching skills. The material to be 'got across' includes complex under-standings, which requires much more than chalk and talk. Consider the following:

> *I'll settle them down with some music, then an introductory spiel: where we were last week, what we're going to do today. Then a video clip followed by a buzz session. The questions they're to address will be on the OH. I'll then fire six questions at them to be answered individually. Yes, four at the back row, finger pointing, that'll stir that lot up. Then I speak to the answers for about seven minutes, working in those two jokes I looked up. Wrap up, warning them there's an exam question hidden in today's session (moans of 'Now he tells us!' yuk, yuk). Mention what's coming up for next week, and meantime they're to read Chapter 10 of Bronowski.*

Plenty of variation in technique here, probably – almost certainly – a good student response, but the focus of this description is entirely teacher-centred. It's about what *I* the teacher am doing, not on what *they* the students are learning.

Traditional approaches to teaching development often work on what the teacher does, as do 'how to' courses and books that provide prescriptive advice on getting it across more effectively:

- Establish clear procedural rules at the outset, such as signals for silence.
- Ensure clarity: project the voice, use clear visual aids.
- Eye contact with students while talking.
- Don't interrupt a large lecture with handouts: chaos is likely.

This may be useful advice, but it is concerned with *management*, not with facilitating learning. Good management is important, but as a means of setting the stage on which good learning may occur, not as an end in itself.

Level 2 is also a deficit model, the 'blame' this time being on the teacher. It is a view of teaching often held by university administrators, because it provides a rationale for making personnel decisions. Good teachers are those who have lots of teaching competencies. Does Dr Jones 'have' the appropriate competencies for tertiary level teaching? If not, he had better show evidence that he has by the time his contract comes up for renewal. However, competencies may have little to do with teaching effectiveness. A competency, such as constructing a reliable multiple-choice test, is useful only if it is appropriate to one's teaching purposes to *use* a multiple-choice test. Likewise, managing educational technology, or questioning skills, or any of the other competencies tertiary teachers should 'have', should not be isolated from the context in which they are being used. Knowing what to do is important only if you know why, when and how you should do it. The focus should not be on the skill itself, but whether its deployment has the desired effect on student learning.

Which brings us to the third level of teaching.

Level 3. Focus: *What the student does*

Teachers at Level 3 focus on what the student does and how that relates to teaching. Level 3 is a student-centred model of teaching, with teaching supporting learning. No longer is it possible to say: 'I taught them, but they didn't learn.' Expert teaching includes mastery over a variety of teaching techniques, but unless learning takes place, they are irrelevant; the focus is on what the student does and on how well the intended outcomes are achieved.

This implies a view of teaching that is not just about facts, concepts and principles to be covered and understood, but also to be clear about:

1 What it means to 'understand' content in the way that is stipulated in the intended learning outcomes.
2 What kind of teaching/learning activities are required to achieve those stipulated levels of understanding.

The first two levels did not address these questions. The first question requires that we specify what levels of understanding we want when we teach a topic. It's just not good enough for us to talk about it or teach with an impressive array of visual aids: the whole point, how well the students have learned, has been ignored. The second question requires the teaching/learning activities to be specifically attuned to helping students achieve those levels of understanding. Then follow the key questions:

- How do you define those levels of understanding as outcome statements?
- What do students have to do to reach the level specified?
- What do you have to do to find out if the outcomes have been reached at the appropriate level or not?

Defining levels of understanding is basic to clarifying our intended outcomes, the subject of Chapter 5. Getting students to understand at the level required is a matter of getting them to undertake the appropriate learning activities, which is a matter dealt with in Chapters 6, 7 and 8. This is where a Level 3 student-centred theory of teaching departs from the other models of teaching. It's not what *we* do but what *students* do that's the important thing. Finally, we need to check that their level of understanding displayed or their performance otherwise are what we intended. This is dealt with in Chapters 9, 10 and 11, on the theory and practice of assessment.

How do students learn?

Learning has been the subject of research by psychologists for the whole of last century, but remarkably little has directly resulted in improved teaching. The reason is that until recently psychologists were more concerned with developing the One Grand Theory of Learning than in studying the contexts in which people learned, such as schools and universities (Biggs 1993a). This focus has been rectified in the last 20 years or so, and there is now a great deal of research into the ways that students go about their learning. Appropriately, the field of study is now designated as 'student learning' research.

Student learning research originated in Sweden, with Marton and Säljö's (1976a, 1976b) studies of surface and deep approaches to learning. They gave students a text to read and told them they would be asked questions afterwards. Students responded in two different ways. The first group learned in anticipation of the questions, concentrating anxiously on the facts and details that might be asked. They 'skated along the surface of the text', as Marton and Säljö put it, using a *surface* approach to learning. What these students remembered was a list of disjointed facts; they did not comprehend the point the author was making. The second group on the other hand set out to understand the meaning of what the author was trying to say. They went below the surface of the text to interpret that meaning, using a *deep* approach. They saw the big picture and how the facts and details made the author's case.

Note that the terms 'deep' and 'surface' as used here describe ways of learning a particular task, they do *not* describe characteristics of students. We can say that Robert might typically use a surface approach, but the whole point of this book is to set up ways of getting him to go deep. We return to this important distinction shortly.

The Marton and Säljö studies struck a chord with ongoing work in other countries; in particular that of Entwistle in the United Kingdom (e.g. Entwistle and Ramsden 1983) and of Biggs in Australia (e.g. 1979, 1987a). Entwistle was working from the psychology of individual differences, Biggs from cognitive psychology, and Marton and Säljö from what they later called phenomenography. However, all had a common focus: studying learning in an institutional context.

Some strong implications for teaching could be drawn from this work, as we explore in this chapter.

Constructivism and phenomenography

Level 3 theories of teaching are based on two main theories: phenomenography and constructivism. 'Phenomenography' was a term resurrected by Marton (1981) to refer to the theory that grew out of his studies with Säljö on approaches to learning and has developed since then (Marton and Booth 1997). Originally used by Sonnemann (1954) in clinical psychology, phenomenography in the student learning context refers to the idea that the learner's perspective determines what is learned, not necessarily what the teacher intends should be learned. This is another reason why our intended learning outcomes should be stated as clearly as possible and their attainment monitored. Teaching is a matter of changing the learner's perspective, the way the learner sees the world and on how learners represent knowledge (Prosser and Trigwell 1998).

Constructivism has a long history in cognitive psychology going back at least to Piaget (1950). Today, it takes on several forms: individual, social, cognitive, postmodern (Steffe and Gale 1995). All emphasise that the learners construct knowledge with their own activities, building on what they already know. Teaching is not a matter of transmitting but of engaging students in active learning, building their knowledge in terms of what they already understand.

In reflecting on our teaching and interpreting our teaching decisions, we need a theory. Whether you use phenomenography or constructivism as that theory may not matter too much, as long as your theory is consistent, understandable and works for you. We prefer constructivism as our framework for thinking about teaching because it emphasizes what students have to do to construct knowledge, which in turn suggests the sort of learning activities that teachers need to address in order to lead students to achieve the desired outcomes. In conceptualizing outcomes-based teaching and learning, constructivism works for us.

Both theories agree that effective learning changes the way we see the world. The acquisition of information in itself does not bring about such a change, but the way we *structure* that information and think with it does. Thus, education is about *conceptual change*, not just the acquisition of information.

Such conceptual change takes place when:

1 It is clear to both teachers and students what the intended outcomes of learning are, where all can see where they are supposed to be going. Outcomes-based teaching and learning requires this of teachers, whereas teaching in the form of 'covering a topic' does not.
2 Students experience the felt need to get there. The art of good teaching is to communicate that need where it is initially lacking. 'Motivation' is as much a product of good teaching as its prerequisite. This question is addressed in the next chapter.
3 Students feel free to focus on the task, not on watching their backs. Attempts to create a felt need to learn by the use of ill-conceived and urgent assessments are counterproductive. The game changes, becoming a matter of dealing with the test, not with engaging the task deeply.
4 Students work collaboratively and in dialogue with others, both peers and teachers. Good dialogue elicits those activities that shape, elaborate, and deepen understanding.

These four points contain a wealth of implication for the design of teaching and for personal reflection about what one is really trying to do, as we examine in the following chapter.

Surface and deep approaches to learning

The concepts of surface and deep approaches to learning are very helpful in conceiving ways of improving teaching. Sometimes it is useful to refer to an 'achieving' approach (Biggs 1987a), or 'strategic approach' (Tait et al. 1998), referring to how ambitious and how organized students are, but we do not go into this here. Our concern is with how learning tasks are handled. The surface and deep approaches usefully describe how Robert and Susan typically go about their learning and studying – up to the point when teaching begins. Our aim is to teach so that Robert learns more like the way Susan does.

Surface approach

The surface approach arises from an intention to get the task out of the way with minimum trouble, while appearing to meet course requirements. Low cognitive-level activities are used, when higher level activities are required to do the task properly. The concept of the surface approach may be applied to any area, not only to learning. The terms 'cutting corners', and 'sweeping under the carpet', convey the idea: the job appears to have been done properly when it hasn't.

Applied to academic learning, examples include rote learning selected content instead of understanding it, padding an essay, listing points instead of addressing an argument, quoting secondary references as if they were primary ones; the list is endless. A common misconception is that memorization in itself indicates a surface approach (Webb 1997). However, verbatim recall is sometimes entirely appropriate, such as learning lines for a play, acquiring vocabulary or learning formulae. Memorization becomes a surface approach when understanding is required and memorizing is used to give the impression that understanding has occurred. When Robert takes notes, and selectively quotes them back, he is under-engaging in terms of what is properly required. That is a surface approach – but the problem is that it sometimes works:

> I hate to say it, but what you have got to do is to have a list of 'facts'; you write down ten important points and memorize those, then you'll do all right in the test . . . If you can give a bit of factual information – so and so did that, and concluded that – for two sides of writing, then you'll get a good mark.
>
> (A psychology undergraduate, quoted in Ramsden 1984: 144)

If the teacher of this student thought that an adequate understanding of psychology could be manifested by selectively memorizing, there would be no problem. But it is unlikely that the teacher did think that – we should hope not, anyway. This is rather a case where an inappropriate assessment task *allowed* the students to get a good mark on the basis of memorizing facts. As it happened, this particular student wrote essays in a highly appropriate way and later graduated with first class honours. The problem is therefore not with the student, but with the assessment task. This teacher was not being reflective while the student was highly reflective: he'd outconned the teacher.

Thus, do not think that Robert is irredeemably cursed with a surface approach if he only lists unrelated bullet points as his understanding of an article. Let us say that *under current conditions of teaching or assessment,* he chooses to use a surface approach. Teaching and assessment methods often encourage a surface approach, because they are not aligned to the aims of teaching the subject, as in the case of the psychology teacher we just saw. The presence of a surface approach is thus a signal that something is out of kilter in our teaching or in our assessment methods. It is therefore something we can hope to address. It might in the end turn out that Robert is a student who is hopelessly addicted to surface learning, but that conclusion is way down the track yet.

In using the surface approach, students focus on what Marton calls the 'signs' of learning; the words used, isolated facts, items treated independently of each other. This prevents students from seeing what the signs signify, the meaning and structure of what is taught. Simply, they cannot see the wood for the trees. Emotionally, learning becomes a drag, a task to be got out of the way. Hence the presence of negative feelings about the learning task: anxiety, cynicism, boredom. Exhilaration or enjoyment of the task is not part of the surface approach.

Factors that encourage students to adopt such an approach include:

1 *From the student's side*:

- An intention only to achieve a minimal pass. Such may arise from a 'meal ticket' view of university or from a requirement to take a subject irrelevant to the student's programme.
- Non-academic priorities exceeding academic ones.
- Insufficient time; too high a workload.
- Misunderstanding requirements, such as thinking that factual recall is adequate.
- A cynical view of education.
- High anxiety.
- A genuine inability to understand particular content at a deep level.

2 *From the teacher's side*:

- Teaching piecemeal by bullet lists, not bringing out the intrinsic structure of the topic or subject. (We hasten to add that some bullet lists, like these two here, for instance, are OK.)
- Assessing for independent facts, inevitably the case when using short-answer and multiple-choice tests.
- Teaching, and especially assessing, in a way that encourages cynicism:

for example, 'I hate teaching this section, and you're going to hate learning it, but we've got to cover it.'
- Providing insufficient time to engage the tasks; emphasizing coverage at the expense of depth.
- Creating undue anxiety or low expectations of success: 'Anyone who can't understand this isn't fit to be at university.'

Points 1 and 2 should not be seen as entirely separate. Most of the student factors are affected by teaching. Is insufficient time to engage properly a matter of poor student planning or of poor teacher judgment? Much student cynicism is a reaction to the manner of teaching busy-work and of assessment. Even the last student factor, inability to understand at a deep level, refers to the task at hand and that may be a matter of poor teacher judgment concerning curriculum content as much as the student's abilities. But there are limits. Even under the best teaching some students will still maintain a surface approach.

It is probably less likely that under poor teaching students will maintain a deep approach. Even Susan. Unfortunately, it is easier to create a surface approach than it is to support a deep approach (Trigwell and Prosser 1991).

The first step in improving teaching, then, is to avoid those factors that encourage a surface approach.

Deep approach

The deep approach arises from a felt need to engage the task appropriately and meaningfully, so the student tries to use the most appropriate cognitive activities for handling it. To Susan, who is interested in mathematics and wants to get to the bottom of the subject, cutting corners is pointless.

When students feel this need-to-know, they automatically try to focus on underlying meanings, on main ideas, themes, principles, or successful applications. This requires a sound foundation of relevant prior knowledge, so students needing to know will naturally try to learn the details, as well as making sure they understand the big picture. In fact, the big picture is not understandable without the details. When using the deep approach in handling a task, students have positive feelings: interest, a sense of importance, challenge, exhilaration. Learning is a pleasure. Students come with questions they want answered, and when the answers are unexpected, that is even better.

Factors that encourage students to adopt such an approach include:

1 *From the student's side*:

- An intention to engage the task meaningfully and appropriately. Such an intention may arise from an intrinsic curiosity or from a determination to do well.
- Appropriate background knowledge.

- The ability to focus at a high conceptual level, working from first principles, which in turn requires a well-structured knowledge base.
- A genuine preference, and ability, for working conceptually rather than with unrelated detail.

2 *From the teacher's side*:

- Teaching in such a way as to explicitly bring out the structure of the topic or subject.
- Teaching to elicit an active response from students, e.g. by questioning, presenting problems, rather than teaching to expound information.
- Teaching by building on what students already know.
- Confronting and eradicating students' misconceptions.
- Assessing for structure rather than for independent facts.
- Teaching and assessing in a way that encourages a positive working atmosphere, so students can make mistakes and learn from them.
- Emphasizing depth of learning, rather than breadth of coverage.
- In general, and most importantly, using teaching and assessment methods that support the explicit aims and intended outcomes of the course. This is the constructive alignment model underlying this book. It is also known as 'practising what you preach'.

Again, the student factors (1) are not independent of teaching (2). Encouraging the need-to-know, instilling curiosity, building on students' prior knowledge are all things that teachers can attempt to do; and, conversely, are things that poor teaching can too easily discourage. There are many things the teacher can do to encourage deep learning. Just what will be a lot clearer by the end of this book.

Desirable student learning depends both on student-based factors – ability, appropriate prior knowledge, clearly accessible new knowledge – and on the teaching context, which includes teacher responsibility, informed decision making and good management. But the bottom line is that teachers have to work with what material they have. Whereas lectures and tutorials might have worked in the good old days when highly selected students tended to bring their deep approaches with them, they may not work so well today. We need to create a teaching context where the Roberts of this world can go deep too.

The second step in improving teaching, then, is to focus on those factors that encourage a deep approach.

What is the difference between learning approaches and learning styles?

Some people speak of students' approaches to learning as if they were learning styles students use whatever the task or the teaching (Schmeck 1988); others speak of approaches as entirely determined by context, as if students walk into a learning situation without any preference for their way of going about learning (Marton and Säljö 1976a).

We take a middle position. Students do have predilections or preferences for this or that approach, but those predilections may or may not be realized in practice, depending on the teaching context. We are dealing with an *interaction* between personal and contextual factors, not unlike the interaction between heredity and environment. Both factors apply, but which predominates depends on particular situations. Have another look at Figure 1.1 (p. 10). At point A, under passive teaching, student factors make the difference, but at point B, active teaching predominates, lessening the differences between students. For an analysis of the differences between learning styles and learning approaches see Sternberg and Zhang (2001). Practically speaking, however, it is more helpful to see approaches to learning as something we as teachers can hope to change, rather than as styles about which we can do little.

Scores on such questionnaires as the *Approaches and Study Skills Inventory for Students* (ASSIST) (Tait et al. 1998) or the *Study Process Questionnaire* (SPQ) in either the three-factor (surface, deep and achieving) (Biggs 1987a) or two-factor versions (surface and deep only) (Biggs et al. 2001), are most usefully seen as outcomes of teaching rather than as measuring student differences. Responses to these questionnaires tell us something about the quality of the teaching environment, precisely because students' predilections tend to adapt to the expected requirements of different teaching environments.

Teaching and approaches to learning

To achieve most intended learning outcomes (ILOs), a range of verbs, from high to low cognitive level, need to be activated. The highest would refer to such activities as reflecting, theorizing and so on, the lowest to memorizing, and in between are various levels of activity. When using a deep approach, students use the full range of desired learning activities; they learn terminology, they memorize formulae, but move from there to applying these formulae to new examples, and so on. When using a surface approach, there is a shortfall; students handle all tasks, low and high, with low level verbs ('two pages of writing, etc.'). The teaching challenge is to prevent this shortfall from occurring, or to correct it where it has occurred (see Figure 2.1).

The conclusion to be drawn is simple but powerful: the surface approach is to be discouraged, the deep approach encouraged – and that is the working definition of good teaching used in this book. Preventing students from using a surface approach by discouraging the use of low level and inappropriate learning activities is the main thrust of the following chapter, while supporting the full range of appropriate learning activities, thus encouraging a deep approach, is what the remainder of the book is about.

Now try Task 2.2 (p. 28) to see how your teaching has helped shape your students' approaches to learning.

Cognitive level of learning activities

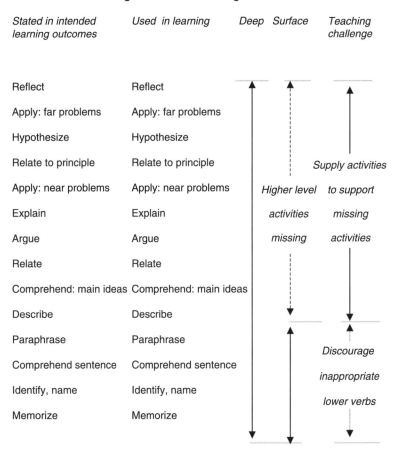

Figure 2.1 Desired and actual level of engagement, approaches to learning and enhancing teaching

Summary and conclusions

Levels of thinking about teaching

We distinguish three common theories of teaching, depending on what is seen as the main determinant of learning: (1) what students are, (2) what teachers do and (3) what students do. These define 'levels' of thinking about teaching. At Level 1, the teacher's role is to display information, the students' to absorb it. If students don't have the ability or motivation to do that correctly, that is their problem. At Level 2, the teacher's role is to explain concepts and principles, as well as to present information. For this they need

---

Task 2.2   Does your teaching encourage surface or deep approaches to learning?

Good teaching *encourages* a deep approach, and *discourages* a surface approach, to learning.

Reflect on your teaching so far, identify aspects of your teaching that have (maybe unintentionally)

a encouraged a surface approach to learning:

_____
_____
_____
_____

b encouraged a deep approach to learning:

_____
_____
_____
_____

What future actions would you take to encourage a deep approach to learning in your students?

_____
_____
_____
_____

---

various skills, techniques, and competencies. Here the focus is on what the teacher does, rather than on what the student is, and to that extent is more reflective and sophisticated. At Level 3, the focus is on what the student does: are they engaging those learning activities most likely to lead to the intended outcomes? If not, what sort of teaching/learning context would best help them? How can I know that they have achieved the intended outcomes satisfactorily?

How do students learn?

It is only in comparatively recent years that researchers into learning have studied learning as it takes place in institutions, by students. There is now a body of theory called 'student learning research' which directly relates to practice, constructivism and phenomenography being the two most influential. Both emphasize that meaning is created by the learner, but constructivism focuses particularly on the nature of the learning activities the student uses and on this account more readily leads to enhanced teaching.

Surface and deep approaches to learning

Learning activities that are too low a level to achieve the intended learning outcomes are referred to as comprising a 'surface' approach to learning, for example memorizing to give the impression of understanding. Activities that are appropriate to achieving the outcomes are referred to as a 'deep' approach. At university, intended outcomes would be high level, requiring students to reflect, hypothesize, apply and so on. Surface and deep approaches to learning are not personality traits, as is sometimes thought, but are most usefully thought of as reactions to the teaching environment.

Teaching and approaches to learning

Good teaching supports those activities that lead to the attainment of the intended learning outcomes, as in constructive alignment. This is the topic for the most of this book. However, there is much in what the teacher does or says that can encourage inappropriate, surface approaches to learning. These are of course to be discouraged. To do so is to set the stage for effective teaching, which is the subject of the following chapter.

Further reading

Biggs, J.B. (1993b) From theory to practice: A cognitive systems approach, *Higher Education Research and Development*, 12: 73–86.
Steffe, L. and Gale, J. (eds) (1995) *Constructivism in Education*. Hillsdale, NJ: Lawrence Erlbaum.
Sternberg, R.J. and Zhang L.F. (eds) (2001) *Perspectives on Thinking, Learning, and Cognitive Styles*. Mahwah, NJ: Lawrence Erlbaum.

The first reading applies the systems approach to student learning, the second is a fairly recent summary of the constructivist positions generally and how they apply to education.

Sternberg and Zhang is a useful collection of chapters on learning/cognitive styles, approaches and orientations. Most contributors argue that styles are relevant to teaching, except Biggs, who argues that styles are a distraction and of little relevance to enhancing teaching.

On applying student learning research to teaching

Dart, B. and Boulton-Lewis, G. (eds) (1998) *Teaching and Learning in Higher Education*. Camberwell, Victoria: Australian Council for Educational Research.
Prosser, M. and Trigwell, K. (1998) *Teaching for Learning in Higher Education*. Buckingham: Open University Press.

Ramsden, P. (2003) *Learning to Teach in Higher Education.* London: Routledge.
Tyler, R.W. (1949) *Basic Principles of Curriculum and Instruction.* Chicago: University of Chicago Press.

Dart and Boulton-Lewis contains a collection of papers that address teaching issues from the general student learning paradigm. Prosser and Trigwell demonstrate the implications for teaching arising from the phenomenographic framework and is in a sense a parallel to the present book, which operates from constructivism. Ramsden's approach is his own, but derives much from phenomenography, Chapters 1 to 7 giving rather more detail on the history and development of the student learning paradigm than is given here and how it may be applied to teaching. Tyler said most of it over 50 years ago, but no one paid any attention. It is under 100 pages in length and is well worth a read, for old time's sake. We hope they pay attention this time round.

3

Setting the stage for effective teaching

Effective teaching requires that we eliminate those aspects of our teaching that encourage surface approaches to learning and that we set the stage properly so that students can more readily use deep approaches to learning. This involves getting students to agree that appropriate task engagement is a good and impelling idea (otherwise known as 'motivation'), and establishing the kind of climate that will optimize appropriate interactions with our students. An important aspect to effective teaching is reflective practice, using transformative reflection, which enables teachers to create an improved teaching environment suited to their own context.

Getting students involved in learning: Motivation

There is no such thing as an unmotivated student: all students not in a coma want to do *something*. Our task is to maximize the chances that what they want to do is to achieve the intended learning outcomes. Unfortunately, there are many aspects of teaching that actually discourage them from doing that: we need to identify and minimize these as far as we can.

The best sort of motivation arises from intrinsic interest, fascination, call it what you will, but, unfortunately, that occurs well down the track, when the student already knows a lot about the topic and, like Susan, is already involved in it. Our problem as teachers is getting students engaged in learning before they have reached that stage or, worse, students like Robert who resort to surface learning strategies to avoid becoming involved. It doesn't help to say such students are 'unmotivated'. Of course they are: that's the problem.

Teachers who have a Level 1 theory of teaching see motivation as a substance that students possess in varying quantities, the Susans having lots, the

Roberts having little or none – and that's the way it is. But surely we can do *something* to encourage Robert to engage? Yes, we can. Two factors make students (or anyone, come to that) want to learn something:

1   It has to be important; it must have some *value* to the learner.
2   The learner needs to *expect success* when engaging the learning task.

Nobody wants to do something they see as worthless. Neither do they want to do something, however valued, if they believe they have no chance of succeeding. In both cases, doing the task will be seen as a waste of time.

This commonsense theory of why students do or do not want to learn is called the *expectancy-value* theory of motivation, which says that if anyone is to engage in an activity, he or she needs both to value the outcome and to expect success in achieving it (Feather 1982). The high value and the expectancy of success both need to be present; if either one is zero, then no motivated activity occurs.

Expectancy-value theory is particularly relevant in the early stages of learning before interest has developed to carry continuing engagement along with it. The following true incident illustrates this clearly:

> When we got to the Psych. I lectures, the Stats lecturer said 'Anyone who can't follow this isn't fit to be at University.' That was the first message I got. I *was* having difficulty with Stats and so I thought, maybe he's right, maybe university isn't for me. I liked the rest of Psych. but couldn't handle the Stats and had to withdraw.
>
> Next year, funny thing, I did Maths I and we came to probability theory, much the same stuff that I'd bombed out in last year. But the lecturer there said 'Probability is quite hard really. You'll need to work at it. You're welcome to come to me for help if you really need it . . .'
>
> It was like a blinding light. It wasn't *me* after all! This stuff really was *hard*, but if I tried it might just work. That year I got a Credit in that part of the subject.
>
> (A mature student, quoted in Biggs and Moore 1993: 272)

This story has important implications for understanding what motivates students.

What makes students expect to succeed or to fail?

The student just quoted had initially been led to believe she had no chance of success. Her first teacher attributed lack of success to lack of ability, she perceived she was not succeeding, so she naturally concluded she didn't have the ability needed. As this was something beyond her control, she concluded she had no chance of ever succeeding. Her second teacher attributed success instead to effort, which is something the student could control. With that came the liberating realization that what was certain failure could now be possible success. So she engaged the task and did, in fact, succeed. The reasons for that transformation are very instructive in the matter of motivating students.

With a history of successful engagement with content that is personally meaningful, the student both builds up the knowledge base needed for deep learning and, motivationally, develops the expectations that give confidence in future success: what are known as feelings of what psychologists call self-efficacy or more simply 'ownership': 'I can do this; this is my thing.'

Expectations of success are instilled on the basis of previous success, but only if the conditions that are believed to lead to success remain unchanged. If a student believes that a particular success was due to factors that might change and that are uncontrollable, such as luck or dependence on a particular teacher, belief in future success is diminished.

For example, westerners differ significantly from the Chinese in their attributions for success and failure. Westerners tend to see success as being attributable more to ability than to effort, while ethnic Chinese see effort as more important. This is possibly one reason that Chinese students do so well in international comparisons of attainment (Watkins and Biggs 1996).

Take methods of assessing students. Norm-referenced assessment is based on grading students against each other, for example by ranking, or 'following the curve': we deal with this in detail in Chapter 9. Students see this sort of assessment as competitive; to get a high grade you have to beat other students. This puts a premium on the importance of relative ability as determining the outcome. In criterion-referenced assessment, where students are assessed on how well they meet preset criteria, they see that to get a high grade they have to know the intended outcomes and learn how to get there, with a premium on attributions involving effort, study skill and know-how. In norm-referenced assessment success depends on the abilities of other students, over which there is no control, while in criterion-referenced assessment, the ball is in the student's court.

Teacher feedback has powerful effects on students' expectations of success, as the story on learning statistics makes very clear. Ironically, the psychology statistics lecturer's comment pre-empted student control, while the mathematics teacher made students see that it was up to them. Feedback as to progress also encourages beliefs in future success, which again is easier with criterion-referenced assessment: 'This is what you did, this is what you might have done, this is how to get a better result.'

But how can norm-referenced feedback, such as 'You are below average on this', help students to learn? What does Robert do with *that* information? This is not to say that some students don't want to be told where they stand in relation to their peers, but that information has little to do with teaching and learning. It is nice to be told that you're cleverer than most other students, but not very helpful for learning how to improve your performance. To be told, directly or indirectly, that you're dumber than most others is simply destructive.

To instil expectations of failure, as did our psychology statistics lecturer with consummate skill, is easy to do. This is classic blame-the-student stuff: attributing failure to lack of ability or to some other entity that lies fixed within the student. A valuable act of self-reflection as a teacher is to monitor what you say, how you say it, and what comments you write in students' assignments. What does the subtext say about future failure?

Task 3.1 asks you to think of the messages you send your students that might leave them feeling hopeful or hopeless about future success.

Task 3.1   What messages of success and failure do you convey to your students?

When students succeed, do you convey the hopeful message that their success will continue: 'You're good at this, aren't you?' Or the hopeless message: 'You had it lucky that time.'

When students fail, do you convey the hopeful message that they can succeed in future: 'This is hard, but with a bit more effort you'll get it right.' Or the hopeless messages: 'I guess you just don't have what it takes.'

Think back on some recent communications to students – such as comments in class, body language, handling questions, writing comments on assignments, describing what it takes to succeed, descriptions of tasks, readings and so on – do you think you convey hopeful, or hopeless, messages? Write down a couple of telling examples:

1 _____

_____

_____

2 _____

_____

_____

What makes a task worth doing?

Next, we look at the value term in the expectancy-value formula. How can we enhance the value of the task to the students? The general answer is clear enough: make their work important to them. Work can be important in various ways, each one producing a familiar category of motivation:

- what the outcome produces (*extrinsic* motivation)
- what other people value (*social* motivation)
- the opportunity for ego enhancement (*achievement* motivation)
- the process of doing it (*intrinsic* motivation).

Extrinsic motivation occurs when students perform the task because of the value or importance they attach to what the outcome brings, either something positive following success, such as a material reward, or something negative, such as a punishment, that would follow failure or non-engagement.

The quality of learning is usually low under extrinsic conditions. The student's attention is not so much on the task as on its consequences. Extrinsic motivation is a standing invitation to students to adopt a surface approach: indeed, the motive component of a surface approach is extrinsic, including a fear of failure (Biggs 1987a). Negative reinforcement is worse than positive, because if the learning is not successful, punishment is implicated, which introduces a range of side issues such as anxiety, anger, shame, desire for revenge, none of which is very helpful in getting the job done.

Social motivation occurs when students learn in order to please people whose opinions are important to them. If the processes of studying, or the fruits of a good education, are valued by other people important to the student, education may take on an intrinsic importance to the student. This is evident in some families, particularly Asian families, who have a high regard for education. Children with this family background are likely to accept that education is a good thing, to be pursued without question.

We can usually trace the beginning of our interest in something to someone who exhibited that interest to us. We want to be like them. This process is called 'modelling', where the models are admired and readily identified with. University teachers are in a good position to be seen as models, especially in the one-to-one situation of dissertation supervision. At the undergraduate level, in today's crowded universities, students are rather less likely to have the opportunity to engage closely with an academic but it can happen, especially if the academic publicly displays great enthusiasm for the subject.

Achievement motivation is about achieving in order to enhance the ego, such as competing against other students and beating them. They feel good about themselves. This can often lead to high achievement, and tends even to be associated with deep learning (Biggs 1987a), but the aims of deep learning and of achievement motivation ultimately diverge. The deep approach is concerned with handling the task as *appropriately* as possible, the achieving approach with handling it as *grade effectively* as possible.

Achievement motivation in the raw is not a pretty sight. It kills collaborative learning. Other students become competitors, not colleagues, and so steps are taken to disadvantage others: key references are hidden or mutilated, hints are not shared, misleading advice is given. Achievement motivation needs competitive conditions in which to work, and while that suits the minority of students who are positively motivated by competition, it actually damages the learning of those who perceive competition as threatening. Achievement motivation, like anxiety, changes the priorities of students, because content mastery plays second fiddle either to winning or to avoiding the appearance of losing. More students are turned off and work less well under competitive conditions than those who are turned on and work better.

Although competition is often touted as the way the 'real' world works, it does not follow that universities should make learning competitive for the general run of students, as happens when using norm-referenced assessments such as 'grading on the curve.'

Intrinsic motivation is the academic ideal but is the rarer for that. Students like Susan learn because they are interested in the task or activity itself. They do mathematics for the intellectual pleasure of problem solving and exercising their skill, independently of any rewards that might be involved. The point is to travel rather than to arrive. Intrinsic motivation drives deep learning and the best academic work.

Intrinsic motivation increases with continuing successful engagement with a specific task. Susan does not turn up at university to study mathematics without having experienced previous success in mathematics. The fact that many students may not have had much previous formal engagement in a subject does not, however, mean they will not develop intrinsic interest in it. Interest in subjects such as psychology or sociology, which may not have been studied previously, arises from curiosity and informal experience or from career plans. If the student sees the area as personally important, intrinsic interest will follow.

The question is: How do we motivate the Roberts, who have no definite career plans, no perception yet of personal importance of the area or even curiosity about related topics?

Involving students who are not yet intrinsically motivated

Rephrase the question: If a student doesn't yet see the task as important, how can we help make it so?

Let us look first at extrinsic motivation, as when the teacher sees assessment as the answer. A common cry is that students will not spend time learning a topic if they think it is not going to be assessed. Very well, some say, see that the topic *is* assessed. But this is an excellent way of devaluing it. The subtext says: 'The only value of this topic is that I have decided to test you on it!'

In an aligned system of teaching, this does not happen. The reason that the topic is being assessed is because it was important enough to be overtly included in the intended outcomes. The fact that it is there establishes its value. Assessing outside, or below, the curriculum gives irrelevant or counterproductive tasks a false value that students will resent or turn to their advantage, as did the student who wrote 'who said what on two sides of paper'.

It also depends on the kind of climate that has been created. One teacher informed his senior undergraduate class: 'You're going to hate the next couple of weeks; I know I am. I see absolutely no point in this form of linguistic analysis, but there it is, it's in the syllabus and we've got to cover it.'

Amazingly, one student reported she found the topic to be the most interesting part of the course, and was designing a dissertation proposal around it! Susan can cope with this kind of thing; she has her own reasons for valuing the topic. But Robert, who has nothing but the teacher's word for it, will indeed see the topic as valueless, hence not worth learning, except for the most cynical of reasons.

Using social motivation is a good strategy. Teachers who love their subject, and show it, can be inspirational. The fact that here is someone who does perceive great value in it will cause the students to be curious, to seek some of that value.

The key to motivation, then, is to ensure that academic activities are meaningful and worthwhile. This is made very clear in problem-based learning, where real-life problems become the context in which students learn academic content and professional skills. When faced with a patient with a suspected broken leg whom they have to help, learning all the necessary knowledge leading to the diagnosis and treatment of the patient is manifestly a worthwhile activity for a medical student. Problem-based learning is usually undertaken enthusiastically.

Teachers might worry less about motivating students and more about teaching better. That, in a nutshell, is what this section means. 'Motivation' is dealt with in two ways. The first is to avoid what not to do, such as devaluing academic tasks by encouraging cynicism and debilitating anxiety or by sending messages that the students have no chance of success. The second is to teach in such a way that students build up a good knowledge base, achieve success in problems that are significant and build up a feeling of 'ownership' over their learning; motivation follows good learning as night follows day. It is a matter of getting the causes and the effects right.

The next step in setting the stage for effective teaching is establishing a productive classroom climate.

The teaching/learning climate

Teachers create a certain learning climate through formal and informal interactions with students, which establishes how we and our students feel about learning. This naturally has strong effects on students' learning.

Theory X and Theory Y climates

Douglas McGregor (1960) was a management psychologist who distinguished between two organizational climates: Theory X and Theory Y. The 'theory' referred to assumptions about human trustworthiness. Managers operating on Theory X assume that workers cannot be trusted, those operating on Theory Y assume that they can and that you get better results when you do – an idea that has little traction in these neo-conservative times.

Nevertheless, the idea transfers readily to the classroom. Teachers operating on Theory X assume that students don't want to learn, they will cheat if given the slightest opportunity and so must not be allowed to make any significant decisions about their learning. They need to be told what to do and what to study, attendances need to be checked every lecture, invigilated examinations must make up most of the final grade, self- and peer-assessments are quite out of the question, deadlines and regulations need to be spelt out with sanctions imposed for failing to meet them.

This way of thinking leads very quickly to a learning climate based on anxiety: put the fear of God in them, *then* they'll shape up! Theory X is essentially a blame-the-student model of teaching, and with that goes all the other baggage associated with the Level 1 theory of teaching.

Teachers operating on Theory Y assume that students do their best work when given freedom and space to use their own judgment, that while bureaucratization of the classroom and of the institution may be necessary to run a tight ship, it may be counterproductive for good learning. Consequently, Theory Y driven teachers take the opposite view on such matters as take-home assessment tasks, self- and peer-assessment, class attendance, allowing students freedom to make their own decisions and so on. You give the benefit of the doubt. Sure, some students may be more likely to cheat when assessed on projects than on invigilated exams, but Theory Y teachers would argue that the educational benefits outweigh that risk. The aim of teaching is to support student learning, not to beat student deviousness.

These are pure cases. An all-Theory X environment would be intolerable for students, while all-Theory Y would be near impossible to run efficiently. Elements of both exist in the learning climates we create, but in our individual philosophies, we tend to lean more towards one theory or the other. Our leanings may be because of our personalities, our own educational history, but hopefully most of all, because of our worked-out theory of teaching. We should create the sort of learning climate that we believe strikes the right balance for optimal learning, given our conditions, our subject and our own students.

The extent to which we lean more towards Theory X or more towards Theory Y translates into action at virtually all levels of student–teacher interaction. For example, when one non-Cantonese-speaking teacher told colleagues at the University of Hong Kong, where English is the official language medium of instruction, that he allowed students to use Cantonese in group discussions, because group interaction was then much livelier, he was met with: 'But they could be discussing the Happy Valley race results for all you know!' True, they could have been. Contrariwise, they could have been engaged in fruitful learning.

It is a question of balancing trust, risk and value. Theory X operates on low trust, producing low-risk but low-value outcomes. You don't trust students so you assess them under high-security, invigilated conditions with little risk of cheating but what is produced under these conditions may not be relevant to the most important intended outcomes (pp. 198–200). Theory Y operates on high trust, producing high-value outcomes but with the risk that some outcomes may be the result of cheating. The following quotation from a part-time student who was a teacher illustrates the balance between risk and value with great self-insight:

> The biggest point I have learned from this course is my biggest flaw as a teacher, that is, I did not trust my students to be able to behave themselves ... (or to be) ... capable of being responsible for their own learning ... I made numerous rules in class for them to follow so as to make sure that they 'behaved', did all the preparations and planning for them, giving them mountains of homework and short tests to make sure that they revise for their lessons and so on – all rooted from my lack of trust in them! And I dared to blame them for being so passive and dependent when all along I helped to encourage them to be so!
>
> (part-time BEd student, University of Hong Kong)

How climate affects learning

Theory X restricts the range of potentially useful ways of learning, particularly self-directed learning, as the last quotation illustrates. Theory X also generates negative feelings, which distract from proper task engagement, directly encouraging a surface approach. Theory X generates two counter-productive emotions in particular, anxiety and cynicism.

Anxiety, produced for example by intimidation, sarcasm, threats of failure or heavy use of sanctions, simply creates an intense need to get out of the situation. The student's behaviour is therefore directed towards that end, rather than towards proper task engagement. Anxiety makes a mess of a student's priorities.

Cynicism works in a more coldly cognitive way. Perceptions that the teacher is degrading the task or belittling students encourages students to be cynical and with that, a deliberate decision not to engage the task honestly. If the teacher doesn't take the task seriously, why should the student? There are many ways in which teachers convey cynicism:

- Showing lack of interest or dislike of a topic ('You'll hate this, but we've got to cover it!').
- Playing games with students when they can't play back, such as setting facetious distracters in multiple-choice test items.
- Theory X by numbers, for example drawing a line after the 2000th word in a 2000 word-limit essay and marking only to that point. But if a student does exceed the limit, it may have been in order to make the argument more clearly. Messages conveyed by marking to the 2000th word include: students will take advantage wherever they can, nit picking is what it's all about, the delirious joy of exercising power, do not bother to make a case, just list points within the word limit.

- Discounting grades or marks for being late or some other offence. This practice conveys such messages as: meeting a deadline is more important than trying to create a product of quality. It also makes genuine criterion referencing impossible. Issues of learning should not be confused with issues of discipline (see Box 9.4, p. 183).
- Busy-work: insisting on trivia, making quality performance secondary to bureaucratic demands or to personal convenience.
- Authoritarianism: refusing to accept student criticisms or suggestions as to content or teaching method, being 'too busy' to attend to reasonable student requests.

Time stress: Coverage

A particular source of both anxiety and cynicism is time stress brought out by an obsession with coverage: too many topics, each taught with equal emphasis. Students become grossly overloaded and deep engagement with any topic is pre-empted. There are many reasons that students are subjected to time stress:

- Lack of coordination between teachers in setting assignment deadlines.
- Insisting on the prime importance of what you teach yourself rather than what colleagues teach.
- Lack of knowledge or even concern about the students' perspective on the workload.
- Shared teaching and particularly shared assessment, where each teacher thinks their own contribution the most important.
- Generally, a lack of care and forethought in designing the curriculum initially. OBTL provides the opportunity of reviewing course outcomes in the context of intended programme outcomes (pp. 68–70).

Deep engagement in a task takes time. If you don't provide the time, you won't get deep engagement:

> The greatest enemy of understanding is coverage – I can't repeat that often enough. If you're determined to cover a lot of things, you are guaranteeing that most kids will not understand, because they haven't had time enough to go into things in depth, to figure out what the requisite understanding is, and be able to perform that understanding in different situations.
>
> (Gardner 1993: 24)

Climate and direction: Summary

Let us bring the two sections on motivation and climate together. A Theory Y climate is a necessary but not a sufficient condition for the cultivation of positive motivation. The teacher must further demonstrate that the task is intrinsically worthwhile and valued.

Expectations of success and failure depend critically on what students are most likely to attribute their success and failure to. How these attributions are built up is partly cultural, partly upbringing and partly what goes on in the classroom. Communicating the message that failure is due to factors that aren't going to go away and that aren't controllable (such as low ability), is to instil an expectation of future failure. Attributing failure to factors that can be changed, such as lack of the appropriate skills (these can be taught) or to insufficient effort (this can be increased next time), help remove the crippling incapacity that failure may induce. Likewise, attributions of success to a special interest, or competence, is likely to increase feelings of ownership and hence positive motivation. Attributing success to luck or to help from someone is likely to decrease feelings of ownership.

Finally, a Theory Y climate does not necessarily mean a disorganized teaching/learning environment. An organized setting, with clear goals and feedback on progress, is important for motivating students and to the development of deep approaches (Entwistle et al. 1989; Hattie and Watkins 1988). Knowing where you are going, and feedback telling you how well you are progressing, heightens expectations of success.

Driving in a thick fog is highly unpleasant. So is learning in one.

So what sort of classroom climate are you creating for your students? Task 3.2 is an exercise to help you identify your classroom climate. But what is more important is how you could improve it to facilitate a more desirable learning approach.

Reflective teaching

Wise and effective teaching is not, however, simply a matter of applying general principles of teaching according to rule; they need adapting to each teacher's own personal strengths and teaching context. A characteristic of award-winning university teachers is their willingness to collect student feedback on their teaching, in order to see where their teaching might be improved (Dunkin and Precians 1992). Expert teachers continually reflect on how they might teach even better.

Let us imagine that Susan and Robert graduated 20 years ago. Susan now is a teacher with 20 years' experience; Robert is a teacher with one year's experience repeated 19 times. Susan is a reflective teacher: each significant experience, particularly of failure, has been a learning experience, so she gets better and better. Robert is a reactive teacher. He goes through the same motions year after year and when things go wrong he tends to blame the students, the administration or government intervention. If it worked last year, but didn't work this year, how can it be his teaching that is the problem?

The kind of thinking displayed by Susan, but not by Robert, is known as 'reflective practice'. Donald Schon (1983) coined the term 'the reflective

Task 3.2   What sort of classroom climate are you creating for your students?

Put a cross on the continuum on a point that best represents what you currently do in your teaching regarding:

	Strict	Negotiable
Classroom management	_____	
Meeting assignment deadlines	_____	
Checking attendance	_____	
Giving invigilated examination	_____	
Trusting students to assess their own work	_____	
Allowing students to take risk	_____	
Your control of all teaching and assessment matters	_____	

Now consider the positions of the crosses. If they are more skewed towards the 'Strict' end, you may be creating a more Theory X classroom climate. If the crosses are more skewed towards the 'Negotiable' end, then your classroom is more a Theory Y one.

So what sort of classroom climate are you creating for your students?

Is your classroom climate conducive to a deep approach to learning? If not, what actions would you take to change the classroom climate that would help your students achieve the intended learning outcomes through adopting a deep learning approach?

practitioner', pointing out that effective professionals, such as architects or medicos, need to reflect when faced with new problems or with difficulties for which they have not been specifically trained to cope. It is the same with university teachers (Brockbank and McGill 1998). A particularly inspiring and personal account of reflective practice in university teaching is given by Cowan (2002).

Reflective practice can be formally encouraged and directed as 'action research' (Kember and Kelly 1993). Action research, or action learning, involves changing teaching systematically, using whatever on-the-ground evidence that you can that the changes are in the right direction, that your students are now learning better than they used to. The target of action research is the teaching of the individual teacher herself or himself. The 'learning' in action learning refers not only to student learning, or even to learning about teaching, but to learning about oneself as a teacher and learning how to use reflection to become a better teacher. Learning new techniques for teaching is like the fish that provides a meal today; reflective practice is the net that provides meals for the rest of your life. We return to how action research may help you evaluate and transform your teaching in Chapter 12.

'Reflection' is, however, a misleading word. *Transformative reflection* is better. When you stand in front of a mirror what you see is your reflection, what you are at the time. Transformative reflection is rather like the mirror in Snow White: it tells you what you might become. This mirror uses theory to enable the transformation from the unsatisfactory what-is to the more effective what-might-be.

Theory makes us aware that there is a problem and it helps to generate a solution to that problem. This is where many tertiary teachers are lacking; not in theories relating to their content discipline, but in explicit and well-structured theories relating to teaching their discipline. Reflecting on your teaching, and seeing what is wrong and how it may be improved, requires you to have an explicit theory of teaching. We will return to this issue of reflective practice in Chapter 12, when readers' theories of teaching will have been elaborated with the contents of this book.

As noted earlier, all teachers have some kind of implicit theory of teaching, but we need something more upfront, a consciously worked-out theory that generates answers to teaching problems. The initial jolt that says 'there's a problem here' has to be defined in such a way that the problem becomes soluble. 'My stuff isn't getting across' doesn't define a soluble problem. 'The students are only giving me back what I said in my lectures' does. The last statement is based on the theory that when students only give back what is in the lectures, something is wrong. A good theory would suggest that the something resides in the teaching, rather than as some defect inherent in the students. It might be that the assessment procedures are letting students get away with repeating the lectures. So we need to present them with assessment tasks where this will not work.

To recognize and then to solve problems in teaching involves reflecting on what is happening, using a framework that gives you an angle on what is going on in your teaching, and that helps you to design an improvement. Such a framework is presented in the next chapter.

Task 3.3 asks you to reflect on a critical incident of your teaching or assessment and see how your response to the situation is related to your theory of teaching and learning as identified in Task 3.1. We will repeat this task later in Chapter 12.

Task 3.3   Reflection on a critical teaching/assessment incident

Reflect on a critical incident in your teaching – a situation in which you thought that your teaching or assessment had not gone quite how you would have liked it to have gone. Consider the following questions.

a What was the problem? What went wrong? What was the evidence for the problem?

_____

_____

_____

b What was (were) the cause(s) of the problem?

_____

_____

_____

c How did you deal with the problem then?

_____

_____

_____

d How did your solution to the problem relate to your theory of teaching and learning?

_____

_____

_____

Improving your teaching

One step towards improving teaching is to find out the extent to which you might be encouraging surface approaches in your teaching. Table 3.1 summarizes the aspects of your personal teaching that might lead to surface approaches.

The list comes under the two headings: motivation and learning climate, although they do interrelate. Some of these things listed here as leading to surface learning – and therefore to be removed – you might think to be necessary, such as deducting marks for late submissions of assignments.

While this is a common solution to the problem of late submission, it can get out of hand, as Box 9.4 (p. 183) tells us.

Table 3.1 Aspects of teaching likely to lead to surface approaches

---

Motivation

1 Conveying expectations of a low probability of success:

- Oral and written comments suggesting failure is due to lack of ability, success due to luck or other factors outside the student's control; not suggesting how a poor result might be remedied
- Norm- rather than criterion-referenced assessment
- Lack of clear direction, no feedback, no milestones of progress

2 Conveying low evaluations of tasks, cynicism:

- Playing games with students at a disadvantage, especially in the context of assessment ('funny' MC alternatives; busy-work)
- Displaying personal dislike of content being taught
- Assessing in a trivial way: low-level tasks requiring memorizing only, marking only to the literal word limit, discounting grades for non-academic or disciplinary reasons, assessments not based on content taught
- Emphasizing rules and regulations beyond their functional utility. *Subtext*: Rules are more important than learning
- Not practising what is preached. *Subtext*: You lot can do it, but it's not worth me doing it

The learning climate

3 Aspects suggesting Theory X:

- Negative reinforcement, use of anxiety to 'motivate'
- Blame-the-student explanations of student behaviour
- Time stress: failure to consider or appreciate student workload, no time available to students for reflection
- Students given little input in decisions that affect them
- Anxiety: engendered by harsh sanctions, bullying, sarcasm, lack of consideration of students' perspective, work/time pressure
- Cynicism: engendered by students feeling that you are not playing straight with them, that you don't actually believe in what you are telling them

---

If you are committed to Level 3, you need to structure a predominantly Theory Y learning climate, with student learning as the top priority. This means using such features as time for reflection, trying to eliminate anxiety and cynicism and adopting the principles and practices of constructive alignment. We are dealing with a package: individual components that don't fit our constructively aligned package have to go. Late submissions will have to be handled another way.

The first set of decisions, then, is to remove those aspects of your teaching that are actually encouraging surface approaches in students. Information on this or on other aspects of your teaching may be obtained from four possible sources:

1 Your own reflections on your teaching.
2 Your students.
3 A colleague in the role of 'critical friend'.
4 A staff developer who can offer informed advice.

Much can be achieved by transformative reflection. We can reflect on the suitability of our intended learning outcomes and on what alternative teaching/learning activities and assessment tasks we might best use. The constructive alignment framework is intended to encourage exactly that sort of reflection. The *Approaches to Teaching Inventory* (Prosser and Trigwell 1998; see also Chapter 12) is a very useful instrument for clarifying your conceptions (views) of teaching and how consistent your practices are with those conceptions.

Task 3.1 (p. 34) is a reflective task based on this chapter, the messages you convey to your students. Think about it and see what you conclude about the feedback you give your students.

It is hard for us to see what is wrong with some aspects of our teaching. We are likely to be blind to the more personal aspects. What we intend as humour might come across as sarcasm; attempts at being friendly as patronizing. Both are fertile breeding grounds for anxiety and cynicism. We need somebody to tell us such things.

Our students are the most direct source of this kind of information: it is, after all, their perceptions that structure the intention to use a surface approach. This is quite a different issue to the usual student feedback questionnaire, which is about how you teach particular courses. Obtaining student feedback in this context is best done anonymously, providing you are capable of putting up with the jibes of the facetious or the negativism of the disgruntled. You can use an open question: 'What aspects of my teaching do you like most? What would you like to see changed?' A positive note is better than: 'What do you see wrong with my teaching?' You might as well walk around with a 'Kick me' sign on your backside.

Another perspective on teaching may be provided by our colleagues. A 'buddy system' or peer review (pp. 269–71) is useful, in which two teachers in the same department – and who trust each other – visit each other's classes as critical friends. They will need a common framework and a common set of assumptions about what is good teaching to do this well.

Yet another perspective is provided by the teaching and learning development centre, if your university has one. Staff developers have the expertise to act as critical friend and to provide important insights on all stages of teaching where your own perspective might be limited.

Some problems may be located in your own personal style of teaching, which is what we are concerned with here. Task 3.4 asks you to list what at this stage you see to be major problems in your teaching that you'd like to solve.

You'll have a chance to revisit this task in Chapter 12.

Task 3.4 What are the major problems in your own teaching that you would like to solve?

Take a semester- or year-long unit that you are currently teaching and that presents you with particular difficulties or problems that you want to solve (e.g. teaching large classes, motivating students, lecturing successfully, dissatisfied with current assessment methods, covering the syllabus, getting students to understand etc.). What are the *three most worrying* problems in teaching that unit, which you would realistically hope to minimize by reading this book?

1 _____

_____

_____

2 _____

_____

_____

3 _____

_____

_____

Comment _____

_____

In the following chapters, bear this unit in mind, even if the material being addressed is not particularly problematic. At the end, you have the chance to revisit these problems.

Summary and conclusions

Getting students involved in learning: Motivation

Motivation has two meanings: it refers to initiating learning, and to maintaining engagement during learning. To initiate learning, students need to see the cost-benefits: that engaging in learning has evident value and that engagement is likely to realize that value. Value accrues to a task for a variety of reasons: *extrinsic*, where the consequences either bring something we want, or avoid something we don't want; *social*, where the value comes from what other important people think; *achievement*, where the value is ego enhancement; *intrinsic*, where we don't even think to ask where the value comes from: it's the journey, not the destination. Teachers can make use of these values to bring about positive results. Extrinsic reinforcement in the form of rewards and punishments needs to be used carefully, punishment can be quite counterproductive. Likewise, competition may turn on some of the Susans but none of the Roberts. Teachers can act as enthusiastic role models – and if they want to motivate their students intrinsically, they should teach constructively.

The teaching/learning climate

The quality of the relationship set up between teacher and students, or within an institution, is referred to as its 'climate', the way the students feel about it. A Theory X climate is based on the assumption that students cannot be trusted, a Theory Y climate on the assumption that they can. If Level 1 and Level 3 theories of teaching describe two cognitive views of teaching, Theory X and Theory Y climates are their affective counterparts. The tight formal structures of a Theory X climate, with sanctions for non-compliance, result in anxiety and cynicism; both lead to surface learning. A Theory Y climate allows students freedom to make their own learning-related choices, which, as we shall see, is important if students are to become independent lifelong learners.

Reflective teaching

Improving teaching under these conditions is not a matter of simply learning a swag of teaching competencies. Teaching is personal and the context in which each teacher works is different. What is effective for this teacher, for that subject, at this level, for those students, may not apply to other teachers, working under their own conditions. Individuals have to work out their own solutions. This requires *transformative reflection*, a theory of teaching to reflect with and a context of experiences as the object of reflection. This process may be structured in action research, in which possible solutions are carefully monitored to gauge their success.

Improving your teaching

The two big questions for any individual teacher are: What do I believe in, a Theory X or a Theory Y climate? What am I doing, unwittingly, that might be creating the opposite climate to what I want? Teachers trying to implement aligned teaching must answer the first question with Theory Y. Information on the second question may come from one's own transformative reflections, from the students, from informed advice such as that of a colleague or of a staff developer. Each source provides a different perspective, but reliance on your own reflections isn't likely to be a productive source of information on those aspects of your teaching of which you are unaware. These can be supplemented with questionnaires, observations, and interviews, their focus on aspects of teaching discussed in this chapter. The factors that are likely to lead to poor motivation and surface learning are summarized in Table 3.1.

Further reading

Biggs, J. and Moore, P. (1993) *The Process of Learning.* Sydney: Prentice-Hall Australia.
McGregor, D. (1960) *The Human Side of Enterprise.* New York: McGraw-Hill.

Further reading for this chapter is a tough one. There is plenty of theoretical material on motivation, but readers who don't know this literature already will have no time to read it now and transform it into functioning know-how. Most of the work on climate is either directed at school classroom level or at big business. The recent literature addressed to business persons is hairy-chested achievement motivation stuff, not Level 3 oriented at all. The exception is McGregor's original work on Theory X and Theory Y, which is well worth reading, but it needs translating into the tertiary context. The general principles of both foci of this chapter are given a more in-depth treatment in Biggs and Moore.

4

Using constructive alignment in outcomes-based teaching and learning

Constructive alignment arose out of an experiment with portfolio assessment. Students were faced with the intended outcomes of a course – mainly that their professional decision making had been improved by taught theory – and asked to provide evidence from their own professional experience as to if and how it had. The results provoked a rethink of the design of teaching: the students couldn't be 'taught' the evidence, they had to reflect on their experience and provide it themselves. The 'teaching method' became a series of negotiations as to how that evidence might be obtained, the assessment the quality of the evidence provided. The course was a success, and in reflecting on it later, it seemed that two principles were involved: a constructivist theory of learning, and alignment between the intended learning outcomes, the teaching/learning activities and the assessment tasks.

What is constructive alignment?

Constructive alignment came about as a result of an experiment with portfolio assessment in a bachelor of education programme. The course, entitled *The Nature of Teaching and Learning,* was a senior-level course in educational psychology for in-service teachers. It followed the then usual model: topics drawn from the psychology of learning and development that were considered relevant to the improved practice of teaching were taught and assignments given that would assess how well the theory and the relationship between psychology and education were understood: a typical academic assignment.

Then the penny dropped. This was not the major intended outcome of the course at all. The assignment was also 'academic' in a less worthy sense: it had nothing to do with the experience and working space of the students. The ultimate aim of any professional education course, by the same token, has everything to do with the direct experience of the students: it is to improve their professional competence. What evidence was there that it was indeed having that effect? The assignments didn't address that question. What caused the penny to drop and events that happened thereafter are contained in Box 4.1.

Box 4.1   How constructive alignment came into being

In 1994, one of the authors, John, returned from study leave in Canada to teach *The Nature of Teaching and Learning*, an evening course in the third year of an in-service, part-time BEd programme. He had been very impressed with the use of 'authentic' assessment and assessment portfolios in Canadian elementary schools. He thought portfolio assessment would be ideal for this course, which was about how knowledge of psychology might improve teaching. As the students were teachers during the day, they had plenty of opportunity to see how psychology might be working for them. However, when told that the assessment would comprise a portfolio of items, selected by them, demonstrating how psychology had improved their teaching, the students felt threatened:

> How am I supposed to do it well when I'm not sure exactly what the professor wants to see in it? . . . though he did say that we can put what means much to us in the portfolio, yet how can I be sure that he agrees with me?

John suggested item types for their portfolios and after a trial run, they got the idea. When they finally submitted their portfolios, John was stunned. They were rich and exciting, the class achieved more A and B grades than ever before, the student feedback the best he'd ever received. Here are a couple excerpts from their diaries:

> All [the teacher] said was 'show me the evidence of your learning that has taken place' and we have to ponder, reflect and project the theories we have learnt into our own teaching . . . How brilliant! If it had only been an exam or an essay, we would have probably just repeated his ideas to him and continued to teach the same way as we always do!

> Instead of bombing us with lengthy lectures and lecture notes, we have to reflect on our own learning experiences and to respond critically . . . I feel quite excited as this course is gradually leading me to do something positive to my teaching career and to experience real growth.

John didn't know it at the time, but he'd just implemented an example of outcomes-based teaching and learning.
Only he'd called it 'constructive alignment.'

Source: Biggs (1996)

Reflecting on why the experiment with portfolio assessment worked so well, John decided that it was because the learning activities addressed in the intended outcomes were mirrored both in the teaching/learning activities the students undertook and in the assessment tasks. This design of teaching was called 'constructive alignment' (CA), as it was based on the twin principles of constructivism in learning and alignment in the design of teaching and assessment.

It is 'constructive' because it is based on the constructivist theory that learners use their own activity to construct their knowledge or other outcome. It extends in a practical way Shuell's statement that 'what the student does is actually more important in determining what is learned than what the teacher does' (1986: 429). The intended outcomes specify the *activity* that students should engage if they are to achieve the intended outcome as well as the content the activity refers to, the teacher's task being to set up a learning environment that encourages the student to perform those learning activities, and then assess the outcomes to see that they match those intended.

The 'alignment' in constructive alignment reflects the fact that the learning activity in the intended outcomes, expressed as a verb, needs to be activated in the teaching if the outcome is to be achieved and in the assessment task to verify that the outcome has in fact been achieved. Take driving instruction. The intention is that the learner learns how to drive a car. The teaching focuses on the learning activity itself: driving a car, not giving lectures on car driving, while the assessment focuses on how well the car is driven. Car driving is the verb that is common to all components of instruction: to the intended outcome of learning, to the learner's activity during teaching and to the assessment. The alignment is achieved by ensuring that the intended verb in the outcome statement is present in the teaching/learning activity and in the assessment task.

By focusing on what and how students are to learn, rather than on what topics the teacher is to teach, we need to phrase the learning outcomes that are intended by teaching those topics not only in terms of the topic itself but also in terms of the learning activity the student needs to engage to achieve those outcomes: we specify not only what students are to learn, as we always have, but what they are supposed to do with it and how they are to learn it. The outcome statement also informs students how they are expected to change as a result of learning that topic. The *intended learning outcome*, or ILO, contains a helpful verb such as 'reflect on X' or 'apply theory to Y' to achieve the outcome. Once those verbs are specified, it is clear what the teaching/learning activities (TLAs) that should engage the student might be, and what the student needs to perform in the assessment task (AT).

The idea of aligning assessment tasks with what it is intended that students should learn is very old – and very obvious. It's called 'criterion-referenced assessment' in the jargon and it's what anyone outside an educational institution does when teaching anyone else anything. Yet as we see in Chapter 9, educational institutions became enamoured of 'norm-referenced assessment', where assessment tasks performed quite a different role: to see who learned better than who. That is an important function when selecting from many people for few positions, such as making an appointment to a job from a large field of applicants or awarding university places or scholarships. However, when the aim of teaching is that students learn specified content to acceptable standards, aligning the test of learning to what is to be learned is not only logical, it is more effective in getting students to learn, as Cohen (1987) concluded after reviewing a raft of studies on the matter. Cohen was so impressed that he called such alignment between the assessment and the intended learning outcome the 'magic bullet' in increasing student performance.

That is all very well for a skill like car driving, you might say, where the learner's activities are explicit, but how can that apply to something that is conceptually of a high level and abstract like learning a theory? The example of 'The nature of teaching and learning' course (see Box 4.1, p. 51) illustrates that it can.

The theory in any course is not only meant to be 'understood', whatever that all-purpose word might specifically mean, but as was argued in the previous chapter it is intended to change the way students see the world and thence to change their behaviour towards it. It isn't only in professional courses that this applies, although it is more obvious in these cases. Virtually all sound learning, whether in medical education or in subjects like pure physics, gives the student a different view of the world, together with the power to change some aspects of it. That view, and instances of the empowerment that learning gives the student, are the outcomes of learning.

All good teachers have some implicit idea of how they want their students to change as a result of their teaching, so they work towards achieving that change when teaching. Constructively aligned teaching systematizes what good teachers have always done: we state upfront what we intend those outcomes to be in the courses we teach – always allowing that desirable outcomes will emerge that we may not have anticipated. Unlike some outcomes-based education, such as competency-based, constructively aligned teaching is not closed loop, focusing only on what is predetermined. As explained later, we use outcomes statements and open-ended assessment tasks that allow for unintended but desirable outcomes.

Another difference between constructive alignment and other outcomes-based approaches is that in constructive alignment, the connections between intended learning outcomes (ILOs), teaching/learning activities (TLAs) and assessment tasks (ATs) are aligned intrinsically, a 'through train' if you like, on the basis of the learning activities expressed in the outcomes statements. In other outcomes-based models, alignment exists only between the ILOs and the assessment tasks, not additionally between the ILOs and the TLAs.

Constructively aligned teaching is likely to be more effective than unaligned because there is maximum consistency throughout the system.

While the curriculum initially contains lists of content topics that are judged desirable for students to learn, those topics are translated into outcome statements that both the teaching/learning activities and the assessments tasks directly address. All components in the system address the same agenda and support each other. The students are 'entrapped' in this web of consistency, optimizing the likelihood that they will engage the appropriate learning activities, helping the Roberts learn more like the Susans but leaving them free to construct their knowledge their way.

Where assessment is not aligned to the intended or other desired outcomes, or where the teaching methods do not directly encourage the appropriate learning activities, students can easily 'escape' by engaging in inappropriate learning activities that become a surface approach to learning. Constructive alignment is a marriage between a constructivist understanding of the nature of learning and an aligned design for teaching that is designed to lock students into deep learning.

A critic of the first edition of this book described constructive alignment as 'spoon feeding'. Spoon feeding, like the other Level 1 metaphors with their curious affinity to metabolic processes – 'regurgitating', 'chewing it over', 'stuffing them with facts', 'ramming down their throats', 'getting your teeth into' – puts a stranglehold on the student's cognitive processes. Spoon feeding does the work for the students, so that they have little left to do but obediently swallow. Constructive alignment, by way of contrast, makes the students themselves do the real work, the teacher simply acts as 'broker' between the student and a learning environment that supports the appropriate learning activities.

It is also important to remember that while the term 'intended' learning outcomes is used, the teaching and assessment should always allow for desirable but unintended outcomes, as these will inevitably occur when students have freedom to construct their own knowledge. The assessments tasks should be open enough to allow for that: an issue we address in Chapters 9 and 11.

Design of constructively aligned teaching and assessment

Let us now unpack the prototypical example of constructive alignment in the course *The Nature of Teaching and Learning*. There are four stages in the design:

1 Describe the intended learning outcome in the form of a verb (learning activity), its object (the content) and specify the context and a standard the students are to attain.
2 Create a learning environment using teaching/learning activities that address that verb and therefore are likely to bring about the intended outcome.

3 Use assessment tasks that also contain that verb, thus enabling you to judge with the help of rubrics if and how well students' performances meet the criteria.
4 Transform these judgments into standard grading criteria.

Intended learning outcomes (ILOs)

The ILOs are statements, written from the students' perspective, indicating the level of understanding and performance they are expected to achieve as a result of engaging in the teaching and learning experience. The ILOs of *The Nature of Teaching and Learning* were, in order of cognitive level, with the learning activities or verbs italicized:

1 *Explain in depth* why a particular course topic is important to teaching.
2 *Explain* how the component course topics interrelate.
3 *Reflect* on your teaching in terms of a working theory you have gained from the course.
4 *Evaluate* a situation that has gone wrong and *apply* a solution.

Each of these verbs addresses 'understanding' at some level: which is why using 'understand' as the verb for your ILOs is inadequate. In the following chapter we shall elaborate on this important question of the level of the outcomes by presenting two taxonomies of verbs that are classified in terms of their cognitive level. For the moment, let us stay with explain, reflect, evaluate and apply.

The first ILO, 'explain in depth', requires that the students choose a topic, say expectancy-value theory, and in their own words relate it to the practice of teaching. The second, 'explain', requires students to view the whole course and explain how the various topics interrelate to form a workable conceptual framework. 'Reflect' in the third ILO is at a higher cognitive level, requiring students to apply that framework they have constructed from the course to their own teaching as reflective practice. The fourth ILO, 'evaluate and apply', requires the students to spot a problem, evaluate it, then suggest how it might be rectified in light of material taught in the course: this too is at a high cognitive level.

The next question is how students were helped to activate these verbs.

Teaching/learning activities (TLAs)

The verbs the students needed to enact are italicized in our list of ILOs. The TLAs were obtained through negotiation with the students, who quickly saw that the usual situation of the teacher lecturing to them wasn't going to help them achieve the outcomes of the course. The following dialogue, condensed from several sessions, illustrates how this happened (S are students, T is teacher):

S How do we show we can reflect?

T Keep a reflective diary or journal.

S What do we put in it?

T What you think are critical incidents in your teaching, anything that might indicate how your teaching has improved, such as samples of conversations with your students, lesson plans, samples of student work.

S That's too vague. We need help to decide what to put in.

T Talk it over with your colleagues. A learning partnership's a good idea. Choose a friend, maybe two, and get their phone number, sit next to them in class. Talk it over together. You can help each other. You can see me in a group if you are in real difficulty.

S Wouldn't it be better if we had discussion groups of students teaching the same subjects as we do? Then we can share experiences on similar problems.

T Certainly. I thought you'd want that. I've already booked the room next door. You can meet there.

S But we'll need direct teaching on some things. Won't you lecture us?

T Yes, but only when that's suitable. There's a topic for each session, I'll give you some pre-reading, just a few pages, before each session with some written answers needed. I'll then meet half the class at a time, while the other half is having a discussion group. We can clarify each topic in the lecture, as necessary.

And so on.

In short, instead of the teacher doing the work of teaching, the students were helped to do what *they* needed to do in order to meet the intended learning outcomes of the course.

The first two ILOs are about 'explaining', which require first that the theories in the course needed to be learned and understood at a sufficient level to allow the two kinds of explanation: in depth, and to integrate the different topics of the course. The TLAs are italicized, as follows.

The content was presented in notes and readings to be *read* before each class. The readings contained self-addressed questions to be *answered*: before the class: 'What do I most want to find out in the next class?' and after the class: 'What is the main point I learned today?' and 'What was the main point left unanswered in today's session?' The questions were *reflected on* and the answers *written* in note form in a journal. Class time, including mass lecture, was used for *questioning, clarifying* and *elaborating*. Each student chose a learning partner to help in *clarifying* and *elaborating* and *interacting* in whatever ways they thought might be helpful.

'Reflection' was encouraged by the journal, which contained the self-addressed questions for each day. Students were asked to *record* learning-related incidents, particularly critical incidents, and to *reflect* on them.

'Evaluation' and 'application' were addressed also with the learning partners (who were also teachers) and to extend the range of exposure to different views and professional experiences, they *discussed* in groups of around 10 students, teaching in the same general content area. The groups had a question to address, but were basically self-directed and students had to *draw their own conclusions.*

Thus, all the learning activities mentioned in the ILOs were embedded in the TLAs in one way or another. Table 4.1 summarizes the alignment between ILOs and the TLAs.

Table 4.1 Intended learning outcomes (ILOs) for *The Nature of Teaching and Learning* and aligned teaching/learning activities (TLAs)

---

1 *Explain in depth* why a particular course topic is important to teaching
TLAs: Plenary sessions with pre-readings and notes used for learning information, clarification and elaboration. Application to teaching by partners and small groups

2 *Explain* how the component course topics interrelate
TLAs: As for (1)

3 *Reflect* on your teaching in terms of a working theory you have gained from the course
TLAs: Keep reflective diary; discuss with group/learning partner

4 *Evaluate* a situation that has gone wrong and *apply* a solution
TLAs: Use workplace resources, group/learning partner comparing perspectives on evaluating and applying

---

Assessment tasks (ATs)

The portfolio required items that addressed each ILO, the highest level having to do with how students' teaching had changed as a result of being informed by theory. The students were to decide on the evidence for their achievement of the ILOs in the form of items for their portfolio and to explain why they thought the portfolio as a whole met the ILOs. Specifically, the requirements were:

1 Four pieces of evidence selected by the student, which they thought addressed most of the ILOs.
2 A reflective journal, including answers to the self-addressed questions for each plenary session.
3 A justification for selecting each portfolio items and the overall case they were supposed to make as a learning package, showing how each ILO had been addressed one way or another. This provided further evidence of students' reflective awareness of their learning.

A list of suggested item types was provided, but original items were encouraged.

Table 4.2 shows the alignment between the ILOs and the items in the portfolio.

Table 4.2   ILOs for *The Nature of Teaching and Learning* and aligned assessment tasks (ATs)

---

1 *Explain in depth* why a particular course topic is important to teaching
AT: Set yourself a 2000-word essay on one of two nominated topics

2 *Explain* how the component course topics interrelate
AT: Concept map of course; letter-to-a-friend

3 *Reflect* on your teaching in terms of a working theory you have gained from the course
AT: Present selected parts of diary with comments: explain how your portfolio items meet ILOs and self-evaluate

4 *Evaluate* a situation that has gone wrong and *apply* a solution
AT: Write a case study of a critical incident in your own teaching and how you dealt with it

---

One student referred to the assessment portfolio as 'a learning tool'. In fact, it was difficult to separate what was a TLA and what an AT, as is the case in an aligned system. For example, students learned how to reflect by using the journal, which was used later as evidence of reflection; the self-addressed questions ('What was the most important idea') are both learning activities and evidence for the quality of learning. Grappling with the task you want students to learn is automatically both a learning process and a learning outcome.

Grading

The final step is to obtain a final grade for the student from the evidence presented in the portfolio as to how well the ILOs have been achieved. There are normally two aspects to grading: assessing the student's outputs against the stated criteria and combining results from several ATs to form a final grade. This can be done quantitatively, as is usually the case, or qualitatively: these issues and the pros and cons are discussed in Chapter 9.

In the case of *The Nature of Teaching and Learning*, a qualitative approach was taken as being the most suitable for the task and the context. Each letter grade represents a qualitatively different level of thinking, as follows:

A Able to reflect, self-evaluate realistically, able to formulate and apply theory to problematic classroom situations, clear mastery of course contents.
B Can apply theory to practice, a holistic understanding of course and components, barely failed **A**.
C Can explain the more important theories, can describe other topics acceptably, barely failed **B**.
D Can only explain some theories, barely failed **C**.
F Less than **D**; plagiarism.

The grading was simple, involving no quantitative 'marking' or averaging to calculate a final grade. The portfolio items were assessed as to whether they provided 'evidence' for A qualities, B qualities, and so on. If the evidence collectively did not reveal realistic self-evaluation, for example, but did show an ability to form a working theory and apply it to classroom situations, then here was a clear B.

Summary and conclusions

This chapter described how constructive alignment came about and how the unit in which it was first used illustrates the important stages. By way of summary let us generalize by reference to Figure 4.1, which can be used as a general framework for teaching. Although it arose in a professional programme, it can be implemented in virtually any course at any level of university teaching.

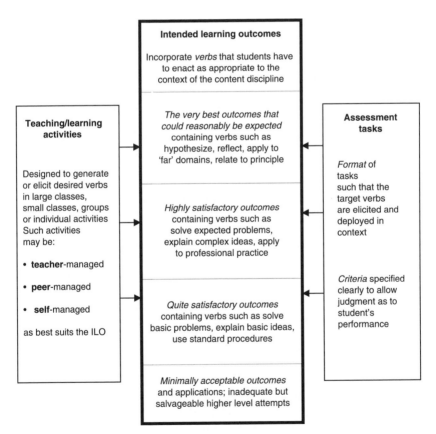

Figure 4.1   Aligning intended learning outcomes, teaching and assessment tasks

The intended learning outcomes are central to the whole system. Get them right and the decisions as to how they are to be taught and how they may be assessed follow. We express the ILOs in terms of what constructive activities are most likely to achieve them. Activities are *verbs*, so, practically speaking, we specify the verbs we want students to enact in the context of the content discipline being taught.

Turn back to Figure 1.1 (p. 10). We see that Susan tended spontaneously to use high-level outcome verbs such as theorize, reflect, generate, apply, whereas Robert used lower level outcome verbs such as recognize, memorize and so on. Their level of engagement is expressed in the cognitive level of the verbs used: reflection is high level, memorizing low level. Note that these verbs are examples only. Precisely what is meant by 'level', and how to determine it, is a key issue addressed in Chapter 5.

Those verbs take objects, the content being taught. We explicitly reject the one-dimensional notion of 'covering' the topics in the curriculum, by specifying the *levels* of understanding or of performance that should be manifested in the learning outcomes intended for the particular content discipline.

Once we have sorted out the ILOs, we design TLAs that are likely to encourage students to engage the verbs that are made explicit in the ILOs, thus optimizing the chances that the intended outcomes will be achieved. Next, we select assessment tasks that will tell us whether and how well each student can meet the criteria expressed in the ILOs. Again, this is done by embedding the verbs in the ILOs in the assessment tasks. ILOs, teaching and assessment are now aligned, using the verbs in the ILOs as markers for alignment.

Finally, a grading scheme needs to be constructed according to how well the ILOs have been met. A grade of A denotes a quality of learning and understanding that is the best one can reasonably expect for the course. Obviously, that level will become increasingly higher from first year to more senior years. In the final year, one would expect the sorts of verbs in the top box ('generalize', 'reflect'), B is highly satisfactory, but lacks the flair that distinguishes A. C is quite satisfactory, while D denotes what is minimally acceptable; anything less is fail (F). What that range will be for any particular course is a matter of judgment. The criteria, or rubrics, defining the final grades will need to be much more specific than this and will need to be developed for each course. The important thing is that the categories are defined by a particular *quality* of learning and understanding, not by the accumulation of marks or percentages.

Grading on the *quality* of learning is not new. The term 'first class honours' has been used for a long time to capture the idea that a student with first-class honours *thinks differently* from a student with an upper second. This difference is not captured by saying that a first has to obtain *x* more marks than an upper second. We have more to say on this in Chapter 9.

To sum up, in an outcomes-based aligned system of teaching, the teacher's task is to see that the appropriate learning activities, conveniently expressed as verbs, are:

1 nominated in the intended learning outcome statements
2 embedded in the chosen teaching/learning activities so that performing them brings the student closer to achieving the ILOs
3 embedded in the assessment tasks enabling judgments about how well a given student's level of performance meets the ILOs.

Because the TLAs and the ATs now access the same verbs as are in the ILOs, the chances are increased that most students will, in fact, engage with the appropriate verbs, which is by definition a deep approach. Had Ramsden's psychology teacher (see pp. 22–3) included in the ILOs such verbs as 'theorize', 'generalize' or 'explain the contribution of particular founders of modern psychology', an assessment task that required only paraphrasing 'a bit of factual information for two pages of writing' would immediately be seen to be inadequate.

Constructive alignment is common sense. Mothers, like driving instructors, use it all the time. What is the intended outcome? That the child can tie her shoes. What is the TLA? Tying her shoes. What is the assessment? How well she ties her shoes. It is so obvious, yet most university teaching is not aligned. There are several reasons for this:

1 Traditional transmission theories of teaching ignore alignment. A common method of determining students' grades depends on how students compare to each other ('norm-referenced'), rather than on whether an individual's learning meets the intended outcomes ('criterion-referenced'). In the former case, there is no *inherent* relation between what is taught and what is tested. The aim is to get a spread between students, not to see how well individuals have learned what they were supposed to have learned.
2 'If it ain't broke, don't fix it.' Some teachers genuinely do believe there's nothing wrong with current practice. As we saw in Chapter 1, however, there are problems of teaching that are arising in the rapidly changing university scene. In any case, a situation doesn't have to be 'broke' before we may profitably start improving matters. The difference between reflective and unreflective teachers is that the former teachers believe they can always teach better than they are at present. Indeed, a major feature of award-winning university teachers was that they were continually seeking feedback from students on ways in which they could improve their teaching (Dunkin and Precians 1992).
3 Some administrative factors, such as resource limitations, appear to dictate large classes with mass lecturing and multiple-choice testing. These make alignment difficult, but not impossible. Some administrative requirements, however, such as requiring teachers to use norm referencing by grading on the curve, do make alignment impossible. If constructive alignment is to be implemented such policies and practices need be changed, as we discuss in Chapter 12.
4 People hadn't thought of it before. Many of these matters may not have occurred to teachers.
5 Others might like to use the principle but they don't know how to.

These points are addressed throughout this book. We shall see how the principle of alignment can be applied to the design of most units.

Further reading

Biggs, J.B. (1996) Enhancing teaching through constructive alignment, *Higher Education*, 32: 1–18

This paper outlines in detail the original course that gave rise to constructive alignment.

DVD

Teaching Teaching & Understanding Understanding, an award-winning DVD from the University of Aarhus, Denmark, written and directed by Claus Brabrand. In less than 20 minutes, Claus takes the viewer through the basics of constructive alignment with Doina and Rune, Danish versions of Susan and Robert. Available from Aarhus University Press (www.unipress.dk) in English, French, Spanish, Italian, Portuguese, German and Danish.

Websites

The Engineering Subject Centre, Higher Education Academy, UK: http://www.engsc.ac.uk/er/theory/constructive_alignment.asp

An excellent overview of constructive alignment, with links to related topics such as 'Assessment', 'Approaches to learning' etc.

University of Wales at Bangor, North Wales: http://riel.bangor.ac.uk/the/Testing%20a%20Model%20of%20Constructive%20Alignment%20-%20planning_files/frame.htm/

A nice easy PowerPoint presentation by Romy Lawson.

National Council of Open and Distance Education and the Teaching and Learning Centre, Southern Cross University: http://www.scu.edu.au/services/tl/sd_online/consalign.html

A version of constructive alignment in an online course on course design, with examples.

What is the evidence on constructive alignment?

http://www.ed.ac.uk/etl/project.html

This is the website for the ETL project led by Noel Entwistle and Dai Hounsell of the University of Edinburgh. The project, which has been running since 2001, seeks to develop subject-specific conceptual frameworks to guide institutional and faculty or departmental development of teaching–learning environments. Constructive alignment is one of the key concepts underlining the thinking of the project.

Other

The home page of the Higher Education Academy http://www.heacademy.ac.uk/ is well worth visiting for a browse. The recently established HEA is just so resource rich: click 'Supporting learning'.

Outcomes-based learning in general

http://merlin.capcollege.bc.ca/mbatters/whatsalearningoutcome.htm

A very good discussion of outcomes-based learning, as these authors call it. The difference between this and constructive alignment is that the *means* of tuning teaching and assessment to achieving the outcomes is left open, whereas in constructive alignment we progress using the verbs.

If you want more, Google 'constructive alignment' and browse.

5

Designing intended learning outcomes

Intended learning outcomes (ILOs) apply at the *institutional* level as graduate attributes, and at the *programme* and *course* levels.* Graduate attributes can provide useful guidelines for designing programme outcomes, which, in turn, are addressed by the outcomes of specific courses. Most of this chapter is taken up with the design and writing of course ILOs, as these are the ones with which teachers are specifically concerned and to which teaching and assessment are aligned. It is important to stipulate the kind of knowledge to be learned, declarative or functioning, and to use a verb and a context that indicates clearly the level at which it is to be learned and how the performance is to be displayed. The SOLO taxonomy is a useful tool for selecting verbs of an appropriate level of complexity.

Intended learning outcomes at different levels

As we saw in the previous chapter, an intended learning outcome (ILO) is a statement describing what and how a student is expected to learn after exposure to teaching. Such an outcome statement can be made at three levels:

- the *institutional* level, as a statement of what the graduates of the university are supposed to be able to do
- the degree *programme* level, as a statement of what graduates from particular degree programmes should be able to do
- the *course* level, as a statement of what students should be able to do at the completion of a given course.

* We use 'programme' to refer to the whole degree pattern. Some universities refer to this as a 'course', as in a course of study. We use 'course' to refer to the units of study making up a programme, whereas others refer to this as a 'unit', 'module' or 'subject'.

Let us now look at each in turn.

Graduate attributes

It has long been believed that university study has an effect on the way graduates think and act, over and above the knowledge and skills that have been learned in the official curriculum of the degree programme. For example, graduates are thought not to accept 'spin' as readily as non-graduates, to feel a need to seek and evaluate evidence before coming to a conclusion, to question the status quo, to show intellectual curiosity about the physical or social world. Public opinion used to expect certain moral behaviour from graduates ('He ought to know better with his education!'). The public service, too, used to recruit graduates, without stipulating any particular area of study, on the grounds that they would be employing a certain sort of person. This sort of thinking has the following view of education: 'When you have forgotten everything you were ever taught, what is left is education' (Anon.).

The Higher Education Council (HEC) of Australia defines the attributes a graduate should possess as:

> The skills, personal attributes and values which should be acquired by all graduates regardless of their discipline or field of study. In other words, generic skills should represent the central achievements of higher education as a process.
>
> (HEC 1992: 20)

The Dearing Report for its part referred to a culture that demanded similar attributes, but also that students should 'become part of the conscience of a democratic society' (Dearing 1997: 1). Both reports are looking to employability at a time when students are more than ever seeing a university degree as a lifelong meal ticket and, more broadly, to qualities that responsible citizens in a global society should have. Such attributes include 'critical thinking', 'ethical practice', 'creativity', 'independent problem solving', 'professional skills', 'communications skills', 'teamwork', 'lifelong learning' and the like. But what are these qualities really and, more to the point, how are they supposed to be acquired in such varied fields as accountancy, veterinary science or social work? Or are they simple generic abilities that apply across the board to any subject?

And this is the problem. We are clearly dealing with more specific residues than what is left after you've forgotten everything you were ever taught. There are several different conceptions of graduate attributes, which makes it difficult for universities to agree on an institution-wide policy in fostering them (Barrie 2004). Barrie, after a phenomenographic analysis of teachers' conceptions of graduate attributes, arrived at a hierarchy of conceptions. The lowest sees attributes as *generic* foundation skills that are unrelated to any particular discipline area, such as numeracy and communication skills that can be taught in standalone courses. At the other extreme are attributes as abilities that are deeply *embedded* in particular disciplines: for example, problem solving strategies that involve thinking like a physicist won't be of much help in solving problems of medical diagnosis. Teachers who hold the latter view are not going to be very concerned about fostering a generic problem solving ability, only that they make sure that their students are required to show evidence of the appropriate problem solving strategies in their academic performances, especially in the higher years. Otherwise, they do not see developing graduate attributes as their responsibility.

A major issue is that if these attributes are to be taught, then how: in standalone courses or as embedded in normal courses? Or perhaps some attributes can be taught as standalone, others as embedded – and if so, which should be handled in what mode of delivery? Some attributes can reasonably be seen as generic and standalone, literacy skills for example, but rather more are seen as standalone when they are best not seen that way, creativity being an example. Should there be a course in Creativity 101 that all students must pass? We hope not, because you can't teach creativity that way, not in any significant sense, because genuine creativity requires significant substantive knowledge in a given area. Others are not quite so clear cut, such as critical thinking and possibly independent problem solving. There are two separate issues here that are often confused:

1 Are there such things as general problem-solving or critical-thinking abilities that work across the board? There almost certainly are. In fact, one of our aims is that graduates can transfer skills learned in one domain to another.

2 If that is the case, then can they be taught out of context, in standalone or foundation courses? The research on this question is discouraging: some minor skills probably can be directly taught, but it is far better to teach them in one context, learning any generic problem-solving or critical-thinking skills in that context, then encouraging transfer to another context. This is much preferable to teaching all-purpose problem-solving and critical-thinking skills in a vacuum, out of context. In fact, 'far transfer', from one domain to another, should be in the ILOs of many higher level courses. It may be helpful to provide some generic courses in study skills and metacognitive study strategies (pp. 149, 150–1), but these are better regarded as 'top-ups', not as substitutes for teaching problem solving in embedded contexts.

Most universities want both kinds of attributes to be addressed, as do quality assurance agencies, not to mention employers who want to be assured that graduates have the attributes claimed. However, if attributes such as creativity or critical thinking are embedded in general teaching, they are less visible; they may not even be directly assessed. Attributes in standalone courses (e.g. Critical Thinking 101) can be seen to have been addressed and assessed, so the quality assurance committee is duly impressed at the next institutional audit or process review. The fact that the critical thinking may not necessarily apply in depth to the content area in which the graduate has studied, but only to across-the-board exercises in the standalone class, may easily be overlooked.

A rather ruthless approach to attribute assessment is given by Yuen-Heung et al. (2005) in a US university. The attributes, or 'university learning goals', are not an atypical list: 'leadership', 'independent lifelong learning', 'values-based decision making', 'develop service potential', 'critical thinking' 'logical reasoning', 'written communication' and 'oral communication'. Students are rated by teachers on goals and each goal's sub-goals. Independent lifelong learning has 14 sub-goals, critical thinking 13, and so on, making 74 goals and sub-goals in all. Students not meeting a satisfactory level on any goal or sub-goal are 'lifted' until they do. One must be forgiven for thinking that the time and effort going into this might be better spent in simply teaching.

Knight (2006), by way of contrast, takes a strong embedded view. He says that attributes such as reasoning, creativity, ethical practice, teamworking and collaboration and so on are complex 'achievements' or 'wicked competences' that develop rather than are taught. They have no single cause, are slow growing and need a complex environment, an *ethos* – a particular climate, a sequence of role models – in which to develop. They are unlikely to be achieved if they are only addressed in one or a few courses. Their assessment cannot be measured with what Knight calls 'high-stakes assessment' instruments of high reliability, such as tests. Self- and peer-assessment, and particularly portfolios, in which students make claims that they themselves try to substantiate are more suitable. In this view, graduate attributes are desirable outcomes that need continually looking to, such that they are fostered in teaching over a range of subjects and interactions with students.

How do we resolve these contradictory positions and derive an internally consistent policy for any given institution? Barrie (2004) proposes an interactive model that sees two levels of attributes. The first are holistic and overarching 'attitudes or stances', as he refers to them:

1 *Scholarship*, relating to academic knowledge, competence and openness to inquiry.
2 *Global citizenship*, relating to societal responsibilities and obligations.
3 *Lifelong learning*, relating to the self as committed to continuous learning and reflection and dealing with new problems and issues as they arise.

The next level has five attributes:

1 Research and inquiry.
2 Information literacy.
3 Personal and intellectual autonomy.
4 Ethical commitment, socially and professionally.
5 Communication skills and commitment.

The interrelations are given in Figure 5.1.

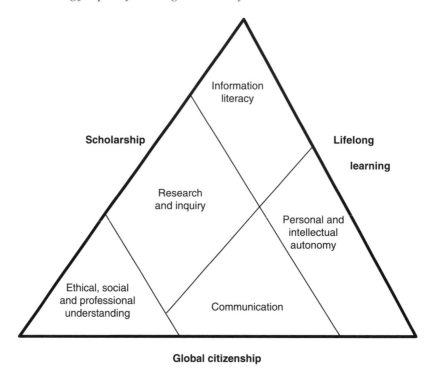

Figure 5.1   Interrelations between two levels of graduate attributes

Source: Adapted from Barrie (2004)

We return to this structure in Chapter 8 with respect to designing teaching/learning activities for lifelong learning. But before we start thinking about how to teach lifelong learning, programme committees need first to deal with these levels and interrelations in order to derive programme, then course, ILOs. This is a complex question that will differ from university to university according to their mix of attributes and their policies on addressing them.

Even before the problem is relegated to the programme level, we might return to Knight's point that the institutional climate itself has a formative effect on some attributes. Ethical behaviour, lifelong learning, creativity and so on are more likely to thrive in a Theory Y institutional climate that itself values such attributes in the very real sense that it enacts them in its own policies and procedures. Constructively aligned courses, where both teaching and assessment address the ILOs, some at least of which are specifically tuned to these attributes, are important too. A consistent message can then be maintained across courses with respect to the overall programme design.

We turn to that level next.

Intended learning outcomes at the programme level

In translating graduate attributes to programme outcomes, two aspects need to be reconciled. The first is mapping the graduate attributes onto the programme. The second is designing the programme ILOs from the aims of the particular degree programme itself. Any degree programme is established in order to achieve a definite aim that will itself generate course ILOs – that many academics will see as more important than ILOs generated to serve graduate attributes. The claims of these two determinants of ILOs, graduate attributes and specific programme aims, need to be reconciled.

Let us start with the aims of the programme itself: what is it meant to achieve, and what is its focus and its context? For example, take a bachelor of business management, BBM (accountancy). The focus, let us say, is on accounting and the programme graduates are to serve the professional, commercial and industrial sector. This aim is served if graduates can achieve the following outcomes:

1 Describe and explain the conceptual framework and practical skills of the accounting profession.
2 Analyse this framework of accounting and apply the practical skills to real-life accounting situations.
3 Communicate effectively as a professional with clients and colleagues in real-life accounting situations.
4 Operate effectively and ethically as a team member in real-life accounting situations.

These programme ILOs are in effect the reasons for establishing the programme. There would usually be only a few such reasons; rarely would they exceed, say, six. However, when graduate attributes address a whole range of outcomes classified under knowledge, skill, values and social concerns (e.g. Ewell 1984), it is very difficult to use these to drive programme, then course, ILOs because it is not possible to align teaching/learning activities and assessment tasks to all these possible outcomes.

Having derived these programme-specific ILOs, the next question is how to reconcile these with general graduate attributes. A simple solution is to see that programme committees and course teachers check that where *possible and appropriate* the intended learning outcomes address the listed graduate attributes, grounded in the content and context of the degree programme. Thus degrees in education, social work, fine arts, computing science or business and management would address different mixes of graduate attributes. The meaning of 'creativity', say, is then confined to the particular areas the student has studied – with hopefully some overflow to a way of thinking, but no promises – but most or all degree programmes would address 'creativity' in some way or another. Here, the focus is on the programme and course outcomes, the graduate attributes being used only to jog the memory when writing ILOs and deriving the criteria for assessing assessment tasks. A hardline approach to accountability may not, however, consider this rigorous enough.

One problem with being too rigorous is that attributes, particularly in the social/value domain, have varying degrees of relevance to different programmes. Empathy, say, is highly appropriate in a social work degree, rather less so in, say, computer programming. A social worker lacking empathy clearly should not be awarded a degree in social work, but one would be inviting big trouble withholding a degree from a computer scientist on the basis of lack of empathy. To insist that inappropriate or irrelevant attribute/outcomes are forced into all programmes irrespective of suitability is to invite resistance and cynicism from students.

Reconciling specific programme ILOs with the requirements of the university's graduate attributes policy is a question specific to each institution and there are various ways of handling it (Bath et al. 2004; Sumsion and Goodfellow 2004).

The important question, as far as teaching itself is concerned, is deriving the course ILOs from programme ILOs and graduate attributes, however that is done.

Intended learning outcomes at the course level

In previous editions of this book, we used the term 'curriculum objectives' or just 'objectives' for the intended outcomes of a course. We now think the term 'intended learning outcome' (ILO) is better because it emphasizes more than does 'objective' that we are referring to what the student has to learn rather than what the teacher has to teach. 'Intended learning outcome' clarifies what the student should be able to perform after teaching that couldn't be performed previously – and there may well be outcomes that are a positive outcome of teaching that weren't intended. 'Objective' was intended to have the latter, student-centred, meaning but ILO makes it absolutely clear that the outcomes are from the student's perspective. The term 'objective' also may recall in older readers the problems associated with 'behavioural objectives'.

'The student will understand expectancy-value theory' might be a teaching objective, but it is not an ILO. Likewise the following example, taken from the objectives for an occupational therapy unit: 'At the end of this unit, students will be able to understand the concept of muscle tone and its relation to functional activity.' What does it mean 'to understand the concept of muscle tone'? What learning activities are involved? What level of understanding are the students to achieve? Here is an objective that is not an ILO.

With an ILO we need to make a statement about what students' learning would look like after they have learned expectancy-value theory to the acceptable standard. Defining that standard of the outcome of learning is important. Verbs like 'understand', 'comprehend', 'be aware of' are unhelpful in ILOs because they do not convey the *level* of performance we require if the ILO is to be met. Even the quite common 'demonstrate an understanding of' leave important questions unanswered: what does the student have to do to demonstrate 'an' understanding? What level of understanding does the teacher have in mind – simple acquaintance? Able to point to an instance of? Apply in a real-life situation? One of the key criteria of a good ILO is that the student, when seeing a written ILO, would know what to do and how well to do it in order to meet the ILO. Box 5.1 presents the conventional objectives of a course in engineering, then the same course expressed in ILOs.

Box 5.1 From objectives to intended learning outcomes in an engineering course

Objectives (old)	ILOs (new)
1 To provide an understanding of the kinematics and kinetics of machines and the fundamental concepts of stress and strain analysis	1 To *describe* the basic principles of kinematics and kinetics of machines and the fundamental concepts of stress and strain analysis
2 To develop an analytical understanding of the kinematics and kinetics and elastic behaviours of machine elements under loading	2 Using given principles, to *solve* a mechanical problem that involves loading and motion
	3 To *select* relevant principles to obtain the solutions for mechanical problems
	4 To *present* analyses and results of experiments in a proper format of a written report such that a technically qualified person can follow and obtain similar findings

Source: Patrick Wong and Lawrence Li, Department of Mechanical and Electrical Engineering, City University of Hong Kong

---

The main reasons for teaching a course – as with a programme – usually amount to no more than five or six. Each ILO might be regarded as one of these reasons. The more ILOs, the more difficult it becomes to align teaching/learning activities and assessment tasks to each. Trying to impose a knowledge, skill, value and attitude template, with all their sub-domains, is as inappropriate at the course level as we saw it was at the programme level.

When writing course ILOs, we need specifically to:

1 decide what kind of knowledge is to be involved
2 select the topics to teach and decide the level of understanding desirable for students to achieve and how it is to be displayed.

We now turn to these important issues. This will enable us to start writing the course ILOs themselves. Finally, we address the question of alignment itself, involving all three levels of institution, programme, and course outcomes.

Kinds of knowledge and levels of understanding

Kinds of knowledge

Knowledge, as the object of understanding at whatever level, comes in two main kinds. *Declarative*, or propositional, knowledge refers to *knowing about* things, or 'knowing-what': knowing what Freud said, knowing what the terms of an equation refer to, knowing what kinds of cloud formation can be distinguished, knowing what were the important events in Shakespeare's life. Such content knowledge accrues from research, not from personal experience. It is public knowledge, subject to rules of evidence that make it verifiable, replicable and logically consistent. It is what is in libraries and textbooks and is what teachers 'declare' in lectures. Students' understanding of it can be tested by getting them to declare it back, in their own words and using their own examples. Such knowledge is basic to applications and creations, but is separate from them.

Functioning knowledge is based on the idea of performances of various kinds underpinned by understanding. This knowledge is within the experience of the learner, who can now put declarative knowledge to work by solving problems, designing buildings, planning teaching or performing surgery. Functioning knowledge requires a solid foundation of declarative knowledge.

These distinctions tell us what our curricula might address. Curricula in many universities are overwhelmingly declarative with teaching methods correspondingly expository. One study from the University of Texas found that university teachers spent 88% of their teaching time in lecturing students (cited by Bok 2006), yet students are supposed to be educated so that they can interact thoughtfully with professional problems; to use functioning knowledge, in other words. Unfortunately, often it is only the foundation declarative knowledge that is taught, leaving it to the students when they graduate to put it to work.

The traditional way of teaching psychology to education students illustrates this problem. The reason for teaching psychology is that teachers should know something about such topics as human learning and motivation, child development, the nature of intelligence, and so on and on, not for the good of their souls, but so they may *teach better*. However, until recently, these topics were taught and the students assessed on how well they had learned them – on their declarative knowledge of the topics – not on how well they applied their topic knowledge to their teaching. With the exception of courses using problem-based learning, the *application* of the theoretical content to teaching or to any other professional practice was left up to the student, when 'out there, in the real world'. When this happens, the most important intended outcome of the course and of the whole programme – that students would teach more effectively by virtue of having learned all that theory – has been ignored in both the teaching and the assessment of the theory courses. It was this realization that prompted the use of portfolio assessment as reported in the last chapter (Box 4.1, p. 51).

This is a problem not only of teacher education. The theory component in professional programmes in general is often treated as an end in itself, not as a means to performing in a more informed and effective way. While some courses in a degree programme, and some topics in probably all courses, need to be taught and assessed in their own right, the higher levels of 'understanding', involving reflection and application, need to be assessed in terms of how students' learning is manifested in better professional practice as their functioning knowledge.

Leinhardt et al. (1995) make a similar distinction between 'professional' knowledge and 'university' knowledge:

- *Professional knowledge* is functioning, specific and pragmatic. It deals with executing, applying and making priorities.
- *University knowledge* is declarative, abstract, and conceptual. It deals with labelling, differentiating, elaborating and justifying.

In other words, would-be professionals are trained in universities to label, differentiate, elaborate and justify, when what they need out in the field is to execute, apply and prioritize!

Entwistle and Entwistle (1997) found that the forms of understanding encouraged by university accreditation and assessment procedures are not those that are professionally relevant (see later). The rhetoric is right, but, in practice, universities tend to focus on declarative knowledge, which students often see as irrelevant and hence worthy of only a surface approach.

The problem is lack of alignment between intended learning outcomes and the means of teaching and assessing them. Graduates need to face new problems and to interact with them, reflectively and thoughtfully. Predicting, diagnosing, explaining, and solving non-textbook problems are what professionals have to do, so this is what university teachers should aim to get their students to do, particularly in senior years. Building such performances of understanding into the course ILOs, aligning teaching to them and designing assessment tasks that confirm that students can or cannot carry out those performances, is a good way to start.

But first, the question of understanding 'understanding'.

Performances of understanding

Ask any teacher what they want of their students and they will say they don't want their students just to memorize, they want them to *understand*. Consequently, that verb is the first they think of when designing the intended learning outcome statements. The trouble is that 'understand' can mean very different things, from the trivial to the complex.

Does the previously mentioned teaching objective, 'The student will understand expectancy-value theory', mean that the student is able to:

1 write a textbook definition of expectancy-value theory
2 explain how it works in the student's own words
3 watch a video of a teacher–student interaction and be able to predict what is likely to happen to the student's motivation afterwards
4 reflect on the student's own teaching to illustrate that a problem that had occurred could be accounted for and rectified in terms of expectancy-value theory?

All these are examples of 'understanding' at some level or other. Clearly, we need to pin down the level of understanding we want when stating the ILO. The ILO needs to make a statement as to that standard, which is done by selecting a suitable verb.

Entwistle and Entwistle (1997) conducted a series of studies on what students meant by 'understanding' and then asked them how they attempt to understand when preparing for examinations. The students described the experience of understanding as *satisfying*; it was good to have the feeling that you understood at last. It also felt *complete*, a whole, as previously unrelated things were suddenly integrated. The experience was irreversible; what is now understood cannot be 'de-understood'. Students thought a good practical test of understanding was being able to explain to someone else or to be able to adapt and to use what had been understood. These are pretty good definitions of sound understandings that probably fit most teachers' requirements: you want students to interrelate topics, to adapt and use the knowledge so understood, to explain it to others and to feel satisfied and good about it.

Unfortunately, when it came to the examinations, these indicators of understanding evaporated. Students attempted instead to understand in ways that they thought would meet assessment requirements. Understanding then took on much less desirable forms. The Entwistles distinguished five:

1 Reproduces content from lecture notes without any clear structure.
2 Reproduces the content within the structure used by the lecturer.
3 Develops own structure, but only to generate answers to anticipated examination questions.
4 Adjusts structures from strategic reading of different sources to represent personal understanding, but also to control examination requirements.

5 Develops an individual conception of the discipline from wide reading and reflection.

Only the last form of understanding, described by a small minority of students, is anything like the students' own definitions. All other forms focused on meeting examination requirements. The examinations actually prevented students from achieving their own personal understandings of the content, which the Entwistles understandably found 'worrying'. Many of these students were in their final year, just prior to professional practice, yet the assessment system pre-empted the very level of understanding that would be professionally relevant. Worrying indeed.

To use our learning in order to negotiate with the world and to see it differently involves understanding of a high order. It is the kind of understanding that is referred to in the rhetoric of university teaching, yet seems hard to impart. If students 'really' understood a concept they would *act differently* in contexts involving that concept and would use the concept in unfamiliar or novel contexts: these are called *performances of understanding* (Gardner 1993; Wiske 1998).

The challenge is to conceive our intended learning outcomes in terms of these performances of understanding, rather than in verbal declarations of understanding. The difference between meeting the requirements of institutional learning and 'real' understanding is illustrated in Gunstone and White's (1981) demonstrations with Physics I students. In one demonstration, two balls, one heavy and one light, were held in the air in front of the students. They were asked to predict, if the balls were released simultaneously, which one would hit the ground first and why. Many predicted that the heavy one would 'because heavy things have a bigger force' or 'gravity is stronger nearer the earth' (both are true but irrelevant). These students had 'understood' gravity well enough to pass HSC (A Level) physics, but few understood well enough to answer a simple real-life question about gravity. They could correctly solve problems using the formula for g – which does not contain a term for the mass of the object falling – while still reacting in the belief that heavy objects fall faster. They didn't *really* understand gravity in the performative sense – and why should they if their teaching and assessment didn't require them to? These physics students hadn't changed their commonsense conceptions of gravity, but had placed alongside them a set of statements and formulae about physical phenomena that would see them through the exams. To really understand physics or mathematics, history or accountancy is to *think like* a physicist, a mathematician, a historian or an accountant; and that shows in how you behave. Once you really understand a sector of knowledge, it changes that part of the world; you don't behave towards that domain in the same way again.

Gunstone and White's physics students were good at verbally declaring their knowledge, for example, explaining what gravity, or the three laws of motion, are about. But is this why we are teaching these topics? Is it for acquaintance, so that students know something about the topic and can answer the sorts of stock questions that typify examination papers? In that case, declarative understanding will suffice. Or is it to change the way (sooner or later) students can understand and control reality? If that is the case, then a performative level of understanding is implicated.

Levels of understanding

So far we have been talking about the end point, 'real' understanding. However, understanding develops gradually, becoming more structured and articulated as it develops. Undergraduates will not attain the level of precision and complexity of the subject expert, but we want none to retain the plausible misunderstandings that marked Gunstone and White's physics students' understanding of gravity.

We thus need to define understanding in ways that do justice to the topics and content we teach, as appropriate to the year level taught. The task is to define what is acceptable for each stage of the degree programme, given a student's specialization and degree pattern. That is a highly specific matter that only the teacher and subject expert can decide, but a general framework for structuring levels of understanding helps teachers to make those decisions and it also provides a basis for discussing levels across different years and subject areas. Once a sound understanding of the basic structural framework is achieved, adapting it to particular course ILOs is straightforward.

The SOLO taxonomy is based on the study of outcomes in a variety of academic content areas (Biggs and Collis 1982). As students learn, the outcomes of their learning display similar stages of increasing structural complexity. There are two main changes: *quantitative*, as the amount of detail in the student's response increases; and *qualitative*, as that detail becomes integrated into a structural pattern. The quantitative stages of learning occur first, then learning changes qualitatively.

SOLO, which stands for **s**tructure of the **o**bserved **l**earning **o**utcome, provides a systematic way of describing how a learner's performance grows in complexity when mastering many academic tasks. It can be used to define course ILOs, which describe where students *should* be operating and for evaluating learning outcomes so that we can know at what level individual students actually *are* operating.

To illustrate, let us take some content with which you are all now familiar and see where you stand on your level of understanding of it.

What are approaches to learning? How can knowledge of approaches to learning enhance university teaching?

In a few sentences, outline your answer to these questions. **Stop reading any further until you have completed the task.** Then turn to Task 5.1 and try to evaluate your own response and against the model responses.

Task 5.1   SOLO levels in approaches to learning question and why

The following levels of response could be observed (but, it is to be hoped, the first three responses were not):

1 *Prestructural*

'Teaching is a matter of getting students to approach their learning.'

This response could have been written by somebody with understanding at the individual word level, but little understanding of what was discussed in the previous chapter. Prestructural responses simply miss the point or, like this one, use tautology to cover lack of understanding. These responses can be quite sophisticated, such as the kind of elaborate tautology that politicians use to avoid answering questions, but, academically, they show little evidence of relevant learning.

2 *Unistructural*

'Approaches to learning are of two kinds: surface, which is inappropriate for the task at hand, and deep, which is appropriate. Teachers need to take this into account.'

This is unistructural because it meets only one part of the task, defining what approaches to learning are in terms of just one aspect, appropriateness. It misses other important attributes, for example that they are ways of describing students' learning activities and what might influence them, while the reference to teaching adds nothing. Unistructural responses deal with terminology, getting on track but little more.

3 *Multistructural*

'Approaches to learning are of two kinds: surface, which is inappropriate for the task at hand, and deep, which is appropriate. Students using a surface approach try to fool us into believing that they understand by rote learning and quoting back to us, sometimes in great detail. Students using a deep approach try to get at the underlying meaning of their learning tasks. Teaching is about getting students to learn appropriately, not getting by with shortcuts. We should therefore teach for meaning and understanding, which means encouraging them to adopt a deep approach.'

We couldn't agree more. The first part is quite detailed (but could be more so); the second part is also what good teaching is about. So what is the problem with this answer? The problem is that this response does not address the key issue: *how* can knowledge of approaches enhance teaching? not *that* they can enhance teaching. This is what Bereiter and Scardamalia (1987) call 'knowledge-telling': snowing the reader with a bunch of facts, but not structuring them as required – and don't be misled by the odd connective like 'therefore'. Here, the students

see the trees but not the wood. Seeing trees is a necessary prelimi-
nary to adequate understanding, but it should not be interpreted as
comprehending the wood.

4 Relational

*'Approaches to learning are of two kinds: . . . (etc.) The approaches come about
partly because of student characteristics, but also because students react differently to their teaching environment in ways that lead them into surface or deep
learning. The teaching environment is a system, a resolution of all the factors
present, such as curriculum, assessment, teaching methods and students' own
characteristics. If there is imbalance in the environment, for example a test that
allows students to respond in a way that does not do justice to the curriculum, or
a classroom climate that scares the hell out of them, the resolution is in favour of
a surface approach. What this means is that we should be consistent.'*

And so on. Here we have an explanation. Both concepts, approaches
and teaching, have been integrated by the concept of a system; examples have been given, and the structure could easily be used to generate
practical steps. The trees have become the wood, a qualitative change
in learning and understanding has occurred. It is no longer a matter of
listing facts and details, they address a point, making sense in light of
their contribution to the topic as a whole. This is the first level at which
'understanding' in an academically relevant sense may appropriately
be used.

5 Extended abstract

We won't give a lengthy example here. The essence of the extended
abstract response is that it goes beyond what has been given, whereas
the relational response stays with it. The coherent whole is conceptual-
ized at a higher level of abstraction and is applied to new and broader
domains. An extended abstract response on approaches to learning
would be a 'breakthrough' response, giving a perspective that changes
what we think about them and their relationship to teaching. The
trouble is that today's extended abstract is tomorrow's relational.
Marton and Säljö's original study was such a breakthrough; linking
approaches to learning to systems theory was another, but now both are
conventional wisdom.

The examples illustrate the five levels of the taxonomy. Uni- and multistructural levels see understanding as a quantitative increase in what is
grasped. These responses were deliberately constructed to show that the
higher level contains the lower level, plus a bit more. The 'bit more' in the
case of multistructural incorporates the unistructural, then more of much
the same – a purely quantitative increase. The 'bit more' in the case of

relational over multistructural involves a qualitative change, a conceptual restructuring of the components, the recognition of the systems property as integrating the components, while the next shift to extended abstract takes the argument into a new dimension. SOLO describes a hierarchy, where each partial construction becomes the foundation on which further learning is built.

This distinction between knowing more and restructuring parallels two major curriculum aims: to *increase knowledge* (quantitative: unistructural becoming increasingly multistructural); and to *deepen understanding* (qualitative: relational, then extended abstract). Teaching and assessment that focus only on the quantitative aspects of learning will miss the more important higher level aspects. Quantitative, Level 1, theories of teaching and learning address the first aim only, so that the deepening of understanding is left to Susan's predilections for spontaneous deep learning activities. The challenge for us is to highlight the qualitative aim in the ILOs and support it by both teaching and assessment methods. Then Robert's understanding is likely to be deepened too.

Using SOLO to design particular intended learning outcome statements is helped considerably by using verbs that parallel the SOLO taxonomy. A visual representation is given in Figure 5.2, with some verbs typical of each level.

The verbs in the staircase are general, indicating what the students need to be able to do to indicate achievement at the level in question. Table 5.1 provides many more verbs from SOLO.

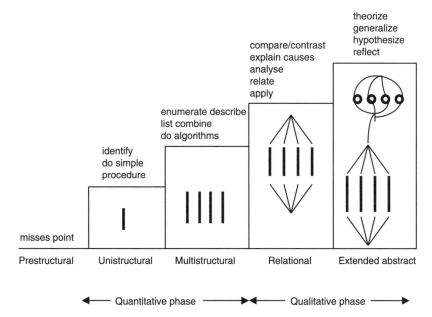

Figure 5.2 A hierarchy of verbs that may be used to form intended learning outcomes

Table 5.1   Some verbs for ILOs from the SOLO taxonomy

Unistructural	Memorize, identify, recognize, count, define, draw, find, label, match, name, quote, recall, recite, order, tell, write, imitate
Multistructural	Classify, describe, list, report, discuss, illustrate, select, narrate, compute, sequence, outline, separate
Relational	Apply, integrate, analyse, explain, predict, conclude, summarize (précis), review, argue, transfer, make a plan, characterize, compare, contrast, differentiate, organize, debate, make a case, construct, review and rewrite, examine, translate, paraphrase, solve a problem
Extended abstract	Theorize, hypothesize, generalize, reflect, generate, create, compose, invent, originate, prove from first principles, make an original case, solve from first principles

This gives us a wide range of levels that can be adapted to the levels appropriate to particular courses, from first to senior years. Particular content areas and topics would have their own specific verbs as well, which you would need to specify to suit your own course. Some verbs could be either extended abstract or relational, depending on, for example, the degree of originality or the context in which the verb was deployed: 'solve a problem', for example. And whether 'paraphrase' is relational or multistructural depends on how the student goes about paraphrasing: replacing with like-meaning phrases or rethinking the meaning of the whole text and rewriting it. Writing ILOs is one thing but when it comes to assessing them it needs to be done in a context so that these ambiguous verbs can be pinned down: to 'show your working', as maths teachers are wont to say.

For another set of verbs, based on Bloom's revised taxonomy (Anderson and Krathwohl 2001), see Table 5.2.

The original Bloom taxonomy was not based on research on student learning itself, as is SOLO, but on the judgments of educational administrators, neither is it hierarchical, as is SOLO. Anderson and Krathwohl's revision is an improvement, but even then under 'understanding' you can find 'identify', 'discuss' and 'explain', which represent three different SOLO levels. This is exactly why 'understand' and 'comprehend' are not helpful terms to use in writing ILOs. However, the Bloom taxonomy is a useful adjunct for suggesting a wider list of verbs, especially for a range of learning activities.

Designing and writing course ILOs

In designing outcomes, there are several points to consider.

Table 5.2   Some more ILO verbs from Bloom's revised taxonomy

Remembering	Define, describe, draw, find, identify, label, list, match, name, quote, recall, recite, tell, write
Understanding	Classify, compare, exemplify, conclude, demonstrate, discuss, explain, identify, illustrate, interpret, paraphrase, predict, report
Applying	Apply, change, choose, compute, dramatize, implement, interview, prepare, produce, role play, select, show, transfer, use
Analysing	Analyse, characterize, classify, compare, contrast, debate, deconstruct, deduce, differentiate, discriminate, distinguish, examine, organize, outline, relate, research, separate, structure
Evaluating	Appraise, argue, assess, choose, conclude, critique, decide, evaluate, judge, justify, predict, prioritize, prove, rank, rate, select, monitor
Creating	Construct, design, develop, generate, hypothesise, invent, plan, produce, compose, create, make, perform, plan, produce

Source: Anderson and Krathwohl (2001)

Decide what kind of knowledge is to be involved

Is the ILO in question about declarative knowledge only: knowing about phenomena, theories, disciplines? Or functioning knowledge: requiring the student to exercise active control over problems and decisions in the appropriate content domains? The ILO should be clear as to what kind of knowledge you want and why. Declarative knowledge in a professional education programme may be taught for various reasons:

- As general 'cultural' content, as in the liberal arts notion of an educated person; e.g. a business management student must take an arts subject for 'broadening'. There is no functioning knowledge involved here.
- As content specifically related to the profession: e.g. the history of western architecture in an architecture degree. This is important background for architects to have, but again there may be little direct bearing on functioning knowledge.
- As content that does bear on functioning knowledge, but is not a key priority. In this case, students might be taught the basic outlines and where to go for more details as and when the need arises.
- As content that definitely bears on everyday decision making. The ILO should be written specifically for seeking the functioning knowledge concerned.

All these different purposes for teaching a topic or course require careful thought as to the balance between coverage and depth. The curriculum is not a plateau of topics, all 'covered' to the same extent, but a series of hills and valleys. In an international phone call, you don't just chat about the weather. We need similarly to prioritize our classroom communications by deciding the depth, or level of understanding required, for each topic, as discussed later.

Select the topics to teach

Selecting the actual topics to teach is obviously a matter of specific content expertise and judgment. You, as the content expert, are best able to decide on this, but when doing so note the tension between coverage and depth of understanding.

There is almost always strong pressure to include more and more content, particularly when teachers share the teaching of a course and in professional faculties where outside bodies validate courses. All concerned see their own special topic or interest as the most important. Over-teaching is the inevitable result:

> The greatest enemy of understanding is coverage – I can't repeat that often enough. If you're determined to cover a lot of things, you are guaranteeing that most kids will not understand, because they haven't had time enough to go into things in depth, to figure out what the requisite understanding is, and be able to perform that understanding in different situations.
>
> (Gardner 1993: 24)

If we conceive the curriculum as a rectangle, the area (breadth x depth) remains constant. Take your pick. Breadth: wide coverage and surface learning giving disjointed multistructural outcomes. Depth: fewer topics and deep learning giving relational and extended abstract outcomes. Do you want a curriculum 'a mile wide and half an inch deep', as US educators described the school mathematics curriculum following the abysmal performance of US senior high school students in the Third International Mathematics and Science Study (quoted in Stedman 1997)? Or do you want your students to *really* understand and be able to use what you have taught them?

Actually, the area of the curriculum needn't be entirely constant. Good teaching increases the area, maintaining depth. But there are limits, and there is little doubt that most courses in all universities contain more content than students can handle at little more than the level of acquaintance – which, it is to be hoped, is not an intended outcome. However, when modes of assessment go no deeper than acquaintance, as is likely with multiple-choice tests, the problem remains invisible.

Level of understanding intended

Is it an introductory or an advanced course? In first year, an extended abstract or theoretical level of understanding of a topic may be too high for even an A grade. The answer also varies according to why students are enrolled in a common first year subject. Anatomy 101, for example, might contain students enrolled in first-year medicine and students enrolled in a diploma in occupational therapy. The ILOs, the required levels of understanding and the assessment tasks should be different for each group.

Next, it is necessary to ask why you are teaching this particular topic:

- to delineate boundaries, giving students a broad picture of what's 'there'
- to inform on a current state of play, to bring students up to date on the state of the topic or discipline
- to stockpile knowledge, of no perceived use for the present, but likely to be needed later
- to inform decisions that need making in the near future, as in problem-based learning?

Each of these purposes implies a different level and kind of understanding; each can be nominated by identifying the appropriate outcome action verbs.

One way of addressing the importance of a topic is to spend more or less time on it. A better way is that important topics should be *understood at a higher level* than less important topics. An important topic might be understood so that students can use it or solve problems with it; a less important topic, just that it is recognized. We can signal importance by choosing a verb at the appropriate level of understanding for each topic.

Writing the course ILOs

We are now in a position to start writing course ILOs. These need to be stated in such a way that they stipulate:

- the *verb* at the appropriate *level* of understanding or performance intended
- the topic *content* the verb is meant to address, the object of the verb in other words
- the *context* of the content discipline in which the verb is to be deployed.

The ILOs for the course *The Nature of Teaching and Learning* illustrate these points:

1 *Explain in depth* why a particular course topic is important to teaching.
2 *Explain* how the component course topics interrelate.
3 *Reflect* on your teaching in terms of a working theory you have gained from the course.
4 *Evaluate* a situation that has gone wrong and *apply* a solution.

The first two refer to declarative knowledge: the students have to reach a level of understanding that requires them to *explain* something, not just describe or list it: the latter only display multistructural levels of understanding. In one, explanation is in depth (1), requiring students to relate the topic to the context of teaching and is at a relational level of understanding, as is the form of explanation in (2), requiring students to integrate the topics in the context of the course itself.

The second two are about functioning knowledge and should be at the relational to extended abstract level of understanding, depending on the originality of the student's response. The content in (3) is the student's own working theory and the context the student's own teaching, and in (4), the content is the theory used in evaluating and the context the problematic situation in teaching.

You should now be in a position to design and write your own ILOs for a course you are teaching (Task 5.2).

Task 5.2   Writing course ILOs

Take a course that you are teaching. Consider the course aim and write the course ILOs by identifying:

a the kind of knowledge to be learned (declarative or functioning)
b the content or topic to be learned
c the level of understanding or performance to be achieved.

The following grid may be a useful framework to help you think.

Kind of knowledge	*Content or topic*	*Level of understanding or performance (outcome verb)*

Now go across the rows and write out the course ILOs by stating the intended level of understanding or performance (outcome verb) and the content or topic in which the verb is to be enacted. You do not need to include the kind of knowledge in the course ILOs as they are only meant to help you clarify your thinking and decision making.

To recap an example of a course ILO from our course *The Nature of Teaching and Learning*:

Students should be able to:
Reflect (*level of understanding and performance*) on your teaching in terms of a working theory you have gained from the course *(content).*

Now write your course ILOs.
Students should be able to:
ILO1:_____
ILO2:_____
ILO3:_____
ILO4:_____
ILO5:_____
ILO6:_____

Review the ILOs to see if:
a the kind of knowledge, content and level of understanding or performance are relevant to achieve the course aim
b they cover all the main reasons for teaching the course
c they are clearly written, especially in identifying the level of understanding or performance to be achieved by the students
d the number is manageable for designing aligned teaching/learning activities and assessment tasks.

You may now wish to review your existing course 'objectives'. Do they need to be rewritten as course ILOs?

Aligning intended learning outcomes at three levels

Now that we have written the course ILOs, we have the task of checking to see that all these levels of intended outcomes, starting with the programme ILOs and the graduate attributes, are aligned.

Graduate attributes and programme ILOs

Table 5.3 shows a simply way of checking the alignment between graduate attributes and programme ILOs.

The table is a device to ensure that the match between programme ILOs and graduate attributes has at least been considered. Our view is that programme ILOs should not be forced to match attributes that don't belong in the programme. Because of the different natures of different disciplines or professions, different programmes may have different emphases in addressing the graduate attributes. It is not necessary that every programme should address all graduate attributes because some graduate attributes may not be relevant to the programme. Programme ILOs are simply the reasons that the programme is being taught, which is a matter of professional and academic judgment. However, university policy will prevail on this.

Table 5.3 Aligning programme ILOs with graduate attributes

Graduate attribute	Programme ILO
Competent professional practice	Apply principles to real-life accounting situations
Communicate effectively	Communicate as a professional with clients and colleagues in real-life accounting situations
Teamwork	Operate effectively and ethically as a team member in real-life accounting situations
Ethical professional	As above

Task 5.3   Aligning programme ILOs with graduate attributes

1 Take a programme in which you are teaching and *either* list the programme ILOs if they are already articulated *or*, if they are not, sit down with the programme coordinator or programme committee chairperson and first write the aims of the programme and a list of programme ILOs that meet those aims.

2 What are the graduate attributes of your university? List them in the left-hand column in the grid.

3 Now list the programme ILOs that would address the attributes.

Are all attributes addressed somewhere? What are not? Does it matter?

Graduate attribute	Programme ILO
1	
2	
etc.	

Task 5.3 parallels Table 5.3: it asks you to align programme ILOs with the graduate attributes of your university, if it has any. List them in the left-hand column, as in Table 5.3. If the intended outcomes of a programme you are teaching have already been articulated, go to the right-hand column and match them with any graduate attributes each might address. If the

programme ILOs haven't yet been articulated, discuss them with the programme coordinator and derive a set, then match them with the graduate
attributes. This should give you a clearer idea of how graduate attributes can
suitably be addressed in your teaching. How does your attempt gel with your
university's policy on this?

Programme ILOs and course ILOs

The next level of alignment is between the programme and the course ILOs.
As each programme is served by its constituent courses, it is important that,
when aligning course ILOs to the programme ILOs, the course ILOs in total
address all aspects of the programme ILOs. Often a programme ILO will be
addressed by several courses, from different and increasingly more complex
angles. You may attempt this in Task 5.4.

The great advantage of this level of alignment is that it guards against
complaints:

- from students that through sloppy programme design the same issue is
  addressed in different courses
- from employers or professional bodies that some important issues aren't
  addressed at all by any course.

Course ILOs, teaching/learning activities and assessment tasks

The final alignments are between the course ILOs and (a) the teaching/
learning activities (TLAs); and (b) the assessment tasks (ATs). These are
the critically important tasks for the design of a constructively aligned
curriculum. They are dealt with in the next few chapters.

Summary and conclusions

Intended learning outcomes at different levels

ILOs exist at three levels: as graduate attributes, as programme outcomes
and as course outcomes. Graduate attributes are conceived mainly in two
ways: as generic skills or abilities that are to be displayed in all circumstances
or as attributes embedded in the content area of a discipline. Reconciling
these interpretations and dealing with them in an accountable way is a
complex issue. Programme ILOs need to address the graduate attributes
in an accountable way and to reconcile this with the reasons that the
degree is being offered in a substantive sense. They are expressed as
the central outcomes intended for the programme and that are to be met by

88   *Teaching for quality learning at university*

Task 5.4   Aligning course ILOs with programme ILOs

For individual teachers

1 List the programme ILOs of the programme.

2 List the course ILOs of the courses that you are teaching in a given programme. It may be one or more.

3 Consider what programme ILO(s) each of the course ILOs addresses.

Programme ILOs	Course 1 ILOs	Course 2 ILOs	Course 3 ILOs
1			
2			
3			
4			

Do your course ILOs address the programme ILO(s)?

For the programme coordinator

After all the courses of the programme have been considered, the programme coordinator needs to consider the following:

a Are all the programme ILOs being addressed by the courses?

b Is the alignment between the programme ILOs and the course ILOs balanced? In other words, are any of the programme ILOs being overemphasized or vice versa?

c Are there any gaps in the programme ILOs that are not being addressed?

---

the particular courses in a balanced way. Course ILOs determine the teaching and assessment that takes place in the classroom and consequently need to be designed and written with a view to the kind of knowledge and the level of understanding intended.

Kinds of knowledge and levels of understanding

Declarative (propositional) knowledge refers to knowing about things and is 'declared' in the spoken and written word. Functioning knowledge is knowledge based on the academic declarative knowledge base that is put to work. These distinctions are important in sorting out whether students need to understand, as in 'know about', or, as in 'put to empowered use'.

But whether declarative or functioning knowledge is in question, we need to specify the *level* of understanding intended. This can be done by selecting a verb and a context for demonstrating the desired level. The SOLO taxonomy can be helpful in specifying those levels.

Designing and writing course ILOs

Before designing particular ILOs it is necessary to:

1 Decide what kind of knowledge is to be involved.
2 Select the topics to teach. But beware: 'The greatest enemy of understanding is coverage.'
3 Decide the purpose for teaching the topic, and hence the level of understanding or performance desirable for students to achieve. We need to prioritize, by requiring that important topics are understood at a higher level than less important topics.

Prioritizing ILOs is done in terms of the verbs related to each level of understanding: important topics are assigned a higher level of understanding than less important. The SOLO taxonomy is useful for providing a 'staircase of verbs' that can be used selectively to define the ranges of understanding needed. Using verbs to structure the ILOs emphasizes that learning and understanding come from student activity and they are used to align ILOs, teaching/learning activities and assessment tasks.

Aligning ILOs at three levels

Once ILOs have been finalized, they need aligning: programme ILOs with graduate attributes, course ILOs with programme ILOs and teaching/learning activities and assessment tasks with course ILOs. These last alignments with course ILOs are dealt with in following chapters.

Further reading

Biggs, J.B. and Collis, K.F. (1982) *Evaluating the Quality of Learning: The SOLO Taxonomy*. New York: Academic Press.

Boulton-Lewis, G.M. (1998) Applying the SOLO taxonomy to learning in higher education, in B. Dart and G. Boulton-Lewis (eds) *Teaching and Learning in Higher Education*. Camberwell, Victoria: Australian Council for Educational Research.

Toohey, S. (2002) *Designing Courses for Universities*. Buckingham: Open University Press.

The first goes into the derivation of SOLO in detail, Boulton-Lewis with several applications of SOLO in higher education. Toohey focuses more on programme (which she calls 'course') design than on course ('unit') design, which usefully complements the present chapter, which concentrates more on writing ILOs for courses.

Graduate attributes

Higher Education Research & Development, 23, 3: August 2004. This whole issue is devoted to graduate attributes.

The graduate attributes site at University of Sydney: http://www.usyd.edu.au/ab/policies/Generic_Attributes_Grads.pdf

The Graduate Attributes Project, Institute for Teaching and Learning, University of Sydney: http://www.nettl.usyd.edu.au/GraduateAttributes/ and how each faculty has developed its own statement of graduate attributes based on the university's framework: http://www.nettl.usyd.edu.au/GraduateAttributes/interpretations.cfm

How the Faculty of Commerce and Economics contextualizes the UNSW graduate attributes: http://wwwdocs.fce.unsw.edu.au/fce/EDU/part3.pdf

Writing course ILOs

The following guides to writing ILOs elaborates the above:
University of Glasgow: http://senate.gla.ac.uk/academic/ilo/guide.pdf
Oxford Brookes University: http://www.brookes.ac.uk/services/ocsd/2_learntch/writing_learning_outcomes.html

On the SOLO taxonomy

A rather nice diagrammatic presentation of SOLO by James Atherton: http://www.learningandteaching.info/learning/solo.htm
As SOLO might apply to children's ethics and to zoology from the University of Queensland's TEDI: http://www.tedi.uq.edu.au/downloads/Biggs_Solo.pdf
A paper by Hargreaves and Grenfell on SOLO and 'The use of assessment strategies to develop critical thinking skills in science': http://www.unisa.edu.au/evaluations/Full-papers/HargreavesFull.doc

And Google 'SOLO taxonomy' for 20,000 more results.

6

Contexts for effective teaching and learning

While particular teaching/learning activities (TLAs) need to be aligned to the target verbs in the ILOs they are to facilitate, there are also general criteria all TLAs should meet, whatever verbs they address. We look at these general criteria in this chapter. All teaching/learning activities set for students should be seen as having value and to be readily performable; students should be required to build on what they already know, to be relevantly active, to receive formative feedback and to be engaged in monitoring and reflecting on their own learning. A potential teaching/learning activity should meet these general criteria before it is aligned to the particular ILOs it is to facilitate.

Characteristics of rich teaching/ learning contexts

In Chapter 1, good teaching was defined as 'getting most students to use the level of cognitive processes needed to achieve the intended outcomes that the more academic students use spontaneously'. Traditional teaching methods – lecture, tutorial, and private study – do not in themselves require students to use these high-level cognitive processes; Susan uses them but she does anyway, no thanks to the teaching. These teaching methods do not intrinsically provide support for appropriate levels of learning; they leave Robert floundering with a pile of lecture notes, a lot of trees but no wood. The challenge for teaching, then, is to select teaching activities that will encourage Robert to use learning activities that Susan uses and that will achieve the ILOs.

There is no such thing as one 'best' all-purpose teaching method: what is 'best' depends on what ILO is being addressed and, at the practical level, on what are the available resources. However, some general characteristics of good teaching/learning contexts emerge from the literature, and that are common to the achievement of a range of ILOs. These are:

1 an appropriate motivational context
2 a well-structured knowledge base
3 relevant learner activity
4 formative feedback
5 reflective practice and self-monitoring.

Appropriate motivational context

When we discussed motivation in Chapter 3, three major points emerged:

1 A Theory Y climate is best for quality learning. Learners learn best when they feel free to move, are trusted and are able to make decisions and take responsibility for their own learning – *consistent with* clear policies and procedures and with an organized environment for learning. 'Consistent with' is the rub. Different teachers, and especially administrators, will disagree about the right balance between a Theory Y climate and an organized environment. Many teaching/learning activities and assessment tasks that address higher level outcomes require an extent of student involvement and a lack of constraints on space and time, such that colleagues, heads of department or boards of examiners may well regard as unacceptably messy: not in the interests of running a tight ship.
2 The task provided – the teaching/learning activity itself – must be *valued* by the student and not seen as busy-work or trivial. In outcomes-based teaching and learning, where the TLA is aligned to the ILO, this is much easier to achieve than in unaligned teaching, because what the student is asked to do is patently in service of achieving the intended outcomes of the course.
3 The student must have a reasonable *probability of success* in achieving the task. Again, this is patently the case in constructive alignment – if an outcome is *intended,* then presumably the teacher has set a task that is achievable. Nevertheless, in their informal interactions with students and in their comments on student performances, teachers may convey messages to students that they have little hope of succeeding; for example, by attributing a poor performance to lack of ability rather than to lack of persistence.

Constructing a base of interconnected knowledge

The teaching context could be regarded as a construction site on which students build on what they already know. Sound knowledge is based on *interconnections.* Everything that has been written so far in this book about understanding, deep learning, the growth and development of knowledge and intrinsic motivation reiterates this. Sound understanding is itself the realization that what is separated in ignorance is connected in knowing.

Cognitive growth lies not just in knowing more, but in *restructuring* what is already known in order to connect with new knowledge.

Building on the known

The physics professor is greeting the new intake of freshers, still glowing from their A level successes:

'Now, do you remember the physics you were taught in sixth form?'
Two hundred heads nod enthusiastically.
'Well forget it. You're here to learn *real* physics, not the simplicities you were taught in school!'

This true exchange is a good example of how not to teach. Teaching builds on the known, it must not reject it: proceed from the known to the unknown, as the old saying has it. In deep learning, new learning connects with old, so teaching should emphasize the interconnectedness of topics. It helps to make the connections explicit ('Last week we. . . . Today, I am taking that further'), to choose familiar examples first, to ask students to build on their own experiences when discussing a principle or topic, to draw and explain parallels while teaching, to use cross-references in presenting material, to present topics by showing where they connect to other topics.

This is easier in an outcomes-based rather than in a topic-based curriculum. With only five or six ILOs, instead of a dozen or so topics, dealing with an ILO will inevitably draw on a wider range of relevant material than teaching topic by topic.

Maximizing structure

The connections we were talking about above are drawn horizontally, but the most powerful connections are drawn vertically or hierarchically. That is, we should help students to *reconceptualize*, so that what are seen as differences at a subordinate level become related at a superordinate level. Take the concept of motivation (Chapter 3). Extrinsic and intrinsic motivation have different effects on learning; one is associated with poor learning, the other with high-quality learning. Two different phenomena? Not so: each is incorporated within expectancy-value theory. The different effects are not because they are different forms of motivation, but because the student reads the value component differently: in one case the task itself is valued, in the other the task is only a means of acquiring something else that is valued.

Specific concepts that seem irreconcilably different to students may frequently be interpreted as different instances of the same higher order principle, the differences the students see are because they are focusing at a lower order node. In teaching, we should see that the students understand what the nodes in the structure are. Teaching using bullet lists, for example, is useful only when the points listed are at the same level or node in the structure. If they are not, the bullet list hides the real conceptual structure. In SOLO terms, they are describing in a multistructural way what is a relational or extended abstract structure.

New information should not be just dumped on the learner, in rambling lessons, in poorly constructed texts or as bullet lists. Good teaching always contains a structure, hidden away, but there to be found. Teaching from lists is like sawing the branches off a tree, stacking them in a neat pile, and saying: 'There! See the tree?'

The chances of students coming to grasp the structure can be maximized in many ways. In some circumstances, it is appropriate to present the structure upfront. An 'advance organizer' is a preview of a lecture that mentions the main topics to be dealt with and the overriding conceptual structure to which they may be related (Ausubel 1968). The student then has a conceptual framework from the start: as material is introduced, it can be fitted into place. For example, a diagram based on expectancy-value theory could be used as such an organizer to a lesson on motivation.

A 'grabber', by the same token, doesn't rely on structure for its effect but on its emotional impact. Starting a class with a cartoon, an interesting slide or video clip elicits interest in the topics to follow. Whereas the advance organizer is *conceptual*, the grabber is *affective*, appealing to shock or to humour. Both have their place but work on different principles – our interest here is in the structure of the material, not in its shock value.

Some teachers fall into the trap of talking down to students with an in-your-face conceptual structure, all answers and no questions. Lessons that are too well structured encourage students simply to take on board the given structure and memorize that, thereby establishing one of the lowest of the forms of understanding mentioned by Entwistle and Entwistle (1997; see pp. 74–5). In the end, the student must *always* do the structuring – it's what the student does that is important. The challenge for teachers is to strike the right balance between presenting students with chaos, on the one hand, and with cut-and-dried conclusions, on the other, where all the interesting conceptual work has been done. The question of how much structure to present, given your students and their existing knowledge base, may be gauged from using formative feedback while they are learning – questions, trial runs, even the inter-ocular test (look them in the eyes for signs of life) – as discussed later.

Relevant learner activity

Being active while learning is better than being inactive. Activity is good in itself: it heightens physiological arousal in the brain, which makes performance more efficient. Physical exertion has quite dramatic effects on mental performance. Typically, four minutes of brisk exercise, such as running or pedalling on a bicycle, improves performance in such tasks as mental arithmetic. Longer periods, however, see performance worsen in the unfit, but continuing to improve in the fit (e.g. Tomporowski and Ellis 1986). Getting the adrenalin to flow increases alertness. This is one very good reason for breaking up long periods of lecturing with interspersed activities. Even just stopping the class and doing stretching exercises does more for students' learning than droning on.

In one study, students were required to learn from text in increasingly active ways: reading silently, underlining important words, writing out the key sentences containing those words, rewriting sentences in one's own words, to the most active, teaching somebody else the material. There was a strong correlation between extent of activity and efficiency of learning (Wittrock 1977).

Better still is when the activity addresses specific intended learning outcomes. Excursions are generally regarded as useful extensions to in-class learning, but their best use is when the activities in the excursion are aligned to the intended outcomes of the excursion. MacKenzie and White (1982) devised an excursion on coastal geography in which each of the intended outcomes was linked to quite dramatic actions, such as chewing mangrove leaves, wading through a muddy swamp, jumping across rock platforms and so on. Performance on a written test on what they had observed and learned three months later was near perfect. Spiegel describes a similar approach of 'adventure learning' to legal studies (see Box 6.1).

Box 6.1   Adventure learning in the School of Law

Nadja Siegel, lecturer in law at Queensland University, is the winner of the law section of the Australian University Teaching Awards. Through adventure learning she tries to develop in students the skills they will need to apply professionally. . . . She creates activities with an element of risk – physical, social or emotional – so that the experience is more real. Crossing a river using blocks as rafts, with one team missing equipment, forces them into deciding whether to adopt a competitive or cooperative approach. But she says adventure learning is not just games. '. . . [Y]ou really need to be aware of how you're using the activity and be able to direct the students' experiences to the focus of their learning . . .'

Source: *The Australian Higher Education*, 26 November 1997

Such activities need to be energetic and memorable in themselves, as well as being aligned to an academic outcome. If discovering the role of salt in the ecology of mangrove swamps is an intended learning outcome, chewing mangrove leaves for their salt content is a teaching/learning activity directly addressing that outcome. If managing a team is an ILO, showing initiative in obtaining cooperation in building a raft is a relevant TLA.

We learn through activating different sense modalities: hearing, touch, sight, speech, smell and taste. The more one modality reinforces another, the more effective the learning. It is like trying to access a book in a library. If all you know is the author, or the title, or the publisher or the year of publication, you could be in for a long search, but the more those 'ors' become 'ands', the faster and more precise the search becomes. Just so in accessing or remembering what has been learned. The more TLAs tie down the topic to be learned to multiple sensory modes, the better the learning.

Table 6.1 puts this very neatly. Don't take the percentages mentioned there too literally, but the messages are clear, simple, and basically right. Some sensory modalities are more effective for learning than others; the more they overlap, the better; and best of all, you learn through teaching, which requires all the previous activities.

Table 6.1   Most people learn . . .

10%	of what they read
20%	of what they hear
30%	of what they see
50%	of what they see and hear
70%	of what they talk over with others
80%	of what they use and do in real life
95%	of what they teach someone else

Source: Attributed to William Glasser; quoted by *Association for Supervision & Curriculum Development Guide 1988*

Table 6.1 is well worth remembering when designing TLAs – peer teaching being a particularly powerful way of learning for the teacher.

It may help to conceptualize this by realizing that the outcomes of learning are stored in three memory systems (Tulving 1985):

- *Procedural* memory: remembering how to do things. Actions are learned.
- *Episodic* memory: remembering where you learned things. Images are learned.
- *Semantic* memory: remembering meanings, frequently from statements about things. Declarative knowledge is learned.

When we learn something, each system is involved; we learn what we *did, where* it was and how to *describe* what it was. However, they are not equally easily accessed. Actions are easiest to remember (do we ever forget how to ride a bicycle?) and semantics, what was actually said, are hardest. That sequence probably reflects the sequence of psychological development: first actions, then images, then semantics. Be that as it may, recalling the context or the actions can often bring back the semantics. If you can *picture* where you learned it and what you were doing, you are more likely to recall what it was that you learned. It's like accessing the book in the library. Thus even learning straight declarative knowledge, the stuff of academia, is best done in association with a rich store of images and actions. The adventure learning studies do exactly that.

Lecture theatres admittedly offer less scope for activity than wilderness areas, but as we see in the following chapter, students can be kept relevantly active in the classroom and rather more so than they usually are.

Formative feedback

Arguably the most powerful enhancement to learning is feedback during learning. This is also called formative assessment – not to be confused with summative assessment. The purposes and effects of these two forms of assessment are so different it is a pity the word 'assessment' is used for both. It tends to confuse issues – and sometimes teachers. Formative assessment is provided *during* learning, telling students how well they are doing and what might need improving; summative *after* learning, informing how well students have learned what they were supposed to have learned. In one project we were involved in, teachers regarded the comments they wrote on final assessment tasks as 'formative', despite the fact that the course was over, let alone that students rarely pay attention to comments given at the end of a course so that they may generalize them to how they learn in future courses.

There have been numerous studies of the effects of feedback (for example, Black and Wiliam 1998; Hattie 2003) and it tops the list of those factors leading to good learning. Running close is whole-class interactive teaching, followed by self- and peer-assessment and cooperative learning, with class size way down the list: all of which we come to in the next chapter.

So important is formative feedback that the effectiveness of any particular teaching/learning activity can be judged by how well it provides feedback to students as they learn. In a large lecture, students may receive little or no feedback, while one reason that interactive class teaching works so well is because it more readily provides students with contemporary information about how well they are going along the road to learning.

Effective feedback requires that students have a baseline knowledge of where they are and knowledge of where they are supposed to be heading – what the ILOs are, in fact – and the feedback is meant to slot into that gap in their self-knowledge. Feedback can be provided by the teacher, by other students and by the students themselves, each such source giving a different aspect to the feedback.

Using error constructively

Errors are important learning opportunities, but formative feedback is essential in learning from error. In the course of learning, students inevitably create misconceptions that need to be corrected so that any misunderstandings can be set right, literally in the formative stage. To do this requires a Theory Y climate, where students will feel free to admit error. If they think that the information will be used summatively or that they will be judged on the result, they will be defensive about admitting to any error. In that case, an opportunity for learning has been lost. This must make one cautious about using formative test results in the final grade.

In a tutorial or group session where the tutor is censorious or sarcastic students will keep quiet, preferring not to make themselves vulnerable. This is independent of any particular teaching method. In an otherwise fine problem-based learning (PBL) course at a particular university, one tutor completely wrecked the process. The aim in PBL is for students to pose questions and to follow through with plausible answers to a given problem. This they do by reference to theory, past experience, similar cases, etc., asking questions and testing possible answers in discussion. But in this particular case, the tutor replied to every question put to her with an all-knowing sneer: 'That's for me to know and for you to find out!' So the students in this group gave up asking questions and problem-based learning acquired a bad name. So did the tutor.

Some teachers feel awkward about drawing attention to students' errors. In wanting to create a Theory Y climate, where students can feel free to explore possibilities and ask far-out questions, these teachers are reluctant to publicly correct students' errors.

This is the dilemma teachers have to face: Do I correct mistakes and risk discouraging students from expressing their understandings in public? Or do I let them go uncorrected in the interests of maintaining a productive working atmosphere? Not to correct seems to be abdicating from an important teaching function: misconceptions are allowed to pass unquestioned and uncorrected. One technique is to smile encouragingly, with 'Yes, not bad. Can anyone else elaborate on that?' This signals that there is a problem, that we are part-way there, that it is a collective job to achieve a better outcome and that individuals are not to be blamed for not having a perfect answer first time round. It's a matter of the interpersonal chemistry, the rapport, that a teacher can create. With good rapport, public correction is cheerfully accepted and appreciated.

Japanese teachers do exactly this in what Hess and Azuma (1991) call 'sticky probing', which westerners might see it as a little drastic. A single problem is discussed for hours by students, with teacher adjudicating, until a consensus acceptable to teacher and students is reached. The focus of the probing is a particular student's error, with the student the focus of public correction. Japanese students, however, don't appear to see this as a punishment for making a mistake; they understand that learning is a collective activity and that learning from mistakes is part and parcel of learning.

Using error constructively thus involves two challenges:

- requiring students to expose their erroneous thinking without risk of ridicule, loss of face or low grades
- correcting them nicely so that they feel positive about being corrected and not ashamed or resentful.

This is a personal matter that every teacher needs to resolve in a way that each can feel comfortable with.

Reflective practice and self-monitoring

In Chapter 3 we discussed reflective practice and transformative reflection, whereby teachers monitored their own practice and used their theory of teaching to see how they could teach better. The same thing applies to learning itself. When self-monitoring, learners keep a watching brief over their learning: How am I doing? Am I making mistakes here? Any pattern in my errors? If so, what is it and how can I avoid it in future? Is there any way I can approach this more effectively than I am now?

These are the sorts of questions that good learners ask themselves, like good practitioners of any sort. Formal, top-down ways of teaching discourage self-questioning. If the teacher always assesses how well the student is doing and never allows the student to self-assess, the student lets it go at that and consequently doesn't see the need for or acquire the skills of reflection. Indeed, the longer many undergraduate students stay at university – the Susans excepted – the less deep and the more surface oriented they tend to become. This has been observed in several countries: Australia (Biggs 1987a; Watkins and Hattie 1985), the UK (Entwistle and Ramsden 1983), and Hong Kong (Gow and Kember 1990). It seems that Robert's learning as it becomes institutionalized becomes unreflective, performed by rule of thumb and with minimum effort. All the decisions, especially about assessment, have been made for him in formal top-down teaching.

Where the teacher expounds the material and assesses it at the end, the teacher is in effect the masterbuilder for constructing the student's knowledge base, the student an apprentice bricklayer only. The student is left in a passive role both in receiving information and in monitoring what has been learned. They come to believe – or rather, they have the belief they acquired in school confirmed – that keeping track of their learning is the teacher's job, not their own. They are unlikely to become very good independent or lifelong learners.

Learning to 'monitor the construction site' is another name for those study skills that involve self-management, including self-assessment, dealt with in Chapter 8 under the heading of self-directed TLAs that are so important for addressing an attribute such as lifelong learning (see also Figure 5.1, p. 68).

A checklist for designing teaching/ learning activities

Any TLA should meet the following criteria for a good learning context (see Table 6.2).

When you have decided what would be the most suitable TLAs for a particular course, given the ILOs and the practical considerations of resources and class size, Table 6.2 suggests the TLA be screened to meet the following criteria:

- Is the general climate in which it is deployed Theory Y?
- Do the students see the task as relevant and important; do they see themselves as likely to succeed at it?

- Does the task build on previous relevant knowledge?
- Does it require the learner to be relevantly active?
- Does it allow for the learner to be reflective as learning progresses?

If the task falls short on any of these criteria, it should be redesigned.

Table 6.2   Some important general criteria for any TLA: a checklist

	Motivational climate	*Does it build on or require*
	Theory X/Y	Prior knowledge?
	Value	Learner activity?
	Success	Reflection?
TLA1		
TLA2		
TLA3		
etc.		

Task 6.1 is a reflective exercise to help you see what type of teaching/ learning context you have created for your students.

In the next two chapters we turn to the central issue: what learning outcomes are the TLAs intended to achieve?

Summary and conclusions

If we are to devise and implement effective teaching/learning activities (TLAs), we need first to ask if there are any general criteria they should meet. There are. They need to be grounded in an appropriate motivational context, to work from a base of interconnected knowledge, to require relevant learner activity and to encourage reflective practice and self-monitoring. The power of a teaching method or TLA depends on the extent to which it embodies these characteristics.

Establishing an appropriate motivational context

The general context needs to be Theory Y so that students can take more responsibility for their learning, but some colleagues and more administrators will see this differently. Specifically, tasks need to be valued by students and to be attainable.

Constructing a base of interconnected knowledge

A powerful knowledge base is complex in structure and error free, built on accessible interconnections. Creating such a base involves: building on the

Task 6.1   The teaching/learning context you have created

Select one of the teaching methods that you commonly use and evaluate it in light of its effectiveness in relation to the characteristics of a good teaching/learning context. Provide evidence to substantiate your evaluation.

a Establishing an appropriate motivational Theory Y context for your students.

_____

_____

_____

b Creating an interconnected knowledge base for your students.

_____

_____

_____

c Providing learning activities relevant to engage your students with the ILOs.

_____

_____

_____

d Providing formative feedback on your students' learning progress.

_____

_____

_____

e Encouraging your students to self-monitor and reflect on their learning.

_____

_____

_____

What changes would you like to make in the future to further enhance the effectiveness of your teaching/learning context?

_____

_____

_____

_____

known, making use of students' existing knowledge and emphasizing structural interconnections between topics. These points should infuse teaching whatever the particular teaching activity.

Relevant learner activity

Knowledge is constructed through learner activity and interaction. Activity has two main roles. The fact of being generally active in and of itself provides general alertness and efficiency. Second, and more specifically, activity specifically keyed to the intended learning outcomes, using different sensory modes of learning to provide multiple access to what has been learned, is a very powerful way of learning.

Formative feedback

If there is any single factor that supports good learning it is formative feedback: teaching is good or poor depending on how readily students receive feedback on how they are doing. For feedback to be effective students need to be clearly aware of what they are supposed to be learning and as they are unlikely to be perfect first time, they need information as to where their deficiencies lie and misconceptions students may have need to be confronted and corrected. Teachers, other students and students themselves can be useful sources of feedback, depending on the intended learning outcome.

Reflective practice and self-monitoring

Whatever the TLA, it should encourage students' awareness of their own knowledge construction, largely by placing them in situations that require them to self-monitor and self-direct their own learning. This is the way to achieve lifelong learning.

Further reading

On good teaching/learning contexts and principles of good teaching

Biggs, J. and Moore, P. (1993) *The Process of Learning*. Sydney: Prentice-Hall Australia.

Fuller, R. (1998) Encouraging active learning at university, *HERDSA News*, 20, 3: 1–5.

Gibbs, G. (2006) On giving feedback to students. http://www.brookes.ac.uk/services/ocsd/firstwords/fw21.html

Hattie, J.A. (2003) Teachers make a difference. http://www.arts.auckland.ac.nz/faculty/index.cfm?P=8650

Petty, G. (2006) *Evidence-based Teaching*. Cheltenham: Nelson Thomas.

Ramsden, P. (2003) *Learning to Teach in Higher Education*. London: Routledge.

Biggs and Moore describe rich learning contexts and the conditions for good learning and summarize research on expert teaching. Ramsden deals with six key principles of effective teaching. Fuller's article is rich with practical suggestions for active learning. Hattie's paper is a summary of meta-analyses on a huge scale: this is a technique that combines research results from hundreds of studies enabling stable generalizations over a variety of contexts about what factors are most important in enhancing student learning. By far the most important are giving proper feedback, as discussed in this chapter, and active teaching, as discussed in the next. Petty's book shows how to put into practice the teaching methods with the biggest 'effect sizes' in Hattie's work: feedback, interactive teaching, graphic organizers and various examples of group work are among the best. We elaborate on all of these in following chapters.

Gibbs's paper describes how feedback is best provided.

Links to educational development centres worldwide

http://learningandteaching.dal.ca/ids.html. This URL provides very useful links to centres in most western countries. You can navigate to most topics dealt with here and in other chapters on university teaching that will discuss the topic in the context and vocabulary of your own country.

7

Teaching/learning activities for declarative knowledge

We discuss aligning teaching/learning activities (TLAs) to ILOs relating to declarative knowledge in this chapter, and to functioning knowledge in the following one. Teaching declarative knowledge by lecture, followed by tutorial, has become so established that 'lecturing' has become the generic term for university teaching, to be carried out in 'lecture theatres', particularly for dealing with large classes. We suggest that the term 'lecture' describes a situation, not a teaching/learning activity, and that within the situation of the large class there are far more effective ways of achieving course ILOs than talking at students. In this chapter, we show how interactive teaching, which is a highly effective mode of teaching, can be used in even large classes. We also deal with interactive learning, and teacher questioning, in smaller classes. We end with a discussion of some of the teaching/learning activities that can be supported by educational technology.

Three changes needed in the way we usually think about teaching

When we turn to the matter of designing teaching/learning activities, we find that to implement constructive alignment requires changing the ways we have previously thought about teaching. First, we, as teachers, need to stop thinking about the next lecture that we have to give or the tutorial we have to design. These are only situations for student learning. It is only when we have clarified our intended learning outcomes that we should start thinking about the teaching/learning activities we might most appropriately use, within our resources. This will probably not mean giving lectures. Many academics start from the assumption that their major activity is to give a 'lecture', which is after all what the timetable says they should be doing. University planners and architects accordingly designate these rooms 'lecture theatres', equipping them with stage and spotlight, as if skilled performers are to provide some pleasant entertainment there. What goes on is only rarely carried out by people skilled in the performing arts and only sometimes is it entertaining.

The assumption that the lecture method, and its satellite the tutorial, should be the defaults that academics use in discharging their teaching duties needs examining. The lecture and tutorial do have their uses, but they are limited in what they can effectively achieve. There are more effective ways of using the space in those large 'lecture' theatres. It helps to think of lectures and tutorials as *situations*, in which a range of teaching/learning activities can take place, rather than as prescriptions for a manner of teaching.

The second change in thinking is to shift the focus from what the teacher does to what the student should best be doing. Teaching is, if you like, a service activity, we teach so that students may learn and what they learn depends on how they go about learning. That sounds obvious, but all too frequently the messages from administration downwards are that teaching is only about what teachers do. We actually have a two-sided ledger sheet: (a) what the teacher is doing and (b) what at the same time the students are doing. Attaining the intended outcomes depends rather more on (b), than on (a). It's a pity that in English we have two separate words for 'teaching' and 'learning'. Some languages, such as Russian, have one word for both so that you can't then say: 'I taught them but they didn't learn.' One feature of constructive alignment is that it brings teaching and learning closer together, even if in English we don't have a single word for it.

The third change is that we need to stop assuming that learning is only taking place when it is located inside a teacher-directed classroom. If you want your students to be the lifelong learners that the mission statement of your institution almost certainly requires, some learning should certainly be taking place outside a formal teacher-directed environment.

In sum, designating teaching sessions as 'lectures' and 'tutorials' should not be seen as prescribing what teachers have to do, but as situations in which a variety of teaching/learning activities can take place. And it must not be forgotten that there will be some intended learning outcomes, often the most important ones, where the best situation for relevant student learning activity is *outside* the classroom, not inside.

We need to make a clear distinction between appropriate teacher activity and appropriate student activity.

What teachers do: What students do

Let us say teaching takes place in a typical lecture situation, where the intended outcome contains that very common verb 'explain'. What are teacher and student most likely to be doing (see Table 7.1)?

The teacher talks to the usual structure of the lecture: introduces the topic, explains, elaborates, takes questions and winds up. The students are engaged in receiving the content, listening, taking notes, perhaps asking a question – but not necessarily 'explaining'. Although this is what the students are intended to be able to do, here the teacher is doing all the explaining. The students are usually only required to explain the theory or topic in question when it comes to exam time – but by then it's too late. The students haven't been given the opportunities to learn to explain before they are assessed on their ability to explain. There's a distinct lack of alignment between the ILO and the students' learning-related activities.

Table 7.1   What teachers and students do in a lecture leading to an ILO containing 'explain'

Teacher activity	Student activity
Introduce	Listen
Explain	Take notes
Elaborate	Understand (but correctly? deeply enough?)
Show some PPT slides	Watch, note points
Questions on slides	Write answers to questions
Wind up	Possibly ask a question

What does it mean to 'explain', as opposed, say, to 'describe'? In order to 'explain' something, the student must understand how the components of the topic/theory are related to each other, which is a relational level of understanding, whereas to 'describe' requires only that the components of the topic can be listed, which is a multistructural level of understanding. The teacher's task is therefore both to present the information itself and how it is structured; the student's is to receive the information and to structure it. In our example, neither teacher nor Robert monitors that double task. Susan would structure her understanding enough for her to be able to explain the topic but only because that's what she usually does, explaining to another student what she thought the teacher meant or reflectively explaining to herself while reviewing and revising. Susan's learning-related activities are aligned to the ILO, if only by default, whereas Robert's are not. In constructively aligned teaching, the teacher might use teaching/learning activities such as peer teaching or buzz groups within the class to ensure that everyone does some explaining; the TLAs are then aligned to the ILO containing that verb 'explain'. Box 7.1 (p. 113) gives another example of 'explain'.

We should now consider teaching/learning activities that relate to constructing the declarative knowledge base.

Constructing the declarative knowledge base

Building a well-structured knowledge base involves what Ausubel (1968) calls 'reception learning', that is, the reception of declarative knowledge and structuring it meaningfully. As we have seen in the 'explain' example, lecturing by the teacher leaves that structuring activity up to the student – Susan does it, Robert usually does not. It is important to use TLAs that help all students, particularly the Roberts.

Teaching/learning activities for reception learning can be managed by the teacher, by groups of students or by the individual student:

- *Teacher managed*: lecturing, tutorials, setting assigned readings or text-books, laboratories, concept mapping, one-minute essays, teaching study skills in context.
- *Teacher managed but with active student participation*: peer teaching, peer-assisted study sessions (PASS), interactive work in class, bulletin boards, various group work.
- *Student managed*: collaborative learning groups, chat rooms.
- *Individually managed*: reading, searching the web, soliciting advice, listening to a lecture.

Many of these are not teaching/learning *activities* so much as teaching/ learning *situations*, in which the appropriate student learning-related activities may or may not occur. The situation – be it lecture, tutorial, laboratory or excursion – simply defines the broad parameters within which learning takes place. It would be a poor physiotherapist who told a patient with a problematic knee joint: 'Go to the gym and do some work with weights.' The proper response would be to find out what the problem was: that, say, one of the muscles supporting the kneecap was weak so the kneecap 'wandered'. Working the whole of the knee in the gym would exacerbate the problem because the other muscles would do the work for the weak one, thus worsening the imbalance. The weak muscle needs to be singled out and exercised.

Just so, hitting all the ILOs with one method, lecturing, is likely to call out the learning activity of memorizing to do the work meant for genuine understanding – especially is this so if the assessment is by examination. In short, the learning activity most appropriate to each ILO needs to be singled out and 'exercised'. Dumping the student in an overall teaching/learning situation will in many cases result in over-exercising inappropriate learning 'muscles'.

Let us illustrate with that very common situation, the large class lecture followed by a tutorial, as a means of constructing a base of well-structured declarative knowledge.

Teaching declarative knowledge in large classes

The lecture/tutorial

A lecture is where the subject matter expert tells the students about the major topics that make up the discipline or professional area, and what the latest thinking is on a topic or discipline. The flow of information is one way, the students' contributions usually being limited to questions and requests for clarification. Elaborating the material, removing misconceptions, applying to specific examples, comparing different interpretations, are left to the complement of the lecture, the tutorial. This seems like a good combination for effective reception learning: the lecture is like the Tasmanian tiger making the kill, the tutorial like the Tasmanian devil doing the mopping up. But sadly, for our simile, the tiger is already extinct, and the devil is heading that way.

Probably because it conveniently accommodates large fluctuations in student numbers, the lecture has become the method for all seasons. It is assumed that if you know your subject, and do not have any speech defects, you can deliver a passable lecture. But take the case of Dr Fox, who did a circuit of several US university medical faculties. He was hugely successful; the student ratings were highly positive and he was praised as an inspirational teacher in total command of his subject matter. It turns out that Dr Fox was a professional actor, whose only knowledge of the field was supplied by a *Reader's Digest* article (Ware and Williams 1975). Dr Fox's escapade has been used to support several conflicting positions:

- Good teaching isn't a matter of how much you know but of how well you put it across. (Wrong on both counts. 'Putting it across' is not what good teaching is.)
- It just goes to show how unreliable student ratings are: they only want to be entertained. (It doesn't show this: these students were rating a one-off presentation, not a complete semester of teaching.)
- Lecturers should be trained in thespian skills or at least in public speaking, as in Box 7.3 (p. 124). (Helpful, no doubt, but could the majority of academics perform centre stage, day after day, inspiring students every time?)
- We should subcontract large class lecturing to professional actors. (Why not, if an academic writes the script?)
- Lectures may motivate and inspire students – if they have the appropriate thespian skills. (Partly correct.)
- There must be better ways of teaching large classes than lecturing. (Correct.)

Years ago Donald Bligh (1972) reviewed nearly 100 studies comparing lecturing with other methods, mostly group discussions or reading. He found the following:

1 Lectures are relatively effective for *presenting information*, but unsupervised reading is more effective. Since Bligh's time, accessing information has been hugely facilitated by search engines.
2 Lectures are quite ineffective for stimulating *higher order thinking*.
3 Lectures cannot be relied on to inspire or to change students' attitudes favourably, although many lecturers believe their own do.
4 Students like *really good* lectures; otherwise they prefer well-conducted group work.

Psychological constraints on learning

Why are lectures so ineffective? Here are some pointers from the nature of human learning:

1 Sustained and unchanging low level activity lowers concentration. Sitting listening to a lecture is such an activity yet it requires concentrated effort to follow lecture content.
2 The attention of students is typically maintained for about 10 to 15 minutes, after which learning drops off rapidly (see Figure 7.1).
3 A short rest, or a change in activity, every 15 minutes or so restores performance almost to the original level (see Figure 7.1).
4 A period of consolidation after prolonged learning greatly enhances retention. Getting students to review at the end of the lecture what has been learned leads to much better and lasting retention than simply finishing and dismissing the students (see Figure 7.2).

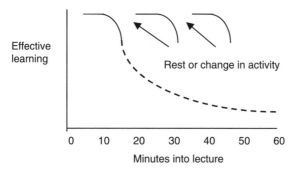

Figure 7.1   Effect of rest or change of activity on learning
Source: After Bligh (1972)

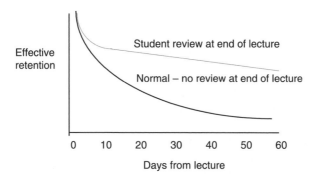

Figure 7.2   Effect of testing at end of lecture on retention
Source: After Bligh (1972)

The time periods in Figure 7.1 depend on the students, the skill of the lecturer, the pace of the lecture, the difficulty of the material, the use of educational technology involving a change of activity, the time of day and so on. But the basic point remains: Do not talk for longer than 15 or 20 minutes without a pause unless you are *certain* you still have their attention. When you pause, get the students to change their activity.

The effect of consolidation in Figure 7.2 may be achieved by asking students to *actively review* what they had just learned. That does not mean that you tell them what you've just told them, as in the conventional summary: that's you being active. *They* are the ones who should do the reviewing: get them to tell you or a neighbour what you have just told them. The problem is that both teacher and students see the lecture as a matter of teacher performance, not of learner performance. It is a perception that has to be reversed. Today, there's a further argument against the lecture: students are so mixed and selective, and so media wise, they far prefer to obtain information from the web at their own pace, rather than at the pace dictated by someone talking at them (Laurillard 2002).

Given all this, what *can* the lecture do that books and the web cannot?

Many university teachers, through their research and scholarship, have developed a perspective on their field of expertise that is not to be found in textbooks. Through publication lag, textbooks are easily two or more years out of date while active researchers are not. In any event, textbooks do not usually have an 'angle', a perspective, but are typically a multistructural list of things that every first-year student might ever need to know. Who better to provide a critical perspective on that bland smorgasbord of knowledge than the teacher at the cutting edge of the topic and in person? The best defence of the lecture, particularly in senior undergraduate years, thus lies not in doing what other media do as well – and usually better – but in exposing students to the most recent developments in the field, and to the ongoing workings of a scholarly mind.

The teacher should be an agent for transforming knowledge, helping students to interpret and to construct their own knowledge, not a passive substation that relays preformed messages to them. Unfortunately, as noted in Chapter 1, the credit transfer system in universities may well result in courses being designed to be equivalent to courses taught in other universities, a consequence that would severely discourage cutting-edge teaching of the kind we are talking about here. The pressure is to teach in style and content that is compatible with what is being taught in other universities, not to build on locally concentrated excellence.

Where does this leave lecturers who *aren't* frontline researchers? Looking for alternatives to the lecture, we hope. Heaven forbid that teachers have reached the demeaning point where all that remains for them to do is to tell students about content that they can read more effectively.

Since practicalities dictate that large numbers of students will be scheduled to meet one teacher in a big room, it is better to see this as a *plenary session* in which – and out of which – excellent learning can take place, using teaching/ learning activities that directly address the intended learning outcomes.

So how can we transform the lecture theatre into a learning theatre?

Interactive teaching

The teaching of Eric Mazur

The last question is something Eric Mazur (1998) asked himself. He was lecturing in physics at Harvard and regularly received good student evaluations. Then he read an article saying that when physics students were lectured to, they relied on memory not on understanding. Not in my class they don't, Eric thought, and tested them on basic principles. The result told him that they were, indeed, relying on memory.

He decided to stop lecturing, forcing the students to rely not on memory but on understanding. He set readings that had to be read before the class. He also gave the students two or three simple questions to be answered by email the night before the class: no answers, no admission to class. His email also said: 'Please tell us what you found difficult and confusing. If you found nothing difficult or confusing, please tell us what you found most interesting.' Thus he discovered what might need clarifying in class. He emailed replies to each student, with an appropriate comment from a database of generic comments.

In class the next day, the students were presented every 10 minutes with a multiple-choice question based on the readings. Each student seat in the theatre had a personal digital assistant (PDA) so that students could record their response to each question; responses were automatically tallied for the whole class and projected on a screen. Other questions addressed a 'trick' physical phenomenon, for example: 'A flat plate of cast-iron, two feet square and one inch thick, has a large circular hole, diameter four inches, drilled in the center. The plate is then heated. Does the hole in the center (a) increase in diameter, (b) decrease, or (c) remain the same, as the plate expands with heating?' While all the relevant physical principles were known by this stage, a wide diversity of opinion as to the outcome of the heating occurred. The students were asked to find someone nearby who voted differently and then to convince their neighbour that their own response was the correct one. After discussion, another vote was taken and this time there was usually much more consensus, in the direction of the correct answer. Mazur reports that the learning was powerful and the students enjoyed it. He was consistently voted best teacher of the year.

Two features of Mazur's approach stand out: feedback and good alignment requiring student activity relevant to the course ILOs. He wanted high level understanding, he gave the students teaching/learning activities that required them to think about novel problems and apply the knowledge they had gained from reading – not from listening to his lectures – and he supplied feedback to each student, individually from himself and from other students.

Course preparation assignments

David Yamane (2006), like Mazur, was also bothered by the inefficiencies of lecturing, when the material could be read before class more efficiently than listening to it in class. The problem was that students didn't read when they were told to. His subject was sociology. He posted 'course preparation assignments' (CPAs) on the course web page to be completed before each class, the time in class being spent in discussions on the assignment in groups of about four. The CPA required students to read and think about a chapter in the course textbook and to produce a written response to a question or problem based on the reading. The CPAs had the following general structure:

1 an introductory statement
2 an objective (ILO) for the assignment
3 the background information for the topic
4 the written assignment.

The first 10 minutes of class were spent in small groups, where individual members pooled their assignments and synthesized one for the group, which was then presented to the whole class. Yamane acted as coordinator and produced a large diagram on the whiteboard that drew together all the points raised and led to a conclusion about the problem. This product was frequently used as the starting point for the next CPA.

This is an example, like the concept map, where what is usually an assessment task – the assignment – becomes the teaching/learning activity. However, instead of assessing the assignment, Yamane looks at each one to check that it has been carried out honestly. If it has, he awards a pass and, if not, the student has to repeat it (all repeats pass in his experience).

This technique worked well within classes of 30 to 80, but Yamane does not recommend it in classes larger than this. He compared the CPA method with a lecture course, taught by himself and using the same material, on students' responses to a questionnaire on their level of thinking and their sense of responsibility and involvement and found strong evidence for the effectiveness of the CPA approach.

Box 7.1 gives an example of an adaptation of CPA by Catherine Chiu in her teaching of sociology at City University of Hong Kong.

How the large class lecture can become interactive

Mazur's and Yamane's teaching are examples of getting students relevantly active with teaching/learning activities that facilitate the intended outcomes. Such teaching, along with formative feedback, has the largest effect on student learning (Hattie 2003). We now look at a range of TLAs that are suitable in large class teaching for constructing a declarative knowledge base in different content areas.

Box 7.1   Course preparation assignments in the teaching of sociology

Introduction to sociology

Course preparation asssignment for Week 5

Lecture two: Culture

1 Read Macionis, Chapter 2, and familiarize yourself with these key concepts:

a Culture, symbols, language, values, beliefs, norms, mores, folkways, cultural integration.
b Cultural changes, cultural lag.
c Cultural diversity, subculture, counterculture.
d Ethnocentrism, cultural relativism.

Assignment 1

a Objective (ILO): To define the key values of Hong Kong culture.
b Background: On pp. 43–44, you read that Robin Williams identifies two key values of US culture.
c Assignment: Identify at least five key values of Hong Kong.

Assignment 2

a Objective (ILO): To apply two theoretical approaches to explain why certain key values exist in Hong Kong.
b Background: On pp. 54–56, Macionis presents analysis of culture using two perspectives – structural-functional and social-conflict.
c Assignment: Pick two of the key values of Hong Kong you have identified and explain why they exist in Hong Kong from the structural-functional point of view. Then do the same by using the social-conflict approach.

Source: Catherine Chiu, City University of Hong Kong

Note taking

Note taking is widely misused when students take notes for the purpose of obtaining a record of what the teacher says. Students, especially the Roberts, have a twofold problem: of following what they are hearing and of writing notes for later reference. They can't do both simultaneously so they alternate between listening and writing. But while they are writing the gist down, the lecturer is sentences ahead. Their notes are therefore a random sample of a fraction of what the teacher was saying. And with only a fraction of the trees, they have to reconstruct the whole wood. Difficult. If note taking is primarily intended as a record for later revision, it is both inefficient and wasteful. Why not just hand out readings?

Note taking may, however, be a useful TLA, for example for immediate review and reflection. If students are to take notes, comprehension time should be separated from recording time, and students should be allowed a time slot to check their notes. Students can swap notes with their neighbour, discuss differences and rewrite their own notes. They can thus review the main ideas about what has been said and elaborate their own understanding to their neighbour and reflect on their neighbour's interpretation if it is different from their own.

Note taking should be used as a teaching/learning activity, in other words, not as a horribly inefficient recording device. The sorts of notes students might best take depend on the content area, the use to which they are to be put and any ILOs they are to serve. For these reasons, the skills and purposes of note taking, as with other study skills, are usefully incorporated into the teaching of particular content (Chalmers and Fuller 1996): we discuss this further later.

Changing activities

As for other large class activities, remember that concentration flags after 15 minutes or so, particularly if the ongoing activity is straight listening. You might set a timer to ring every 15 minutes; when it rings, stop whatever is going on and change the activity or consolidate (Gibbs et al. 1992):

- Students reflect on what they think they have just learned, then in pairs tell each other what they saw as the most important point in the preceding 15 minutes of lecturing. Here's a TLA that gets *them* to 'explain'.
- Each student writes down a question or a comment sparked by the previous 15 minutes for their neighbour to respond to. They can hand in their question/comments sheet at the end of the session; it will also be useful feedback to you – and an attendance check.
- You pose questions for them to answer, either individually or discuss with a neighbour.
- You set a problem for them to work on, either individually or in discussion with a neighbour.
- Towards the end of the lecture, allow five minutes for each student to tell their neighbour or learning partner (see later) what they think was the thrust of the session. This achieves the consolidation by active review and also gives them a different perspective to think about, other than their own interpretation of your perspective. Further, they are giving and receiving feedback, and enacting that ubiquitous ILO 'explain'.

Linking diagrams and key points can be achieved by handouts using PowerPoint software, three or so slides per page, with space beside each where the students can write their notes and comments. This gives students accurate basic notes and diagrams, but requires them to actively search for the main idea, and put it in their own words with an example or two.

Work-along exercises

Olivia Leung, of the Department of Accountancy at City University of Hong Kong, links student activity to her lecturing by devising work-along exercises that accompany her discussion of each topic. These exercises help students follow the lecture closely and actively visualize the application of concepts. Box 7.2 shows some examples of work-along exercises used in an Accounting class of over 200 students.

One-/three-minute essay

The one- or three-minute essay is a technique whereby students write brief answers to such questions as:

At the start of the lecture: What do I most want to find out in this class?
Towards the end: What is the main point I learned today?
Also at the end: What was the main point left unanswered in today's session?

Allow a couple of minutes for students to swap and read what their neighbour said. The students' responses may be handed in, with names, and each can be read in a few seconds. The answers can be used as formative assessment both for them and for you – and as an attendance check. The cumulative record gives a very good, and quick, indication of the development of students' thinking through the course.

These ultra-short essays at the beginning of the class forces students, as did Mazur, to actually *do* the pre-reading and to reflect on it. The second question can tell you something about their learning and your teaching: if some quite minor aside is seen as 'the main point', either you or they have a problem. In either case, it will need to be addressed in the next class. The last question also provides fodder for the next class. Students are provided with feedback on how their thinking is in line with other students' and with your own. You can no doubt think of other questions that would better suit your intended outcomes. Some may find it more convenient for students to use personal digital assistants (PDAs) to record and transmit their one-minute essays.

Concept maps

Concept maps were originally designed both to present a structure and to find out how students see the structure (Novak 1979). They can be used by teachers for both teaching and assessment purposes and by students for organizing their ideas, for example for reviewing the semester's work, for planning and writing essays or for clarifying difficult passages. They are useful for ILOs requiring students to see the whole, perceive relationships, integrate and organize and can be demonstrated and used by students inside or outside the classroom.

In creating concept maps, students singly or in groups are presented with a central concept or principle. Either they themselves generate sub-concepts that relate to it, or the sub-concepts are supplied. The students then arrange the sub-concepts, either drawing them or arranging cards on which they

Box 7.2   Some examples of work-along exercises for a class in accounting of over 200 students

Review question: Debit and credit effects on assets and liabilities

What accounts below are decreased by debits?

- Inventory
- Accounts payable
- Dividends
- Cash
- Notes payable
- Accounts receivable

Answer: _____

Why? _____

Review question: Adjusting entry supplies

The trial balance shows supplies of $2000 and supplies expense of $0. If $750 of supplies are on hand at the end of the period, what is the adjusting entry?

Account	Debit	Credit
	$1250	
		$1250

The balance in supplies after adjustment is $750, the amount remaining unused. The amount used is transferred to expense.

Review question: Closing entries

Which of the following accounts will have a zero balance after the closing process?

- Unearned revenue
- Advertising supplies
- Prepaid insurance
- Rent expense
- Income summary

Answer: _____
are temporary accounts. All temporary accounts are closed and thus have a zero balance after the closing process.

Source: Olivia Leung of City University of Hong Kong

have been written, in a way that makes best sense to them, the distance between sub-concepts reflecting their perceived degree of interrelation. Lines are then drawn linking sub- and central concepts with a brief explanation of what the link or relationship is.

Creating concept maps is a learning experience for the students, helping them to explicitly structure their thinking and, at the same time, the resulting maps give an indication of how the student sees the way in which individual concepts relate to each other. They can therefore be used for assessment purposes (p. 235). As concept maps present an overall picture, a holistic representation of a complex conceptual structure, they are best evaluated by judging the complexity of the arrangement and the correctness of the interrelations, rather than by analytic 'marking' (see Chapter 9). They can be used as feedback, to see how teaching might be adjusted, as part of the final assessments of student learning or for students in their own studying.

Santhanam et al. (1998) found that first-year science and agricultural students saw the value of using concept maps but not their relevance. They thought that memorization was the best approach to study in first year and so did not use concept mapping in their own studying; a depressing finding, suggesting that the students had obtained the wrong cues from the way they had been taught and assessed (see also Ramsden et al. 1986).

Think-aloud modelling

When presenting new tasks or problems, it can be very helpful for the teacher to think out loud while handling it, so that the students are clearer about what they are supposed to be doing. The teacher is doing the self-analysis and reflection publicly, letting the students know how an expert does it, so that eventually they do so themselves. Many teachers think aloud for their students automatically, but many others do not. Modelling is handy whenever you get the inevitable: 'But what are we supposed to do?' But then, for it to be an active TLA, they must then be required to do it, not just watch a demonstration.

An overhead projector enables you to face and interact with the class while thinking out loud, showing your notes and revisions and mistakes. For example, you could show how you write an article at the various stages of planning, composing and revising, to demonstrate the various techniques that academic writers use. Students are brought face to face with processes and possibilities that they themselves would not think of and, if the class is not too large, the students can call out contributions to the ongoing composing or problem-solving process. In large classes, you could nominate a particular row or rows of students to call out their suggestions.

The various techniques just mentioned meet many of the objections raised about the lecture and they can take place in the lecture situation and focus on what the *students* are doing, not what the teacher is doing. Students are not confronted with loads of information at too great a rate for many of them to handle, but are required to work with that information, to elaborate, correct and consolidate it.

Peer teaching

What do you perceive when you enter the door of a large crowded lecture theatre: 400 students sitting there waiting to be taught by you or 400 teaching assistants waiting to be brought in on the action? Peer teaching is a very powerful ally when you have large classes to teach. There may be no single best method of teaching 'but the second best is students teaching other students' (McKeachie et al. 1986: 63).

Peer teaching is greatly under-utilized, although both tutor and tutee benefit academically, the tutor more than the tutee (as you would expect on the grounds of active learning), while the tutor is also likely to have increased social skills and attitudes to study and self (Goodlad and Hirst 1990; Topping 1996). The reasons for these benefits are clear:

- The content to be taught has to be viewed not from one's own perspective, but from that of someone whose conceptions of the topic to be taught are different and less satisfactory.
- The teacher reflects on how they learned the topic, which means that peers, being closer to that process and more aware of the traps and difficulties than the expert, can teach more empathically.
- The teacher 'owns' the material, publicly taking responsibility for its validity. There is heavy loss of face if they get it wrong – so they are more careful about getting it right.

Two New Zealand tertiary institutions give course credit for peer tutoring, the practical work being carried out tutoring secondary school students (Jones et al. 1994). No, not education students, destined for a teaching career, but law, science, and business students. The assumption is simply that teaching the subject deepens students' understanding of it. Compared to teacher-led groups, student-led groups range wider in their discussion and produce more complex outcomes (McKeachie et al. 1986; Tang 1998). In cross-year tutoring, the tutor is in a higher year than the tutee. Both tutors and tutees like the process, and the achievement of the tutees is little different from conventionally taught (Topping 1996): a positive and cost-effective finding, when you think about it.

The peer assistance supplementary scheme or peer-assisted study sessions (PASS in either case) is a common scheme for cross-year tutoring, designed to alleviate the problem of large first-year classes. The tutors are second-year or third-year students who passed the first-year subject exceptionally well and are judged to have appropriate personal qualities. They are trained to 'model, advise and facilitate' rather than to address the curriculum directly and are either paid or given course credit. Data involving 295 courses in the USA show improved achievement and higher re-enrolment and graduation rates (National Center for Supplemental Instruction 1994). Outcomes in the UK are likewise encouraging (Topping 1996). At the University of Queensland, over many thousands of student, regular attendees of PASS averaged a whole grade higher than students who did not attend, while of the students gaining high distinctions, 85% attended PASS, 14% did not (Chalmers and Kelly 1997).

PASS employs two tutors or student leaders per group of 25 first years and they are paid also to attend at least one lecture that the tutees receive (Chalmers and Kelly 1997; Watson 1996, 1997). Leaders receive one full day of training and ongoing weekly meetings with the staff coordinator. Leaders are required to keep a reflective diary, with which they provide feedback to the departmental staff coordinator. This ongoing information was found to be far more useful to lecturers in meeting problems than end-of-semester course evaluations.

Attendance from the first-year classes is voluntary, ranging from 20% of the class to over 80%. The agenda is up to the students, frequently involving a review of what has gone on in class that week. No new material is presented.

Following are some of the benefits that students see (Chalmers and Kelly 1997):

- a friendly environment in which they can comfortably ask 'the dumbest questions'
- weekly study that keeps them up to date
- insight into the range of material other students are covering and the difficulties they have
- a mentor who can give information and who has inside knowledge of how they coped
- international students particularly like the opportunity to discuss without staff present.

PASS is considered particularly useful in subjects having:

- large classes, particularly when unsupported by other group work
- highly technical content
- a failure rate of more than 10%
- high international student enrolments
- a service role as a core subject for a number of degree courses.

To sum up, then, if two major principles are adopted, that lecture theatre can indeed become a learning theatre:

1 Keep the students active with relevant teaching/learning activities.
2 Supply them regularly with feedback from yourself, from other students, and from reflective self-assessment.

Where does this leave the tutorial?

Active learning of this kind meets many if not all of the outcomes the tutorial is intended to achieve – elaboration and clarification of what the students had understood from the preceding lecture. And given that 'tutorials' of 30 and 40 students, as sometimes occurs, can't possibly do what they are supposed to do, and that tutors are frequently the least experienced staff members, one begins to question why we should have tutorials at all. Essentially, the tutorial is a relic of an older academic ecosystem, when the Susans outnumbered the Roberts and when classwork needed only to be held in big or small rooms.

If we replace the lecture with more flexible teaching/learning activities involving interactive learning, as suggested earlier, the conventional tutorial may follow the Tasmanian tiger into extinction unless it is rethought. In the School of Experimental Psychology at the University of Sussex, for example, tutorials are mainly student-led tutorials. Students give a brief 15-minute presentation that has been assessed by the teacher beforehand, each tutorial has assigned questions for discussion and each student must put to the group at least one point in the lectures they didn't understand. Beyond that, the students run the main proceedings themselves, except that the teacher turns up for the last 10 minutes, which has a good effect on morale and allows unresolved issues to be put to the teacher (Dienes 1997).

Interactivity in smaller classes

In classes under 30, sometimes the formal lecture becomes the formal lecture with a looser, more conversational script. Some inspirational lecturers like students to interrupt with comments or ask unplanned questions. They can think up answers on their feet: the lightning riposte, *that's* the stuff of good teaching! Maybe, but there could be a role confusion here between stand-up comic and teacher; the attention in this case is on the teacher, not on what the students are supposed to be doing. The students are simply the means for showing how brilliant the teacher is.

Good interactive teaching nevertheless requires on-the-spot improvisation in response to events as they occur. Questions and comments from students can be the basis for rethinking and reconstructing new and exciting ideas, if the ball is picked up and taken in an appropriate direction. The experience gives the phrase 'the social construction of knowledge' real meaning. Papers have originated that way.

Dealing with questions from students

In more intimate surroundings than the large lecture theatre, questioning by students presents a different challenge. Dealing effectively with questions requires a knowledge of topic structure that is sufficiently rich and flexible that you can recognize the students' perspective of it and their access to it. It's not only a matter of having expert knowledge of your subject – that goes without saying – but of understanding where they are coming from in asking it in the way they did and how the understanding they displayed in asking the question can be orchestrated in harmony with your own expert knowledge.

Questions put to students

Convergent questions

Convergent questions are asked with a correct answer in mind and students are steered towards that answer, while divergent questions are open ended, seeking input from the students' perspective. Convergent questions are not necessarily low level. Socratic questioning is a case in point. The teacher goes round the class asking questions that lead subtly to the answer the teacher requires. This is the social construction of knowledge, where all contribute and agree on the structure as it emerges.

Divergent questions

Divergent questions are useful for probing student experiences and using them for constructing fresh ideas and interpretations, for incorporating them as examples of the case in point and for student reflection. In professional programmes, where the students have hands-on experience, there is a wealth of functioning knowledge to be tapped, to be located in a conceptual structure and generalized. Divergent questions can also lead to aimless rambling and that needs controlling. Good questioning skills are required.

High- or *low-level* questions

High-level questions probe the high-level verbs: theorizing, reflecting, hypothesizing; low-level questions enact the low-level verbs: recalling factual answers. High-level questions need *wait time*. High-level thinking takes more time than low-level thinking. Whether out of fear of silence, impatience or bad judgment, the fact is that in most classrooms nowhere near enough wait time is allowed. When allowed unlimited time to answer, tertiary students averaged nine seconds to answer a convergent question, over 30 seconds to answer a divergent question (Ellsworth et al. 1991). The longer students took, the better quality of the response. If you might feel embarrassed by 30 seconds of silence, work out ways of not being embarrassed.

The fact that high-level responding needs time is a major advantage of the asynchronous use of educational technology, that is when students respond to online questions and issues in their own time (see later).

Now for a reflective task about who is doing what in your classes (Task 7.1). How would you redesign your next large class 'lecture' (Task 7.2)?

Managing large class teaching

Large classes require effective and quite specific management skills. It is quite shameful that the least experienced and junior staff members are often allocated to the largest classes to spare the more experienced teachers from this unpopular teaching situation.

Large classes need *meticulous preparation*. The larger the class, the slower

---

Task 7.1   What happened in your large class 'lecture'?

Reflect on the 'lectures' you have been giving in the last semester. Write down what activities occurred and who was engaged in those activities (the 'doers').

Activities	The 'doers'			
	Teacher	Students as a class	Students as peers	Students alone

Now compare the activities and who the 'doers' of those activities are, with the intended outcomes of the 'lecture'. Who was doing the activities that led to achieving the ILOs?

---

things get done. A spur-of-the-moment change of direction, perhaps in response to a student question, highly desirable and manageable with a group of 30, becomes perilous with 300. Most teachers find large class teaching a 'performance', with the increased likelihood of stage fright (see Box 7.3, p. 124).

As few teachers have any training in public speaking, providing such training would no doubt be helpful. However, even with training, the majority of academics would be pushed to be able to perform centre stage, day after day, inspiring students every time: even Dr Fox would have trouble doing that.

This slow-heaving hulk needs to be carefully directed otherwise it will crush your plans. Establish your procedural rules at the outset: signals for silence, procedures for questioning (how are you going to deal with the forest of hands or with the clown who always asks questions to class groans?), signals for starting and stopping, if you are going to use buzz groups who is to discuss with who, who is to be spokesperson on report back, and how to bring them back to order when it's time. Establish these rules in the first session.

The size and buzz of a large class requires a smooth start:

- Don't just sail straight in. Signal that class has started and wait for quiet. Try playing music while students enter, then when you are ready to start, stop the music. It creates a nice air of expectancy.
- Start with a proper introduction: 'Following from last week when we . . . What we are going to do today.' Why lecture when the topic is in the

---

Task 7.2   Redesigning your next large class 'lecture'

Take your next large class session, which you would normally regale with a long and carefully prepared lecture. Now is the time to have a go at restructuring the session. Assume the time period is one hour. If more than this, make allowance in your plans.

1 Stage a striking introduction that will grab their attention and be relevant to what follows.

_____

_____

_____

2 Allow for three breaks after 10 to 15 minutes of solid talk by you. What will you do, or rather what will the students do, in each break? One of the activities should involve something you collect at the end and ponder for the next session.

Break 1 _____

_____

Break 2 _____

_____

Break 3* _____

_____

[* if applicable]

3 Consolidate with an active review in the last five minutes by getting them to do something _____

_____

_____

---

textbook? Because you are going to do something the textbook can't? What is that? Tell them. Then they'll know what they should be getting from this particular lecture (Gibbs et al. 1984).

- If lecture you must, preview with a slide giving the subheadings of the lecture, and some explanation of the sequences of subheadings, or a diagram if that is appropriate.

Following are a few points to watch while talking to a large class:

- Eye contact students while talking; no head buried in notes.
- Ensure clarity: project the voice, check it can be heard at the back. Cordless radio mikes are best.
- Focus on the 'U' rather than the 'T'. Susan and her friends tend to sit along the front row and up the middle (the T), Robert and his friends at

---

Box 7.3   Dons struggle with stage fright

Brendan O'Keefe

It happens to the best of them. As lecture time approaches, on come the cold sweats and the nerves as confidence departs.

An underperforming student, scared of being found out? No. An experienced lecturer, who has been in the limelight for years, with stage fright? Yes.

One who knows plenty about it – and who wants to know more – is University of Canberra marketing communication lecturer Amanda Burrell.

Ms Burrell has a degree in creative arts (acting) from the University of Wollongong and was a professional performer for a decade before turning to lecturing about 10 years ago.

Returning to the lectern this year for the first time in 15 months after having a baby, Ms Burrell found herself in dread of fronting a class . . . A straw poll of colleagues revealed that many felt the same way. 'People told me stories about losing confidence, how they lost their voice in a presentation, how they fainted or got so muddled they couldn't read their notes,' Ms Burrell said. 'I thought: "There's something worth looking at here".'

Ms Burrell believes stage fright among lecturers is a widespread but little talked about problem. She has set herself the task, as a research project, to find out how many suffer and how they cope. She even rigged up a colleague with a heart-rate monitor to check stress levels. The woman, whose resting heart rate was 80 beats per minute, was described by a third-party observer to be 'as cool as a cucumber' during a presentation. But her heart rate had peaked at 175bpm.

Ms Burrell said she wanted universities to include public speaking as part of their training for new lecturers. Ms Burrell has plans to visit acting schools. 'I'd like to see how the training of professional actors can inform our practice,' she said.

Source: *The Australian Higher Education*, 19 April 2006

---

the back and down the sides (the U). Focus on grabbing Robert and you will automatically include Susan.

- Handouts should be collected up on entry or exit. If possible, organize the schedule at least a week ahead so that the end of the previous session can be used for handouts for the next. Distributing handouts during class is messy and time wasting.

- Consider putting any lectures on WebCT or BlackBoard and then ask yourself this question: Why give that lecture at all if they all have access to it anyway? Can't you use that time more effectively than merely repeating what they can read at their own pace? Yes, you can: we've just been through that.

Questions provide a break that many students perceive as chat-to-neighbour-time while the nerd has a heart-to-heart with the teacher. To prevent this, the whole class must be included and involved. This means *distancing* yourself, not doing the personable thing and leaning towards the questioner. Move back so that the questioner is part of the class, repeat the question so that it becomes a whole class question. In a very large class, it may be better to ask them to write down their questions and pass them up to the front, rather than shouting them at you. You could take them on the spot or answer them in the introduction to the next session. In *very* large classes – what have we come to? – you might use the large meeting technique, with microphone stands in the aisles.

Most students dislike the *impersonality* of large class teaching: it's a short step from there to a cold Theory X climate. To warm things up a bit, try the following (Davis 1993):

- Stand in front of the lectern, not behind it. Walk about, up and down the aisles if feasible. Get students to leave a few rows empty, so you can move along them. Convey accessibility, not distance, but stand still when delivering important points.
- Do not in your friendly wandering be seduced by a *sotto voce* question. Make it a question coming from the whole class (see earlier).
- At the beginning of the class get neighbouring students to introduce themselves to each other. These may or may not lead to formal learning partnerships (see next section).
- Get students to complete a short biographical questionnaire, giving names, reasons for taking the unit, hobbies, etc. You can then refer to students by name occasionally, selecting examples to illustrate points to match their interests. They'll feel good about that, although not everyone may get a mention.
- Arrive early, and/or leave late, to talk with students. Make your hours of availability in your office known and keep those times sacred. Some teachers may be comfortable inviting groups of students, in circulation to cover everyone, to coffee.
- Where tutors assess assignments, make sure you read a sample and discuss it in class. Let them know you are not delegating entirely.
- Use humour and topical references but take care where there are large numbers of international students. They are likely to be confused by topical references, colloquialisms and culturally specific jokes.

Eric Mazur, he who decided lectures were a waste of time (p. 111), kept the photographs of the 160 students in his physics class in his address file.

When they emailed in their answers to his questions on reading, the tasks were such that errors fell into few categories, so that there were essentially only five generic emails to be sent, to groups of 30 or so students. By clicking on the student's address, up would come their face reminding him who he was talking to. He then tuned the opening and the close to the individual: 'Hi there Jenny. You slipped up a bit here, after last week's great effort. Here seems to be the problem . . . (then he pasted the appropriate generic email). Let me know if it's not clear now. Best.'

Learning partners

A great help for both students and teacher, especially in large classes, is to require students to form a partnership with another student or a small group of students. Partnerships are not so much for working towards a particular goal, such as a group assignment, but for mutual general support. Students need someone to talk to: to share concerns, to seek clarification over assignment requirements, to check their own insecure interpretations of procedure or of content (Saberton 1985).

Partners could be matched by the teacher, perhaps on the basis of the way students complement each other (high performing/at risk, international/ local, mature age/straight from school, those with access to desirable resources/those with little access). Alternatively, students could each choose their own partners, which has some advantages but particularly with the presence of international students, there are excellent reasons for ethnically mixed partnerships. Partners then agree to sit next to each other in class and to consult out of class, exchanging telephone numbers, email, etc. They can also collaborate on suitable assessment tasks. Partnerships that do not work because of the personal chemistry should be reformed. Some students may prefer to remain loners and that should be respected: it is their loss, which in time they come to realize.

Learning partners permanently sitting next to each other makes life much easier for the teacher when implementing the kinds of note swapping, active review and so on mentioned earlier. The teacher's out-of-class time in dealing with queries is actually rather more than halved, because the chances are that one partner can put the other partner straight without consulting the teacher.

Large class teaching is difficult, but it doesn't have to follow the pattern of the standard lecture. If you are not convinced already, read *Twenty Terrible Reasons for Lecturing* (Gibbs 1981b). Certainly, large class sizes provide no reason to abandon the principle of alignment, either in designing teaching/ learning activities to suit your intended learning outcomes or, as we shall see in Chapter 11, in selecting the assessment tasks needed.

Educational technology

The University of Western Australia has developed 'Lectopia', a system whereby lectures are recorded and posted on the net. With podcasting, lectures can be downloaded at any time on computers, iPods or mobile phones. The system is now used by several Australian universities, allowing students whose work commitments clash with scheduled lectures to listen to the lectures at their convenience. This is a great convenience for them, but it might reinforce the idea that the main function of university teaching is lecturing: the transfer of information, without the interactive learning that – one hopes – took place in the lecture.

Educational technology (ET) opens up a whole new world domain for student activity, of which replaying lectures and downloading gigabytes of information is only a fraction of its potential usefulness. BlackBoard and WebCT, apart from being used as a management platform for all teaching on and off campus, also have supports for interactive teaching/learning activities and for different types of assessment, as we discuss in Chapter 11. The use of these platforms for interactive teaching, perhaps especially intended for off-campus teaching, can be a boon for teachers and students alike with respect to large classes.

The interactive use of ET literally dissolves the boundaries of time and space, allowing many different kinds of interaction between people:

1 *Synchronous and asynchronous use.* Synchronous use is when teacher, or learning package, interact with the student in the same time frame. This is the case when teacher and student are online at the same time, as in tele- or videoconferencing. Students attending a PowerPoint lecture is also a synchronous use. With asynchronous use, participants make their communication in their own time, such as happens when using email or a bulletin board. For example, the teacher may post questions on the board and the students respond with answers or comments, as is convenient to them, prior to the stated deadline. Asynchronous use is particularly valuable in off-campus teaching, so that individuals with full-time jobs can enter their learning space at evenings or weekends or whenever suits them.

2 *Individual and social use.* We normally think of online teaching as involving a lonely individual at a keyboard responding asynchronously to a distant information source. This is only one, limited, use. When used synchronously, student and teacher may converse one to one, or one to many and students may interact with each other at the same time. The social advantages can be enhanced by having pairs or even larger numbers at the same keyboard so that they may discuss their comments, questions or responses before sending them. These groupings can be used synchronously or asynchronously.

The combinations of individual and group, and synchronous and asynchronous use, are many. Each combination has its own advantages and dis-advantages; as always, it depends entirely on what and how you want your students to learn. A disadvantage of asynchronous online discussion is that that those who place their views first on online discussion can frustrate others who wanted to make the same points. This might be obviated by requiring students to post to a closed address, which would then be opened on a specified date. It helps considerably if groups can meet face to face first, so that when online discussion begins, people can put a face to the name and feel that they are genuinely conversing.

Personal digital assistants (PDAs) can be used in the classroom, as did Mazur for instant responding to MC-type questions, but the most recent versions have telephone, still, video and internet-accessing options, which make them incredibly flexible as learning and assessment tools. Teacher–student and student–student communication can be maintained outside the classroom in workplace or other learning situations in real or in virtual time.

Bulletin boards, either with PDA or computer, can be used to consolidate and elaborate material. Students can, in their own time – that is, asynchronously – post comments about a reading or lecture, which can lead to conversations about the content, different interpretations, elaborations, corrections. This can provide a tremendous amount of feedback both to the teacher and to the students themselves. An example of enlightened bulletin board use with teachers attending a postgraduate educational psychology course is given by Chan (2001), who integrated computer-supported collaborative learning with regular teaching. The students were asked to post their learning notes and responses to questions on a bulletin board and to comment on the notes and responses of others. The distinctive feature of her use of the bulletin board was the way she posted reflective prompts, such as:

- Is there anything interesting or useful you have learned?
- What are some things that are difficult to understand?
- How did reading these notes help you think about X and Y?
- Have the comments on your ideas made you rethink the issue?

Students did not have to address each as an assignment question, but as reminders to guide their thinking. Students were also asked about their conceptions of teaching and learning at the beginning and at the end of the course; the difference became a measure of the growth of their complexity of thinking about teaching and learning.

Chan found that the frequency of contribution to the bulletin board in itself was unrelated to a gain in complexity of thinking, but when the comments were divided into those that were derived collaboratively or were simply posted as individual contributions, those who entered into collaborative engagement gained most in complexity of thinking. This replicates a finding that face-to-face collaborative learning leads to better structured assignments than individually written ones (Tang 1998).

Knowledge Forum is a powerful program for encouraging collaborative knowledge construction (Scardamalia et al. 1994). Knowledge Forum involves students contributing to a bulletin board by generating their own problems, posing their own questions and commenting on each other's work, rather like Chan's usage. The computer helps search all comments written by a student at different periods, which can then be rated in terms of the quality of the comments. The software comes with a program called Analytical Toolkit that can generate quantitative indices, such as how much each student has written, how much the individual has read others' notes, how often their comments are revised or elaborated, how one student's notes relate to others' notes, who is writing to whom, and so on. However, the program cannot recognize the quality of the comments written and so analyses still need to be done by teachers; in some respects, these analyses are not unlike SOLO. The main difference between Knowledge Forum and other discussion platforms is that it includes thinking prompts and other devices to help students reflect deeply as they contribute and it provides formative assessment of students' ideas as they are posted on the platform continually. One can also make a summative statement about students' growth and learning outputs at the end of the course.

Virtual environments, many available commercially on CD-ROM, provide interesting interactive environments for students to explore. For example, 'Virtual Dig' can take archaeology students through excavating a site; they can alter factors such as time of dig, method, whether to screen dirt for relics and so on. There are many science laboratory virtual environments where students can try expensive or dangerous experiments at a fraction of real cost and with no risk of something going badly wrong.

Computer-mediated conferencing (CMC) is a general term for teaching online with an 'e-moderator', who is in effect a tutor who 'chairs' asynchronous sessions with distance learning students (Salmon 2003). Salmon suggests a five-stage model for CMC:

1 Access and motivation: making sure all participants can go online, keeping them motivated over the inevitable blips and providing technical support.
2 Online socialization: getting to know each other and building a group sense.
3 Information exchange: helping participants with searching, downloading and organizing the relevant information.
4 Knowledge construction: participants become authors, sharing views and contributions. There are many ways of organizing this phase, with individual, dyad and group work, depending on the purpose.
5 Development: participants now become responsible for their own learning, using self-critical and reflective strategies, developing where they want to go.

There is a view popular among politicians, among others, that online teaching is the answer to large classes. This view assumes a Level 1 theory of teaching as a one-way transmission: teaching is merely providing information. But as we have seen, effective teaching involves engaging students in relevant activity, so there are obvious limits to the numbers that can be handled appropriately. The difference between a teacher responding interactively to 30 students online and 3000 is obvious. Salmon's five stages of online teaching should put paid to that view. As student enrolments in a course increase, it becomes correspondingly necessary to engage online teaching assistants or e-moderators who are both computer wise and content expert.

Box 7.4 tells of a nice example of reflective practice, which led to a Level 2 theory of using ET becoming Level 3, where what mattered was what the students did – and assessment became a TLA.

Box 7.4   How reflection led to assessment being used as a TLA

Problem: 90 per cent of nursing students experience difficulty in understanding the topic: oedema associated with cardiac failure.

Hypothesis: A visual approach is more suited to the subject and to students' learning styles.

Solution: Develop 'a multisensorial approach from which there could be no escape'. It has to have visual appeal and movement: hence *multimedia*, an animated slide show.

Result: Only a 'slight' improvement in students' understanding.

Reflection: 'I had wasted my time'

But then Tyler read the first edition of this book and learned:

1 Don't blame the students.
2 Don't blame the teacher.
3 Don't blame the teaching tool.
4 Do blame the lack of alignment.
5 Do blame the lack of assessment.

On further reflection: 'The multimedia program was worthwhile . . . what it lacked was alignment and assessment.'

Students now:

1 Complete an assessable worksheet at home (marked and assessed by peers).
2 Complete a similar worksheet in class (again marked by peers).

Result: Pass rates in clinical studies increased from 80 per cent to 99.5 per cent.

Source: Tyler (2001)

Before leaving this chapter, you can now try to design teaching/learning activities for some of your course ILOs relating to declarative knowledge. Task 7.3 gives a framework that should help you.

Task 7.3   TLAs for declarative knowledge

Select two of your course ILOs relating to declarative knowledge. Design TLAs that would facilitate achievement of these ILOs.

Course ILO1: _____

Course ILO2: _____

Number of students in the course:

Course ILO	Teaching situation	Teaching activities (what the teacher does)	Learning activities (what the students do)
1			
2			

Now doublecheck if the student learning activities are aligned with the verbs nominated in the respective course ILOs.

Compared with the teaching situations that you have been using so far for the same course ILOs:

a What changes have you made?
b What do you expect to achieve through these changes?

Summary and conclusions

Three changes needed in the way we usually think about teaching

We need to question three assumptions:

1 That lectures and tutorials are the default teaching methods. Rather they are types of *situation* in which different teaching/learning activities can be organized, depending on the learning outcomes that are intended.
2 That the focus should be on what teachers are doing. The term 'lecture' focuses on what teachers should be doing. In the lecture or any teaching/learning situation it is more important to focus on what the students are doing.
3 That relevant learning occurs only when inside the classroom with a teacher orchestrating the proceedings.

What teachers do: What students do

The term 'lecture' is teacher-centred: it says what teachers do. The important thing is what students are doing while the teacher is lecturing. Even in a simple ILO involving the verb 'explain', students are unlikely to be doing any explaining themselves in the typical lecture situation. This needs turning around, so that the ILO prescribes what *students* should be doing in a teaching/learning situation if they are to build the solid, well-structured knowledge base that is prerequisite even to such ILOs as 'explain'. Such a knowledge base is even more important to achieving yet higher order ILOs.

Teaching declarative knowledge in large classes

Lecturing is logistically convenient, being able to handle large numbers of students simultaneously, but it has no advantage over other teaching situations, except that when given by an active researcher it exposes students to a scholar's ongoing thinking. Otherwise the learning that takes place in lecturing is demonstrably worse than in other teaching situations. A more articulated focus on ILOs and the TLAs that foster them is needed. This requires interactive teaching.

Interactive teaching

Interactive teaching can be brought to the large class quite readily. The most prolific resource in large classes is the students themselves; using them appropriately engages a different lot of verbs that address a range of ILOs scarcely touched by teacher-directed TLAs. Creating semi-permanent learning partnerships can make life easier for both you and them, providing a continually accessible resource for discussing, reciprocal questioning and mutual support in an otherwise anonymous environment. In resource-starved times, it is amazing that peer teaching in its various forms, including the use of paid students as in PASS, is not used more widely. In smaller classes, interactivity between teacher and students is more personal and requires in particular effective questioning skills.

Managing large class teaching

Large classes raise management problems of their own. A plenary session demands management strategies quite different from those appropriate to small classes. Such things as preparing before class, commencing the session, effective strategies of talking and questioning during the session and ensuring that students know what to do and who is to report back after student–

student interaction sessions are important to work out in advance. A management issue of a different kind is overcoming the anonymity and alienation that many students feel and dislike in large classes.

Educational technology

Educational technology offers a range of TLAs addressing ILOs for both declarative and functioning knowledge; we concentrate on the former here. ET can support TLAs that mimic standard classroom TLAs, while others offer possibilities of engaging learners that are not possible in the classroom. Computer-mediated conferencing and Knowledge Forum are examples that belong in the latter group. Both may operate in real time or asynchronously, the latter allowing students to go online at their own convenience and to post contributions after serious reflection. ET may obviate some problems of large class teaching, but effective online interaction with students demands teacher time just as much as offline teaching.

Further reading

On lecturing in large classes

Bligh, D.A. (1972) *What's the Use of Lectures?* Harmondsworth: Penguin.

Elton, L. and Cryer, P. (1992) *Teaching Large Classes.* Sheffield: University of Sheffield Teaching Development Unit.

Gibbs, G. (1981) *Twenty Terrible Reasons for Lecturing.* Oxford: Oxford Polytechnic.

Gibbs, G. and Jenkins, A. (eds) (1992) *Teaching Large Classes in Higher Education.* London: Kogan Page.

O'Neill, M. (Project Director) *Teaching in Large Classes.* A very comprehensive CD-ROM, produced at the University of Western Australia, showing examples of expert teachers in action at all stages of teaching, from getting prepared for lecture to closing elegantly. Has interviews with novice teachers, expert teachers and students at each teaching stage.

Teaching and Educational Development Institute, University of Queensland, Project on Teaching Large Classes. http://www.tedi.uq.edu.au/largeclasses/

On interactive teaching

Chalmers, D. and Fuller, R. (1996) *Teaching for Learning at University.* London: Kogan Page.

Race, P. and Brown, S. (1993) *500 Tips for Tutors.* London: Kogan Page.

Salmon, G. (2003) *E-moderating: The Key to Online Teaching and Learning.* London: Kogan Page.

Chalmers and Fuller remind you to teach students how to handle the information you are teaching them. The 'tips for . . .' genre contains useful collections of procedures, but you must use your own judgment as to their applicability to your own problems. There is a danger of falling into the Level 2 mode: tell me what are good teaching techniques and I'll use them. You know by now it doesn't work like that. Salmon gives solid practical advice for using computer-mediated conferencing, an interactive technique developed from the Open University for teaching distance learning students.

Websites

Making active learning work, University of Minnesota: http://www1.umn.edu/ohr/ teachlearn/tutorials/active/index.html
Active learning: http://alh.sagepub.com/cgi/reprint/5/1/87 (this item requires a subscription to Active Learning in Higher Education Online).
The enterprising James Atherton's website on university teaching. Browse contents: http://146.227.1.20/~jamesa//teaching/contents.htm

On peer tutoring

Goodlad, S. and Hirst, B. (eds) (1990) *Explorations in Peer Tutoring.* Oxford: Blackwell.
Topping, K.J. (1996) The effectiveness of peer tutoring in further and higher education: a typology and review of the literature, *Higher Education*, 32: 321–45.

The first book provides case studies of peer tutoring, Topping provides a useful classification of different types of peer tutoring and a summary of research results.

On e-learning and teaching

Oliver, R. and Herrington, J. (2001) *Teaching and Learning Online: A Beginner's Guide to E-learning and E-teaching in Higher Education.* Mt Lawley, WA: Centre for Research in Information Technology and Communications, Edith Cowan University.
Salmon, G. (2003) *E-moderating: The Key to Online Teaching and Learning.* London: Kogan Page.

8
Teaching/learning activities for functioning knowledge

In this chapter we are concerned with teaching/learning activities that put knowledge to work, with particular reference to professional contexts. The teaching/learning situations that may be used are much more diversified than 'lecture' and 'tutorial' while the TLAs, which are located within them, are quite specific. We need therefore to be selective: we focus here on TLAs for 'apply', 'create', 'solve problems' and for 'lifelong learning'. The students themselves provide a rich source of many of these TLAs, in various forms of specially designed groups and in the workplace. Creativity has often been regarded by teachers as a 'gift' the student either has or hasn't, and therefore cannot be taught. We argue that creativity can indeed be fostered as it must be, given its status as a common graduate attribute. Lifelong learning is a broad concept that interfaces between institution and the workplace from pre-university to continuing professional development after graduation. We focus here on what the university can do to prepare students for lifelong learning in the undergraduate years. One example is problem-based learning, which was designed so that students would enter the professional world as independent lifelong learners.

Functioning knowledge and professional education

In many courses in the humanities or basic sciences the intended learning outcomes may appropriately focus mainly on building a base of declarative knowledge. In other courses, however, the more important ILOs refer to putting that knowledge to work in practical contexts. This is clearly the case in professional programmes such as in architecture, business, dentistry, engineering, fine arts, medical and healthcare programmes, psychology and social work, to name just a few. In these, much of the declarative knowledge is learned, not for its own sake so much but to construct a platform for launching informed decision makers and performers into the workforce. A major difference between a professional and a technician is not so much about what each might *do* – a dentist and a dental technician will often perform identical tasks – but about the basis for doing it. Essentially, the technician does what he does because he has been trained to do it: the professional does what she does because she has thought about it and made an informed decision to do it this way and not that way.

There are thus two broad steps in educating students for such professional decision making. The first is to build up the appropriate declarative knowledge base, which was the subject of the previous chapter, and the second is to put that to work, which is our present concern. Thus far, this follows the traditional fill-up-the-tanks model: declarative knowledge is built up first, the application of that knowledge second. Another model is just-in-time learning: students' declarative knowledge base is built up as need arises. This is the case in problem-based learning (PBL), where professional knowledge is rooted in practice from the outset. PBL is used in many professional programmes and we deal with it in a later section. Just-in-time learning is now conceived more broadly in connection with lifelong learning in the workplace, with particular reference to the role of information technology (Brandenburg and Ellinger 2003).

But whether the fill-up-the-tanks or the just-in-time model is used, the teaching/learning activities facilitating the ILOs relating to functioning knowledge require more overt performance than those relating to declarative knowledge and they will often best be situated beyond formal teacher-directed situations. Often, the teaching/learning activity and the assessment task will be identical. For example, a reflective diary may be used as a TLA to the ILO addressing 'reflect', but it, or sections of it, can also become the assessment task. In such cases, the alignment is obvious: the ILO is about reflection, the TLA is carrying out a reflective task, and the assessment task is how well the reflection has been carried out, on the basis of (selected) diary entries.

Unfortunately, many ILOs that are in the domain of functioning knowledge are addressed with TLAs more suitable for declarative knowledge. For example, in dealing with an ILO containing the verb 'apply', teachers may only *talk about* applying the knowledge instead of getting the students to *do* the applying (see Table 8.1).

After first addressing the ILOs that establish the relevant declarative knowledge, let us say that the teacher, when addressing the ILO 'apply', discusses what is meant by 'application' in the context in question and models an example or gives a demonstration. Here, the students are doing what they do when taught declaratively: they listen and take notes. They are not doing any applying themselves and, as always, it is more important that the students' activities are aligned to the ILO in question than the teacher's. The students may be required to 'apply' in the final examination but by then, as we saw with 'explain' in the last chapter, they were not explicitly given that opportunity before they were assessed. In our consulting work, we have come

Table 8.1   What teachers and students do in a lecture leading to an ILO containing 'apply'

Teacher activity	Student activity
Introduce	Listen
Explain	Listen, take notes
Elaborate	Understand (but correctly? deeply enough?)
Discuss application in area	Listen, take notes
Give examples of application	Listen, take notes
Show some PPT slides	Watch, note points
Questions on slides	Write answers to the questions
Wind up	Possibly ask a question

across teachers who are quite convinced that she or he is dealing with 'application' as mentioned in the ILO – but *they* are dealing with it, not the students. It's that mindset, once again, that sees teaching being about what teachers do, not about what learners do.

In later sections of this chapter, we suggest teaching/learning activities that are more clearly aligned to ILOs for functioning knowledge. Table 8.2 suggests some of the teaching/learning situations where each is likely to be developed.

Table 8.2   Some areas for developing functioning knowledge with sample ILOs and the teaching/learning situations where they may be located

Programme ILOs relating to	Sample ILOs	Teaching/learning situations
Professional competence	Apply, solve problems	Laboratory, workplace, placement
Creativity	Design, invent	Workplace, home
Communication	Explain, write	Everywhere
Teamwork	Cooperate, lead	Simulated, workplace, classroom
Lifelong learning	Reflect, develop	Everywhere
Ethical sense	Explain codes of practice	Classroom
	Behave ethically	Workplace, placement

We see that the teaching/learning situations are now highly diverse, some located in the classroom, but others are best located in the workplace or its substitute, the placement or practicum, while others again can be at home, in front of the computer or virtually anywhere. Certainly we can move out of those large lecture theatres. We can gather with our students in more personably arranged rooms, sprawl under the trees in companionable groups, log into chat rooms in the comfort of our homes and, perhaps most important, let our students report back to us about their learning in the world of work.

The task is to develop TLAs within these teaching/learning situations to suit the ILOs, which now are quite specific to the particular professional programme concerned. We can only discuss general principles with a few particular examples here. In designing TLAs it helps to consider them as the assessments tasks as well – then you have excellent alignment. For example, say the ILO requires the application of a concept to a real-life case, the teaching/learning activity is simply applying that concept to a case study and the most appropriate assessment task is how well that concept is applied to the case study.

Let us say we are teaching a course in client relationships in a bachelor programme of social work and the ILO is to establish rapport with a client. We could give a lecture explaining what rapport is and then give the students a written test on what they think good rapport is. This is poor alignment: the students learn *about* rapport, not necessarily how to *create* rapport, which is one intended outcome of the course. No, let us give the lecture by all means – but call it an explanation of the need for rapport or a briefing – but the most appropriate learning will take place when the students are themselves required to create rapport with a client and the assessment is how well they do that. Here you have perfect alignment throughout: the intended outcome becomes the activity of teaching and of learning, the TLA, and it is also the assessment task. A different assessment task might address an ILO about their ability to explain why rapport is essential.

Let us now take a few ILOs, starting with 'apply'.

Teaching/learning activities for 'apply'

'Apply' is one of the most common verbs, but it is too wide ranging on its own and is focused down to apply *something* to *something* or *someone*. We offer a range of teaching/learning situations where application is involved, some of which will better suit a particular context than others.

Case-based learning

Case-based learning of some kind or another has been around for some time in law and business schools. It can apply to most professional education. There are several variants, a common one having two stages: (i) presenting cases that have already been carried out and (ii) requiring students to carry out their own cases.

Documents presenting the case to students may be in the form of narratives, outlining a real-life situation or an event – the court proceedings, the person or business with a problem – and through teacher–student, and student–student interactive discussion, draw out what happened, who the participants were and their differing perspectives of the issues. Many ILOs could be addressed: application, the role of theory in the decision making involved in the case, the role of teamwork and collaboration, critical thinking, creativity. Box 8.1 presents a case in environment education.

Box 8.1   A case in environmental education

The ILOs addressed in this case study are:

1 Apply relevant ecological principles to conservation and exploitation of natural resources to solve real-life problems and explain the rationale for doing so.

2 Critically evaluate the merits, limitations and future trends and apply techniques in environmental conservation and resources management.

Mr Wong and his family are indigenous villagers in Yuen Long. Mr Wong owns three hectares of land and five hectares of fishponds inherited from his ancestors. With assistance of his two sons, Mr Wong manages to produce vegetables and freshwater fish for sale at the local markets. To keep up with production, he, like many farmers and fishermen in the New Territories, has been applying fertilizers and pesticides to the field, and trying to stock as many fish as possible in his ponds. However, in recent years, he sees his harvest decline gradually. One day, he woke up to discover that a great quantity of his fish were floating belly up. He could not believe his eyes!

What is going wrong? What can he do? How can he be assured that he is doing the right thing?

Provide reasons to support your answers.

Source: Dr Paul Shin, Department of Biology and Chemistry,
City University of Hong Kong

Case-based learning can be used to illustrated particular issues or, as in problem-based learning (see later), it can be used throughout a course to address the whole syllabus, the cases being carefully selected so that the contents areas that are to be addressed are represented and sequenced in the logic of the build-up of knowledge.

The second stage of case-based learning more closely addresses the verb 'apply': the students experience the various roles in the appropriate case themselves, either through role play or in a more advanced way by dealing directly with a real-life case, as in problem-based learning. This time round, the students, through role play or directly, enact the activities that lead to the desired ILOs. The first stage may be viewed as the declarative stage of case-based learning, in the sense that to the students it is second hand, while the second stage addresses our concern, functioning knowledge.

Group work

Case-based learning makes a great deal of use of group work, so here is a good place to discuss various kinds of group. Most TLAs for functioning knowledge make use of student–student interaction, both in the form of role play or of a variety of kinds of group work, which require students to apply their knowledge and to address functioning knowledge in general learning.

Although the essence of group work is student–student interaction, the initiating, orchestrating and managing of many kinds of group need to be performed by teachers. The following outcomes are likely in effective student–student learning interactions in small groups (Collier 1983; Johnson and Johnson 1990; Topping 1996):

- *Elaboration of known content.* Students hear of different interpretations, things they themselves hadn't thought of. This facilitates:
- *Deriving standards for judging better and worse interpretations.*
- *Reflective awareness of how one arrives at a given position.* How did that guy arrive at that conclusion? How did she? How did I get to mine? Which is better?
- *Applying theory to practice.*

The reflective aspects are sharpened because students readily identify with each other's learning in a way they do not do with top-down teacher-directed learning (Abercrombie 1969). Abercrombie herself used this style of group work with medical students in applied areas such as interpreting X-rays, as described below (pp. 141–2).

In all group work, the students must have sufficient background to contribute, either from reading enough to have an informed discussion or where the topic relates directly to personal experience. Above all, the group leader needs to be able to create the right sort of atmosphere so that students can discuss uninhibitedly. Some teachers find it hard not to correct a student, not to be seen as the expert or to arbitrate in disputes between students. But to become Expert Arbitrator kills the point of the exercise, as students then tend to sit back and wait to be told what to think.

As to the optimal size of a group, there is no set answer as it depends on the nature of the group task and the group dynamics. The principle is that each member should feel responsibility and commitment. The larger the group, the more likely 'social loafing' will take place, one jerk leaving it to the others to do the work. Interestingly, this is a western phenomenon – in ethnic Chinese groups, members work harder in larger groups (Gabrenya et al. 1985). If the architecture permits, students can be allocated to groups of 10 or so in the same room, but it can be awkward where lecture rooms are tiered, with fixed seats – outside under the trees is preferable, weather permitting. When the groups have reached their conclusions, one person speaks to the plenary session on their behalf, making sure that spokesperson is nominated in advance. When reporting back, individuals then need not feel shy about saying something others might criticize: it comes from the group.

In forming groups, Yamane (2006) strongly recommends assigning students to groups randomly. He found groups formed by friends or voluntary membership much more likely to gossip or otherwise discuss off-task. Random assignment 'solved the problem', as he puts it.

Buzz groups

Students are given a question or problem or issue to discuss in the course of a class or asked to apply theory to analyse and solve a case study. The success of free ranging depends on the size of the group and making absolutely sure the students are clear about what they have to do. Brainstorming groups have a topic and no rules, except to say whatever comes to mind. Brainstorming can be used wherever the verbs 'generate', 'hypothesize', 'speculate' and the like are on the agenda.

Syndicate groups

These are formed out of a class of 30 or so into four to eight students each (Collier 1983). Each group has an assigned task, which could be part of a larger project, a problem or a case study. The heart of the technique is the intensive debate that is meant to go on in the syndicates. The assignments are designed to draw on selected sources as well as on students' first-hand experiences, so that everyone has something to say. The syndicates then report back to plenary sessions led by the teacher to help formulate and to consolidate the conceptual structures that have emerged from each group. Collier reports that student motivation is high, and that higher level skills are enhanced, as long as they are addressed in assessment.

Jigsaw groups

Here the groups are allocated sub-tasks and the plenary is to put the finished sub-tasks back together to solve the main task. This is a good way of getting a complex task handled where every person has had some active input into the solution. The downside is that each group only gets to see the working of their own sub-task, and may miss the whole. Again, assessment is the answer: the assessment task must address the whole. Each student could be asked to write a reflective report on the task and their role in it. Concept maps are also useful here, as they are what the whole complex is about, not just the sub-concept.

Problem-solving groups

Abercrombie (1969) worked with medical students in problem-solving groups. Her groups consisted of 10 or so students, and the task was diagnosis, mostly using X-ray films as content (about what the X-ray may be of and what it might mean). The principle is applicable to any situation where students are learning to make judgments, and where there is likely to be a strong difference of opinion. Students have to construct a hypothesis where the data are insufficient to reach an unambiguous conclusion. Different individuals typically seize on different aspects of the data or use the same data to draw different conclusions, so that astonished students find themselves at loggerheads with others equally convinced of the correctness of their own interpretations. The shock of that discovery can be powerful, forcing students to examine closely the basis of what theories they used and how they arrived at their own conclusions. Students taught in this way made better diagnoses, based more firmly on evidence, and they were less dogmatic, being more open to consider alternative possibilities (see also Abercrombie 1980). In addition to increased professional competence, she found motivational and social outcomes that are also professionally relevant, such as increased self-concept, communication skills and self-knowledge.

Learning cells

Learning cells are dyads formed not so much for mutual support, as are learning partners, but for working jointly on a problem or skill. The justification is simply that students work better when working in pairs (McKeachie et al. 1986). This is particularly useful in laboratory situations, learning at the computer terminal or question–answer on set tasks.

Many of the common group structures discussed earlier can be replicated online. Some groups work better online, some worse. For example, going from student to student, seeking the opinion of each on the discussion topic, works much better asynchronously online than synchronously, either online or face to face. In the asynchronous use, students are not under pressure to say something – anything – when it is their turn, but rather they can take their time to think out their view first and then post it on the bulletin board after due reflection. Buzz groups, by the same token, work better face to face, where oral spontaneity is an important feature (Maier and Warren 2000). Syndicates also work well online, which can work synchronously at first, then subgroups may confer and then report back, which can be synchronously for some phases and asynchronously for others.

Reciprocal questioning

Students are trained to ask generic questions of each other, following the teaching of a piece of content (King 1990). Generic questions get to the point of the content; in SOLO terms they are relational. For example:

- What is the main idea here?
- How would you compare this with . . .?
- But how is that different from . . .?
- Now give me a different example.
- How does this affect . . .?

King compared answers to these kinds of question presented in the reciprocal teaching situation to answers to the same questions presented in open-ended discussion that took the same time. While the latter were often longer, they were almost all low level. On critical thinking and high-level elaboration, the questioning groups were far superior. These findings emphasize that when getting students to interact in order to reach specific outcomes, make sure there is a clear and high-level agenda for them to address.

Spontaneous collaboration

Some student groups are unofficial, formed spontaneously to focus on coping with specific tasks, such as set assignments (Tang 1996, 1998). Tang studied spontaneous collaborative learning among physiotherapy students, who after the announcement of an assignment formed their own groups, deciding who would check out what set of references, what ideas might be included and so on. The collaborative effort extends variously through the planning phase of the assignment or project, but the final detailed plan and write-up is conducted individually. Over 80% of Tang's students collaborated to some extent and those who did showed greater structural complexity (higher SOLO levels) in their assignments. Such a high proportion of spontaneous collaboration may not occur with western students, but Goodnow (1991) reports that Australian students at Macquarie University formed syndicates, mainly for the purpose of exchanging wisdom on examination questions. An interesting question is how far teachers might encourage, or have any interaction with, these groups (Tang 1993).

ICQ ('I seek you') and MSN are used by students mainly for non-academic purposes, but many students use them for spontaneous collaboration over set work such as assignments.

Workplace learning

Workplace learning, variously known as 'placement', 'attachment', 'practicum', 'clinical' or 'internship' according to discipline, is an integral component, even the apex of, professional education.

Depending on the nature of individual professions, each professional education programme has its own specific ILOs. However, the major ILOs of workplace learning which would likely be applicable to many professional programmes are for the students to be able to:

1 integrate knowledge and skills learned in university to real-life professional settings
2 apply theories and skills to practice in all aspects of professional practice
3 work collaboratively with all parties in multidisciplinary workplace settings
4 practise with professional attitudes and social responsibilities in their respective professions.

Workplace learning is an active learning experience focusing on student participation in situated work activities (Billet 2004). It provides a teaching/ learning situation where students learn through experiencing and active participation in learning (usually under supervision) in various aspects of professional practice situated in the real-life professional context. It could be a hospital clinical placement of internship in medical and healthcare programmes, field placement in social work, industrial attachment in business and engineering or law firm placement for law students. This teaching/ learning situation is most suited to facilitate the functioning ILO of applying theories and concepts to perform professional practice such as making clinical decisions and diagnosis, planning and implementing treatment or intervention programmes, conducting industrial projects, producing a stage play and making a legal case etc.

To enable students to achieve these outcomes, teaching/learning activities that are aligned to the ILOs must be designed. In most workplace learning situations, these activities include the following.

Teaching activities, conducted by placement educators:

1 Plan and coordinate the logistics of the placement.
2 Design appropriate learning activities.
3 Select cases or projects.
4 Provide appropriate level of guidance and scaffolding to learning.
5 Provide feedback to learning.
6 Assess the learning outcomes.

Learning activities, conducted by the students either in groups or individually:

1 Interview a patient or client to collect relevant data.
2 Analyse the data to identify a situational problem or issue.
3 Formulate solution to the problem through application of theory to the problem or situation in hand.
4 Implement actions to effect the solution.
5 Evaluate effectiveness of intervention or project.
6 Collaborate with other team members either intra- or inter-disciplinary.
7 Reflect on own performance to identify areas for improvement.

It is important to ensure the alignment between these student learning activities and the ILOs for that particular workplace learning situation.

A learning contract, a negotiated agreement between the student and the placement educator regarding the particular learning experience, may well form part of the placement. In such contracts, students are actively involved in designing their learning experience, in identifying their learning needs, their ways of fulfilling those needs and how they will be assessed. A learning contract provides an authentic and contextualized learning experience that students will encounter in a real-life situation.

Although workplace learning involves experiences in the workplace, it is closely integrated with classroom learning. It is important that the ILOs for workplace learning are clearly defined and understood by all parties concerned. In particular, the need for students to integrate and apply theory to practice should be explicitly emphasized to help them understand the link between classroom and workplace learning. It is important that students should see the common ILOs in both learning situations and how they are interrelated and mutually supportive to provide a holistic professional learning experience.

Workplace learning naturally enough is closely related to 'apply' in the sense of lifelong learning. We look at that connection in a later section.

Teaching/learning activities for creativity

Creativity is not only an intended learning outcome in the fine or performing arts. Graduate attributes make it clear that creativity is required in all disciplines and professional areas. So what is meant by creativity in higher education?

We have already used the terms 'convergent' and 'divergent' in connection with student questioning. They were originally coined by Guilford (1967) to describe two different forms of ability:

- *Convergent* ability, as in solving problems that have a particular, unique answer, as in most intelligence and ability test items. Convergent thinking is 'closed'. A common perception is that convergent thinking is what academic ability is about: knowing a lot and getting it right, but that should be only part of the academic story.
- *Divergent* ability, as in generating alternatives, where the notion of being correct gives way to other assessments of value, such as aesthetic appeal, originality, usefulness, self-expression, creativity and so on.

We prefer to see the terms 'convergent' and 'divergent' as describing processes, ways of going about thinking, that are involved in most high-level thinking and in professional work, rather than as simple abilities. However, it is difficult to 'generate', 'hypothesize', 'theorize' or 'reflect' without prior content mastery. You have to know what you are to hypothesize about or to reflect on. But, by the same token, having a solid knowledge base is no guarantee that one will be creative in using it. Many, perhaps most, academics focus on establishing that knowledge base, but neglect the next step of making it function creatively.

Creativity also requires, or at least is accompanied by, intense interest and involvement in a specific area, the end result of which is a product, a 'creative work', as Elton (2005) puts it, comprising something new, a synthesis that didn't exist quite like that before. The job of teachers is thus not to help students 'be' creative, but to help them create works, products, outputs, that are founded in the discipline or area and that add to it in an original way.

A common perception is that outcomes-based teaching and learning is antithetical to creativity on the ground that the outcomes are predetermined, specified in advance and so form a 'closed loop'. The essence of creativity, by way of contrast, is to concentrate on process and produce outcomes that are unexpected and often unintended (Jackson 2005). This is true when the intended outcomes are low level, such as competencies, or are convergent, working towards the one correct answer. However, when the outcomes are high level, at the extended abstract end, they contain verbs such as 'design', 'invent' or the verb 'create' itself. Here the outcome is itself an open-ended process, the product not being pre-determined at all.

Addressing open-ended verbs like these with an appropriate teaching/learning activity is igniting a creative process with an unspecified outcome. A common TLA for the ILOs just examined is brainstorming in groups, after which students can individually work on their ideas and possibly regather to provide mutual feedback. There are many ways of triggering the creative verb, as appropriate for each discipline or area: an engineering TLA for 'design' will obviously be very different from a TLA for a creative writing course for 'create a character . . .'. 'The Imaginative Curriculum' is a large-scale project designed to help teachers whatever their teaching area to foster students' creativity through specific examples of teaching practice (Jackson et al. 2006).

Some areas, such as dramatic art, require situations in which TLAs are reflective and improvised. Box 8.2 provides an example.

Box 8.2   An example of teaching/learning activities in acting skills

TLAs in drama involve private rehearsal and reflection and public interaction with the teacher in workshop, skills classes and before-the-camera situations. Both student and teacher are looking for organic application and generation. The quality of reflection, whether intuited or consciously thought through, can be measured by repeating the exercise; and by making sure that the doing of the exercise is connected/aligned to the thinking of the reflection. Self-control, which includes extensive private preparation, is paramount.

ILO: *Create a character and establish credible relationships.*

TLA: *Character object exercise.* The student seeks the core of the character by being in a character-familiar space (e.g. bedroom), using meaningful objects and carrying out physical activities, e.g. getting dressed.

ILO: *Achieve an organic perception of action and of the sequence 'reaction–action–variation'.*

TLA: *Playing the action*: Generating interaction through trying to make another character do something, as opposed to simply saying the lines and 'indicating' (not effecting an activation). When an action is played, the actor induces curiosity and, most significantly, becomes a storyteller, i.e. what will happen next? The TLA ought to be self-controlled or the student will lack ownership/authenticity. An element of peer control can be a great support. If the partner is activated, the student will at least receive a good energy-inviting reaction, which also amounts to interaction (the result of action playing). Proaction and reaction are the two halves of activation (or action playing). In dramatic terms, action playing, with its character-informed variations, naturally represents alignment.

A good piece of material can be found in Act I, scene vii of *Macbeth.* Lady

---

Macbeth tries to make Macbeth kill the king. That is her action. To get what she wants, she must be proactive. She will have to use more than one approach or variation (otherwise, the scene would be resolved after only a line or two) and that is obtained by drawing on a range of so-called psychological activities (transitive verbs). These must generate tempo rhythms that can organically affect and potentially change a partner. High-level verbs must be sought, e.g. flatter, rebuke, encourage, humiliate. 'Beg' is self-indulgent, 'persuade' or 'question' are generalizations, 'shout' is intransitive. Applying these verbs and then reflecting on the exercise with a view to progressing should be givens. But sometimes the student may only pay lip service to the verbs; or struggle with reflection.

Source: Alan Dunnett, Drama Centre, Central Saint Martins,
University of the Arts, London

Powerful TLAs can be constructed using educational technology. In her discussion of e-learning, Laurillard (2002) outlines *adaptive* media that change their state in response to users' actions thus giving intrinsic feedback, internal to the action, as opposed to a commentary which is external. Simulations allow students to change parameters and see what happens, which encourage the 'what would happen if?' enquiry. *Productive* media allow students to construct micro-worlds, where they may build their own systems.

Unfortunately, it is much easier to stifle creativity than to encourage it. Whatever the TLAs relevant to a creative ILO, the right climate for encouraging creativity is one where the students can feel they can take risks and can feel free to ask 'what would happen if?' without being ridiculed either by the teacher or by other students for making a 'silly' response (Box 8.3).

Box 8.3   How not to encourage creativity

Teacher: And now, who can tell me what infinity means? (*Silence*). What is infinity?
Billy: Uh, I think it's like a box of Creamed Wheat.
Teacher: Billy, you're being silly.

Source: Jones (1968: 72)

Billy is, of course, quite right, infinity *is* like a box of Creamed Wheat breakfast cereal, on which there is a picture of a man holding a box of Creamed Wheat who is holding a box of Creamed Wheat . . . *ad infinitum.* It is likely, however, that Billy will in future keep his insights to himself, at least in that teacher's class. This homely example illustrates some further points that also apply to tertiary teaching. Snap value judgments by teachers are not a good idea. The teacher in the box might better have picked this up with (laughs): 'Good, but can anyone explain what Billy might mean?' and an enlightening discussion could ensue. We can too easily dismiss an insight that at first glance seems irrelevant.

A Theory X climate of criticism, mistrust and high anxiety is death to creative responses from most people. An example of this, familiar to all academics, is the difference in adventurousness, originality and freshness between a term assignment and the answer to a question on the same topic held under invigilated examination conditions: we return to this later when discussing the assessment of creativity.

Teaching/learning activities relating to lifelong learning

Lifelong learning, the ultimate aim of university teaching, has the generic and the embedded meanings of many other graduate attributes (pp. 65–6). The generic meaning – that graduates can learn to handle whatever life throws at them – is vacuous, empty rhetoric. The embedded meaning, however, that students can learn to handle unseen problems in their chosen field of study is significant and attainable. One somewhat blinkered interpretation is that lifelong learning is 'a political response to a need to upskill the working population in order to obtain a competitive advantage in the economy' (Burns and Chisholm 2003: 179).

Burns and Chisholm relate lifelong learning to work-based learning in the context of engineering. They propose an ongoing interface between educational institutions and engineering firms, but they claim their models of work-based learning can be applied to any professional area. The general principle is just-in-time learning where, as in PBL but now in the workplace proper, people seek to learn what they have to know when need arises, most frequently now with the aid of e-technology (Brandenburg and Ellinger 2003).

A somewhat related but more flexible idea is the *emergent* curriculum (Jackson et al. 2006). The 'curriculum' here comprises problems that emerge in real life and that cannot be predicted and that usually require ongoing 'conversations' to invent, create and implement new enterprises that work in a business sense. As Jackson (private communication) elaborates:

> No-one knows where we are heading until an idea or a perception of needs begins to crystallise. We are trying to establish the conditions and resources for co-operative just-in-time learning and then respond to what emerges. We have students on year long placements scattered all over the world experiencing a multitude of cultures and problem working situations. The emergent curriculum is driven by a highly contextualised situation and need and the way it is met is not through

text-book knowledge but by creating conditions, relationships and net-works for purposeful and sympathetic conversation informed by experiences of dealing with similar situations or operating from principle-based positions.

These views of work-based and just-in-time learning can apply to pre-university, undergraduate, postgraduate and continuing professional development in the workforce. Important though lifelong learning is in this sense, we must limit ourselves here to our focus: what can be achieved within the general run of institutional undergraduate programmes.

The role of the institution in this context is twofold: what it can achieve externally by locating teaching/learning activities and assessments in work-based placements wherever feasible; and what it can achieve in providing students with the skills needed for independent lifelong and just-in-time learning. The latter addresses both second-tier attributes of 'information literacy' and 'personal and intellectual autonomy' that Barrie (2004) suggests comprise 'lifelong learning' (see Figure 5.1, p. 68). Students need to learn how to seek new information, how to utilize it and evaluate its importance and how to solve novel, non-textbook, professional problems. They will need high-level reflective skills and an abstract body of theory on which to deploy them, so that they can judge how successfully they are coping with novel problems, and how they may do better. Action learning for life, if you like.

As for Barrie's 'personal and intellectual autonomy', we are dealing with three levels of self-directed learning:

1 generic study skills
2 study skills that relate to learning particular content
3 reflective learning.

Generic study skills

Study skills are ways of managing time and space. For example:

- Keeping notes and references neatly and systematically so that they can be found when needed.
- Apportioning time and keeping track of deadlines, so that all topics and subjects are given adequate time, and in proportion to their importance.
- Seeking new information without being overwhelmed, using search engines strategically and relevantly, prioritizing searches.

Adults are very much better at such organizing and planning than are students straight from school, while women are generally better than men (Trueman and Hartley 1996). Teaching generic study skills, particularly long-term planning, has positive effects on performance (Hattie et al. 1996).

Study skills that relate to learning particular content

These skills include:

- Underlining/highlighting the key words in a passage.
- Reading for main ideas, not details, as in SQ4R (Thomas and Robinson 1982).
- Taking notes properly, by capturing the main idea of several sentences in own words, rather than copying every second or third sentence.
- Using concept maps to derive a major structure.
- Composing essays according to a pre-planned structure; using review and revise, not first drafts.

But consider this experiment. Ramsden et al. (1986) taught study skills to first-year undergraduates from a variety of faculties, focusing on reading and note taking, examination preparation and writing skills. The effects were the opposite of what was intended: in comparison to a control group, the students increased their use of *surface* approaches. Subsequent interviews with the students revealed that they believed that to be successful in first year you needed to retain facts accurately, so they selected from the study skills course just those strategies they believed would help them memorize better. You will recall first-year students rejected concept maps for the same reason (pp. 115, 117). Students get these ideas from the way they have been taught and assessed and from the general culture of the class. No doubt the teachers did not at all intend that the students would interpret their first-year experience in this way, but they did.

This misalignment, between what the teachers intended and what the students perceived, can be overcome if teachers embed useful study skills in their teaching so they are not only teaching *what* they want their students to learn, but *how* to learn it. Chalmers and Fuller (1996) suggest teachers teach strategies for *acquiring* information (note making, memorizing, skim reading), strategies for *working with* information (explaining ideas, organizing ideas, writing summaries), strategies for *confirming* learning (handling assessment tasks) and so on. These are adapted to suit the particular unit or course content.

If study skills are supported by the context in which they will be used, it becomes clear why those strategies are useful. Building knowledge is so much more effective when the tools needed for building are used on the spot, thoughtfully.

Reflective learning

Lifelong learning and just-in-time learning require *informed self-direction*. That is, students need to operate from a sound knowledge base and use reflective or metacognitive skills to work strategically towards solving novel problems, to self-monitor their emerging solutions. The outcomes are not spelled out, they are emergent: one doesn't know what the intended outcome is to be until it emerges from a fuzzy problem situation. The teaching/learning activities are entirely self-managed or negotiated with others in the field and the ongoing formative assessment has also to be entirely self-managed. The judgment has to be made that *this* is the best solution in these complex circumstances.

When faced with such a novel situation, the learner might consider the following questions:

- This is a 'fuzzy' problem; how can I reformulate it in a way that relates to first principles leading to good solutions?
- What do I know that might be relevant? What problems like this have I met before? What did I do then?
- How can I find out further information? From where? How do I test it?
- I'll try this solution; does it work? How could I improve it?

These constitute a different order of question, using study skills in order to organize and conceptualize what is known prior to *re*-conceptualizing it. The verbs involved are open ended and extended abstract: planning, theorizing, hypothesizing, generating.

Alongside these divergent processes, it is also necessary to monitor what is going on, to test ongoing outcomes for adequacy, to see that learning is on track. Evaluating one's own work, of prime importance in everyday professional life, is one skill that graduates feel their university education least prepared them to do (Boud 1986). Self-evaluation or self-monitoring skills therefore need to be addressed. Accordingly, self- and peer-assessment are as much teaching/learning activities as assessment tasks. Other relevant TLAs are reflective diary, selecting critical incidents and suggesting how to deal with them.

If dealing with emergent problems is what graduates are supposed to be able to do, undergraduate teaching should foster self-managed learning and assessment. The generic and content-specific study skills mentioned earlier only challenge students to apply, generalize and refine their understanding of what is given. Reflective learning skills and strategies require students to go further: to manage problems and questions that they have *not* previously addressed.

This is also the aim of problem-based learning.

Problem-based learning

Problem-based learning (PBL) reflects the way people learn in real life; they simply get on with solving the problems life puts before them with whatever resources are to hand. They do not stop to wonder at the 'relevance' of what they are doing, or at their 'motivation' for doing it: it is the traditional model of education that gives birth to these questions.

Education for the professions for years followed the fill-up-the-tanks model of knowledge acquisition and much of it still does. The disciplines are taught first, independently of one another, and, armed with all that declarative knowledge and with some professionally relevant but atheoretically taught skills, the student is accredited as ready to practise as a professional. Professional practice, however, requires functioning knowledge that can be put to work on the spot. Traditionally taught graduates manage to do that with varying degrees of success and, with experience in the real world, become increasingly better at it. However, if students graduate with that functioning knowledge already to hand, their induction into real-life professional practice is that much quicker. The problem in the traditional model is that the programme ILOs nominate professional competence on graduation but declarative knowledge is the main output: curriculum, teaching and assessment are not aligned.

PBL is alignment itself. If the aim is to become a doctor – PBL originated in a school of medicine – then the best way of becoming one is being one, under appropriate guidance and safeguards. If the ILO is to make clinical diagnoses then making clinical diagnoses is the obvious teaching/learning activity and how well they are made is the obvious assessment task. And so it goes for any professional problem.

Savin-Baden (2000) argues that problem-based learning is commonly confused with problem-solving learning. The latter simply means setting problems for students to solve after they have been taught conventionally and then discussing them later. In PBL, contrariwise, 'the starting point for learning should be a problem, query or a puzzle that the learner wishes to solve' (Boud 1985: 13). The problem, or a series of problems, is where learning starts and, in going about solving those problems, the learner seeks the knowledge of disciplines, facts and procedures that are needed to solve the problems. The traditional disciplines do not define what is to be learned, the problems do. However, the aim is not only to solve those particular problems, but in the course of doing so, the learner acquires knowledge, content-related skills, self-management skills, attitudes, know-how: in a word, professional wisdom. This means the problems had better be carefully selected.

Although PBL is used most commonly in education for the professions, it can also be used in the teaching of basic disciplines (see 'Further reading' at end of this chapter, where a couple of websites on PBL for teaching physics and biology are provided).

In a fully blown PBL programme, the problems are selected so that by the end of the programme, the learner is ready to move directly into the workforce. Less content may well be covered than in a traditional programme, but the knowledge so gained is acquired in a working context and is put back to use in that context. Coverage, so dominant in discipline-centred teaching, is considered less important. Instead, students learn the skills for seeking out the required knowledge as the occasion demands.

A typical PBL sequence goes like this:

- The *context* is pressing. In a typical medical programme, students in their first week of first year are faced with the responsibility of a real patient with, say, a broken leg. The felt need to learn is strong.
- Learners become *active* very quickly. They are assigned to small problem-solving groups and begin *interacting* with teachers, peers and clients (who present the problem).
- Learners start from what they already know and *build a knowledge base* on that. They learn where to go to check what they know and to seek out more. They are variously guided towards resource materials, including films, videos, the library and lecture room. Knowledge is *elaborated and consolidated*. Students meet with a tutor and discuss the case in relation to the knowledge they have obtained.
- The knowledge is functioning: it is *applied* to the problem in hand. *Feedback* is ongoing.
- The problem is reviewed and learners develop *self-management* and *self-monitoring skills*, which they review throughout the programme.

The italicized words may remind you of the characteristics of a rich learning context described in Chapter 6.

PBL makes use of them all.

Goals of PBL

There are several modifications and versions of what is called 'PBL', but all should address the four goals distinguished by Barrows (1986):

1 *Structuring knowledge for use in working contexts.* Professional education is concerned with functioning knowledge. PBL is concerned with constructing knowledge that is to be put to work.
2 *Developing effective reasoning processes.* Such processes refer to the cognitive activities required in the professional area concerned and include: problem solving, decision making, hypothesizing, etc. Each professional area has its own specific processes to be developed as relevant problems are solved.
3 *Developing self-directed learning skills.* Included here are the three levels of skill mentioned earlier (pp. 149–51): generic study skills, content-specific study skills and especially the metacognitive or self-management skills for lifelong learning are specifically addressed in PBL, where they are learned in context, as they should be.
4 *Increased motivation for learning.* Students are placed in a context that requires their immediate and committed involvement. Thus, in terms of motivational theory (see Chapter 4), the value is high, the expectation of success is high, as problems and cases are selected in which students are likely to be successful, so motivation is high.

To these four may be added a fifth:

5 *Developing group skills, working with colleagues.* Many professions require

teamwork, so this becomes a goal in many PBL programmes. It might be noted that such teamwork takes place in a workplace-like context, unlike much group project work.

PBL varies according to two major variables (Barrows 1986):

1 *The degree to which the problem is structured.* Some problems are tightly structured, with all the information needed to solve it. Others have some facts provided, the student having to find the rest. Open or 'ill-defined' problems present no data, it being entirely up to the student to research the case and decide what needs to be found out and what to do to handle it.
2 *The extent of teacher direction.* The most conservative case, arguably not PBL, is where the teacher controls the amount and flow of information. In the case of 'ill-defined' problems, teacher direction is minimal, the students going off on their own to solve the problem. Variations in between depend on how much the teacher provides clues and information handling support.

The optimal amount of structure of the problem, and of teacher direction, depends at least initially with the educational philosophy of the teachers and tutors participating, and what freedom the students can initially handle (Ryan 1997). In a study at the Polytechnic University of Hong Kong modifications were introduced to fit the aims of six departments and the different expectations of full- and part-time students (Tang et al. 1997). The full-time students found most difficulty with assessment, not surprisingly given their exam-dominated school background. As one student put it, 'It is difficult to guess what is the marking scheme of the lecturer' (Tang et al. 1997: 586). Part-time students, by way of contrast, took to PBL straight away because it mimicked the workplace: 'When I encounter a problem, I will have a solution, like that in my workplace' (Tang et al. 1997; Tiwari et al. 1999).

Nature and construction of the problems

A good problem has the following characteristics (Johnston 2002):

1 It calls on different disciplines and integrates them in solving the problem.
2 It raises options that promote discussion.
3 It activates and incorporates previous knowledge.
4 It requires new knowledge the students don't yet have.
5 It stimulates participants to elaborate.
6 It requires self-directed learning.
7 And, of course, it meets the course ILOs.

Such problems are open ended and 'ill structured'; that is, they do not present the students with enough information.

Here's a problem for you: 'You plan to use PBL in teaching your unit. What are you going to do?' Ill structured, definitely. You see straight away that you don't have enough information, while seeking a solution involves higher order thinking, such as hypothesizing, evaluation, reflection. It also involves divergent thinking, as there is likely to be more than one way of reaching a solution. A sensible first step, then, might be to read the rest of this chapter, then some of the readings. Are there any colleagues in your institution using PBL? If so, talk to them.

The characteristics of a good problem are given in Box 8.4.

Box 8.4   Designing a problem

1 Map all the *concepts* likely to be involved from different disciplines, including the *knowledge* and *skills* required to solve the situation. Maybe a knowledge tree would help.

2 Write the *ILOs*. What do you expect the students to do with the new knowledge and skills?

3 Identify a *real problem* from a real-life situation that is important to students, such as one they are likely to meet in their future employment. Authenticity is highly motivating.

4 Repeat (3) until all your ILOs are addressed.

5 When *writing* problems make sure to:

- Use the present tense. Otherwise problems look like another textbook exercise.
- Provide a context and specific role of practitioner: what, when, where.
- Provide specific rather than vague data.
- Require the students to deliver something: a decision or report.

6 Many situations or problems *evolve over time*. It might be appropriate to provide an extended problem (called 'roll-out' problem or case). Such a problem is in parts, covering a sequence of events or the problem is addressed in stages as more data become available and may last over more than one semester.

7 Write a *facilitator guide* for others involved in the PBL, including:

- the problem
- the ILOs
- the learning issues, including all the new knowledge you expect participants to learn and discuss
- content background information for the facilitators
- suggested resources for students.

With permission of David Johnston, Director, Hong Kong Centre for PBL

So there you have it. For those interested in trying PBL, you can now handle Task 8.1.

Task 8.1   Getting going with PBL

Take a topic you are teaching and turn it into PBL.
Be guided by Box 8.4.

We deal with assessment issues in PBL in Chapter 11.

Does PBL work?

The goals of PBL have already been listed as: structuring knowledge for professional use, developing effective reasoning processes, developing self-directed learning skills, increased motivation for learning and effective teamwork. How effectively does PBL attain these goals?

Albanese and Mitchell (1993) conducted a major meta-analysis of all studies published between 1972 and 1992. The following conclusions emerge:

1 Both staff and students rate PBL higher in their evaluations and enjoy PBL more than traditional teaching.
2 PBL graduates perform as well and sometimes better on clinical performance. More PBL (medical) graduates go into family practice.
3 PBL students use higher level strategies for understanding and for self-directed study.
4 PBL students do worse in examinations of basic science declarative knowledge.
5 PBL students when compared to traditionally taught students become progressively deeper in their approaches to learning (McKay and Kember 1997; Newble and Clarke 1986).

Hmelo, Gotterer and Bransford (1997) argue that PBL by its nature requires a *different way* of using knowledge to solve problems. They distinguish two strategies in clinical decision making:

• *Data driven*: 'This patient has elevated blood sugar, therefore he has diabetes.'
• *Hypothesis driven*: 'This patient has diabetes, therefore blood sugar should be up, and rapid respiration, "fruity" breath odour . . .'

Experienced and expert doctors use the data-driven strategy, except for unfamiliar or complex problems. Novice doctors, such as students in training, lack that experience and should therefore work top-down from first principles, with longer reasoning chains: 'If this, then because of that, it would follow that we should find symptoms X, Y, and Z. . . .' The traditionally taught students tried to follow the experts – and couldn't, they didn't have the background. PBL taught students increasingly used hypothesis-driven reasoning, with longer and clearer reasoning chains. PBL students also used a wider variety of knowledge resources, whereas traditionally taught students stuck with the textbook. Such findings are completely in line with what PBL is trying to do.

An important aspect of evaluating PBL is its implementation, particularly cost benefits. The economies of large lectures are offset by the economies of self-directed learning and on the size and number of tutorial groups complementing the lectures. Albanese and Mitchell (1993) estimate that for fewer than 40, and up to around 100 students, PBL once set up can be equivalent in cost to traditional teaching. Savin-Baden (2000) is more optimistic still, saying that because of the move to mass education, fee-paying students from diverse backgrounds are more likely to be attracted to interesting ways of learning like PBL than to mass lectures.

Let's hope so.

Problem-based problems

PBL is particularly sensitive to context and climate. Remember the disastrous effect a know-it-all tutor had on the questioning strategy needed for the problem-solving process ('That's for me to know and you to find out') (pp. 97–8). An equally devastating effect was achieved in another case when the course coordinator decided to retain the traditional final-year examination, leaving the students unsure whether their conclusions drawn from case study work would be relevant to the final exam. They weren't. Not surprisingly, performance was low and the course evaluation of PBL was unfavourable (Lai and Tang 1999).

Both cases are examples of poor alignment. The tutor was creating affective misalignment in that the climate created was incompatible with the spirit of PBL, while the coordinator was creating instructional non-alignment in that the assessment matched neither the ILOs nor the TLAs used.

Albanese and Mitchell (1993) say that in PBL, students cover only 80% of the traditional syllabus and do not perform as well in standard examinations. That worries traditional critics more than PBL teachers. The latter would prefer the PBL graduate to know less declarative knowledge but be able to put what they do know to work more readily. When what they know is insufficient, the students have the self-directed skills to know just-in-time where to go and how to acquire what knowledge they will require when attending to a particular case.

PBL is undoubtedly an effective approach to teaching. It exemplifies a high degree of alignment. To practice as a particular professional requires solving problems that belong to that profession. Thus, professional knowledge and skill are the intended learning outcomes, professional practice comprises the teaching/learning activities, professional knowledge and skill are what are assessed (among other things). It is distinguished from apprenticeship in that it is theory based; it is not just a matter of performing the skills in an uninformed manner.

There are two major reasons that PBL is not used more widely. First, PBL requires teachers to adopt a different philosophy of professional education; that education is something more than the acquisition of separate bodies of knowledge, in one of which the teacher is professed expert. The teacher has to be prepared to drop the role of expert. Many find this hard to do: their very career path is expedited by their demonstrating their specific expertise. It is much easier for experts to give lectures on their specialty, leaving integration and application as the students' problem to solve. Most students probably will, but years down the track.

Second, PBL requires considerable institutional flexibility. Most universities are organized into departments with specific content foci. PBL is multidisciplinary as usually the problems presented require knowledge from several areas: it therefore challenges the traditional model of university organization.

So where do you place the horse – before or after the cart?

Now design a TLA to help your students put knowledge to work (Task 8.2, p. 159).

Summary and conclusions

Functioning knowledge and professional education

Professional education is chiefly concerned with putting declarative knowledge to work as functioning knowledge. The usual means of doing this is to build the declarative knowledge base first, as we saw in the last chapter, but in problem-based learning, that knowledge base is built in the process of its being applied. 'Apply' is the most typical verb in functioning knowledge. It is important to see that the TLAs used ensure that the students themselves do the applying and not just watch someone else doing it or telling them about it. Functioning knowledge may be used in teacher-managed, student-managed or self-managed situations.

Teaching/learning activities for 'apply'

Case-based learning has had a long history in applying theory to practice. A common teaching/learning situation for 'apply', depending on applying what to what, is groupwork. We looked at different types of group: syndicate, jigsaw, buzz groups, brainstorming, learning cells, or reciprocal questioning, to name a few. Students may on their own initiative set up their own spontaneous learning groups. The suitability of which type will, of course, depend on the ILO in question. Workplace learning is used precisely because it is concerned with application and also in service of lifelong learning.

Task 8.2   ILOs and TLAs in putting knowledge to work

Take one of your course ILOs relating to functioning knowledge, where students are expected to put knowledge to work in practical contexts. Identify what teaching/learning situations you use and identify the teacher and student activities. Are the student activities aligned to the ILO? Would they really help the students achieve that ILO?

ILO relating to functioning knowledge in my course: _____

_____

_____

Teaching/learning situation	TLAs	
	Teacher activities	Student activities

Are the students performing the ILO verb(s)? _____

Do I need to change the TLAs? _____

_____

What changes would I make? _____

_____

Teaching/learning activities for creativity

Almost all graduate attributes mention 'creativity' in some form or another, but most university teaching emphasizes convergent rather than divergent thinking. Both ways of thinking are important in all high-level functioning. Creativity is characterized by open-ended thinking based on a sound knowledge base, resulting in products with some degree of originality. Such creative work can be positively encouraged in a number of ways. Unfortunately, it is all too easily discouraged by insisting on a regimen of correct answers rather than experimenting with ideas and creating a Theory X type of climate in which students are fearful of taking risks and exploring different possibilities.

Teaching/learning activities relating to lifelong learning

Lifelong learning opens a range of learning: just-in-time learning, work-based learning and continuing professional education, which go well beyond undergraduate education. Undergraduate courses can, however, prepare students for later just-in-time and work-based learning – as indeed PBL has been already doing for many years. TLAs for ILOs preparatory for lifelong learning need to emphasize learner information literacy and reflective self-direction. The latter may be achieved by teaching students both generic and content-specific study skills and by reflective practice. Students need to be able to manage their space and time effectively, to be able to seek new information, especially by using search engines strategically and to carry out effectively those strategies that are specific to their content area. Additionally, they need to be able to reflect on past practice, with the intention of improving what they have done and of solving new problems they haven't met before.

Problem-based learning (PBL)

PBL is an example of a total approach to the main aims of lifelong learning. In solving the selected curriculum problems, the intended outcomes that students will acquire are: the necessary declarative knowledge and applications to real problems; the skills and strategies needed for acquiring new knowledge; and the metacognitive skills for applying that knowledge to unseen, 'fuzzy' problems and evaluating the effectiveness of problem solutions. Students taught by PBL think differently from traditionally taught. They may have less declarative knowledge, but use what they have to reason more effectively and to apply the products of their reasoning; they have greater self-awareness and self-direction; and they enjoy learning more, as indeed do their teachers. However, PBL is sensitive to insensitive teaching. An institutional problem is that the infrastructure for PBL is not discipline based, whereas most universities are organized on disciplinary lines. Teachers tend to identify themselves as scholars in their home discipline and PBL might seem to threaten their academic identity.

Further reading

On group work

Abercrombie, M.L.J. (1980) *Aims and Techniques of Group Teaching*. London: Society for Research into Higher Education.
Collier, K.G. (1983) *The Management of Peer-Group Learning: Syndicate Methods in Higher Education*. Guildford: Society for Research into Higher Education.

Johnson, D.W. and Johnson, R.T. (1990) *Learning Together and Alone: Cooperation, Competition and Individualization*. Englewood Cliffs, NJ: Prentice-Hall.
    The first two are very practical accounts of using groups effectively. Johnson and Johnson is the classic on setting up cooperative learning groups.
Working in Groups – A Note to Faculty and Quick Guide for Students. Derek Bok Centre for Teaching and Learning, Harvard University.
The following website has links to all aspects of classroom teaching and assessment: http://www.brookes.ac.uk/services/ocsd/2_learntch/2_learnt.html

On case-based learning

Lynn, L.E. (1996) *What is the Case Method? A Guide and Casebook*. Tokyo: The Foundation for Advanced Studies on International Development.
Rangan, K. (1995) Choreographing a case class. http://www.hbsp.harvard.edu/ products/cases/casemethod/rangan.pdf; www.queensu.ca/ctl/goodpractice/ case/resources.html; www.use.edu/programs/cet/resources/casebased; www.healthsci.utas.edu.au/faculty/cases/newindex.html
On the effectiveness of case-based learning: www.cuhk.edu.hk/sci/case-learning/ doc/reflections.pdf

On creativity

Jackson, N., Oliver, M., Shaw, M., and Wisdom, J. (eds) (2006) *Developing Creativity in Higher Education: The Imaginative Curriculum*. London: Routledge.
Laurillard, D. (2002) *Rethinking University Teaching*. London: Routledge Falmer. See references to adaptive and productive media.

Jackson et al. derives from the Imaginative Curriculum Project. Concerned that current quality assurance, peer review, pressures on research output and so on were discouraging innovation and creativity, academics teaching across all disciplines show how creativity can be integrated into normal university teaching. The chapters by Jackson and Sinclair on a pedagogy for creativity and Baillie on art, science and engineering are noteworthy for deriving TLAs. Laurillard shows how technology can be used with conversations between student, teaching and machine to advance high-level and creative thinking.

Mycoted, on teaching for creativity: 'The A to Z of creativity techniques': http:// www.mycoted.com/creativity/techniques/
And the link to creativity on the Higher Education Academy website: http:// www.heacademy.ac.uk/creativity.htm
Mycoted has an extensive range of 'creativity techniques' that will provide a source of ideas; the Higher Education Academic website has many useful links.

On workplace learning

The Journal of Workplace Learning. http://www.emeraldinsight.com/info/journals/ jwl/jwl.jsp

Guidelines for workplace learning from the University of Tasmania: www.utas.edu.au/
tl/supporting/workplace_learning.html

On lifelong learning

Knapper, C. and Cropley, A. (2000) *Lifelong Learning in Higher Education*. London:
Kogan Page.
http://www.lifelonglearning.co.uk/
http://www.adelaide.edu.au/clpd/materia/leap/leapinto/LifelongLearning.pdf

Where do we start selecting? Knapper and Cropley's book is one of the classics in
this area. The two home pages are of lifelong learning sites, one in the UK, the other
in Australia, with plenty of links.

On problem-based learning

Boud, D. and Feletti, G. (eds) (1997) *The Challenge of Problem-based Learning*. London:
Kogan Page.
Savin-Baden, M. (2000) *Problem-based Learning in Higher Education: Untold Stories*. Buck-
ingham: The Society for Research into Higher Education/Open University Press.
Research and Development in Problem Based Learning. The Australian Problem-Based
Learning Network c/o PROBLARC, CALT, The University of Newcastle, NSW
2308.

Boud and Feletti contains contributions by users in many different areas. Savin-
Baden introduces a little-discussed aspect: what happens *inside* when teachers and
students experience PBL. Both books are important for anyone seriously interested
in PBL. The last is a serial publication of the Australian Problem-Based Learning
Network, which holds biennial conferences, of which these volumes are the
proceedings.

Waters, L. and Johnston, C. (2004) Web-delivered, problem-based learning in organisation behaviour: a new form of CAOS, *Higher Education Research and Development*,
23, 4: 413–431.

An e-version of PBL in teaching organizational behaviour is based on *Case Analysis
of Organisational Situations*.

PBL in biology (20 case examples): www.saltspring.com/capewest/pbl.htm
PBL in physics, chemistry, biology and criminal justice: www.udel.edu/pbl/problems
PBL in engineering: http://fie.engrng.pitt.edu/fie2001/papers/1102.pdf

9

Aligning assessment tasks with intended learning outcomes: Principles

What and how students learn depends to a major extent on how they think they will be assessed. Assessment practices must send the right signals to students about what they should be learning and how they should be learning it. Current practice, however, is distorted because two quite different models of summative assessment have, for historical reasons, been confused and the wrong signals to students are often sent. In this chapter, these issues are clarified. We examine the purposes of assessment, the relation between assessment and the assumed nature of what is being assessed, assessing for desirable but unintended or unexpected learning outcomes and who might usefully be involved in the assessing process. The underlying principle is that the assessment tasks should comprise an authentic representation of the course ILOs.

Formative and summative assessment

There are many reasons for assessing students: selecting students, controlling or motivating students (the existence of assessment keeps class attendance high and set references read), satisfying public expectations as to standards and accountability, but the two most outstanding reasons are for *formative feedback* and for *summative grading*. Usually – and perhaps unfortunately – both are referred to as types of 'assessment'. Both are based on seeing how well students are doing or have recently done, which is what assessment is, but the purposes of the two forms of assessment are so different.

In formative assessment, the results are used for *feedback* during learning. Students and teachers both need to know how learning is proceeding. Formative feedback may operate both to improve the learning of individual students and to improve the teaching itself. Formative feedback is inseparable from teaching: as we have already noted (p. 97), the effectiveness of different teaching methods is directly related to their ability to provide formative feedback. The lecture itself provides little. The improvements to the lecture mentioned in Chapter 7 were almost all formative in function: they got the students learning actively and feedback was provided on their activity, either from teacher or from peers. Formative feedback is a powerful TLA that uses error detection as the basis for error correction: if error is to be corrected, it must first be detected. Thus, students must feel absolutely free to admit error and seek to have it corrected. Students also need to learn to take over the formative role for themselves, just as writers need to spot error and correct it when editing a text by reflecting critically on their own writing. Self- and peer-assessment are particularly helpful TLAs for training students to reflect on the quality of their own work.

In summative assessment, the results are used to grade students at the end of a course or to accredit at the end of a programme. Summative assessment is carried out after the teaching episode has concluded. Its purpose is to see how well students have learned what they were supposed to have learned. That result, the grade, is final. Students fear this outcome; futures hinge on it. They will be singularly unwilling to admit their mistakes. Error no longer is there to instruct, as in formative assessment; error now signals punishment. This difference between formative and summative reminds us that continuous assessment (see later) is problematic when it is used for both formative and summative purposes. What then does the student do about admitting error? This is one area where the same word 'assessment' leads to confusion.

Nevertheless, there is one similarity: in both we match performance as it is, with performance as it should be. When the student is aware of the immediate purpose to which it is being put, the same task can act as a TLA, in the formative sense, and as the assessment task when it is time to do the summative assessment: 'When the chef tastes the sauce it is formative assessment; when the customer tastes, it is summative' (Anon.). Figure 9.1 places tasting the sauce in a classroom context.

Say four topics are to be learned in a semester. The ILOs of each are symbolized as IL01, IL02, IL03 and IL04. At the start of the semester (labelled 'baseline') students enter with little or some knowledge, which the TLAs nurture until the end of the semester. Formative assessment checks that growth and sees that it is on track. Then it is time to see where each student now stands with respect to each of the four topics; this is the task of summative assessment. Finally, there is the administrative matter of converting those four positions into a grade, taken here as A, B, C and D.

A caution in interpreting Figure 9.1. While the same assessment task may be used formatively throughout the course and summatively at the end, it must be clear to the students when it is being used for what purpose. To use it for *both* formative and summative purposes, as may happen in continuous assessment, creates a conflicting situation for the students: they are being asked to display and to hide error simultaneously. When assessment is continuously carried out throughout a course, and it is intended to use some of the results summatively, the students must be told *which* assessment events are formative and which summative. They can then decide how they will handle the task to best advantage.

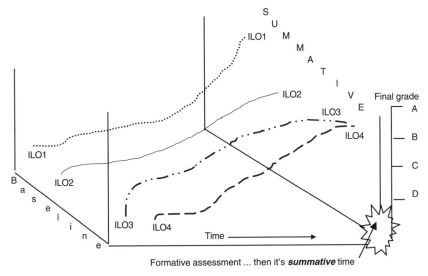

Figure 9.1   Learning in four topics and their formative and summative assessment

Two quite different models of summative assessment have become confused. Our intended learning outcome of this chapter is that readers will unconfuse themselves so that they may apply the appropriate model to their own assessment practices.

But before we do this, Task 9.1 present six dilemmas ('cases') relating to assessment practice. Go through these, writing your responses down. When you have completed this chapter you might like to revisit what you wrote to see if your thoughts might have changed.

Task 9.1   Some cats to place among your collegial pigeons: six assessment dilemmas for you to consider

Case 1. Misunderstanding the question

You are assessing assignments and find that one student has clearly misunderstood the question, the only one to have done so. It is now past the due date for handing in. If you assess it as it is, she will fail. What do you do?

a   Fail her.
b   Hand it back, explain that she has misunderstood and give her an extension.
c   As in (b), but assess it pass/fail only or deduct a grade.
d   Set her another assignment, to be assessed later. Meantime record 'result withheld'.
e   Other. What?

What are the reasons for your decision? _____

_____

_____

_____

Would you have decided differently if she would otherwise graduate with distinction?

_____

_____

Case 2. Grading on the curve

The guidelines for awarding a grade of A are outlined in a programme document:

> *Outstanding.* Demonstrates thorough understanding and interpretation of topics and underlying theories being discussed, and shows a high level of critical thinking and synthesis. Presents an original and thorough discussion. Well organized and structured, fluently written and correctly documented. There is evidence of substantial studies of the literature.

You use these guidelines in grading the assessment tasks of your class of 100 students and find to your delight that 35 (35%) meet these criteria, so you award A to all of them. Your departmental head, however, is unhappy about this because you are 'not showing enough discrimination between students and we don't want this department to get a reputation for easy marking'. The results have not been announced yet, so he suggests that you regrade so that only 15% of your students are given an A. What do you do? Why?

a You agree you must have been too lenient, so you do as he says, giving A to the top 15 only, the remaining of the original As being given B.
b You compromise, splitting the difference: you give As to 25 students.
c You say something like: 'Sorry, but the guidelines are clear. I must in all conscience stick with the original. The conclusion to be drawn is that this was an exceptionally good group of students and that they were taught well.'
d 'I must stick with the guidelines. However, I am prepared to entertain a second opinion. If I can be persuaded that I have been too lenient, I will change my grades.'
e Other.

_____

_____

_____

_____

Case 3. A matter of length

It is policy that the maximum word length of assignments is 1000 per credit point. You are teaching a 2-credit point module. One of your better students has handed in an assignment of 2800 words. What do you do and why?

a Count up to 2000 words, draw a line and mark or assess up to that point only.
b Hand it back to the student with the instructions to rewrite, within the limit, with no penalty.
c As for (b) but with a penalty. (What would you suggest?)
d Hand it back unassessed.
e Assess or mark it but deduct a grade or part-grade, or marks, according to the excess.
f Other.

_____

_____

Would your decision have been any different if it were a poor student?

_____

_____

Case 4. Exam strategy

You are discussing the forthcoming final exam with your first year class. You explain that, as usual, there will be five sections in the paper, each section covering an aspect of the course, and there are two questions per section. They are to choose one of the two, making a total of five questions, to be completed in three hours. You alone will be doing the assessing. A student asks: 'If I think I will run out of time, is it better to answer four questions as best as I can, or to attempt all five, knowing I won't finish most questions?'

What do you say in reply and why?

_____

_____

Case 5. Interfering with internal affairs?

You are the head of a department that has decided to use problem-based learning in the senior level subjects. In PBL, the emphasis is on students applying knowledge to problems, rather than carrying out detailed analyses of the research literature, as has been the tradition in the past. Faculty regulations require you to set a final examination for the major assessment of the course, despite your own judgment and that of your staff that this format is unsuitable for PBL. It is therefore decided that the final exam will contain questions that address application to problem solving rather than questions that require students to demonstrate their familiarity with the literature.

On seeing the paper, however, the external examiner insists that the questions be reworded to address the research literature. You argue, but he insists that 'academic standards' must be upheld. If they are not reworded, you know that he will submit an adverse report to the academic board, where there are vocal critics of your foray into PBL.

What do you do?

_____
_____
_____
_____

Case 6. What is the true estimate of student learning?

A department is trying to arrive at a policy on the proportion of final examination to coursework assignments. In discussing the issue, the head collates data over the past few years and it becomes very clear that coursework assessments are consistently higher than examination results. In discussing this phenomenon, the following opinions are voiced. Which argument would you support?

a Such results show that coursework assessments may be too lenient and because the conditions under which they are undertaken are not standardized, and are unsupervised, the results may well be inflated by collaboration and outright plagiarism. Examination conditions control for these factors. Therefore final exams must be a higher proportion of the final grade than coursework assessments.

b The conditions under which final examinations are conducted are artificial: working under time pressure, little and often no access to tools or data sources, and mode of assessment limited to written expression or MCQ, means that exam performances are sampling only a narrow range of students' learning. Therefore coursework assessments must be a higher proportion of final grade than exams.

c Other. What?

_____
_____
_____

Effects of assessment on learning: Backwash

We teachers might see the intended learning outcomes as the central pillar in an aligned teaching system, but our students see otherwise: 'From our students' point of view, assessment always defines the actual curriculum' (Ramsden 1992: 187). Students learn what they *think* they will be tested on. This is *backwash*, a term coined by Lewis Elton (1987: 92), to refer to the effects assessment has on student learning, to the extent that assessment may determine what and how students learn more than the curriculum does.

Backwash is almost invariably seen negatively (Crooks 1988; Frederiksen and Collins 1989). Recall the 'forms of understanding' that Entwistle and Entwistle's (1997) students constructed to meet presumed assessment requirements (see pp. 74–5). Negative backwash always occurs in an exam-dominated system. Strategy becomes more important than substance. Teachers actually teach exam-taking strategies, such as telling students to attempt all questions even if they don't finish any because they gain more marks than by thinking deeply over a question and providing a complete answer. Students go through previous papers, best-guessing what questions they will encounter and then rote learning answers to them. This sort of backwash leads inevitably to surface learning. Yet learning for the assessment is also inevitable; students would be foolish if they didn't. So, what do we do about it?

In fact, backwash can work positively, encouraging appropriate learning. This is when the assessment is aligned to what students should be learning (Figure 9.2).

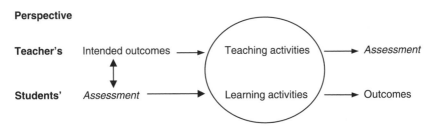

Figure 9.2 Teacher's and student's perspectives on assessment

To the teacher, summative assessment is at the end of the teaching–learning sequence of events, but to the student it is at the beginning. If the intended outcomes are reflected in the assessment, as indicated by the downward arrow, the teaching activities of the teacher and the learning activities of the student are both directed towards the same goal. In preparing for the assessments, students will be learning the intended outcomes.

It sounds easy, but there is a long tradition of thinking about assessment, and some time-honoured assessment practices, that complicate matters. In this chapter, we clarify some of the conceptual issues involved; in the next, we deal with designing and grading assessment tasks for declarative knowledge and, in the chapter after that, designing and grading assessment tasks for functioning knowledge.

Measurement model of assessment

Two quite different models of assessment underlie current thinking and practice: the *measurement* model and the *standards* model (Taylor 1994). Understanding the difference between the two models is basic to effective assessment.

In the Chinese Han Dynasty in the 4th century BC, the purpose of education was selective. Students were required to master a huge classical curriculum, in order to put into effect Confucius' belief that 'those who excel in their study should become officials' (quoted in Zeng 1999: 21). The winners, however lowly their background, were motivated by a rich prize: a lifetime of wealth and prestige. The idea was to select the best individuals in terms of stable characteristics: 'not only intelligence, but also character, determination, and the will to succeed' (Zeng 1999: iv).

Twenty-three centuries later, psychologists in the 19th century also became interested in sorting people out. Sir Francis Galton (1889) found that physical and mental differences such as height, weight and performance on various mental tests, which he called 'traits', were distributed in 'an unsuspected and most beautiful form of regularity' (Galton 1889: 66). He was of course referring to the normal curve, a distribution that occurs inter alia as a result of the extent of the polygenetic inheritance of such traits. Galton's assumptions, not only about statistical techniques, but also about the inheritance of ability and of educability, were built into the burgeoning industry of mental testing in the early part of the 20th century.

Educability was assumed to be about how bright people were and, back to the Han Dynasty, education was seen as a device for sorting people out: usually the brightest, but sometimes to sort out those who weren't educable in normal schools. The present so-called 'parametric' statistical procedures such as correlation and factor analysis were based on Galton's work and are used for constructing educational tests, establishing their reliability and validity and interpreting test scores. Taylor (1994) refers to this individual differences model as 'the measurement model' of educational assessment.

The measurement model was originally designed by psychologists to measure stable traits and abilities and to express that measurement along a graduated scale so that individuals could be compared, either against each other or against population norms. This is fine for research, or for diagnosis when dealing with individuals – for example to say how atypical a person is on reading ability – but the model was hijacked and applied to assessing *educational* outcomes in the form of norm-referenced assessment (NRA).

In NRA, results of assessment are reported in terms of comparisons between students. The rank order is the simplest example, which tells who performs better than who, but there are sophisticated versions of NRA, such as grading on the curve, which we discuss later.

For now, let us examine some of the assumptions the measurement model is based on when applied to assessing classroom learning.

Some assumptions of the measurement model

(*Note*: Beware the following subheadings: all are either wrong or misleading.)

Knowledge can be quantified

Measurement requires that the learning outcomes of individual students are quantified as scores along a single dimension or continuum so that individuals may be compared with each other. In practice, this means that learning is evaluated according to *how much* material has been learned correctly. Good learners know more than poor learners. The Level 1 view of teaching makes essentially quantitative assumptions, as we noted in Chapter 2: teaching involves transmitting the main points, assessment involves marking students on their ability to report them back accurately. The uni- and multi-structural levels of the SOLO taxonomy are quantitative, where learning is a matter of finding out more and more about a topic. But if you assess only using quantitative techniques, what happens to the higher levels of the SOLO taxonomy: to our ILOs addressing critical analysis or hypothesizing?

Percentages are a universal currency

One of the commonest forms of quantification is the percentage, derived either as the ratio of number right to maximum possible multiplied by 100, or as sets of ratings the maxima of which total 100. When this transformation is carried out, it is assumed that percentages are a universal currency, equivalent across subject areas and across students, so that different students' performances in different subjects can be summed, averaged and directly compared. This is completely unsustainable, yet that doesn't stop university senates having long and earnest debates about one faculty using 75% as the cut-off for an A grade and another using 70% as the cut-off: 'We must level the playing field across faculties! It's not fair if it's easier to get an A in arts than it is in science!' Such debates are silly: they are trying to extract certainty from the unknowable. There is simply no way of knowing if 75% in physics is the 'same standard' as 75% in history; or even if a student's result of 75% in Psychology 201 this year represents an improvement over 70% the same student obtained in Psychology 101 the previous year.

Educational tests should be designed to clearly separate the high and low scorers

Measurement experts used to maintain that a good attainment test yields 'a good spread', following the bell curve (back to Galton). However, grades follow the bell curve only if two conditions apply: that ability is normally distributed, and that ability is the sole determinant of academic attainment. But the ability of our students is not likely to be normally distributed because students are not randomly selected – not quite yet, anyway. And neither is ability the sole determinant of students' learning outcomes. Other factors are called 'teaching' and 'learning'. As argued in Chapter 1, good teaching narrows the initial gap between Robert and Susan therefore producing a *smaller* spread of final grades than that predicted by the initial spread of ability. The distribution of results after good teaching should not be bell shaped but skewed, with high scores more frequent than low scores. At university level there is therefore every reason *not* to expect a bell curve distribution of assessment results in our classes. Forcing assessment results to follow the curve actually prevents us from seeing how students are really performing.

Quantitative approaches to assessment are scientific, precise and objective

Numbers mislead. The measurement model yields an extended continuous scale that invites us to make minute distinctions between students, but we have to be careful. The error of measurement in our usual class sizes is bound to be rather more than one percentage point. Worse, the way we use the scales prevents them from being equal interval scales, where the difference between any two adjacent numbers is the same as any other two. This is an *essential* property if we are to average and accumulate marks. The difference between 73 and 74, say, must be the same as the difference between 79 and 80, if marks are to be added or averaged. But the difference between 79 and 80 often becomes zero if first class honours is awarded to a dissertation of 79 marks when the cut-off is 80 (see Box 9.3, p. 182). Many times, teachers and boards of examiners are faced with the borderline case and argue that as the scale is not accurate to one mark, we'll give the student the benefit of the doubt. This, however, makes our scale elastic, distinctly more rubbery at some points along the scale than at others.

Do such decisions show how human we are or just how sloppy? We are both and neither. We are being wonderfully inappropriate, like cooking dinner in the chemistry lab. The precision of the parametric measurement model is just as out of place in the classroom as is weighing sugar in milligrams. It is worse, actually, because the procedure of quantifying qualitative data, such as shifts in students' understandings, requires arbitrary judgments as to what is a 'unit', what is 'worth' one mark, what is worth five or however many marks. These judgments are not only subjective; they often do not even have an explicit and examinable rationale, beyond a vague norm referencing: 'I am marking out of five, this is the best so it gets five, this is average so it gets three marks.' What the *criteria* are that allow the judgement that this one is 'best' and that one 'average' may not be examined.

What happens, then, is that a series of independent minor subjective judgments – a mark for this, a mark for that – accumulate. The big decision – pass or fail?, first class or upper second? – is made on the aggregate of numbers, which includes the aggregate of error in all those minor judgments. That big decision should be made, not on the accumulation of unknowably flawed minor judgments, but on a reasoned and publicly sustainable judgment about the performance itself. This requires a holistic judgment made on publicly stated criteria.

The application of a precise, scientific model to an area where it does not apply cannot be scientific.

University education is selective

Comparing students with each other assumes that universities are a selective device to find the intellectuals in the population, as in Han Dynasty China, or that the purpose of the undergraduate years is to weed out the 'pass' level students from the potential postgraduate research students.

The only place for assessing students selectively in the university context is for entry to university or to graduate school. At entry, a convenient estimate of scholastic ability is obtained by summing a student's best three, or best five, HSC or A level subjects, with or without adjustments for second attempt. What you get is a measure of scholastic ability, which is robust enough to allow direct comparisons between students in different subject areas. It is rough, but it works over large numbers. Once students have been selected, however, the aim of undergraduate teaching is to get students to learn what is in the curriculum, an enterprise in which the measurement model has no place.

But shouldn't the entry into university, and especially into graduate school, be based on whether the students are able to meet the criteria or standards necessary for doing graduate work? You don't answer that question by comparing students with one another.

The above assumptions give rise to some common practices.

Grading on the curve

After ranking, a common form of norm-referenced assessment is 'grading on the curve'. The top 10% of the class, say, are awarded 'high distinction', the next 15% 'distinction', the next 25% 'credit' and 45% 'pass'. The results will appear to be stable from year to year and from department to department. If there is a query from the odd student about the grade awarded, it is easy to point to an unarguable figure: all objective, very precise. 'You didn't earn enough marks to beat the others. They were too good for you. Sorry.'

The very term 'high distinction' is comparative, applicable only to that blessed few who are highly distinguished. This puts the brake on the number of HDs awarded. Even if one-third of the class met the criteria set for obtaining a high distinction, it would be seen by colleagues on the board of examiners, with the bell curve tolling in their heads, as a contemptible fall in standards, not as it should be a cause for congratulation. Rather than calling the highest grade a 'high distinction', the neutral term 'A' makes it easier to accept that a high proportion of students could reach that high standard.

Many people, teachers, administrators, and even students, feel it 'fitting' that a few should do extremely well, most should do middling well and a few do poorly, some failing. This feeling comes straight from the assumptions that ability determines learning outcomes and that ability is normally distributed. Both assumptions are untenable, as we have seen.

Unfortunately, grading on the curve is so easy. All you need is a test that will rank order the students – a quick and dirty MCQ will do – and then you simply award an A to the first 10%, B to the next 25%, or whatever has been decided, and so on. Alignment is irrelevant.

Grading on the curve also appeals to administrators, because it conveys the impression that standards over all departments are 'right', not too slack, not too stringent, so that a few do really well, most middling and a few poorly: we have got it *right*, year after year. But that result is an artefact: the distribution has been defined that way, whatever the actual results in any given year or department.

Grading on the curve precludes aligned teaching and criterion-referenced assessment. It is a procedure that cannot be justified on educational grounds.

Marking

Marking is an assessment procedure that comes directly from quantitative assumptions and is so widespread as to be universal. It is, however, a procedure that needs to be examined closely. Marking is quantifying learning performances, either by transforming them into units (a word, an idea, a point), or by allocating ratings or 'marks' on a subjective if not arbitrary basis. For marking to be acceptable, we have seen that one mark must be 'worth' the same as any other, so that they can be added and averaged and a grade is awarded on the number of marks accumulated. Two most peculiar phenomena are associated with marking:

1 Half the total number of marks available is almost universally accepted as the pass mark.
2 It does not matter *what* is correct, as long as there are enough of them.

Multiple-choice tests enact these assumptions exactly. Learning is represented as the total of all items correct. Students quickly see that the score is the important thing, not how it is comprised, and that the ideas contained in any one item are of the same value as in any other item. The strategy is to focus on the easy or trivial items; and of the alternatives you don't know, check the ones that seem vaguely familiar. You'll almost certainly get more than half correct – and by defintion you'll pass.

The essay format, technically open ended, does not preclude quantitative means of assessment. When multiple markers use marking schemes, they give a mark or two as each 'correct' or 'acceptable' point is made, possibly with bonus points for argument or style. This too sends misleading messages to students about the structure of knowledge and how to exploit its assessment. A good example is the strategy in timed examinations of attempting all questions and finishing none. The reasoning is that the law of diminishing returns applies: the time spent on the first half of an essay nets more marks than the same time spent on the second half. The more facts the more marks, never mind the structure they make. But students don't learn 'marks', they learn such things as structures, concepts, theories, narratives, skills, performances of understanding. These are what should be assessed, not arbitrary quantifications of them. It is like examining architects on the number of bricks their designs use, never mind the structure, the function or the aesthetic appeal of the building itself.

Assessment separated from teaching

In the measurement model, assessment is a standalone activity, unrelated to teaching as such. Accordingly, it attracts its own context and culture. One feature is the need for standardized conditions including the same assessment tasks for all, a necessary condition when students are to be compared with each other. Guaranteeing standardized procedures leads to a Theory X, bureaucratic assessment climate: emphasis on decontextualized assessment tasks that address declarative, not functioning, knowledge.

In universities that work in this way, teaching occupies the greater part of the academic year, assessment a frantic couple of weeks at the end. Both the present writers can recall, now with shame, not even thinking about the final examination until the papers were due to be sent to the central examinations section. You teach as it comes, you set an examination, the examination centre invigilates it for you, you allocate the marks.

Alignment doesn't come into it.

Effects of backwash from the measurement model

Measurement model procedures send unfortunate messages to students:

- *The trees are more important than the wood.* Maximizing marks is the important thing, not seeing the overall structure of what is being learned. Put another way, the measurement model encourages multistructural thinking, not relational or extended abstract.
- *Verbatim responses will gain marks.* Although a verbatim replay of a unit in the text or in the lecture may not be very noble, it has to be given some credit when using a multistructural marking scheme, given cheating has been ruled out. This happens even when the teacher warns that verbatim responses will be penalized (Biggs 1973 (regrettably)).
- *Success or failure is due to factors that are beyond the student's control.* An individual's result under NRA depends on the competition, who is more able. Thus, in the event of a poor result, the student can either blame bad luck or, more damagingly, come to the conclusion that he or she is simply not as able as other people. Students can't do anything about luck or ability,

so why bother? The attribution under the standards model is different: 'Here is what I am supposed to have achieved, I didn't achieve it, so what went wrong?' The answer to that could be: 'I didn't put in enough effort', 'I didn't know how to do it' but, at worst: 'I am dumb.' The first two attributions are under the students' control and they can do something about doing better next time. The last couldn't be more discouraging.

The case against the measurement model is pretty convincing, so why do its procedures remain? Box 9.1 suggests some answers.

Box 9.1   Why measurement model procedures remain

1 *Tradition, habit.* Why question what has worked well in the past, especially when administrative structures and procedures make change difficult?

2 *Bureaucratic convenience*

- Dealing with numbers gives the illusion of precision. Any appeal or disagreement is over trivial issues. Let the numbers make the big decisions.
- Grading on the curve gives the illusion of constant standards, no egregious departments or results.
- The language of percentages is generally understood (another illusion).
- Given the tight security of exams, avoidance of plagiarism can be assured.
- Combining results from different departments needs a common framework: the percentage and normalized scores (both illusions, see earlier point).

3 *Teaching convenience*

- You teach, the exam questions can be left until well into the teaching, exams section will see to the details. It is flexible on coverage, what questions you set.
- You can easily average and combine marks across tasks and across courses.
- You can use marks for disciplinary purposes (deduct for late submission).
- It's easier to argue numbers with students in case of dispute than to argue 'subjective' structures.

4 *Genuine belief in the measurement model.* My job *is* to sort the sheep from the goats.

Let us now turn to the alternative, the standards model.

Standards model of assessment

The standards model of assessment is designed to assess changes in performance as a result of learning, for the purpose of seeing what, and how well,
something has been learned. Such assessment is criterion-referenced (CRA),
that is, the results of assessment are reported in terms of how well an individual meets the criteria of learning that have been set. This model is the
relevant one for assessment at university (Taylor 1994). The point is not to
identify *students* in terms of some characteristic, but to identify *performances*
that tell us what has been learned, and how well. Unlike in NRA, one student's
result is quite independent of any other student's.

In 1918, R.L. Thorndike made it very clear that CRA was most appropriate
for educational purposes, and predicted that CRA would displace NRA from
public schooling (Airasian and Madaus 1972). He was right about the first
point, but, unfortunately, his prediction was wrong. The idea still lurks that
education *is* a selective exercise, and that norm-referenced examinations
are appropriate. But even where this idea is not explicit, the procedures of
constructing and administering tests, establishing reliability and validity and
interpreting and reporting test scores are based on parametric statistics, as if
the biological assumptions of polygenetic inheritance, which produce the
normal curve, are appropriate for educational assessment. As already argued,
for purposes of classroom assessment such statistics as the correlation and
the usual tests of reliability and validity are entirely inappropriate. Reliability
and validity of assessments are important, but they have entirely different
meanings in the standards model (pp. 188–90).

Outside educational institutions, the standards model is assumed whenever anyone teaches anyone else anything at all. The teacher has a standard,
an intended outcome of their teaching, which the learner is to learn satisfactorily. Parents intend their children to learn to dress themselves to a given
standard of acceptability, swimming instructors have standards they want
their learners to achieve. Parents don't lecture a toddler on shoe tying, and
give a multiple-choice test at the end to see if their child ties her shoes better
than the kid next door. The parent's ILO, the teaching/learning activity and
the assessment are all the same: it is tying a shoe. In the case of driving
instruction it is driving a car. The alignment is perfect. Outcomes-based
teaching and learning is placing this approach back into the institution.

The logic is stunningly obvious: Say what you want students to be able to
do, teach them to do it and then see if they can, in fact, do it. There is a
corollary: if they cannot do it, try again until they can. This principle is used
in 'mastery learning' (Bloom et al. 1971) and the Keller Plan, a mastery
model for universities (Keller 1968). Students are allowed as many tries at
the assessment as they need – within reason – in order to pass the preset
standard. Some students pass in short order, others take longer. The main
objections to mastery-learning models were not to the principle, but to the
fact that the preset criteria were defined quantitatively, mainly because quantitative criteria are easy to define. In one study with high school biology

students, the Roberts who focused on memorizing detail performed well in such a mastery-learning approach, but not the Susans who were bored stiff (Lai and Biggs 1994).

Such objections do not apply when the standards are defined *qualitatively*. Qualitative assessment does not directly address the question of *how much* the student knows, but *how well*. This requires an explicit classification of learning quality that needs to be derived for each topic or skill taught. The SOLO taxonomy is a general model of learning quality that can be adapted to suit particular content (see Chapter 5).

Let us now look at the assumptions needed to make the standards model of assessment work.

Some assumptions of the standards model

We can set standards (criteria) as intended learning outcomes of our teaching

Yes we can, as outlined in Chapter 5. If the intended learning outcomes are written appropriately, the job of the assessment is to state how well they have been met, the 'how well' being expressed not in 'marks' but in a hierarchy of levels, such as letter grades from 'A' to 'D', or as high distinction through credit to conditional pass, or whatever system of grading is used. Deciding at the level of a particular student performance is greatly facilitated by using explicit criteria or rubrics (examples on pp. 210–Table 10.2, 214–Table 10.4, 226–Table 11.2). These rubrics may address the task, or the ILO.

Different performances can reflect the same standards

While standardized conditions are required when individuals are to be compared to each other, when we are seeking to find the optimum performance of individuals, the more standardized the conditions the less valid the test is likely to be for any given individual. Individuals learn and perform optimally in different conditions and with different formats of assessment. Some work better under pressure, others need more time. As in professional work itself, there are often many ways of achieving a satisfactory outcome. Individual students demonstrate their best work in different ways; assessment tasks such as portfolios allow for that.

Teachers can judge performances against the criteria

This is critical when using the standards model but it is skirted when using the measurement model. In the latter, teachers need to answer the following question: 'How many marks do I give this section?' and in the former: 'How well does this performance as a whole meet the criteria for high distinction (or whatever)?' In order to make these holistic judgments teachers need to know what is poor quality performance, what is good quality and why.

Constructive alignment operates on these same assumptions and addresses how they may work in practice.

Norm- and criterion-referenced assessment: Let's get it straight

Differences between NRA and CRA

Because of the universality of many NRA practices in assessing students, and the educational logic of CRA, we should be clear about the differences. To recap briefly:

1 In NRA, the results are expressed in terms of comparisons between students after teaching is over. CRA results are expressed in terms of how well a given student's performance matches criteria that have been set in advance.
2 NRA makes judgments about *people*, CRA makes judgments about *performance*.

Task 9.2 presents a criterion-referenced test to sort the sheep from the goats (joke).

Task 9.2   NRA or CRA?

A teacher assesses two students in a CRA system and notes that Robert has been awarded a B and Susan an A. On a recheck of the papers, the teacher notes with a shock that Robert's paper *is* as good as Susan's! He is reassessed and given an A too.

Is this now NRA (comparing students) or CRA (judging on standards)? Why?

The answer is at the end of this chapter.

A summary of the differences between CRA and NRA is captured in Table 9.1, which lists a lexicon of NRA and CRA words. The only word common to both? Summative assessment.

Nevertheless, it is easy to blur the two models. Box 9.2 (p. 181) represents a valiant attempt by an arts faculty at one university to move towards the standards model. Previously, a marks system was used to define 'A+', 'A' and 'A–' and so on, and the attempt was made at faculty board to devise a scheme that defined the grading categories, avoiding marks. The following was issued to all teachers in the faculty.

You work out what the problem is. Then turn to Box 9.3 (but no peeking!) (p. 182).

Table 9.1   Two lexicons

Norm-referenced assessment

Mark, percentage, decile, rank order,* summative assessment, decontextualized assessment, standardization, 'fairness', quantitative, average, grade-point average, normal/bell curve, normal distribution, grading on the curve, a good spread of scores, parametric statistics, test–retest reliability, internal consistency, discrimination, selection, competition, high flier, ability

Criterion-referenced assessment

Assess, authentic/performance assessment, contextualized, standards, formative assessment,* summative assessment, criteria, individualization, optimal performance, student-centred, qualitative, grading categories, ILOs, alignment, judgment, distribution free, non-parametric statistics, effort, skill, learning, competence, expertise, mastery

---

* The one word in common!

A double problem

Despite the prevailing norm-referenced cast of mind at undergraduate level, the sheer logic of criterion-referenced assessment is generally seen in assessing theses and dissertations. We expect a dissertation to display certain characteristics: coverage of the literature, definition of a clear and original research question, mastery of research methods, and so on. The categories of honours (first class, upper second, lower second) originally suggested qualities that students' work should manifest: a first was qualitatively *different* from an upper second, it was not simply that the first got more sums right. Today, this approach might be in jeopardy, as these categories seem increasingly to be defined in terms of ranges of marks, which is unfortunate. In Box 9.4 (p. 183) we see a doubly unfortunate instance: defining the level of honours in terms of marks, and allowing non-academic factors to influence the judgment of academic quality.

In the standards model, and in constructive alignment in particular, this double problem could not occur. The ILOs would refer to academic qualities only, not sexual harassment, lateness or anything else, and the assessment would be aligned to those ILOs. There are other and more appropriate ways of dealing with the non-academic issues than by adjusting final grades.

Some important concepts in assessment

Authentic and performance assessment

In assessing functioning knowledge in particular, the assessment tasks need to represent the knowledge to be learned in a way that is authentic to real life. Verbal retelling is not often authentic; for example, we do not teach

---

Box 9.2   How Faculty Office suggests final grades should be determined (and the best of British luck!)

The following guidelines were issued to all staff in the faculty. They were to use these in arriving at their final grade distributions:

A (A+, A, A–)	Excellence, up to 10% of students. The student must show evidence of original thought as well as having a secure grasp of the topic from background reading and analysis
B (B+, B, B–)	Good to very good result, achieved by next 30% of students who are critical and analytical but not necessarily original in their thinking and who have a secure grasp of the topic from background reading and analysis Occasionally, a student who shows originality but is less secure might achieve this result
C (C+, C, C–)	Satisfactory to reasonably good result. The students have shown a reasonably secure grasp of their subject but probably most of their information is derivative, with rather little evidence of critical thinking Most students will fall into this category
D	Minimally acceptable. The students have put in effort but work is marred by some misunderstandings, but not so serious that the student should fail Students falling into this category, and outright failures, would not normally comprise more than about 10%

Source: Faculty of Arts Handbook, the University of . . .

What is the problem here? _____

_____

_____

_____

---

psychology or any other subject just so that students can tell us in their own words what we have told them. We need some sort of 'performance of understanding' (see pp. 74–6) that reflects the kind of understanding that requires an *active demonstration* of the knowledge in question, as opposed to talking or writing about it. This is referred to as 'authentic assessment' (Torrance 1994; Wiggins 1989). The term 'authentic' assessment may imply that all other forms of assessment are inauthentic, so many prefer the term 'performance assessment' (Moss 1992). It reminds us of what we already know in aligned teaching, that the assessment task should require students to do more than just tell us what they know – unless, of course, declarative knowledge is all that we require in this instance.

Box 9.3   The problem in Box 9.2

The intention is to assess according to quality, but the thinking is still measurement model. Where there is a conflict, it seems that the NRA guidelines would be expected to prevail. For instance, if 30% of students 'showed evidence of original thought as well as having a secure grasp, etc.' that would be seen in this scheme to be anomalous, but as teachers we should be happy if this is what we found. Likewise, we should be disappointed if not ashamed that most students displayed 'derivative information' (C): it looks like they hadn't been taught properly, but here we are told that that is what we should expect. What is wrong here is that the definitions of learning outcome appear to be based on expected distributions of ability. Major departures from that distribution suggest either that there is something wrong with our teaching or that we are too soft in assessing.

Decontextualized assessment

A related issue is whether the assessment tasks should be decontextualized, requiring students to perform in the abstract, out of context. Where the ILOs target declarative knowledge, it is quite appropriate to assess it using decontextualized assessments, such as written examinations. We thus arrive at an important distinction in assessment formats:

1 Decontextualized assessments such as a written exam, or a term paper, which are suitable for assessing declarative knowledge.
2 Performance assessments, such as a practicum, problem solving or diagnosing a case study, which are suitable for assessing functioning knowledge in its appropriate context.

While both decontextualized and contextualized learning and assessment have a place, in practice decontextualized assessment has been greatly overemphasized in proportion to the place declarative knowledge has in the curriculum. As we saw in Chapter 5, functioning knowledge is underwritten by declarative knowledge and we need to assess both. A common mistake is to assess only the lead-in declarative knowledge, not the functioning knowledge that emerges from it. The following ILOs are taken from rehabilitation science, with their SOLO level and type of knowledge assessed:

1 Describe the bones and the muscles of the hand (multistructural, declarative).

Box 9.4   How not to 'mark' a dissertation

A student's postgraduate thesis, carried out at an Australian university, was submitted late, and given a mark of 76. However, during an oral examination, in which the student left the room in tears, one examiner persuaded the other two examiners that because of 'supervisory difficulties', the thesis be upgraded to 79, which meant a classification of second class honours for the degree. The student then raised other issues, including sexual harassment and claimed her thesis was worthy of first class honours. An internal enquiry suggested that 79 be converted to 80, so the dissertation was now awarded first class honours. But the case was then referred to the deputy ombudsman, who advised that the 'real' mark should have been 73, when readjusted for lateness and the bonuses for stress.

A 'real' mark is surely that which reflects the genuine worth of the work done, but here we have a thesis variously marked at 73, 76, 79 and 80, ranging from second to first class honours. The variation is due not so much to differences in staff opinion on the intrinsic academic worth of the thesis, as to differences in opinion on non-academic matters – lateness, stress, supervisory difficulties and sexual harassment – which were factored in arbitrarily and after the event. The public, employers, other universities – not to mention the poor student – would simply have no idea whether the thesis demonstrated those qualities of flair and originality that are associated with first class honours or of the less dazzling but high competence that is associated with good second class honours. It is ironic that a lay person, the deputy ombudsman, seems to have been the one who was least swayed by non-academic issues.

Source: 'From a flood of tears to scandal', *The Australian*,
26 January 2001: p. 4

---

2   Explain how the bone and muscle systems interact to produce functional movement of the hand, for example in picking up a small coin from the floor (relational, but still declarative).
3   Given a trauma to one muscle group *(x)* rendering it out of action, design a functional prosthesis to allow the hand to be used for picking up a coin (relational, functioning).

Holistic and analytic assessment

Analytic marking of essays or assignments is a common practice. The essay is reduced to independent components, such as content, style, referencing, argument, originality, format, and so on, each of which is rated on a separate scale. The final performance is then assessed as the sum of the separate ratings. This is very helpful as *formative* assessment (Lejk and Wyvill 2001a); it gives students feedback on how well they are doing on each important aspect of the essay, but the *value* of the essay is how well it makes the case or addresses the question as a whole. The same applies to any task: the final performance, such as treating a patient or making a legal case, makes sense only when seen as a whole.

A valid or authentic assessment must be of the total performance, not just aspects of it. Consider this example from surgery. You want to be sure that the student can carry out a particular operation with high and reliable competence. An analytic assessment would test and mark knowledge of anatomy, anaesthesia, asepsis and the performance skills needed for making clean incisions and then add the marks to see if they reach the requisite 50% (or in this case perhaps 80%). Say a student accrues more than the number of marks needed to pass but removes the wrong part. On the analytic model a pass it must be.

Absurd though this example may seem to be, in an analytic marking scheme some aspects of knowledge are inevitably traded off against others. The solution is not to blur the issue by spreading marks around to fill in the cracks, but to require different levels of understanding or performance, according to the importance of the sub-topic. In this example, the student's knowledge of anatomy was insufficient to allow the correct performance, hence the proper judgment is 'fail'. Assessment of components certainly should be undertaken as formative assessment but, at the end of the road, assessment should address the whole.

In making holistic assessments, the details are not ignored. The question is whether, like the bricks of a building or the characters in a novel, the specifics are tuned to create an overall structure or impact. This requires a *hermeneutic* judgment; that is, understanding the whole in light of the parts. For example, an essay requiring reasoned argument involves making a case, just as a barrister has to make a case that stands or falls on its inherent plausibility. The judge does not judge the barrister's case analytically: uses legal terms correctly (+10 marks), makes eye contacts with jury members (+5 marks), for too long (−3 marks) and then aggregates, the counsel with most marks winning the suit. The argument, as a whole, has to be judged. It is the whole dissertation that passes, the complete argument that persuades, the comprehensive but concise proposal that gets funded, the applicant's case that wins promotion. That is what holistic assessment is about.

Critics argue that holistic assessment involves a 'subjective' judgment. But as we have seen, awarding marks is a matter of judgment too, a series of mini-judgments, each one small enough to be handled without qualm. The numbers make the big decisions: if they add up to 50 or more, then it is a pass. At no point does one have to consider what is the *nature* of a passing grade as opposed to a fail or of a distinction level of performance as opposed to a credit. One of the major dangers of quantitative assessment schemes is that teachers can shelter under them and avoid the responsibility of making the judgments that really matter: What is a good assessment task? Why is this a good performance? (Moss 1992).

The strategy of reducing a complex issue to isolated segments, rating each independently, and then aggregating to get a final score in order to make decisions, seems peculiar to schools and universities. It is not the way things work in real life. Moss (1994) gives the example of a journal editor judging whether to accept or reject a manuscript on the basis of informed advice from referees. The referees don't give marks, but argue on the intrinsic merits of the paper as a whole and the editor has to incorporate their advice, resolve conflicting advice and make a judgment about what to do with the whole paper: reject it, accept it or send it back for revision. Moss reports that one of her own papers, which argued for a hermeneutic approach to educational assessment, was rejected by the editor of an educational journal on the grounds that a hermeneutic approach was not the model of assessment accepted in the educational fraternity. But it just had been! Moss gleefully pointed out that the editor had used a hermeneutic approach to arrive at that conclusion. Her paper was accepted.

In order to assess learning outcomes holistically, it is necessary to have a conceptual framework that enables us to see the relationship between the parts and the whole. Teachers, like journal editors, need to develop their own framework. The SOLO taxonomy can be useful in assisting that process (see pp. 79–80; Boulton-Lewis 1998; Hattie and Purdie 1998; Lake 1999).

Convergent and divergent assessment: Unintended outcomes

We used the terms 'convergent' and 'divergent' in Chapter 8 in connection with teaching for creativity. A Level 1 view of teaching sees all assessment as convergent: Get right what I have just taught you. When essays are marked with a checklist, marks are awarded only for matching the prescribed points, none for other points that might be just as good or better. This is not what assessment should be about. Virtually all university-level subjects require at least some divergent assessment. Setting only closed questions is like trying to shoot fish in murky water. We need to use open-ended assessment tasks that allow for *unintended outcomes*, that follow from such verbs in the ILOs as 'hypothesize', 'create', 'design', 'reflect' and the like.

A student teacher provided the following metaphor for assessment:

> When I stand in front of a class, I don't see stupid or unteachable learners, but boxes of treasures waiting for us to open.
> (An inservice teacher education student, University of Hong Kong)

What 'treasures' students find in their educational experience is something that can surprise, delight and, of course, disappoint too. When we assess using closed questions something like this occurs:

Teacher   How many diamonds have you got?
Student   I don't have any diamonds.
Teacher   Then you fail!
Student   But you didn't ask me about my jade.

Students' treasures need not be just in diamonds. If you only ask a limited range of questions, then you may well miss the jade: the treasure that you didn't know existed because you didn't ask. Of course, if the ILOs are expressed only in diamonds that is one thing, but frequently they are not, or ought not to be if they are.

Any rich teaching context is likely to produce learning that is productive and relevant, but unanticipated. The value of many formal activities lies precisely in the surprises they generate, such as field trips, practica or lab sessions, while informal activities bring about unanticipated learning in infinite ways. The student talks to someone, reads a book not on the reading list, watches a television programme, browses the net, does a host of things that sparks a train of thought, a new construction. Such learning probably will not fit the questions being asked in the exam, but they could nevertheless be highly relevant to the course ILOs. Most if not all important discoveries came about as a result of paying attention to unintended outcomes.

Assessment practices should allow for such rich learning experiences, but rarely do. One psychology professor included the following in the final exam paper: 'Based on the first-year syllabus, set and answer your own question on a topic not addressed in this paper.' Another was: 'Psychology. Discuss.' You had to answer these questions extremely well. He also used the instruction: 'Answer *about* five questions.' The conservative or insecure students answered exactly five. The more daring answered three, even two. They were, of course, the deep learners. Other ways of assessing unintended outcomes are reflective journals, critical incidents and the portfolio. We look at these in due course.

Some may see a problem of 'fairness' here. Shouldn't all students be assessed on their performance in the same task? This complaint has weight only in a norm-referenced context, when you are comparing students with each other. Then, yes, you have to standardize so that all have a fair crack at however many As or HDs have been allocated. In portfolio assessment, however, the complaint is irrelevant. If student A can justify task X as addressing the ILOs, and student B task Y, where is the problem?

> To treat everyone the same when people are so obviously different from each other is the very opposite of fairness.
> (Elton 2005 on assessing student learning)

If the ILOs specify creativity and originality and the assessment does not allow for them, now that *is* unfair.

Who takes part in assessing?

Three stages are involved in assessing students' performances:

1 *Setting the criteria* for assessing the work.
2 *Selecting the evidence* that would be relevant to submit to judgment against those criteria.
3 *Making a judgment* about the extent to which these criteria have been met.

Traditionally, the teacher is the agent in all three assessment processes. The teacher decides in advance that the evidence for learning comprises correct answers to a set of questions that again in the teacher's opinion addresses and represents the essential core content of the course and the teacher makes the final judgments on meeting the criteria.

Self-assessment (SA) and *peer-assessment* (PA) usually refer to student involvement in stage (3), but students can and often should be involved in stages (1) and (2) as well. Arguments can be made for all or any of these combinations (Boud 1995; Harris and Bell 1986). Students can be involved in discussing with the teacher what the criteria might be, which need not be the same for all students, as happens in a learning contract system (pp. 220–1). Students can also be involved in (2), that is, as the ones responsible for selecting the evidence to be put up against the criteria, as happens with assessment by portfolio. Finally, students can be involved in making the summative judgment (3). This can be as self-assessment or as peer-assessment and either or both can be used as a teaching/learning activity and as an assessment task. Their judgments may also be included in the final grade. All these possibilities are discussed in due course.

Probably the strongest arguments for self- and peer-assessment are that they provide a TLA that engages crucial and otherwise neglected aspects of student learning:

1 First-hand knowledge of the criteria for good learning. Students should be quite clear about what the criteria for good learning are, but when the teacher sets the criteria, selects the evidence and makes the judgment of the student's performance against the criteria, the students may have little idea as to what they should have been doing and where they went wrong. It is too easy for the students just to accept the teacher's judgment and not reflect on their own performance. They should be more actively involved in knowing what the criteria really mean. They should learn how to apply the criteria, to themselves and to others.
2 What is good evidence for meeting the criteria and what is not? Telling students may not engage them. They need to learn what is good evidence being themselves actively involved in selecting it.
3 Making judgments about whether a performance or product meets the given criteria is vital for effective professional action in any field. Professionals need to make these judgments about their own performance (SA) and that of others (PA). It is the learning experience professionals say is

most lacking in their undergraduate education (Boud 1986). Brew (1999) argues that students need to distinguish good from poor information now they are faced with an incredible overload of information from the net: an essential skill in lifelong learning (pp. 148–51). A more general argument along these lines is that conventional assessment disempowers learners, whereas education is about empowering learners and assessment can be made to play an empowering role (Leach et al. 2001).

Reliability and validity

A frequent criticism of qualitative assessment is that it is 'subjective' and 'unreliable'. This is the measurement model talking. Let us rephrase so that it applies to both models of assessment: Can we rely on the assessment results – are they reliable? Are they assessing what they should be assessing – are they valid?

Can we rely on the assessment results?

In the measurement model, reliability means:

- *Stability*: a test needs to come up with the same result on different occasions, independently of who was giving and marking it. Hence, procedure of test–retest reliability: give the same test to the same group again and see if you get the same result.
- *Dimensionality*: the test items need to measure the same characteristic, hence the usual measures of reliability: split-half, internal consistency (Cronbach α).
- *Conditions of testing:* each testing occasion needs to be conducted under standardized conditions.

Here reliability is seen as a property of the test. Such tests are conceived, constructed and used within a sophisticated framework of parametric statistics, which requires that certain assumptions be met, for example that the score distributions need to be normal or bell shaped.

In the standards model reliability means something rather different:

- *Intra-judge reliability.* Does the same person make the same judgment about the same performance on two different occasions?
- *Inter-judge reliability.* Do different judges make the same judgment about the same performance on the same occasion?

Here reliability is not a property of the test, but of the ability of teachers/ judges to make consistent judgments. This requires that they know what their framework of judgment is and how to use it: the criteria need spelling out in what are now known as grading criteria or *rubrics*, which are simply clear criteria of grading standards. We deal with these in Chapters 10 and 11.

Reliability here is not a matter of statistical operations, but of being very clear about what we are doing, what learning outcomes we want, what is to be the evidence for those outcomes and why. In other words, reliable assessments are part and parcel of good teaching. We have been explicating the framework and the specific criteria for making informed and reliable judgments about students' learning from Chapter 5 onwards.

Do the test scores assess what they should be assessing?

In the measurement model, the test needs to be validated against some external criterion to show that the trait being measured behaves as it should if it were being measured accurately. Thus, the scores could be correlated with another benchmark test or used as a variable in an experimental intervention, or in predicting an independent outcome.

In the case of the standards model, by way of contrast, validity resides in the *interpretations and uses* to which test scores are put (Messick 1989), that is, in the test's alignment with the total teaching context. For example, if sitting an exam results in students rote-learning model answers, then that is a consequence that invalidates the test. An aligned, or properly criterion-referenced assessment task is valid, a non-aligned one is invalid. The glue that holds the ILOs, the teaching/learning environment, and the assessment tasks and their interpretation together is, again, *judgment.* There is now quite a good deal of agreement about reliability and validity in qualitative assessment (Frederiksen and Collins 1989; Moss 1992, 1994; Shepard 1993; Taylor 1994).

Table 9.2 draws all these points together, contrasting the measurement and standard models.

Task 9.3 (p. 191) is a reflective exercise to help you see where you stand in your thinking about your assessment practice.

Table 9.2   Comparing the measurement and standards models

	Measurement model	*Standards model*
Theory	Quantitative. Classic test theory, using assumptions of parametric statistics	Qualitative. A theory of learning enabling consistent judgments. No assumptions about distributions
Stability	Scores remain stable over testing occasions	Scores after teaching should be higher than before teaching
Dimensionality	The test is unidimensional. All items measure the same construct	Test multidimensional (unless there is only one ILO) The items address all the course ILOs
Testing conditions	Conditions need to be standard	Conditions reflect an individual's optimal learning in the intended application of the learning

(Continued)

Table 9.2   Continued

	Measurement model	*Standards model*
Validity	External: how well the test correlates with outside performances	Internal: how well scores relate to the ILOs and to the target performance domain
Use	Selecting students. Comparing individuals, population norms. Individual diagnosis	Assessing the effectiveness of learning, during and after teaching and learning

Now take a second look at Task 9.1 (p. 165). Would you make different decisions now?

Answers to Task 9.2   The NRA/CRA problem

Despite the fact that Susan's and Robert's performances were compared, the purpose of comparing was not to award the grades but to check the consistency of making the judgment. What happened here was that the initial judgment of Robert's performance was inaccurate, very possibly because of a halo effect: 'Ah, here's Robert's little effort. That won't be an A!' It took a direct comparison with Susan's effort to see the mistake. The standards themselves were unaltered.

Summary and conclusions

Formative and summative assessment

The first thing to get right is the reason for assessing. There are two paramount reasons that we should assess: formative, to provide feedback during learning; and summative, to provide an index of how successfully the student has learned when teaching has been completed. Formative assessment is basic to good teaching, and has been addressed in earlier chapters. Our main concern in this chapter is with summative.

Effects of assessment on learning: Backwash

The effects of assessment on learning are usually deleterious. This is largely because assessment is treated as a necessary evil, the bad news of teaching and learning, to be conducted at the end of all the good stuff. Students second-guess the assessment and make that their syllabus, and will under-

Task 9.3 Where does your assessment stand?

Reflect on your assessment practice so far, put a cross on the continuum on a point that best represents what you currently do in assessing your students:

Formative	_____ Summative
Involving your students	_____ All teacher controlled
Using open-ended assessment tasks	_____ Using closed-ended assessment tasks
Authentic tasks	_____ Decontextualized tasks
Criterion-referenced	_____ Norm-referenced
Using grading criteria	_____ Using model answers
Awarding grades for quality	_____ Awarding marks for quantity
Assessing the task as a whole	_____ Assessing individual components of the task

If you were to adopt constructively aligned assessment, what changes would you need to make in your assessment practice?

estimate requirements if the assessments tasks let them, so they get by with low-level, surface learning strategies. In aligned teaching, contrariwise, the assessment reinforces learning. Assessment is the senior partner in learning and teaching. Get it wrong and the rest collapses. This and following chapters aim to help us get it right.

Measurement model of assessment

The measurement model of educational assessment was hijacked from individual differences psychology, which is concerned with measuring stable characteristics of individuals so that they can be compared with each other or with population norms. However, when this model is applied to assessing educational outcomes, numerous problems arise. Unfortunately, many procedures deriving from the measurement model are incompatible with constructive alignment but remain in current practice: grading on the curve so that students have to compete for the higher grades; marking, despite its universality, has implications for the nature of knowledge that are unacceptable; separating assessment from teaching, which ignores alignment and imposes a separate culture of assessment as apart from the culture of teaching and learning. The backwash from the measurement model sends unfortunate messages to students about the nature of knowledge and about assessment preparation strategies that lead to surface learning.

Standards model of assessment

The standards model of educational assessment defines forms of knowledge to be reached at the end of teaching, expressed as various levels of acceptability in the ILOs and grading system. This framework requires higher levels of judgment on the part of the teacher as to how well the students' performances match the ILOs than does quantitative assessment. The assessment tasks need to be 'authentic' to the ILOs, stipulating a quality of performance that the assessment tasks demand. The backwash tells students they need to match the target performances as well as they are able.

Norm- and criterion-referenced assessment: Let's get it straight

Although norm- and criterion-referenced assessment are logically different, there is still room for confusion, which we try to dispel with some exercises.

Some important concepts in assessment

We present a list of concepts that are important in thinking about and implementing constructive alignment. Authentic assessment directly engages the student with functioning knowledge in its context, decontextualized assessment is more suitable for declarative knowledge. While formative feedback often should be analytic by informing students how well they are managing different aspects of the task, the summative judgment should be of the whole, not the sum of its parts. Open-ended assessment tasks allow for unintended and divergent outcomes, and students themselves need to be involved in the various stages of assessment, in both peer- and self-assessment.

Reliability and validity

Measurement modelists accuse qualitative assessment methods of being 'subjective' and 'unreliable'. What they fail to recognize is that reliability and validity are not the exclusive domains of number crunchers. As the quantitative scaffolding is dismantled, we find that notions as to reliability and validity depended more and more on the teacher's basic professional responsibility, which is to make judgments about the quality of learning.

Further reading

Dart, B. and Boulton-Lewis, G. (eds) (1998) *Teaching and Learning in Higher Education.* Camberwell: Australian Council for Educational Research.

Moss, P.A. (1994) Can there be validity without reliability?, *Educational Researcher,* 23, 2: 5–12.

Taylor, C. (1994) Assessment for measurement or standards: The peril and promise of large scale assessment reform, *American Educational Research Journal,* 31: 231–62.

Torrance, H. (ed.) (1994) *Evaluating Authentic Assessment: Problems and Possibilities in New Approaches to Assessment.* Buckingham: Open University Press.

The Taylor and Moss articles are seminal, outlining the principles of the rethink on assessment, where the criteria that are qualitatively defined are included. Taylor traces the historical and conceptual roots of NRA and CRA, clearly outlining where the confusions in current practice have crept in, while Moss goes into the conceptual issues in terms of assessment theory. Torrance's book contains some commentaries on the new approach. Dart and Boulton-Lewis contains chapters by Boulton-Lewis, Dart, and Hattie and Purdie, which specifically deal with SOLO as a conceptual structure for holistic assessment.

Websites

University of Melbourne, see especially the Assessment in Australian Universities project: www.cshe.unimelb.edu.au/assessinglearning

The Higher Education Academy: www.heacademy.ac.uk/default.htm

Oxford Brookes University: www.brookes.ac.uk/services/ocsd/2_learntch/2_learnt.html

The Hong Kong Polytechnic University's Assessment project, see especially the Assessment Resource Centre: www.assessment.edc.polyu.edu.hk/

Queensland University of Technology: www.tedi.uq.edu.au/teaching/index.html. Click 'Assessment' and choose your topic.

10

Assessing and grading declarative knowledge

In this chapter, we discuss designing assessment tasks for intended learning outcomes relating to declarative knowledge, and grading students' performance. Assessing declarative knowledge is overwhelmingly by the written essay, under either invigilated or open conditions, and by multiple-choice testing. The latter has its uses for assessment but typically the MCQ addresses only low-level outcomes. We look at the ordered-outcome item, which is an objective format that aims to assess high level ILOs. An important problem in grading the written essay format is its unreliability. We discuss eliminating halo effects and other sources of unreliability and suggest the use of assessment criteria, or rubrics, to use in both the analytic and the holistic assessment of extended prose.

Designing assessment tasks

We now turn to designing assessment tasks that are to be aligned to the learning outcomes we intend to address. An appropriate assessment task (AT) should tell us how well a given student has achieved the ILO(s) it is meant to address and/or how well the task itself has been performed. Assessment tasks should also *support* student learning, not sidetrack students, as do some traditional assessment tasks, into adopting low-level strategies such as memorizing, question spotting and other dodges. The backwash must, in other words, be positive, not negative. It will be positive if alignment is achieved because then, as we saw in the previous chapter, the assessment tasks require students to perform what the ILOs specify as intended for them to learn.

In designing appropriate assessment tasks, the following need to be taken into account:

1 The criteria for the different grades, assigned to describe how well the assessment tasks have been performed, should be clearly outlined as

rubrics that the students fully understand. These rubrics act as signposts to students for preparing for assessment – for examples, see Tables 10.2 (p. 210) and 10.4 (p. 214). After assessment, students can compare their actual grade with the criteria for higher grades and thus reflect on why their actual grade may not have been as high as they would have liked. They wouldn't have the faintest idea of the quality of their actual performance if they received a norm-referenced grade such as 'You were in the 60–70% range.'

2   One assessment task may address several ILOs. One AT per ILO can easily lead to an overload of assessment for the student. *Synoptic* assessment is where a large task addresses several ILOs and may even be used to assess ILOs in different courses, as in a research project or a capstone project. We deal with these modes of assessment in the next chapter. One final exam is traditionally used synoptically, but this is likely to be effective only when the ILOs are all declarative and all the students are Susans.

3   By the same token, one ILO may be addressed by more than one assessment task. For example, an assignment and a reflective diary may each have something to say about an ILO 'reflect and improve'. It helps to see each AT as a *source of evidence* of a student's achievement of any ILO. You can have one source of evidence or several, just as in (2) in this list, one task may provide evidence relating to more than one ILO.

4   In selecting assessment tasks, the time spent by students performing them and by staff assessing students' performances, should reflect the relative importance of the ILOs. This is frequently breached when there are compulsory final examinations ('70% of the final grade must be by final examination'). In this case, most of the assessment is likely to be focusing on ILOs addressing only declarative knowledge ('describe', 'explain', 'argue'), while more important ILOs that can't be easily assessed in the exam situation ('apply', 'design', for example) are assessed by tasks worth only 30% of the final grade.

5   An important practical point is that the assessment tasks have to be *manageable*, both by students in terms of both time and resources in performing them and by staff in assessing students' performances. For example, a portfolio would be impracticable in a large class.

These principles apply to ILOs addressing both declarative and functioning knowledge. Table 10.1 (p. 197) gives lists of typical verbs at different SOLO levels illustrating each of declarative and functioning knowledge.

For the rest of this chapter, we focus on declarative knowledge verbs (in the left-hand column), and in the next, we address some illustrative functioning knowledge verbs.

Table 10.1 Some typical declarative and functioning knowledge verbs by SOLO level

	Declarative knowledge	*Functioning knowledge*
Unistructural	Memorize, identify, recite	Count, match, order
Multistructural	Describe, classify	Compute, illustrate
Relational	Compare and contrast explain, argue, analyse	Apply, construct, translate, solve near problem, predict within same domain
Extended abstract	Theorize, hypothesize, generalize	Reflect and improve, invent, create, solve unseen problems, predict to unknown domain

Assessing declarative knowledge

Typical declarative ILOs would include: identify, describe, list, explain, argue, compare and contrast. In these, the student is required orally or in writing to say something *about* a topic or body of knowledge, not necessarily to *do* anything with that topic. There are two main formats of assessment addressing these ILOs: questions that probe the student's knowledge base, to which students write extended prose in answer; and objective format, usually in the form of the MCQ.

How important is the format of assessment? In a word: very. Different formats produce typical forms of backwash. In preparing for exams, students use memorization-related activities, assignments application-related activities (Tang 1991). Tang found that an assignment required deep learning from the students with respect to one topic; the exam required acquaintance with a range of topics, which allowed a high degree of surface learning. The teachers concerned realized the assignment better addressed their ILOs, but only with respect to one topic. They accordingly adopted a policy to use both: short answer exams to ensure coverage, the assignment to ensure depth.

As for MCQs, students see them as requiring low cognitive-level processes and so they avoid a deep approach when studying for them, while they see essays as requiring higher level processes and so use them (Scouller 1996, 1998). Some students were actually angry at being assessed by MCQs, feeling they did not do justice to their learning (see Box 10.1).

So format is important. The lesson so far is that MCQs address lower order ILOs containing verbs such as 'memorize', 'recognize', 'identify', 'match' and essays have a better potential for assessing higher levels of declarative ILOs such as 'explain', 'argue', 'analyse' and 'compare and contrast'.

Let us deal first with what is the most common format for assessing declarative knowledge, essay-type answers to specific questions, first in invigilated situations – the typical exam – and then in open situations, such as the assignment.

Box 10.1   Two examples of students' views on multiple-choice tests

I preferred MCQ . . . It was just a matter of learning facts . . . and no real analysis or critique was required, which I find tedious if I am not wrapped in the topic. I also dislike structuring and writing and would prefer to have the answer to a question there in front of me somewhere.

A multiple choice exam tends to examine too briefly a topic or provide overly complex situations which leave a student confused and faced with "eenie, meenie, minie, mo" situation. It is cheap and, in my opinion, ineffectual in assessing a student's academic abilities in the related subject area.

Source: Scouller (1997)

Assessment under timed invigilation: 'Exam conditions'

The major reasons for the ubiquity of the standard 'exam' have less to do with assessment theory as with management issues. Because the situation of invigilating students in a timed context effectively minimizes plagiarism, many universities require a percentage at least of the summative assessment leading to a student's final grade to be assessed in this situation (we deal with the question of plagiarism later; pp. 240–3).

Assessment in this context is quite extraordinary when you think about it. It is about the only situation, outside TV quiz shows, when somebody is asked to write answers to questions to which the person who asked the questions already knows the answers! Nobody is telling anything new to anybody. This is not what good communication is about, which implies that new information is conveyed. Such assessment is hardly in keeping with a graduate attribute requiring communication skills.

However, there is a place for such convergent assessment in order to check the depth and accuracy of students' knowledge. No, of course we can't ask all the questions that would tap the sum total of a student's knowledge, but we can sample areas of it. It is a little like shooting fish in muddy water and concluding that the number of fish you hit is an indication of how many fish are there. Not a very edifying metaphor for student assessment, but as shooting fish with pointed questions is so entrenched as to be inevitable, let us go along with that for a while. That same metaphor does, however, remind us that we should also be thinking of complementary formats of assessment that are open to considering evidence that we ourselves had not thought of. For example, portfolio assessment allows students to tell us what they consider to be evidence for their learning in relation to the ILOs and that they would like us to consider.

But apart from all those missed fish, it is very *convenient* to have a time and a place nominated for the final assessment. Teachers, students and administration can work around that: everyone knows where they stand. Further, nobody has an 'unfair advantage': all is standardized. But in that case do you allow question choice in a formal examination? Surely. But then you violate the standardization condition, because all candidates are not then sitting the 'same' examination (Brown and Knight 1994). Does that worry you?

It is sometimes claimed that the time constraint reflects 'the need in life to work swiftly, under pressure and well' (Brown and Knight 1994: 69). However, in real-life situations where functioning knowledge is time-stressed – the operating theatre, the bar (in law courts, that is), or the classroom – this point is better accommodated by performance assessment, rather than by pressurizing the assessment of declarative knowledge in the exam room. Alignment suggests that time constraints be applied only when the target performance is itself time constrained.

Time constraint creates its own backwash. Positively, it creates a target for students to work towards. They are forced to review what they have learned throughout the course, and possibly for the first time see it as a whole: a tendency greatly enhanced if they think the exam will require them to demonstrate how holistic their view of the course is and not just a series of easy-to-predict questions about particular topics. The format can be open ended, so theoretically students can express their own constructions and views, supporting them with evidence and original arguments. The reality, however, is often different.

The more likely backwash is negative, with students memorizing specific points to be recalled at speed (Tang 1991). Even so, there are different ways of memorizing: Susan creates a structure first, then memorizes the key access words ('deep memorizing'), while Robert simply memorizes unconnected facts (Tang 1991). So while timed exams encourage memorizing, this is not necessarily *rote* memorizing or surface learning. Whether it is or not depends on the students' typical approaches to learning and on what they expect the exam questions to require.

Open-book examinations remove the premium on memorization of detail, but retain the time constraint. Theoretically, students should be able to think about higher level things than getting the facts down. Baillie and Toohey (1997) moved from a traditional examination in a materials science course to a 'power test' – an open-book exam, with opportunities for collegial interaction – with positive results on students' approaches to learning. Students need, however, to be very well organized and selective about what they bring in, otherwise they waste time tracking down too many sources.

Does the time constraint impede divergent responses? Originality is a temperamental horse, unlikely to gallop under the stopwatch or to flourish in the climate of a stern regimented silence. One needs only to compare the quality of a term assignment with that of an exam response on the same topic to see that difference. In our experience, Susans excepted, exam texts are dull, crabbed and cloned; most students focus on the same content to memorize and use the same examples as given in class or in the text. And isn't it so boring for us to be told over and over what we know already? The assignments of the same students, contrariwise, are often fresh, frequently telling us something we didn't know before, and sometimes even appear to have been written with pleasure.

It is possible for students to display originality in examinations – especially if they can prepare their original answers at leisure. But then they need to know the questions, at least in general outline. You can encourage this high-level off-track preparation by making it known you intend asking open questions ('What is the most important topic you studied in the course this semester? Why?') or by telling the students at the beginning of the semester what the exam questions will be – but then, of course, they have to be complex questions, open to different interpretations and this strategy is open to the criticism that it could encourage plagiarism and memorization of the plagiarized source. Assessing divergent responses cannot be achieved by using a model-answer checklist, because it does not allow for the well-argued surprise.

In short, while the exam can elicit high-level responding from Susan, Robert underperforms in the timed, invigilated setting, especially when he knows that he can get by with memorization. As we shall see in the section on assessing in large classes (pp. 232–8), there are better ways of using that invigilated space than asking for written answers to closed questions. When universities require a proportion of invigilated assessment in the final grade, it is all the more important that alternatives to the closed-answer format are used.

Exams are almost always teacher assessed, but need not be. The questions can be set in consultation with students, while the assessing and awarding of grades can be done by the students themselves and/or their peers. Boud (1986) describes a conventional mid-session examination, where students in an electrical engineering course were, after the examination, provided with a paper of an unnamed fellow student and a detailed model answer and asked to mark it. They then did the same to their own paper, without knowing what marks someone else might have given it. If the self- and peer-assessed marks were within 10%, the self-mark was given. If the discrepancy was greater than 10%, the lecturer remarked the script. Spot checking was needed to discourage collusion ('Let's all agree to mark high!'). Student learning was greatly enhanced, as the students had access to the ideal answer, to their own match to that and the perspective of someone else on the question – and teacher marking time was slashed by nearly a third.

Oral assessments

Oral assessments have something in common with an invigilated situation. They are used most commonly in the examination of dissertations and theses. In the last case, the student constructs a thesis that has to be defended against expert criticism. These oral defences are most frequently evaluated holistically and qualitatively. The components of the dissertation, such as literature review, methodology and referencing, are usually not examined analytically but are treated as hurdles that have to be cleared before the assessment itself proceeds. The interview is not used in undergraduate assessment as widely as it might be. A properly constructed interview schedule could see a fruitful interview through in 20 minutes or so, while carefully run group interviews could deal with four or five students at a time. Interviews are not necessarily as time consuming as they appear to be and they are even more plagiarism proof than an invigilated exam.

Unstructured interviews can be unreliable, but a major advantage of interviewing, that it is interactive, is lost if the interview is too tightly structured. Teachers are able to follow up and probe and students to display their jade, pearls and opals – their unanticipated but valuable learning treasures. Oral assessments should be tape recorded so that the assessment itself may be made under less pressure, and the original assessment can be checked in case of dispute when student and an adjudicator can hear the replay.

Assessing extended prose under open conditions

Assessing extended prose written under non-invigilated conditions, such as assignments, raises some important questions. Many years ago, Starch and Elliott (1912; Starch, 1913a, 1913b) originated a devastating series of investigations into the reliability of assessing essays. Marks for the same essay ranged from bare pass to nearly full marks. Sixty years later, Diederich (1974) found things just as bad. Out of the 300 papers he received in one project, 101 received every grade from 1 to 9 on his nine-point marking scale.

The problem was that the judges were not using the same criteria. Diederich isolated four families of criteria:

- *ideas*: originality, relevance, logic
- *skills*: the mechanics of writing, spelling, punctuation, grammar
- *organization*: format, presentation, literature review
- *personal style*: flair.

However, different judges disagreed about their relative importance, some applying all the criteria, others applying one or few.

Maximizing stable essay assessment

The horrendous results reported by Starch and Elliott and by Diederich occurred because the criteria were unclear, unrecognized or not agreed on. There should have been some kind of moderation procedure, where teachers need collectively to clarify what they really are looking for when assessing different tasks and use an agreed set of criteria or rubrics. The reliability of their interpretations of the criteria by each may be tested by assessing a sample of the same scripts and repeating this procedure until they reach a high degree of consensus, say of the order of 90% within a range, say, of ± 1 grade. The criteria not only need to be used, the levels of acceptability (A to F) in meeting the criteria need to be defined. 'Ideas', for example, has three subscales: originality, relevance and logic. How do you define an 'A' level of originality? A 'B' level? Table 10.2 (p. 210) gives an example of a set of rubrics for marking an assignment on arguing a case.

Halo effects are a common source of unreliability. Regrettable it may be, but we tend to judge the performance of students we like more favourably than those we don't like. Halo effects also occur in the order in which essays are assessed. The first half-dozen scripts tend to set the standard for the next half-dozen, which in turn reset the standard for the next. A moderately good essay following a run of poor ones tends to be assessed higher than it deserves, but if this same essay follows a run of very good ones, it is assessed at a lower level than it deserves (Hales and Tokar 1975).

Halo and other distortions can be greatly minimized by discussion. There is some really strange thinking on this. A common belief is that it is more 'objective' if judges rate students' work without discussing it. In one fine arts department, a panel of teachers independently awarded grades without discussion, the student's final grade being the undiscussed average. The rationale for this bizarre procedure was the postmodern argument that the works of an artist cannot be judged against outside standards. Where this leaves the assessment process itself is a thought to ponder.

Disagreement between external examiners for research dissertations is best resolved by discussion before the higher degrees committee adjudicates, but this is comparatively rare in our experience. Such disagreements are more commonly resolved quantitatively: by counting heads or by hauling in additional examiners until the required majority is obtained. In one university, such conflicts were until recently resolved by a vote in senate. The fact that the great majority of senate members hadn't even seen the thesis aided their detachment, their objectivity unclouded by mere knowledge.

Once the criteria or rubrics for assessment have been decided (see Table 10.2 for an argue-a-case assignment), the moderation procedures just mentioned should be implemented, whereby all assessors agree on the interpretation and application of the rubrics. The following additional precautions in any summative criterion-referenced assessment procedure suggest themselves:

- Before the assessment itself, the wording of the questions should be checked for ambiguity and clarity by a colleague.
- All assessment should be 'blind', the identity of the student concealed.
- All rechecking should likewise be blind, the original assessment concealed.
- Each question should be assessed across students, so that a standard for each question is set. Assessing by the student rather than by the question allows more room for halo effects, a high or low assessment on

one question influencing judgment on the student's answers to other questions. Criterion-referenced and outcomes-based assessment refers to performances, not to students.

- Between questions, the papers should be shuffled to prevent systematic order effects.
- Grade into the full letter grades, A, B, C, and D first, then discriminate more finely into A+, A, A– etc.
- Recheck borderline cases.

Objective formats of assessment

The objective test is a closed or convergent format requiring one correct answer. It is said, misleadingly, to relieve the marker of 'subjectivity' in judgment. But 'judgment' won't go away. In objective tests, judgment is shifted from scoring items to choosing items and to designating which alternatives are correct. Objective testing is not more 'scientific' nor is it less prone to error. The potential for error is pushed to the front end, in producing items that can address higher order ILOs, which is difficult and time consuming to do properly – and doing it properly includes pilot testing items. The advantage is that the cost benefits rapidly increase the more students are tested at a time. With machine scoring, it is as easy to test 1020 students as it is to test 20: a seductive option.

There are many forms of the objective test: true–false, multiple choice (MCQ), matching items from two lists and ordered outcome. We consider the MCQ and its lookalike, but very different, ordered-outcome format.

Multiple-choice questions

The MCQ is widely used. Theoretically, it can assess high-level verbs, but practically they rarely do. As we saw, some students look back in anger at the MCQ for not doing so (see Box 10.1, p. 198).

MCQs assess declarative knowledge, usually in terms of the least demanding cognitive process, recognition. But probably their worst feature is that MCQs encourage the use of game-playing strategies, by both student and teacher:

Student strategies
1 In a four-alternative MC format, never choose the facetious or obviously jargon-ridden alternatives.
2 By elimination, you can usually reduce to a binary choice, with the pig ignorant having a 50% chance of being correct.
3 Does one alternative stimulate a faint glow of recognition in an otherwise unrelieved darkness? Go for it.
4 Longer alternatives are not a bad bet.

Teacher strategies

1   Student strategies are discouraged by a guessing penalty: that is, deducting wrong responses from the total score. (Question: Why should this be counterproductive?)
2   The use of facetious alternatives is patronizing if not offensive (I-can-play-games-with-you-but-you-can't-with-me). Not nice.
3   You can reword existing items when you run out of ideas: it also increases reliability (if you want that sort of reliability: see p. 188).

MCQs allow enormous coverage (that 'enemy of understanding', Gardner 1993). One hundred items can cover a huge range of topics. Exclusive use of the MCQ greatly misleads as to the nature of knowledge, because the method of scoring makes the idea contained in any one item the same value as that in any other item (see Box 10.2).

The message is clear. Get a nodding acquaintance with as many details as you can, but do not be so foolish as to waste your time by attempting to learn anything in depth.

MCQs can be useful as a minor supplement to other forms of assessment and for quick quizzes. Eric Mazur used them as a TLA, publicly displaying the range of responses and getting their students to discuss them (p. 111). Their potential for wide coverage means items can address anything dealt with in class: they are therefore useful in encouraging class attendance.

When used exclusively, however, they send all the wrong signals.

Box 10.2   What do you remember of Thomas Jefferson?

An MCQ was given to fifth-grade children on the 200th anniversary of the signing of the US Constitution. The only item on the test referring to Thomas Jefferson was: 'Who was the signer of the Constitution who had six children?' A year later, Lohman asked a child in this class what she remembered of Thomas Jefferson. She remembered that he was the one with six children, nothing of his role in the Constitution.
   What else did this girl learn?

There is no need to separate main ideas from details; all are worth one point. And there is no need to assemble these ideas into a coherent summary or to integrate them with anything else because that is not required.

Source: Lohman (1993: 19)

Ordered-outcome items

An ordered-outcome item looks like an item from an MCQ, but instead of opting for the one correct alternative out of the four or so provided, the student is required to attempt all sub-items (Masters 1987). The sub-items are ordered into a hierarchy of complexity that reflects successive stages of learning that concept or skill. The students ascend the sequence as far as they can, thus indicating their level of competence in that topic.

The stem provides sufficient information for a range of questions of increasing complexity to be asked. In the given example, devised by one of the authors (CT), the SOLO taxonomy was used as a guide to the levels of complexity: (a) is declarative unistructural, (b) and (c) are increasingly complex declarative relational and (d) addresses functioning knowledge at a relational level. The levels do not need to correspond to each SOLO level or to SOLO levels at all; here, SOLO is simply a way of helping structure increasingly high level responses that *make sense* in the particular context.

Key situations can be displayed in this format and a (d) or (c) level of performance required (in the example in Box 10.3, anything less would not be of much help to patients).

Box 10.3   An ordered-outcome item for physiotherapy students

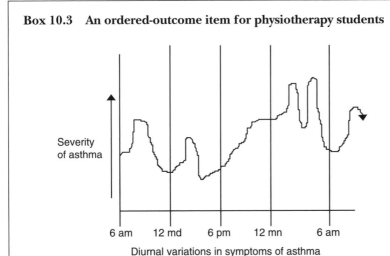

Severity of asthma

6 am   12 md   6 pm   12 mn   6 am

Diurnal variations in symptoms of asthma

a   When is the asthma attack most severe during the day?
b   Is an asthmatic patient physically fitter at 1 pm or 8 pm?
c   Do you expect an asthmatic patient to sleep well at night? Give your reasons.
d   Advise an asthmatic patient how to cope with diurnal variation in symptoms.

A guide to constructing ordered-outcomes items, using a SOLO sequence, follows:

a   *Unistructural*: Use one obvious piece of information coming directly from the stem. Verbs: 'identify', 'recognize'.

b *Multistructural*: Use two or more discrete and separate pieces of information contained in the stem. Verbs: 'list' and, in this example, 'compare', which is nearer relational.

c *Relational*: Use two or more pieces of information each directly related to an integrated understanding of the information in the stem. Verbs: 'interpret', 'apply'.

d *Extended abstract*: Use an abstract general principle or hypothesis that can be derived from, or suggested by, the information in the stem. It is sometimes possible to use a one-correct-answer format ('Formulate the general case of which the preceding (relational) item is an instance') or to use a divergent short-answer sub-item ('Give an example where (c) – the preceding item – does *not* occur. Why doesn't it?'). Verbs: 'hypothesize', 'design', 'create' (not in Box 10.3 example).

An example from chemistry is given in Box 10.4.

Box 10.4   A chemistry ordered-outcome item

In a space shuttle, the exhaled air from an astronaut is circulated through lithium hydroxide filters to remove carbon dioxide according to the following equation:

$$2LiOH(s) + CO_2(g) \rightarrow Li_2CO_3(s) + H_2O(l)$$

(Relative atomic masses: H = 1.0, Li = 6.9, C = 12.0, O = 16.0, K = 39.0; molar volume of a gas at the temperature and pressure of the space shuttle = 24 dm^3).

a State whether the lithium hydroxide in the filters is in the form of a solid, liquid or gas.
b How much greater is the relative molecular mass of carbon dioxide compared to that of lithium hydroxide?
c Calculate the volume of carbon dioxide that could be absorbed by 1gm of lithium hydroxide.
d Suggest how the spent lithium hydroxide in the filters can be conveniently regenerated after use.

[Solubility data: LiOH (slightly soluble), NaOH (soluble), Li$_2$CO$_3$ (insoluble)]

Source: Holbrook (1996)

In the ordered-outcome item, we are seeing what ILOs, applying to a single situation, a student can meet. The ordered-outcome format sends a strong message to students that higher is better: recognition and simple algorithms won't do. Using this format with mathematics items, Wong (1994) found students operated from theory rather than applying algorithms, while Lake (1999) found an ordered-outcome format in biological sciences led students from the basic skills of data retrieval to the advanced skills of critical analysis.

Using the evidence from ordered-outcome items raises the interesting question of what are we assessing: how well the student meets the ILO, or how well the student performs the task? If the former, then the evidence is there immediately according to what levels the student was able to pass. If the latter, we need to be very careful in constructing ordered-outcome items so that we can achieve one final score at the end. The items need to form a staircase: unistructural items must be easier than multi-; multi- easier than relational; relational easier than extended abstract. This can be tested with trial runs, preferably using the Guttman (1941) scalogram model, or software is available (Masters 1988). Hattie and Purdie (1998) discuss a range of measurement issues involved in the construction and interpretation of ordered-outcome SOLO items.

In scoring ordered-outcome items as a normal test, it is tempting to say (a) gets 1 mark if passed, (b) 2 marks, (c) 3 marks and (d) (let's be generous) 5 marks. We then throw the marks into the pot with all the other test results. While this is convenient, it misleads as to a student's level of understanding. If the score is less than perfect, a nominal understanding of one level could be averaged with a high understanding of another, yielding 'moderate' understanding across all levels, which was not the case at all.

Alternatively, we could say that as the items are for all practical purposes perfectly ordered, the final score is the highest level addressed, as all the preceding levels may be presumed to have been passed.

For those who are interested to try out some ordered-outcome items, you can complete Task 10.1.

This discussion of ordered-outcome items has raised two major issues:

1 Do we assess how well each ILO has been addressed or how well the task has been performed?
2 Do we assess quantitatively or qualitatively?

Let us turn to these two questions.

Assessing the task

Do you assess and grade the ILO or the task? The obvious answer in outcomes-based teaching and learning is that you assess how well each ILO has been addressed. But that is not what teachers are used to doing or what students are used to receiving as assessment results. Teachers assess the work that students do, the tasks they perform, whether they are exam questions, lab reports, assignments, final-year projects or whatever. Students for their part want to know how well they did in the exam, in their lab report, in their assignment or in their final-year project.

When each ILO is assessed by only one assessment task, there is no problem: assessing the task and assessing the ILO amount to the same thing. It is

---

Task 10.1   Writing ordered-outcome items

Try the following steps to write some ordered-outcome items for your course.

1 Identify the content area and the ILOs that you expect your students to achieve with that content area.

Content area: _____

ILOs : _____

_____

_____

_____

2 Design the stem to provide adequate information for the students to answer the range of questions. The stem could be in the form of written information, a diagram, a chart or any other form of presentation.

_____

_____

_____

3 Now design four or five questions that the students need to answer based on the information given in the stem. These questions should be of increasing complexity of the ILOs. Double-check if the answers to the questions do reflect the successive stages of learning of the concept or skill as indicated in the ILOs.

_____

_____

_____

_____

_____

4 Now decide how you are going to score the items.

---

only when there are several tasks that might address one ILO or when one task addresses several ILOs that the question arises. Sometimes the task itself is so important that it is an ILO. 'Write a laboratory report' is an example: keeping proper records of laboratory procedures is an intended outcome in itself. Usually, however, assessment tasks are a means, not an end: 'pass the examination' is not an intended learning outcome in itself but a means by which we can assess whether particular learnings have occurred or not.

It could be argued that since the assessment tasks have been aligned to one or more ILOs, that is good enough: alignment is present and so we assess the task, as we have always done. However, where there is more than one task relevant to any given ILO, we would not then know what contribution each task made to that ILO; and where one task addresses several ILOs, assessing the task doesn't give much idea of how well a student has met any particular ILO.

Several positions may be taken:

1 The task is assessed quantitatively, or 'marked', in the traditional way; that is, ratings or percentages are given in the way they always have been. Some teachers feel that this is already adequate for their particular subjects and will continue to assess this way, Chapter 9 notwithstanding. This is a minimally acceptable position, as alignment is present.
2 The task is assessed qualitatively by using rubrics (see Table 10.2), and converted to percentage points for obtaining the final grade for a task or for a course.
3 The task is assessed holistically and graded directly.

Point 1 is standard practice, and nothing further need be said about that. We do, however, need to say more about points 2 and 3.

Assessing qualitatively but reporting quantitatively

Table 10.2 gives an example of point 2, assessing qualitatively and converting to a quantitative scale, for an assignment in which a case is argued, evidence for and against is marshalled, a conclusion is reached and a letter grade from F to A is to be given.

You may notice that the general structure from D to A is in terms of SOLO as applied to the four components of introduction, argument, conclusions and references. Each component is assigned a range of points or marks, weighted so that the argument, the most important component, is allocated most points. Note that the gap between grades is greater than the gap between levels within grades, to emphasize that achieving a grade is more important than achieving a fine grade within grades. Thus, a grade is first awarded according to the rubrics, after which the conversion to a number is made. The task, in other words, is graded, not 'marked'; the conversion to marks is only for administrative purposes. (And notice: we used the term 'points', not 'marks'.)

For example, let us say the introduction in one case describes the topic, refers to past work with some passing evaluation of it but then goes on to state the present case, with no logical progression to the topic. This meets the C criteria, hinting at a B–, so let us say C+, or seven points. Each component is then assessed in this way and totalled. Table 10.3 (p. 211) gives a range of percentage points for a letter grade.

Say a student scored 67 for this assessment task. This is closest to a B (Table 10.3), so B it is. The second row in Table 10.3 is for arriving at the final GPA for a student for the year. The mean percentage points over all courses is calculated and converted to a typical GPA-type scale. All this is fairly arbitrary, but then using numbers in this way always is. Numbers just happen to

Table 10.2 Grading criteria (rubrics) for an argue-a-case assignment

Percentage points	D *1–3*	C– C C+ *5–7*	B– B B+ *9–11*	A– A A+ *13–15*
Introduction 15	Gives enough to tell what the topic is but little prioritizing 5–20	Describes topic, refers to past work, what is proposed to do here 24–28	As in C, but shows what past work has done/not done; logical progression to topic 32–38	Interesting and complex account of why this topic, what questions need to be addressed, foretaste of original contribution 42–50
Argument 50	Some relevant points in descriptive lists, mainly either pro or con 2–4	More relevant points drawn from literature, lists both pros and cons, but has difficulty in making a convincing case 7–10	Most/all relevant points from mainstream literature; uses appropriate structure to resolve issues in convincing argument 13–17	As in B, but makes an original case in own voice, well supported by resources/references going well beyond the mainstream literature 18–20
Summary and conclusions 20	Summary is a list of either pros or cons leading to a lopsided conclusion 1–3	Summary recognizes differences but unable to resolve them, weak conclusion or jumps to conclusion 5–7	Summary is balanced leading to well-reasoned conclusion 9–11	Summary leads to a surprise or original conclusion generating new issues 13–15
References 15	Sparse; little evidence of library skills Incorrect formatting 1–3	Evidence of some search skills Standard references in mostly correct formatting 5–7	Comprehensive, showing care in researching the issue, format correct and clear 9–11	As in B, but uses unusual references to bolster an original argument Formatting as in B 13–15

Table 10.3   Conversions between percentage points, letter grades and GPA

Fail	D	C–	C	C+	B–	B	B+	A–	A	A+
> 45	46–50	52	55	60	65	68	70	75	80	80+
For GPA	1.0	1.7	2.0	2.3	2.7	3.0	3.3	3.7	4.0	4.3

be very convenient for determining final results over a number of tasks or a number of courses.

Holistic grading

Now let us look at the alternative: holistic grading of the task. The argument is that assessment tasks are best assessed as a whole, not as a set of components. The unique benefit of the essay assignment, for example, is to see if students can construct their response to a question or issue within the framework set by the question. The point of the essay is to see how appropriately structured the response is. But there are traps for the unwary teacher. Using an analytic marking scheme, it is very hard not to award high marks, when in fact the student hasn't even addressed the question (see Box 10.5).

Box 10.5   A warning from an ancient history essay

Question: In what ways were the reigns of Tutenkhmen and Akhnaton alike and in what ways were they different?

The student who obtained the highest marks in the class listed the life histories of both pharoahs and was commended by the teacher for her effort and depth of research. But her lists didn't answer the question, which required a compare-and-contrast structure.

Source: Biggs (1987b)

The ancient history teacher failed to distinguish between 'knowledge telling' and 'reflective writing' (Bereiter and Scardamalia 1987). Knowledge telling is a multistructural strategy that can all too easily mislead those assessing the essay. Students tell all they know about the topic content by listing in a point-by-point form. When marking bottom-up, as is so often done by tutors using a common template for a marking scheme, it is very hard not to award high marks for knowledge telling when in fact the student hasn't properly addressed the question.

Reflective writing, on the other hand, transforms the writer's thinking. The novelist E.M. Forster put it thus: 'How can I know what I think until I see what I say?' The act of writing externalizes thought, making it possible to unleash a learning process. By reflecting on what is written, it can be revised in so many ways, creating something quite new, even to the writer. That is what the best academic writing does.

Reflective writing is clearly what the essay should be used for, not knowledge telling. Tynjala (1998) suggests that writing tasks should require students to transform their knowledge actively, not simply to repeat it. The writing should require students to undertake open-ended activities that make use of existing knowledge and beliefs, that lead them to question and reflect on that knowledge and to theorize about their experiences and to apply theory to practical situations, and/or to solve practical problems or problems of understanding. Tynjala gave students such writing tasks, which they discussed in groups. When compared with students who did not do these tasks, the reflective writers had the same level of knowledge as the other students but were far better than the latter in the *use* to which they could put their thinking.

Assessing the discourse structure of the essay requires a framework within which that structure can be judged. SOLO helps in making that judgment. Listing, describing, narrating are multistructural structures; compare and contrast, causal explanation, interpretation, and here, arguing a case, are relational. Inventive students create their own structures, which when they work can make original contributions: these are extended abstract. The facts and details play their role in these structures in like manner to the characters in a play. And the play's the thing. You do not ignore details, but ask of them:

- Do they make a coherent structure (not necessarily the one you had in mind)? If yes, the essay is at least relational.
- Is the structure the writer uses appropriate or not? If yes, then the question has been properly addressed (relational). If no, you will have to decide how far short of satisfactory it is.
- Does the writer's structure open out new ways of looking at the issue? If yes, the essay is extended abstract.

If the answer is consistently 'no' to all of these questions, the essay is multistructural or less and should not be rated highly, no matter how rich the detail. If you want students to 'identify' or 'list', the short answer or MCQ are more appropriate formats, as easier for the student to complete and for the teacher to assess. It may be appropriate to award the grades on this basis: D (bare multistructural), C– to C+ (increasingly better multistructural, hints of relational), B– to B+ (relational), A– to A+ (extended abstract). Each grade is qualitatively different from the next, but within each grade, one can use the '+' and '–' modifiers for a bare C or an excellent C. Table 10.3 (p. 211) can be used to convert the letter grade to a number for collating purposes and for calculating GPA.

The essay assignment can be a powerful tool for learning as well as an assessment task. If it is not used for the purpose of reflective writing, thus addressing ILOs with higher relational and extended abstract verbs, it is simpler to use a listing format.

Assessing the intended learning outcome

The alternative to assessing the task is to use the evidence supplied by the assessment tasks to assess each student's performance with respect to each ILO. The argument here is that since the ILOs are statements of what the student is intended to learn, it makes most sense to report the results of the assessments in terms of the ILOs for each course rather than for the assessment tasks themselves. Again, if there is only one AT per ILO, there is no issue, but where there are several the question becomes: 'What does the available evidence say about this student's performance on the ILO in question?'

Having said that, it is not, of course, a good idea to multiply assessment tasks – we need to watch both our workload and the students' – but frequently an AT that is set primarily to address a particular ILO often has something to say about a student's performance on another ILO. For example, a common verb like 'explain' a particular concept or 'be able to communicate' may be evidenced in an examination and again in an assignment. Do we ignore the evidence from a secondary AT or do we incorporate it in our assessment of how well the student has met the ILO?

Assessing by ILO cannot meaningfully be performed quantitatively, that is by 'marking' the ILO. It is a question of what the evidence from the assessment tasks says about how well the ILO has been achieved by a given student, which has to be a matter of *judgment*. In order to keep our own judgments stable, and in order to obtain maximum reliability between teachers making these judgments, rubrics need to be spelled out clearly. Table 10.4 gives a sample set of rubrics for the verb 'explain' although, of course, these will need to be adjusted according to what is being explained and in what context.

Here, we moved straight from whatever evidence is available to making a graded judgment of how well the student addresses the ILO itself. This could be used as formative feedback to the student or summatively. If the latter, as this is only one ILO out of five or so for a given course, we will need to state a final grade for that course and to calculate a student's GPA. The 'scale score' is actually taken from one university's conversion from grade to GPA-type scale: notice that again as in Table 10.2 (p. 210), the gap between grades is greater than the gap within grades in terms of scale score. When the final result has been calculated, we can convert to GPA score using Table 10.3 (p. 211), as before. It would in fact be most meaningful if on the student's transcript all the assessments of all the course ILOs were retained rather than overall GPA.

In practice, students at present want to know 'How did I do on that midterm assignment?' rather than 'How did I do on the "explain" ILO?' To some extent, then, it will be necessary to assess both the task itself to give student feedback, as well as the ILOs it may address. In time, however, when students and the public generally become used to outcomes-based teaching and learning it may well be that a profile of grades on the ILOs will become perfectly meaningful to all.

Table 10.4 Example of criteria (rubrics) for grading an ILO

	Marginal	Adequate			Good			Excellent		
	D	G−	C	C+	B−	B	B+	A−	A	A+
Scale score	1.0	1.7	2.0	2.3	2.7	3.0	3.3	3.7	4.0	4.3
ILO Explain	Able to identify and briefly write about limited points Very little evidence of using these points to provide reasoning to why they are interrelated	Able to identify a number of relevant points with some details Use these points to provide a fair reasoning or causality No evidence of a comprehensive overview of reasoning or causality			Able to identify a full range of relevant points with details Supported by relevant literature Points are organized to provide a comprehensive and cohesive reasoning or causality			As in 'good' but provides views on possible alternative causes and/or results depending on changes of conditions Able to link current reasoning to situations in real-life professional contexts		

Before we end this chapter, Task 10.2 is an exercise on designing assessment tasks for declarative knowledge of your course.

Task 10.2   Design an assessment task or tasks for one of your course ILOs

Select one ILO relating to declarative knowledge of your course and design assessment task(s) that will appropriately assess this ILO. To help you check the alignment between the task(s) and the ILO, identify what the students are required to do in order to complete the assessment task(s). The task requirements should be aligned to the ILO.

Course ILO: _____

Number of students in the course:

Assessment task	Student activities to complete the task
1	
2	

Now double-check if the student activities are aligned to the verb(s) nominated in the respective course ILO.

After designing the task(s), you will need to write the grading criteria for either the ILO or for each of the tasks.

Summary and conclusions

Designing assessment tasks

In designing assessment tasks there are several things to bear in mind. Clear assessment criteria or rubrics need to be established for each task or for the ILO(s) each AT is meant to address. It is useful to think of ATs as a *source of evidence* of a student's achievement of any ILO. You can have one source of evidence or several, just as one task may provide evidence on more than one ILO, but the ATs have to be *manageable*, both by students in terms of both time and resources in performing them and by staff in assessing students' performances.

Assessing declarative knowledge

Declarative knowledge is typically assessed by writing answers to set questions or in objective formats. Writing is either in the timed and invigilated 'exam' or unrestricted, as in the typical essay assignment. The stress typically felt in the 'exam' situation produces its own distortion in the quality of work done, especially by the Roberts of this world. A particular problem with assessing extended writing is the lack of reliability between assessors. Several suggestions are made to improve this.

Objective formats of assessment

The lack of reliability of assessing essays, plus the time they take to assess, has led many teachers to use objective formats, particularly the MCQ. The major problem with the MCQ, however, is that it is not at all suited to addressing high-level outcomes and that it is prone to encouraging 'strategic' rather than knowledge-driven preparation strategies. An exception is the ordered-outcome format, which encourages students to target higher rather than lower level items.

Assessing the task

Once the AT is aligned to the ILO(s) it is meant to address, the question becomes how, operationally, is the student's performance assessed? Is it assessed against the task or against the ILO(s) the task is meant to address? Teachers and students are used to task assessment and that is what many teachers will continue to do. There are three ways of task assessment: quantitatively, as has been the case traditionally; by assessing the task analytically, addressing the task components using rubrics for each component; or by assessing the task as a whole and grading qualitatively.

Assessing the ILO

The most logical, and operationally the simplest, way of assessing is by using the evidence gained from the various tasks directly to assess the ILO itself, by using rubrics designed for each ILO. The main objection to this method is simply that teachers and students are not yet used to it.

Further reading

Much of the background and enrichment material for this chapter is the same as for the next. Please refer to Chapter 11's further reading section.

11

Assessing and grading functioning knowledge

We now look at aligning assessment tasks to ILOs that address functioning knowledge, and at how they may be graded. Functioning knowledge has particular relevance to professionally related programmes, the assessment of which includes assessing for ILOs for professional problem solving, for creativity and, up to a point, for lifelong learning. We look at a range of assessment formats with special reference to portfolios and capstone projects as these formats allow students to display the full range of their personal learning. Assessment in large classes restricts the range of formats that are practicable, but there are better ways of assessing both declarative and functioning knowledge than cramming large numbers of students into examination halls and relying heavily on MCQs. One of the reasons for invigilating students during assessment is not on grounds of good assessment but to prevent plagiarism. Plagiarism is of increasing concern in today's universities for a variety of reasons. We look at some of the issues here and how plagiarism may be minimized.

Formats for assessing functioning knowledge

Assessing functioning knowledge is in principle much easier than assessing declarative knowledge. Just look at these verbs: 'apply', 'design', 'create', 'solve unseen problem', 'perform a case study', 'reflect and improve' and many others that put knowledge to work. These verbs work as performances of understanding in a context, and in professional faculties, that context is about dealing with real-life professional problems. The assessment in these cases is much more direct than when assessing decontextualized declarative knowledge. How well do the students carry out a case study? Get them to carry out a case study and see how well they do it. How well do the students design a piece of systems software? Get them to design a piece of software and see how well they do it.

Such tasks are, as in real life, often divergent, ill formed or 'fuzzy', in the sense that there are no single correct answers. For example, there are many acceptable ways a software program could be written for use in a real estate office. 'Real life' imposes limitations relating to budget, the costs of a range of materials, time and space and so on, that allow different alternatives. Assessment involves how well the design or creation works within those limitations. What is important is that the student shows a 'real-life' understanding of the situation: how the problem may reasonably be approached, how resources and data are used, how previously taught material is used, how effectively the solution meets likely contingencies and so on. Clearly, this needs open-ended assessment, where students are free to structure their performances as they best see fit.

Various formats may be used for assessing and grading functioning knowledge in terms either of the ILOs addressed or the task itself. As in the case of declarative knowledge, it is a matter of whether the rubrics apply to the task, to the ILO, or to both.

Presentations

Student presentations

As opposed to the traditional seminar, student presentations are best for functioning rather than declarative knowledge. Peer input can be highly appropriate in this case. In one fine arts department, students present a portfolio of their best work to an examining panel that comprises teachers, a prominent local artist and a student (rotating), who view all the student productions. The works are discussed and a final, public, examiners' report is submitted. This is not only a very close approximation to real life in the gallery world, but actively involves staff and students in a way that is rich with learning opportunities.

Poster presentations

Poster presentations also follow a real-life scenario: the conference format. A student, or group of students, displays their work, according to an arranged format, in a departmental or faculty poster session. This provides excellent opportunities for peer-assessment and for fast feedback of results. Poster assessment was introduced as an additional element of the assessment of final-year project in an optometry programme to facilitate and assess reflection and creativity (Cho 2007). Apart from teacher assessing the posters, self- and peer-assessment were also used. To motivate students to do well in the poster assessment, opportunity was given to present the students' posters at a regional conference and a cash reward was awarded to the best poster. Student feedback shows that designing the posters was fun and helped them to be more creative and reflective of what they were doing in the project. The experience of self- and peer-assessment also helped them learn from an assessor's perspective. However, posters 'must be meticulously prepared'

(Brown and Knight 1994: 78). The specifications need to be very clear, down to the size of the display and how to use back-up materials: diagrams, flowcharts, photographs. Text needs to be clear and highly condensed. Assessment criteria can be placed on an assessment sheet, which all students receive to rate all other posters. Criteria would include substance, originality, impact and so on.

Critical incidents

Asking students to keep records of critical incidents in their workplace experience and later to discuss their significance can be very powerful evidence of how well their knowledge is functioning. They might explain why these incidents are critical, how they arose and what might be done about it. This gives rich information about how students (a) have interpreted what they have been taught and (b) can make use of the information.

Such incidents might be the focus of an assessment interview, of a reflective journal or be used as portfolio items (see later).

Individual and group projects

Whereas an assignment usually focuses on declarative knowledge, the project focuses on functioning knowledge applied to a hands-on piece of research. Projects can vary from simple to sophisticated or carried out individually or by a group of students.

Group projects are becoming increasingly common for two major reasons: they aim to teach students cooperative skills, in line with ILOs or graduate attributes relating to teamwork; and the teacher's assessment load is markedly decreased. They are not, however, always popular with students: they often find it difficult to coordinate times; the assessment may not take into account individual contributions, on the one hand, or group processes, on the other; workplace cooperation involves individuals with distinct roles and they may not be assessed individually on their contribution (Morris 2001). The common practice of simply awarding an overall grade for the outcome, which each student receives, fails on all counts.

Group projects need to be used carefully. Peer evaluation of contribution is certainly one way to make them more acceptable, but giving that a miserly 5% towards the final grade is not enough to overcome the problem, as one student, quoted in Morris (2001), put it. Lejk and Wyvill (2001a, 2001b) have carried out a series of studies on assessing group projects, this question of assessing contribution of members being one aspect. They found that self-assessment was not very effective and suggest that the fairest way is to use peer-assessment following an open discussion between students about relative contributions – but the peer-assessment should be conducted in secret, not openly.

Most attempts to assess relative contribution use quantification. A simple version might be to award a global 60%, say, to a particular project. If there are four participants, this means that 240 marks need to be allocated. You may make this allocation, on the basis of interviews with the students, or get them to do it. One problem is that they may decide to divide them equally – some hating themselves as they do so, knowing they are selling themselves short. Lejk and Wyvill use an elaborate matrix where students rate each other on aspects of the task and derive an index for each student, which is used to weight the calculation of the grade of each. The reliability of peer-assessment in assessing group projects is an interesting and neglected issue that is handled by Magin (2001).

A problem with collaborative projects is that individual students too easily focus only on their own specific task, not really understanding the other components or how they contribute to the project as a whole. The idea of a group project is that a complex and worthwhile task can be made manageable, each student taking a section they can handle. However, the tasks should not be divided according to what students are already good at: Mario has read widely, so let him prepare the literature review, Sheila is good at stats so let her do the analysis of results. The problem with this is that little *learning* may take place. We want students to learn things other than what they already know, so a better allocation is that Sheila does the literature review and Mario the stats. This is likely to end up with both helping one another and then everyone learns with some peer teaching thrown in to boot.

Most important, we want the students to know what the whole project is about and how each contribution fits in. To ensure this, an additional holistic assessment is necessary. Students might be required to submit a reflective report, explaining where and how their contribution fits into the project as a whole and explaining how they think they have achieved the ILOs through their participation in the project.

Learning contracts

Contracts replicate a common everyday situation. A learning contract would take into account where an individual is at the beginning of the course, what relevant attainments are possessed already, what work or other experience and then, within the context of the course ILOs, he or she is to produce a needs analysis from which a contract is negotiated: what is to be done and how it is proposed to do it and how it is to be assessed. Individuals, or homogeneous groups of students, would have a tutor to consult throughout and with whom they would have to agree that the contract is met in due course. The assessment problem hasn't gone away, but the advantage is that the assessments are tied down very firmly from the start and the students know where they stand (Stephenson and Laycock 1993).

A more conventional and less complicated learning contract is little different from clear criterion referencing: 'This is what an A requires. If you can prove to me that you can demonstrate those qualities in your learning, then an A is what you will get.' This is basically what is involved in portfolio assessment (see later).

Reflective journal

In professional programmes in particular, it is useful if students keep a reflective journal, in which they record any incidents or thoughts that help them reflect on the content of the course or programme. Such reflection is basic to proper professional functioning. The reflective journal is especially useful for assessing ILOs relating to the application of content knowledge, professional judgment and reflection on past decisions and problem solving with a view to improving them. One teacher told us she had tried journals but found them useless, because the students wrote what was in effect a diary of routine events – which is *not* what a reflective journal should contain. One needs to be very clear about what course or programme ILOs the journals are meant to be addressing. In a course of contact lens clinic in one of the universities in Hong Kong, reflective writing was used as one of the components of assessment to encourage and assess students' reflection during their clinical placement (Cho and Tang 2007). Students were asked to keep reflective diaries on their learning experience from clinical cases, interaction with and feedback from supervisors and peers and application of theory to practice. Students were briefed on this new form of assessment and were also involved in giving suggestions on the design and assessment weighting of reflective diaries. Quantitative and qualitative feedback from students indicated that students found that they learned more because of the reflective component of the assessment, their learning experience was sharpened through the reflective writing. They were motivated to communicate more frequently with their supervisors and peers to critique their own practice and also the application of theory to practice.

Assessing journals can be delicate, as they often contain personal content. For assessment purposes it is a good idea to ask students to submit selections, possibly focusing on critical incidents. Journals should not be 'marked' as a task, but taken as sources of evidence for the ILOs in question, especially useful for the verb 'reflect' to see if the students are able realistically to evaluate their own learning and thinking in terms of course content.

One of the authors used reflective diaries to assess transformative reflection applied to teaching in an inservice masters of education course for tertiary teachers (Tang 2000). As one of the learning activities, students were asked to keep a reflective diary of their learning for every session of the course. They were required to select and include two such diaries as part of their assessment portfolio. Feedback from the students showed that the diaries were a useful tool for transformative reflection, providing them with opportunities to search for and express their learning in a personal way and to relate and apply their learning to their own teaching.

Case study

In some disciplines, a case study is an ideal way of seeing how students can apply their knowledge and professional skills. It could be written up as a project or as an item for a portfolio. Case studies might need to be highly formal and carried out under supervision or be carried out independently by the student. Possibilities are endless.

Assessing the case study is essentially holistic, but aspects can be used both for formative feedback and for summative assessment. For example, there are essential skills in some cases that must be got right, otherwise the patient dies, the bridge collapses or other mayhem ensues. The component skills here could be pass–fail; fail one, fail the lot (with latitude according to the skill and case study in question). Having passed the components, however, the student then has to handle the case itself appropriately and that should be assessed holistically.

Portfolio assessment

Portfolios have long been used in the art world and in job applications: individuals place their best work in a portfolio for judgment. They also need to be wisely selective: dumping in items that do not address the job specifications and qualifications will not impress. Just so, students need to be wisely selective in placing in their portfolios what they think best addresses the ILOs and why. Portfolios allow the student to present and explain his or her best 'learning treasures' and are therefore ideal for assessing unintended outcomes (pp. 185–6). When students give their creativity free rein, portfolios are full of complex and divergent surprises, aligned to the course or programme ILOs in ways that are simply not anticipated by the teacher.

In their explanations for their selection of items, students explain how the evidence they have in their portfolios addresses the course ILOs or indeed their own personal intended aims and outcomes of learning. One danger with portfolios is that students may go overboard, creating excessive workload both for themselves and for the teacher. Limits must be set (see later).

Assessing portfolio items can be deeply interesting. It may be time consuming, but that depends on the nature and number of items. Many items, such as concept maps, can be assessed in a minute or so. In any event, a whole day spent assessing portfolios is existentially preferable to an hour of assessing lookalike assignments.

Following are some suggestions for implementing portfolio assessment:

1 *Make it quite clear in the ILOs what the evidence for good learning may be.* The ILOs to be addressed should be available to the students at the beginning of the semester and discussed with them.

2 *State the requirements for the portfolio:*

- *Number of items.* This depends on the scope of the portfolio, whether it is for assessing one course or several and the size of the items. Four items is about the limit in a semester-long course but that is flexible.
- *Approximate size of each item.* Some items, such as a reflective essay, may reach 2000 words or more, while other items, such as concept maps or other diagrams, require less than a page. A rule of thumb: the total portfolio should not be much longer than a normal project or assignment.
- *A list of sample items* is most helpful when the students are new to portfolios (see Box 11.1) but they should be strongly discouraged from using that list only. Students should show some creativity by going outside the list.
- *Any compulsory items?* This depends on the nature of the course. In most professional courses, a reflective journal is probably a good basis even if only extracts are submitted in the end.
- *Source of items.* Items may be specific to a course or drawn from other courses in the case of evaluating a programme. In some problem-based courses, students will be continually providing inputs, often on a pass–fail basis, over a year, or two years. The final evaluation could then comprise – *in toto* or in part – samples of the best work students think they have done to date.

Box 11.1 Sample items that went into an assessment portfolio in a course for teachers

- Critical incidents from a reflective diary
- Lesson plans, constructed on principles dealt with in class
- Teaching checklists on how teachers may (unconsciously) encourage surface approaches in students as rated by a colleague
- A videotaped peer discussion on teaching with each participant writing up his/her perspective
- Accounts of exemplary teaching/learning experiences and the lessons to be drawn
- Concept maps of the course
- Letter-to-a-friend about the course
- Reviews of articles, self-set essays, to address the declarative ILOs
- A questionnaire on motivation and self-concept

Source: Biggs (1996)

- *Grading the portfolio.* Portfolios are best assessed as a whole (the 'package'), not by marking individual items.

On this last point, if items are graded separately and averaged, the main value of the portfolio is lost: the situation is the same as combining different assessments in the usual way to arrive at a final grade (see p. 209). While each item might address one or more different ILOs, the whole addresses the thrust of the course. The student's selection of items is in effect saying: '*This* is what I got out of your class. I have learned these things, and as a result my thinking has changed in the following ways.' If their package can show that, they have learned well indeed.

Box 11.2 gives a concrete example from a course for educational psychologists at a Hong Kong university; Table 11.1 gives general guidelines for grading a portfolio.

Box 11.2   An example of assessing and grading a portfolio holistically

Curriculum and instruction: A subject in a course for educational psychologists

Grading will be based on your attaining the following ILOs:

1 Apply the principles of good teaching and assessment to chosen contexts.
2 Relate selected aspects of curriculum design and management to the educational system in Hong Kong.
3 Apply the content and experiences in this subject to enhance your effectiveness as an educational psychologist.
4 Show examples of your reflective decision making as an educational psychologist.

Final grades will depend on how well you can demonstrate that you have met all the ILOs (only grades A, B, C and F were awarded):

A Awarded if you have clearly met all the ILOs, provide evidence of original and creative thinking, perhaps going beyond established practice.
B Awarded when all ILOs have been met very well and effectively.
C Awarded when the ILOs have been addressed satisfactorily or where the evidence is strong in some ILOs, weaker but acceptable in others.
F Less than C, work plagiarized, not submitted.

Assessment guidelines

Show evidence that you have learned according to the criteria in the ILOs. Keep a *reflective journal* to record useful insights as you progress through the course. Use as a database. The evidence will be presented in the following forms:

- A *paper*, drawing on principles of curriculum and good teaching, explaining how you would like to see the Hong Kong educational system implement any major educational reforms. You should have ILO (2) in mind.
- A *report* specifically addressing ILOs (3) and (4), a review of those aspects of the course that you think will probably enhance your work as an EP. This can refer both to your way of thinking about your role, as much as to actual skills. Your reflective journal will be an important source for this.
- Your *own rationale* of your group presentation, taking into account the evaluation made at the time of presentation. You should have ILO (1) in mind.
- A *self-evaluation* showing how you have addressed each of the ILOs.

Place these in a portfolio, which will be graded as above. Take 5000 words as a guideline for the complete portfolio.

Handout for students in a masters course for
educational psychologists

Table 11.1 Holistic grading of a portfolio of items

Marginal		*Adequate*			*Good*			*Excellent*	
D		*C–*	*C*	*C+*	*B–*	*B*	*B+*	*A–*	*A*	*A+*
1.0		*1.7*	*2.0*	*2.3*	*2.7*	*3.0*	*3.3*	*3.7*	*4.0*	*4.3*
The pieces of evidence are relevant and accurate, but are isolated, addressing one aspect of the course Demonstration of understanding in a minimally acceptable way Poor coverage, no originality, weak justification of portfolio items		The evidence is relevant, accurate and covers several aspects of the course Little evidence of an overall view of the course Demonstrates declarative understanding of a reasonable amount of content Able to discuss content meaningfully Good coverage but little application or integration Fair justification of items			The evidence presents a good appreciation of the general thrust of the course Good coverage with relevant and accurate support A clear view of how various aspects of the course integrate to form a thrust or purpose Good evidence of application of course content to practice Portfolio items well justified			As in 'good' but with higher degree of originality and evidence of internalization into personalized model of practice Good evidence of reflection on own performance based on theory Generalizes course content to new and unfamiliar real-life contexts		

Notice that the final grade is awarded on the basis of the student's profile on all the ILOs: there is no need for counting and averaging, which greatly simplifies the usual procedure. Because of these points, portfolios are very appropriate for capstone projects (see next section).

For an example of grading a single functional ILO, Table 11.2 presents some rubrics for 'reflect and improve'.

Table 11.2 Grading the ILO 'reflect and improve'

	Marginal	*Adequate*			*Good*			*Excellent*		
	D *1.0*	*C–* *1.7*	*C* *2.0*	*C+* *2.3*	*B–* *2.7*	*B* *3.0*	*B+* *3.3*	*A–* *3.7*	*A* *4.0*	*A+* *4.3*
Reflect	Able to use available information to self-evaluate and identify limited aspects of own strengths and weaknesses in a general sense No evidence of suggestions of ways to improve performance No evidence of theory being used in self-evaluation	Able to use available information to self-evaluate and identify more aspects of own strengths and weaknesses in a general sense Little application of theory in self-evaluation and limited suggestions of ways to improve performance			Able to use available information to self-evaluate and identify the full range of own strengths and weaknesses Self-evaluation is based on theory Increasingly able to suggest ways to improve performance in a specific context			As in 'good' Able to generalize self-evaluation to beyond existing context Suggest ways of improving performance in real-life professional contexts		

Educational technology has enabled the development of e-portfolios with items involving multimedia presentations.

If you are interested in implementing portfolio assessment, try completing Task 11.1.

Capstone or final year projects

Capstone projects are versions of final year projects with the specific intention of addressing programme ILOs that may not have been assessed in individual courses. It is, in fact, a flaw in much programme design that programme ILOs are often seen in practice if not in intention as no more than the sum of individual course ILOs. However, many programme ILOs, 'to make informed professional decisions' for example, may not be addressed by any particular course ILO, but by a combination of several

---

Task 11.1   Design portfolio assessment for functioning knowledge

Have a go at designing portfolio assessment for functioning knowledge for your course by following the following steps:

1 Identify the ILOs relating to functioning knowledge that are to be assessed.
2 Indicate the number of items to be included in the portfolio and the size of each item.
3 Give a list of sample items for students' consideration. However, students should be encouraged to include items outside the list and ones that they think will best evidence their achievement of the course ILOs.
4 Write the grading criteria of the portfolio.

Before you implement the portfolio assessment, discuss with your students so that they clearly understand the rationale, procedural details of the assessment and the grading criteria. It would be helpful if students have access to some samples of portfolios produced by previous students.

ILOs. Many important outcomes – most graduate attributes for example – are not easily teachable in a single semester, but emerge over the years more as a result of 'immersion' than of direct teaching (Knight and Yorke 2004). For this reason, Knight and Yorke recommend that students keep long-term portfolios of their work in which this development may be tracked.

Addressing these broad ILOs, or combinations of ILOs, requires *synoptic* assessment, that is, an assessment that straddles several course ILOs. This is what the capstone project attempts to do. Synoptic assessments enable students to integrate their experiences, providing them with important opportunities to demonstrate their creativity (Jackson 2003). If students' creativity is inhibited by having to address course-specific ILOs throughout their undergraduate career – or if they *feel* it has been inhibited – then they can really let fly in their final year or capstone projects.

The capstone project is thus designed to span several final-year courses or possibly courses over all years, so that students have a chance to show that they can put it all together and use it or, more generally still, to show how they have developed in line with the institution's graduate attributes and of the programme ILOs, which otherwise may never be satisfactorily and holistically assessed. It is particularly well suited to assess those evolving, 'fuzzy' ILOs that are not readily amenable to direct teaching such as lifelong learning and creativity.

Assessing creativity

A deep-seated ambiguity about the nature of creativity and its assessment exists: whether creativity is conceived as generic, applying across contexts, or as embedded in students' chosen *area of specialization*. As when discussing TLAs for creativity, then, we are not assessing here how creative people are, but the creative work that students produce (Elton 2005).

While most teachers in all disciplines believe that it is possible to help students use their creative abilities to better effect, rather fewer think it is possible to assess these capabilities reliably and even fewer are prepared to try and do it. Yet evaluation is critical to the very idea of creativity and creativity is critical in all areas of study.

Let us start with an area where creativity is expected: University College London Slade School BA in Fine Art, Student Handbook 2003/2004 (quoted in Elton 2005). The assessment criteria are as follows:

> You will be assessed on the evidence of ambition, experimentation, innovation and understanding of the subject and its contexts, as developed in the work. Your progress in and development of the following will be taken into account:
>
> * critical awareness;
> * relevant use of processes and materials;
> * the depth and scope of investigation;
> * the ability to realise ideas;
> * contribution to and participation in the course.

'Experimentation and innovation' and 'the ability to realise ideas' imply what creativity psychologists like Guilford (1967) and Hudson (1966) refer to as *originality*: the ability to create something different on a foundation of the known. This can take the form of recombining known elements in a new way or seeing connections between ideas that others have missed. 'Critical awareness' is similar to transformative reflection (p. 43): it looks at what is known with a view to seeing what it might become.

These criteria suggest a sequence, starting with a foundation of solid knowledge, prising it open and generating new possibilities, in a SOLO-type progression from relational to extended abstract. Extended abstract verbs are open ended, such as hypothesize, generate, design, reflect and improve: all are built on prior sound knowledge and they require an object and a context relating to that knowledge. Assessing creativity in this way applies to all disciplines, from accounting to zoology and, accordingly, can be built into course or programme ILOs as appropriate. In higher years, such open-ended assessment should be appropriate whatever the area of study.

Two major conditions apply to assessing creativity:

* The assessment tasks have to be open ended. Invigilated examinations are not good formats for displaying creativity, but portfolios, web pages (an e-version of portfolios), blogs, solving 'far' or 'fuzzy' problems, designs,

projects, case studies, posters, narratives, reflective journals offer excellent opportunities for students to display their creativity in thinking about and applying their learning.

- The climate must be such that students are encouraged to take risks, to dare to depart from the established way of doing things. A Theory X climate, with an insistence on students being *right*, discourages creativity.

Assessments in some areas must insist that students do things the established way: surgery, laboratory practice, for example. But when the ILOs address creativity, the assessment tasks must be open ended.

But to continue with our strategy of assessment, what about the rubrics for assessing such outcomes? Isn't asking creative work to be assessed against set criteria something of an oxymoron? Not really, but as Elton (2005) says, the criteria have to be interpreted 'in light of the work'. One aspect of this, he says, is connoisseurship, the ability of experts to asses work in their own field of expertise, the willingness to employ judgment. Balchin (2006) adds to the reliability of judgment by using consensual assessment by several judges.

An important ingredient of creativity is the *originality* of the product and we can estimate that: is it totally surprising and unexpected, is it original-ish but rather ho hum or is it somewhere in between? Another key attribute of genuine creativity is *appropriateness*. Creative work falls within a context. A design that doesn't work, be it ever so 'imaginative', should not receive an A; a hypothesis that is off the wall as far as the research literature is concerned is not likely to be much of a contribution to knowledge. The rubrics will need to address the constraints that have to be met but be open enough to allow students to display their originality. What other specific aspects of a creative work may need to be taken into account in assessment will depend to a large extent on the discipline area.

John Cowan (2006) suggests a rather more radical model for assessing creativity, based on students' self-assessment according to their own conceptions of what creativity means. The assessment by the teachers is not of the student's creativity on the basis of the creative works the student produces, but to 'decide if they are sufficiently persuaded by the learner's making of their judgment to endorse the learner's self-assessment of their own creative processes, thinking and outcomes, made against the learner's chosen and stated criteria, and following the method of judging which the learner has outlined.' (Cowan 2006: 161). To achieve this requires workshopping with students to help them formulate their ideas of creativity and what constitutes the kind of creative works they might produce and how to self-assess it.

Assessing lifelong learning

Lifelong learning is also one of the graduate attributes that can only really be assessed in its embedded form. The summative assessment of lifelong learning generically will by definition occur rather late in the day for the learner. However, the embedded components of lifelong learning, such as the ability to work independently, to source information selectively, to monitor the quality of one's learning, to reflect transformatively and improve decision making, to use sensible strategies for tackling unseen problems, are assessable in well-designed capstone or independent research projects.

A particular aspect of lifelong learning is workplace learning, of which the *practicum* is a foretaste. The practicum, if properly designed, should call out all the important verbs needed to demonstrate competence in a real-life situation. Examples include practice teaching, interviewing a patient or client in any clinical session, handling an experiment in the laboratory, producing an artistic product. It should be quite clear that the student has to perform certain behaviours to a specified standard. Videotaping students at work is useful, as then students can rate their own performance against the criteria before discussing the supervisor's rating.

The closer the practicum is to the real situation, the greater its validity. The one feature that distorts reality is that it is, after all, an assessment situation and some students are likely to behave differently from the way they would if they were not being assessed. This may be minimized by making observation of performance a continuing fact of life. With plenty of formative feedback before the final summative assessment, the student might nominate when he or she is 'ready' for the final, summative, assessment. This might seem labour intensive, but recording devices can stand in for *in vivo* observation, as can other students.

In fact, this is a situation ideal for peer-assessment. Students will become accustomed to being observed by one another when they give and receive peer feedback. Whether student evaluations are then used, in whole or in part, in the summative assessment is a separate question and one worth considering.

In Chapter 8, we discussed some teaching/learning activities for facilitating functioning knowledge in workplace learning focusing on ILOs such as:

1 integrate knowledge and skills learned in university to real-life professional settings
2 apply theories and skills to practice in all aspects of professional practice
3 work collaboratively with all parties in multidisciplinary workplace settings
4 practise with professional attitudes and social responsibilities in their respective professions.

Because of the multifaceted nature of the different workplace learning situations, there can be no one fixed format of assessment. Assessment tasks and formats must be designed or selected to appropriately address the ILOs. Some common assessment tasks in workplace learning may include:

• observation of students' workplace performance
• placement case reports

- placement case/seminar presentations
- performance records
- reports from other staff in the placement centre
- feedback and evidence from others' relevant sources
- e-portfolio.

The ILOs to be assessed become the criteria of assessment. They should be clearly defined and understood by all parties concerned before the commencement of the workplace learning placement. Individual programme will have to decide on the type of assessment tasks that will require the students to enact the target ILO verbs and provide evidence of their achievement of such ILOs. In most cases, assessment is conducted either by the workplace educators or as a combined effort of the institute academics and the workplace educators. These assessments are teacher-centred. However, we should consider the possibility and feasibility of involving the students in assessing their own performance through peer- and/or self-assessment. These student-centred assessments enable students to have a clearer understanding of the ILOs and also have a shared control of their learning.

Assessing problem solving

Assessing problem solving can vary considerably. Standard problems usually call out a relational response, using conventional and correct paradigms. But even in these problem types, an 'elegant' (extended abstract) solution that is original and concise obviously should be given greater credit: this is creative work even if the format is conventional.

'Fuzzy' problems are those to which there is no definitive correct solution, only better or worse ones. Deciding whether a solution is 'better' or 'worse' depends on the context. All sorts of criteria could come into play: degree of originality, 'elegance', loose strings left hanging, cost etc. Each teacher will have to decide each case on its merits. In this open and complex area, as in the case of creativity, we return to the notion of connoisseurship: the expert should be able to recognize excellence in their field of expertise.

One area where assessing problem solving has well-established practices is problem-based learning itself. The essential feature of a teaching system designed to emulate professional practice is that the crucial assessments should be performance based, holistic, allowing plenty of scope for students to input their own decisions and solutions (Kingsland 1995). Some version of the portfolio, as open ended, may be useful in many programmes, but essentially the assessment has to be suitable for the profession concerned.

Medical PBL developed the 'triple jump' (Feletti 1997), but the structure applies to professional education generally:

1 *Dealing with the initial problem or case:* diagnosing, hypothesizing, checking with the clinical data base, making use of information, reformulating.

2 *Review of independent study*: knowledge gained, level of understanding, evaluating information gained.

3 *Final problem formulation*: synthesis of key concepts, application to patient's problem, self-monitoring, response to feedback.

While these steps emulate real life, Feletti asks:

- Do all steps have to be passed or can you average?
- Is there an underlying 'problem-solving ability'?
- Should performance at the various steps correlate together or not?

At the risk of sounding like a previous UK prime minister, Maggie Thatcher, we would answer 'no', 'no' and 'no':

- 'No', you cannot average because that may mask a crucial weakness.
- 'No', we are not interested in underlying problem-solving abilities, we are interested in whether the student can solve the problems in question.
- 'No', the steps or rather outcomes may well correlate but as teachers that is not our business. We are interested in the answers to each outcome step independently of any other.

All of which goes to show just what a grip measurement model thinking has had on our thinking: even on best practice PBL practitioners.

Assessing in large classes

Many teachers see no alternative to the final exam and the MCQ when assessing large classes. Using varied assessment tasks for higher level ILOs, especially those addressing functioning knowledge, is seen by many teachers as impractical in large classes.

However, it need not be thus. Of course, assessing the projects, assignments and portfolios of 400 students between the end of semester and submission of grades to the faculty board of examiners may be logistically and humanly impossible. But there are alternatives. While rapid assessments are more adapted to assessing declarative than functioning knowledge, we can make some suggestions for assessing both forms of knowledge.

Speeding up assessment procedures

Peer- and self-assessment

Peer- and self-assessment can slash the teacher's assessment load quite drastically, even when conventional assessments such as exam or assignment are used (p. 200). An additional benefit is that self- and peer-assessment are particularly well suited for assessing functioning knowledge and values ILOs such as teamwork and cooperation, because such assessments are what are required in real life.

Let us recap the advantages:

1 Self- and peer-assessment give the students first-hand, active involvement with the criteria for good learning.
2 Students learn how to select good evidence.
3 Judging whether a performance or product meets given criteria is vital for effective professional action.

It is important that these educational justifications are made clear to the students, not only because the rationale for all teaching and assessing decisions should be transparent, but because it is necessary to get the students on side. A common belief is that assessment is the *teacher's* responsibility and some students resent being required to do the teacher's dirty work (Brew 1999). Peer-assessment can also be stressful to some students (Pope 2001). It should be noted too that good students under-assess themselves, compared to what their peers would rate them, while poor students over-assess themselves (Lejk and Wyvill 2001b).

How well do self- and peer-assessments agree with teacher assessments? Falchikov and Boud (1989), reviewing 57 studies, found that agreement was greatest with advanced students, least in introductory courses; and in convergent content subjects, such as science, medicine and engineering, rather than in arts and social science. Good agreement requires explicit criteria of assessment and discussion and training in using them (Fox 1989).

As an operational rule of thumb, Boud (1986) suggests that if self- and/or peer-assessments agree within a specified range, whether expressed as a qualitative grade or as a number of marks, the higher grade is best awarded (collusion can be mitigated by spot checking): he estimates this procedure can cut the teacher's load by at least one-third. Gibbs (1999) cut marking time for the teacher by 18 hours a week by using peer-assessment, while summative marks increased by 20% simply because peer-assessment is itself a powerful TLA.

Group assessment

Group assessment is appealing in large classes. With four students per assessment task, you get to assess almost a quarter the number you would otherwise. But there are problems, particularly of plagiarism and its equivalent, freeloading. It is necessary to be very careful about who does what in the project, which is where peer-assessment helps, and that each student obtains an overview of the whole task, not just of their particular contribution, for example by writing a reflective report on how well each thinks they have achieved the ILOs (pp. 219–20).

Synoptic assessment

We met synoptic assessment earlier in connection with capstone projects. In essence, synoptic assessment is one large assessment task that might serve several ILOs, whether of one course, or of several courses, as in the case of the capstone project. A research project, extended library assignment or a dissertation could address the ILOs of different courses, even though the ILOs themselves are different. It is, however, important that the teachers concerned agree as to the assignment. They may well have different rubrics to assess it by, to suit their own ILOs and purposes. Synoptic assessment is an important way of avoiding over-assessment.

Random assessment

One way of ensuring that students are motivated to put effort into a series of ATs is to use random assessment. In Gibbs (1999), 25 reports through the year were required, but as each was worth only a trivial 1%, the quality was poor. When the requirements were changed, so that students still submitted 25 reports as a condition for sitting the final exam, but only four reports selected at random were marked, two benefits resulted. The students worked consistently throughout the term and submitted 25 good reports and the teacher's marking load was one-sixth of what it had previously been.

Rapid assessment of declarative knowledge

One three-minute essay

This appeared as a TLA for large class teaching and as a learning activity and as feedback for the teacher (p. 115). It can just as easily be used summatively for grading purposes, but if so, the students should be told first as their strategies will be different. An obvious advantage is that the three-minute essay can be answered and assessed in, er, three minutes.

Short-answer examinations

These are answered in note form. This format is useful for getting at factual material, such as interpreting diagrams, charts and tables, but is limited in addressing main ideas and themes. The examiner is usually after something quite specific, and in practice operates more like the objective format than the essay (Biggs 1973; Scouller 1996). However, it has advantages over the standard multiple-choice in that it is less susceptible to test-taking strategies: the answer can't be worked out by elimination, it requires active recall rather than just recognition and it is easier to construct but not as easy to score.

Cloze tests

These were originally designed to assess reading comprehension. Every seventh (or so) word in a passage is deleted and the student has to fill in the space with the correct word or a synonym. A text is chosen that can only be understood if the topic under discussion is understood, rather like the gobbet (pp. 235–7). The omitted words are essential for making sense of the passage.

Concept maps

We have seen concept maps as a teaching/learning activity (p. 115, 117). They can also be used for assessment. They are particularly useful for giving an overview of the course. They need not take a long time to prepare and the teacher can tell at a glance if a student has an impoverished knowledge structure relating to the topic or a rich one.

Venn diagrams

A simple form of concept map, where the boundary of a concept is expressed in a circle or ellipse, and interrelations between concepts expressed by the intersection or overlap of the circles (see Box 11.3). Venn diagrams, like concept maps, are very economical ways of expressing relationships. They can be used for teaching purposes, in conveying relationships to students, and for assessment purposes, so that students may convey their ways of seeing relationships between concepts. Getting students to draw and briefly explain their own Venns, or to interpret those presented, can be done quickly, where the target of understanding is relationships between ideas.

Box 11.3 represents an item for an educational psychologist course ILO relating to professional interaction. There are three domains: psychologist, student and school, with each of which the psychologist has to interact at various times. For the student to be able to explain examples of the inter-actions (1) through (3) would indicate a high level of understanding of the psychologist's role. This item could be adapted to virtually any situation: just label the circles differently. Task 11.2 asks you to think about precisely that.

Letter-to-a-friend

This is written by the student to a friend, imaginary or real, who is supposedly thinking of enrolling in the course in the following year (Trigwell and Prosser 1990). These letters are about a page in length and are written and assessed in a few minutes. The student should reflect on the unit and report on it as it affects them. Letters tend to be either multistructural or relational, occasionally extended abstract. Multistructural letters are simply lists of course content, a rehash of the course outline. Good responses provide integrated accounts of how the topics fit together and form a useful whole (relational), while the best describe a change in personal perspective as a result of studying the course (extended abstract). Letter-to-a-friend also provides a useful source of feedback to the teacher on aspects of the course. Like the concept map, letters supplement more fine-grained tasks with an overview of the course.

Rapid assessment of functioning knowledge

Gobbets

Gobbets are significant chunks of content with which the student should be familiar and to which the student has to respond (Brown and Knight 1994).

Box 11.3   A powerful Venn item

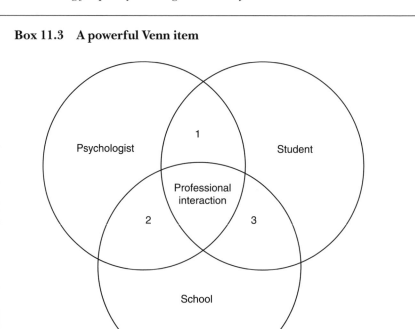

Write a brief sentence describing an interaction that would occur in the sites in relation to professional interactions.

1 _____
  _____

2 _____
  _____

3 _____
  _____

This item is easily adapted to other areas by using different labels in each circle.

They could be a paragraph from a novel or of a standard text, a brief passage of music, a Venn diagram, an archeological artefact, a photograph (a building, an engine part) and so on. The student's task is to identify the gobbet, explain its context, say why it is important, what it reminds them of or whatever else you would like them to comment on.

Gobbets should access a bigger picture, unlike short answers that are sufficient unto themselves. That big picture is the target, not the gobbet itself.

Task 11.2   Venn diagram of TLAs and ATs for functioning knowledge

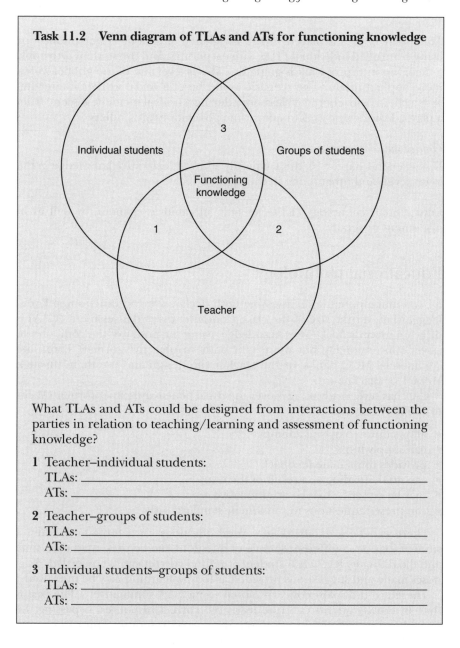

What TLAs and ATs could be designed from interactions between the parties in relation to teaching/learning and assessment of functioning knowledge?

1 Teacher–individual students:
   TLAs: _____
   ATs: _____

2 Teacher–groups of students:
   TLAs: _____
   ATs: _____

3 Individual students–groups of students:
   TLAs: _____
   ATs: _____

Brown and Knight point out that three gobbets can be completed in the time it takes one essay exam question, so that to an extent you can assess both coverage and depth. They could assess either declarative or functioning knowledge.

Video segments

These can easily be played in the invigilated situation, either publicly or using controlled individual PDAs with earphones, and the student is to apply a theory to interpret what is going on. This is a version of the gobbet with a more applied intent. The scenario could be of a social worker interacting with a client, a teacher in a classroom during a critical incident, a scene from a play, a historical re-enactment . . . the possibilities are endless.

Ordered-outcome tests

Discussed in Chapter 10, these typically address declarative knowledge in the lower levels and functioning in the higher.

Educational technology (ET) can help in rapid assessment, as well as in assessment generally.

Educational technology

ET has much potential in assessing both declarative and functioning knowledge, whatever the size of the class. Computer-assisted assessment (CAA) is directed towards declarative knowledge, using the power of the computer to assess conventionally but more efficiently in objective format. There are commercial MCQ banks, or the teacher can design and use them through WebCT or Blackboard.

CAA has several advantages over the usual pencil-and-paper format (Maier et al. 1998) because it:

- allows more than one attempt
- can supply hints
- provides immediate feedback
- can guide reading as a result of the test
- may be either formative or summative
- can present questions in random or standard order.

There can be a databank of several questions on a topic and, when a student logs on, a different sample of questions can be presented each time and the difficulty level each student is getting correct can be recorded, diagnoses made and suggestions provided as to how learning may be improved.

There are two main concerns about using CAA summatively. The first is that, in time, students can rote learn the correct responses, bypassing the mental process required to work out the correct response. This can be mitigated by randomizing the alternatives at each presentation, and, on the principle of alignment, using the system precisely for items that require rote learning, such as terminology, rules and so on. When used on a pass–fail basis, 'pass' requiring 90% correct responding, is identical with mastery learning. And that is the problem: it is too easy to equate good learning with 'knowing more', if that is all CAA is used for.

ET's most exciting use is in assessing functioning knowledge. Complex real-life situations can be given in multimedia presentations and students asked to respond. A video clip, with multiple-choice alternatives, could show a professional scenario, say a psychologist interviewing a client and the student is required to choose from the alternatives what type of situation is represented (Maier and Warren 2000); or in an open-ended version, asking the student to comment on what is going on, a critical analysis of the exchange, what steps the psychologist might take next and so on. Essay assessment can be facilitated by the teacher inserting comments from a bank of comments in appropriate parts of the essay.

Students may be required to set up their own web pages and post their learnings as they would in a learning portfolio and in portfolio assessment. The advantage here is that all the other students in the course can access it and post their own evaluative comments, thus providing formative feedback and self- and peer-assessment much more readily than when assessments are made in hard copy. The UK Open University uses a student-created website in place of a traditional exam; details and discussion of the issues involved such as plagiarism, are discussed in Weller (2002). In one university, each student has their own PDA that they use in a wide variety of ways throughout the course. They are able to take photographs and videos and post them on the net, communicate with their teacher and with one another, thus potentially turning every relevant experience into a learning event, a TLA, that can also be an assessed as an assessment task.

ET can be very sophisticated, as in *productive media*, using microworlds where the student builds his or her own system (Laurillard 2002): here TLA and assessment are intertwined as in real-life learning. In fact, the uses of ET in assessment are limitless, mimicking as it can much authentic assessment and by virtue of its interactivity allowing creativity of a high order.

As far as large class assessment is concerned, however, one must sound a caution. At first blush it sounds like the answer to assessment of high-order ILOs of functioning knowledge in large classes because the students can work away in their own time, but someone has to visit the websites and make the assessments. Certainly a large part of this burden can be solved by self- and peer-assessment and no doubt too programs like Scardamalia and Bereiter's (1999) Knowledge Forum can help to organize the mass of responses and evaluate the contribution individual students make to the forum.

ET may handle both quantitative and qualitative modes of assessment, with considerable logistic and managerial advantages. The potential of ET in assessment is most valuable in open-ended responding, in rich and contextualized situations, particularly with the advent of software like Knowledge Forum, which facilitates both formative and summative assessment at either individual or group level.

A problem with using ET for summative evaluation is that one needs to be sure that the person at the keyboard is the student who should be there. Hopefully, technology will be designed to beat even this problem. There is always the problem of plagiarism, but that exists in both conventional and ET modes when conducted outside an invigilated environment.

Let us now consider that problem.

Plagiarism

Many students do not see plagiarism as a moral issue or that it undermines assessment (Ashworth et al. 1997). In some universities, up to 90% of all students plagiarize their work (Walker 1998). In 2002, the Australian Vice-Chancellors Committee commissioned a survey that found that 14% of students are plagiarists, but the figure is probably much higher because much goes unreported.

Susskind (2006) in a summary of various reports on plagiarism suggests that plagiarism in university essays is so rife that bringing back compulsory exams may be the only way to stop it: 'Plagiarism has knocked the stuffing out of the essay assignment,' Melbourne University's Simon Marginson is quoted as saying. 'It has contaminated the essay badly, making it a waste of time as an educational project. Things have moved beyond the current regimes of assessment. The system has broken down.'

Susskind summarizes the driving forces behind current plagiarism levels:

- The internet, with its 8 to 10 billion pages of information freely available.
- Since universities have gone corporate, passing students affects funding, so that teachers are not encouraged to report plagiarism, because of the fear of scandal and loss of funds from failed students. In one Australian university, the senior administration dismissed the claims made by an external examiner that several students had plagiarized their work as motivated by 'spite', although he had supplied the web addresses from which the students had downloaded their papers. This particular case ended in an independent inquiry that took the administration severely to task, resulting in much clearer definitions of plagiarism and tougher procedures, but the fact that this case even occurred is evidence of the extent to which some institutions not only may tolerate but even seem to condone plagiarism.
- Globalization in Australia has brought an influx of about 240,000 foreign university students, or 25% of the student body, many of whom struggle with English. Many feel it preferable to copy from sources rather than trust their own writing skills.
- Generation Y's tendency to question the value and legitimacy of copyright and intellectual property. Brimble and Stevenson-Clark (reported in Lane 2006) found that 40% of students from four Queensland universities thought that faking the results of research was just 'minor cheating', while 11% did not even regard it as cheating. Students were also very tolerant of copying another student's assignment or downloading from the web.

The true occurrence of plagiarism is hard to estimate: we have estimates here ranging from 14% to 90%. Probably both figures, and all in between, are true in different universities. Plagiarism among international students presents a different problem, due to uncertainty about writing skill. In some cultures, students are taught that it is disrespectful to alter the words of an expert (Ballard and Clanchy 1997).

The hard remedy is to go back to compulsory examinations but the educational cost of that in terms of sound assessment would be huge.

A longer-term remedy is to change the culture from what it seems to be becoming. Students are much readier to cheat if they perceive the staff to be setting 'make-work' assignments or if they know that their assignments will be marked by tutors and part-timers whose heart isn't in it: surface approaches on one side breed surface approaches on the other. Setting worthwhile assessment tasks that draw meaningfully on the experience of the students is much more likely to be treated respectfully.

Smythe (2006) describes a way of successfully reducing plagiarism by requiring students to choose a research topic and a proposal, which is submitted early in the semester. Students are thus forced to think about the assignment from the start and to work on it until about the middle of the semester, when they hand in a first draft. This is not graded but comments and guidelines suggested, which are then built into the final version that is graded. Smythe's technique is labour intensive – 'only manageable in classes of under 100' – but the advantages are that students feel a personal commitment and they have to follow the guidelines provided.

This technique contributes to addressing the fundamental problem. Teachers need to convey a culture of scholarship and what research means. Brimble and Stevenson-Clark's finding that students condone cheating in research simply shows that they don't understand the nature of research or scholarship in general. It doesn't mean producing the results that the corporations who finance the research want to see. It means following the rules of empirical evidence gathering and of their replicability, of logical argument and of recognizing the work of other scholars and building on that in a transparent way: making clear what are the source data, what is the researcher's contribution and its originality. The conventions of citation always make it clear what is previous work and what is the researcher's.

What applies to scholars at the forefront of knowledge applies to undergraduate students when they submit their work. They need to be taught – and to see by example – what the nature of scholarship is and how, therefore, we need to be careful in citing others' work to make clear what is and is not the work of others. Many students plagiarize out of ignorance. They really don't understand the nature of the game.

The game, however, isn't always clear even to academics. Wilson (1997) points out that plagiarism proceeds in stages (that interestingly follow the SOLO levels):

- *Repetition*: simple copying from an unacknowledged source. Unistructural and unacceptable.

- *Patching*: copying, with joining phrases, from several sources. Some general, non-specific, acknowledgment. Weak multistructural and still unacceptable, but harder to spot.
- *Plagiphrasing*: paraphrasing several sources and joining them together. All sources may be in the reference list, but the sources pages are unspecified. Still multistructural and still unacceptable, technically, but a plagiarism programme would not detect it because no single sentence or paragraph can be traced, yet the ideas are all second hand. This shifts almost imperceptibly to the next stage.
- *Conventional academic writing*: ideas taken from multiple sources and repackaged to make a more or less original and relational type of synthesis. Quotes properly referenced, general sources acknowledged; the package may be new but are the *ideas* new? Unoriginal academic writing is plagiphrasing that is properly referenced.
- The extended abstract level would involve a 'far' transformation from the sources – genuine originality – which conventional academic writing should, but does not necessarily, incorporate.

Repetition and patching are clearly unacceptable, but students with poor writing skills of whatever cultural background find it hazardous to attempt to 'put it in your own words' when they are not confident in their use of the language. Lack of confidence in writing skill, especially in second-language international students who may have a good *content* understanding, can easily lead to 'innocent' patching. Such cases need augmented modes of assessment, such as a brief interview, or a less verbal medium such as a concept map.

Plagiphrasing should be unacceptable, but as it is not verbatim it is difficult to detect with software. However, the shift from plagiphrasing to conventional academic writing (presumably acceptable) is not always clear. While it may be sometimes difficult to decide what constitutes genuine and culpable plagiarism, repetition and patching are definite no-nos.

Teachers, on both local and international fronts, need therefore to be extremely clear about these levels of plagiarism and what the rules of referencing and of citation are. And, of course, what the penalties are. The culture of going soft on suspected plagiarism cannot be tolerated as it is anti-scholarship. In the corporatized world, a firm known for its cheating or false labelling in the end loses its market.

In summary, plagiarism can be minimized by the following means:

1 Creating a culture that emphasizes scholarly values.
2 Alerting students to the rules and the penalties for infringing them.
3 Using assessment tasks that use reflective diaries and personal experiences.
4 Using oral assessment and peer- and group assessment.
5 Checking assignments using software. *Turnitin*, licensed to 29 Australian universities, can detect plagiarism from web-based sources.
6 Increased invigilation as a last resort, but widening the range of assessment tasks within that context from the conventional written examination.

To wind up this chapter on assessing and grading functioning knowledge, you might care to tackle Task 11.3.

Task 11.3   Design an assessment task or tasks for one of your course ILOs

Select one ILO relating to functioning knowledge of your course and design assessment task(s) that will appropriately assess this ILO. To help you check the alignment between the task(s) and the ILO, identify what the students are required to do in order to complete the assessment task(s). The task requirements should be aligned to the ILO.

Course ILO: _____

Number of students in the course:

Assessment task	Student activities to complete the task (individually)	Student activities to complete the task (in group)
1		
2		

Now double-check if the student activities are aligned to the verbs nominated in the respective course ILO.

After designing the task(s), you will need to write the grading criteria for either the ILO or for each of the tasks.

Summary and conclusions

Assessing functioning knowledge

Functioning knowledge is readily assessable: it is deployed most often in the student's real-life experience. Assessment tasks include critical incidents, projects, reflective journals; case studies are assessment tasks that mirror professional life, while the formats of assessment such as the portfolio, contract and interviews are used in real-life assessment situations. Often high-level functioning knowledge is not addressed by one course ILO but by several, or by the whole programme, so assessment needs to be synoptic, addressing several ILOs. The portfolio and the capstone project are such assessment devices.

Assessing for creativity

Creativity is not something ineffable and unassessable: it is involved in all subject areas, especially in higher years, and needs to be assessed. Creative thinking requires a sound knowledge base, but beyond that requires critical awareness or reflection and the ability to generate original ideas or products that address critical reflection on what is the case. Assessment needs therefore to be open ended, allowing students to spring their surprises on us, but also they need to be surprises that are assessed within parameters that each situation would define as relevant. One suggestion for assessing creativity without any external 'impositions' of what creativity might be is to monitor students' self-assessments of their own creativity using their own standards of what creativity implies.

Assessing for lifelong learning

One highly defined area of lifelong learning is assessment of work-based learning, starting with the practicum, which is a representation of professional experience. Lifelong learning can also be assessed through its components: ability to work independently, to source information selectively, to monitor the quality of one's learning, to reflect transformatively to improve decision making, to use sensible strategies for tackling unseen problems and the like, all of which are variously assessable in open-ended formats.

Assessing problem solving

Assessing students' ability to solve 'far' or 'fuzzy' problems is similar to assessing the components of lifelong learning. A detailed technology of assessment has developed in problem-based learning itself.

Assessing in large classes

Large class assessment can go beyond MCQs and invigilated examinations. Self- and peer-assessment, synoptic assessment, group assessment and even random assessment can cut down the assessment load for both students and teachers while maintaining the integrity of the assessment. Even in the invigilated context, more exciting assessment tasks than requiring students to write answers to standard questions can be devised that address ILOs for declarative and functioning knowledge, such as gobbets, ordered-outcome items, concept maps and Venn diagrams.

Educational technology

ET has two main roles in assessment. Computer-assisted assessment makes the most out of the standard situation of asking standard convergent questions and providing feedback. Beyond that, interactive ET allows students to give free reign to their creativity by constructing models, using web pages, blogs and chats. Moreover, these formats can use self- and peer-assessment readily.

Plagiarism

Plagiarism is an ancient problem but it seems to be becoming easier and more rife with the use of the internet, with pressures on universities not to fail students and with cultural changes among Gen Yers and some international students in views of what constitutes intellectual property. The best answer to this is to institute a culture of scholarship in which the way of doing research, of submitting assignments and of setting assessment tasks as authentic and personally relevant, becomes the accepted norm. There are better ways of minimizing – but admittedly not eliminating – plagiarism than by increased invigilation.

Further reading

General assessment tasks

Brown, S. and Glasner, A. (eds) (1999) *Assessment Matters in Higher Education.* Buckingham: Society for Research into Higher Education/Open University Press.
Brown, S. and Knight, P. (1994) *Assessing Learners in Higher Education.* London: Kogan Page.
Carless, D., Joughin, G., Liu, N.-F. and associates (2006) *How Assessment Supports Learning.* Hong Kong: Hong Kong University Press.
Gibbs, G., Habeshaw, S. and Habeshaw, T. (1984) *53 Interesting Ways to Assess Your Students.* Bristol: Technical and Educational Services.
Nightingale, P., Te Wiata, I., Toohey, S., Ryan, G., Hughes, C. and Magin, D. (eds) (1996) *Assessing Learning in Universities.* Kensington, NSW: Committee for the Advancement of University Teaching/Professional Development Centre, UNSW.
Stephenson, J. and Laycock, M. (1993) *Using Contracts in Higher Education.* London: Kogan Page.

There are many books of practical suggestions on assessment; this list is a good sample. Brown and Glasner and Brown and Knight talk about the theory and practice of mainly CRA. Carless et al. and Nightingale et al. are both collections of 'best practice': Carless from university teachers across Hong Kong and Nightingale from across Australia. Carless's collection gives 39 case studies, grouped under various headings of self- and peer-assessment, group assessment, building feedback into assessment tasks, addressing higher order thinking and the like. Readers are likely to find several ideas to improve their own teaching and assessment. Nightingale's collection is grouped under convenient 'verb' headings, such as thinking critically, solving problems, reflecting and so on.

Websites

www.cshe.unimelb.edu.au/assessinglearning/
www.assessment.edc.polyu.edu.hk/. Go to Assessment Resource Centre (ARC).
www.heacademy.ac.uk/Assessmentoflearning.htm
www.itl.usyd.edu.au/
www.tedi.uq.edu.au/. Click 'Teaching and learning support' then 'Assessment'.
www.brookes.ac.uk/services/ocsd/2_learntch/2_learnt.html. Especially click link to
    'Computer-Aided Assessment Centre'.

E-portfolio

An overview of e-portfolio: www.educause.edu/ir/library/pdf/ELI3001.pdf
e-portfolio portal: www.danwilton.com/eportfolios/
Rubrics for electronic portfolio: www.uwstout.edu/soe/profdev/
    eportfoliorubric.html

Assessing creativity

Jackson, N., Oliver, M., Shaw, M. and Wisdom, J. (eds) (2006) *Developing Creativity in
    Higher Education: An Imaginative Curriculum.* Abingdon: Routledge.
www.heacademy.ac.uk/2841.htm. See especially the chapters and papers by Lewis
    Elton, Norman Jackson and Tom Balchin.

Assessing workplace learning

www.polyu.edu.hk/assessment/arc. Go to 'Forum' where there are several papers on
    work-based learning and several other topics pertinent to this chapter.

Peer-, self- and large class assessment

Boud, D. (1995) *Enhancing Learning through Self-assessment.* London: Kogan Page.
Carless, D. et al (as on p. 245).
Gibbs, G., Jenkins, A. and Wisker, G. (1992) *Assessing More Students.* Oxford: PCFC/
    Rewley Press.

Plagiarism

Home page for *Turnitin*: www.turnitin.com/static/plagiarism.html
Excellent article on plagiarism and minimizing it: www.library.ualberta.ca/guides/
    plagiarism/

12

Implementing constructive alignment

Now that we know how to put together all the components of constructive alignment – writing ILOs, designing TLAs and assessing and grading students' performance – we have the task of implementing courses and programmes. Introducing educational change into the system is a procedure with its own pitfalls. We look at implementing constructive alignment at two levels: by the individual teacher and by a whole department or faculty. In both cases, the strategy of implementation is similar, using transformative reflection and formative evaluation. Implementation isn't a one-off process but a continuing action learning cycle of reflection, application and evaluation that is basic to all quality enhancement. In fact, all procedures relating to implementing constructive alignment can be generalized to create quality enhancement procedures for the whole institution. The key is that all structures and procedures to do with teaching and learning, from classroom level to procedures and regulations that apply across the whole institution, are founded in the scholarship of teaching and learning to create an organic, reflective institution.

A framework for implementing constructive alignment

So far, we have been presenting the framework of constructive alignment; the next step is the process of implementing it. As 'theories of education and theories of change need each other', as Michael Fullan (1993) puts it, so do frameworks for teaching and learning need a framework for implementing them. This is our concern in this chapter.

As we argued in Chapter 2, the means by which considered professional change takes place is through transformative reflection (p. 43). In the case of implementing constructive alignment, who are involved in this reflective process? We distinguish three major parties: teachers, students and the institution, whether the last refers to teaching or to administration. The intended outcome of this reflection is the successful implementation and continuing enhancement of constructively aligned teaching and learning. Let us put all this together in a Venn diagram (Figure 12.1).

Three parties participate in this transformative reflection: the *teachers*, the *students* and the *institution*, which may variously be the department, the faculty or school or the whole institution and its committees, such as senate or academic board. Each of these participants reflects in interaction with the others in the following three domains or contexts:

1   teacher and students
2   teacher and institution
3   students and institution

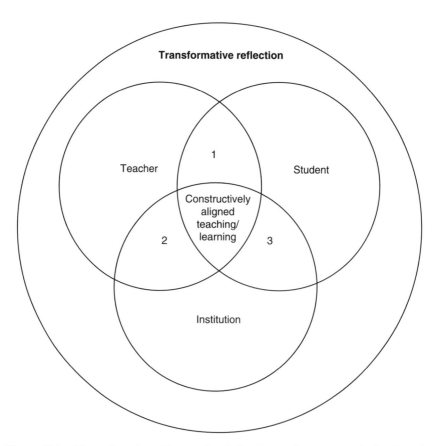

Figure 12.1   Three domains of interaction in implementing constructively aligned teaching and learning

These domains of interaction define foci for facilitating implementation and each of which should have built-in quality enhancement mechanisms, as the aim is not only to constructively align teaching and assessment, but to develop mechanisms for not only assuring quality but for *enhancing* quality. Just as teachers need to eliminate or minimize those factors that encourage a surface approach and to maximize those factors that lead to a deep approach, so those factors that inhibit the implementation of constructive alignment should be minimized and those that support and encourage it should be maximized. But first let us go straight to the engine room: transformative reflection.

Revisiting transformative reflection

We met Stuart Tyler in Box 7.4 (p. 130), but we haven't yet met Stewart Taylor. Both Stuart and Stewart had problems teaching oedema associated with cardiac failure to nursing students; both thought that the problem needed realistic three-dimensional videos, using motion, to model the process rather than lecturing and illustrating with still, two-dimensional diagrams. Both found the videos made little difference to student performance. Stewart concluded that he'd done his best; he'd used the most suitable ET according to all the good books but it turned out not to be worth the extra hassle. He went back to lecturing with diagrams. Stuart, by way of contrast, reflected: 'It didn't work, and it should have worked. *Why* didn't it?' He had a theory, which, when he thought about it, told him that there was lack of alignment between his existing assessment task and his desired outcome. He made an aligned assessment sheet a teaching/learning activity – and failure rates dropped to near zero (see Box 7.4).

This is an example of transformative reflection, using constructive alignment as the theory to effect the transformation from a not-working TLA to a working one. Stuart's case illustrates a very important point. Constructive alignment isn't just a method or a model to be implemented: *It provides a conceptual framework for reflecting on the questions that need to be answered at crucial stages of teaching in general.* Those questions are:

1 What do I want my students to learn?
2 What is the best way in my circumstances and within available resources of getting them to learn it?
3 How can I know when or how well they learned it?

These are the questions, of course, involved in designing ILOs, TLAs and ATs. These components, of curriculum, teaching method and assessment, are present in *any* teaching. What the constructive alignment framework does is invite us to question what we are doing as teachers at those crucial points and to rethink other ways of carrying them out, as did Stuart. But to ask those questions and rethink answers to them as the application of transformative reflection requires a theory. Figure 12.2 illustrates the steps in transformative reflection, here worded for the individual teacher, but which apply equally well *mutatis mutandis* to deans, deputy vice-chancellors and their respective creature committees.

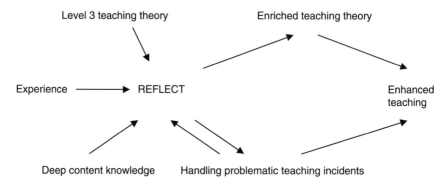

Figure 12.2   Theory and transformative reflective practice in teaching

A reflective teacher starts with three important components:

1 *Experience.* You cannot reflect on a blank slate. When you come across a difficult or challenging situation, the first question is: 'Have I come across anything like this in my past experience? If so, what did I do then? Did it work?' A further set of questions: 'What resources did I need then? What are at my disposal now?'
2 *Deep content knowledge.* You cannot teach effectively if you don't know your subject content very well indeed. So well, for example, that you can see instantly whether an unexpected answer a student confronts you with is original or misconceived (see Billy and the Creamed Wheat in Box 8.3, p. 147), or that you can see – on the run – powerful but simpler ways of expressing an idea.
3 *A Level 3 theory of teaching.* You can reflect with any theory. If you were a Level 1 teacher you might say: 'It didn't work because those students are just so *thick*. I suppose I could talk more slowly.' As a Level 2 teacher you might say (with Stewart): 'Well the video didn't work. I'll do what I know I can do: lecture well.' As a Level 3 teacher you say (with Stuart): 'Why aren't they learning? How can I get them to be relevantly active?' *That* is the sort of theory we want here, one that focuses on what the student does. This is a cyclical process; you keep looking at what they do, what they achieve and link that with what you are doing. You get to know your students as learners very well.

The next stage is to reflect on the teaching incident, using all three points, plus the specifics of this particular incident. There are several outcomes:

1 *Your teaching is enhanced,* eventually. You may need several gos at the problem.
2 *Your experience is enriched.* Each go at the problem adds to your store of experiences.

3 *Your teaching theory is enriched.* Using the theory in action makes you realize what aspects of the theory work and what do not.

This, then, is how transformative reflection enhances the quality of what it is we are doing. When used by individual teachers, as here, it shows the way forward under difficult or changing circumstances. When used by administrators and committees, as it will need to be particularly in the interface between teachers and the institution, (2) in Figure 12.1, the following are the sorts of question that teacher, committee or administrator, as appropriate, need to ask in order to implement constructive alignment effectively:

1 What is the espoused theory of teaching we are operating with here? Chapters 1–11 provide the answer to that.
2 How can the theory provide answers to the problems and issues of implementation? What needs doing to support, facilitate and maintain implementation?
3 What is preventing effective implementation?

In sum, transformative reflection can be used for implementing constructive alignment at two levels:

• In the classroom, by individual teachers in one or more courses for which they are responsible.
• In the institution, at the level of department, faculty, school or the whole institution.

Implementing at either level requires some necessary conditions:

1 A felt need for change by all major participants.
2 A clear conception of what an aligned teaching system is.
3 The operational decisions made concerning ILOs, TLAs, and ATs and how to grade students' performances.
4 A 'willing' climate, in which all participants, and those whose cooperation is necessary for the project to go ahead, will be on side and institutional policies and procedures that support constructive alignment.
5 Sufficient resources: resources such as financial, time for development of constructive alignment, space, educational technology and the like.
6 Formative evaluation of progress, including evidence that the new system is working properly; and, if not, the means of finding out what to do to correct matters.

Implementation in the individual classroom: Teacher and students

We start with the first domain of interaction – teacher and students. Let us assume you are willing to give constructive alignment a go. If you have persisted with this book so far, and have carried out the suggested tasks, then you will have met the first three necessary conditions: you are motivated, you have a clear idea of what you are trying to do and you have made all the main decisions.

Availability of the resources you think you need is limiting rather than lethal. You can always do something with what you have even if it is not what you'd most prefer to do. The first resource is time. You need time to prepare for the first run for planning and writing the ILOs while at the same time continuing to teach in the old way. If your head of department is sympathetic to what you are doing you might get some relief from other duties, which would make life easier. If not, then your commitment and enthusiasm need to be that much greater. However, once the course has run for a semester, it will demand much less time in maintaining and fine-tuning than the first run took.

Personnel and financial resources may present some problem: some ideal decisions are 'expensive' in terms of resources, but if the resources aren't available, it is usually possible to make less expensive decisions. The selection of teaching/learning activities is probably the most resource intensive. You might want to break down a large class into tutor-led groups or to utilize two separate classrooms, but if additional rooms or tutors are not available, those TLAs you had in mind may not be feasible. However, as we saw in Chapter 7, there is a range of TLAs available that you can use yourself in a large class: not ideal, but better than lecturing.

Policies and regulations to do with assessment will probably be your big-gest difficulty. If there is an iron-clad policy of grading on the curve, then a constructively aligned system is in real trouble. You could state your ILOs, align your TLAs and assess with aligned ATs – but then submit your grades according to the required proportions. That is possible, but it is an act of academic infidelity: you'll probably feel guilty afterwards and you'll have some explaining to do to your students. They may never forgive you.

Other regulations may require a fixed percentage of the final grade to be by invigilated exam. The main problem here is that if the proportion is too high, it may severely limit the assessment of the more important, high-order ILOs (see p. 200). However, 'by examination' doesn't necessarily mean you have to use the assessment task of writing answers to questions but that your ATs are to be set in a situation that is timed and supervised, in which case you can use ATs in which some high-level assessment may take place (p. 232 ff.). Another regulation that is a nuisance rather than a critical impediment is being required to report assessment results in percentages or in other quantitative terms. It is important – but again not absolutely *vital* (see p. 209–11) – that the actual assessment is done qualitatively, but having done that, it is simple to allocate numbers to grades (Table 10.3, p. 211) and give admin their precious numbers. They'll most likely convert them back to grades anyway.

As to the willing climate and cooperation of colleagues, that may or may not be a problem. While Lee Shulman (quoted in D'Andrea and Gosling 2005: 67) complains that 'we close the classroom door and experience pedagogical solitude', as opposed to scholarly research where we work in a community of scholars, that also means that you can get on with your teaching as you see fit. Actually, Shulman wrote that 15 years ago and it is almost certainly less true today than it was then. Today's universities, competing for markets, on the one hand, and packaging courses and programmes for credit transfer, on the other, require a degree of homogeneity within programmes and that they address graduate attributes. This requires cooperation between colleagues in planning individual courses within programme requirements. Shulman today would feel less pedagogically lonely, even if he might feel a twinge of loss of what was then quaintly known as the 'academic freedom' to teach as he saw fit. Today's conditions of accountability make the issue of implementation much more an institutional matter than used to be the case, as outlined later.

Before we move onto that, however, there is the question of the formative evaluation of progress. You have designed your course or courses and taught it for one semester. Did you, as an individual teacher, get it right? How would you know if you did and how would you ensure that problems were rectified and ILOs, TLAs and ATs fine-tuned to keep doing it better?

The answer is action research, which we introduced in Chapter 3.

Quality enhancement through action research

Action research is built on the 'action research spiral': 'reflect, plan, act, observe, reflect, plan, act, observe etc.', each such cycle building on the previous one (Kember and Kelly 1993). Applying this to implementing constructive alignment in your own classroom, you might take day one of implementation: to present the ILOs to the students and explain that they are required to produce evidence as to how well they meet them. Box 4.1 (p. 51) explains what happened in John's first implementation: the students hadn't come across this before and many didn't like it. John then reflected and decided to introduce a trial run with the portfolio and to negotiate with them about some teaching/learning activities. It is essentially a cycle of transformative reflection, beginning from day one: you first reflect on the situation or problem, plan what to do, do it, observe the effects it has, reflect on those effects, then plan the next step and so on. Even when the course is running for the first time, you will have your own gut feeling as to how well the students are taking it. Those feelings are important, the antennae that any teacher uses, but in action research you take deliberate steps to obtain harder evidence than your own intuitions, important though the latter are. More formally, the action research cycle goes like this:

1 Obtain evidence of progress.
2 Reflect on what seems to be working and what seems not to be working.
3 Introduce variations at the points in the system that seem not to be working as you had hoped.

4 Obtain evidence on how these changes seem to be working.
5 If they are not working, repeat (3) as appropriate.
6 Use the offices of a 'critical friend' wherever possible.

It may sound rather bothersome, but much of the 'evidence' is there already, it's only a matter of systematically collecting what you think is sufficient for your purposes. Remember that much action research, well carried out, is publishable. If your institution supports publishing the teaching of your content area as well as publishing research in the actual content – as it should (see later) – you can kill two birds with one constructively aligned stone: you improve your teaching and keep on improving it and you add to your publication record (Kember and McKay 1996).

Evidence comes largely from two perspectives: the students' and the teacher's.

Evidence from the students' perspective

Improved student perception of teaching/learning conditions

A questionnaire needs to be designed that tells you such things as: Were the ILOs clear? Did the TLAs help them achieve the ILOs? Which did not? Did the ATs address the ILOs? Were the grading rubrics understood? Students might rate the ILOs themselves for clarity, thus giving a concrete and articulated look at what students think. Further, when teachers write the ILOs knowing that students will be rating them, they write them more effectively (Peter Looker, private communication). Focus group interviews are also valuable sources of evidence. Selected students could be asked to keep reflective diaries in which they comment on their learning environment.

Student reflections

The students should also be brought to the process of reflection, in particular in elaborating on what we have just seen, on the impact that statements of the intended learning outcomes upfront had on their planning for learning, how they went about their learning, whether they had any insights into the way the teaching/learning activities helped them realize the ILOs, whether they thought the assessment tasks were 'fair' (that is, were aligned to the ILOs). Susan constantly reflects on how she is going about learning, on whether her learning and study strategies are fruitful, whereas Robert does not – which is Robert's main problem. Thus requiring students to keep a learning diary, to bring them into the assessment with peer- and self-assessment, to assess by learning portfolio, are situations that encourage students too to carry out transformative reflection. This is not only helpful for them but is very important feedback in action research on constructive alignment.

Grade distributions

Grade distributions can be compared prior to the implementation of constructive alignment and after implementation, but *only if* the same grading criteria are used in assessing student performances. Has the *nature* of the grades changed? Is the 'A' grade after implementation the same kind as previous 'A' grades? Remember, you can't compare the distribution of norm- with criterion-referenced grades, as norm-referenced are artificially held constant year after year.

Samples of student performance

Pre- and post-implementation samples can be kept in a library of assessment tasks representing the worst grades, middle grades and best grades.

Students' approaches to learning

Are the Roberts becoming more like Susan after the introduction of constructive alignment? The shortened two-factor version of the study process questionnaire (SPQ) (Biggs et al. 2001), which has only 20 items and may be copied from the reference, will tell you. The SPQ is designed to reflect students' reactions to teaching in terms of their approaches to learning. We want to be able to say: 'Before I implemented constructive alignment, the students in the class were on average higher on the surface scale and lower on the deep, but after implementation they are higher on the deep and lower on the surface scale. It looks like I'm on the right track'.

Evidence from the teacher's perspective

Teaching portfolio

The best source of evidence is a teaching portfolio. A general portfolio is described later (p. 166–8) but sections of that would be appropriate for keeping a record of reflections on implementation, with the following additional foci, compiled preferably while still teaching the course before constructive alignment was implemented, and of course continued afterwards:

1 Difficulties you have had in implementation: with ILOs, TLAs, assessment tasks or with any other aspect.
2 Insights into teaching and learning you have gained.
3 Evidence of successful teaching incidents with constructive alignment.
4 Comparisons with the 'old way'.
5 Suggestion for further improving implementing constructive alignment or your teaching in general.

Role of 'critical friend'

Reflection is often not best carried out alone. So, as the fish is the last to discover water, it is helpful to have a 'critical friend' on dry land. This is a complex role, part partner, part consultant, but most of all a mirror to facilitate reflection (Stenhouse 1975). Your own reflections are sharpened if shared with someone with a different perspective – and with some technical expertise. Different people can take the role of critical friend: a colleague in the same department is particularly convenient as critical friend, because they know the context and at the right time can gently feed in suggestions to be reflected on; if they have educational expertise, so much the better. We look at peer review later as a normal part of quality enhancement; part of that process could well include the role of critical friend. Teaching developers are ideal as critical friends, especially in the early stages or where specific technical advice is required, but not the head of department, even if he or she is a friend.

Changes to your own teaching are more likely to be sustained and effective the more those changes are supported by departmental/institutional policy. Say that in your first run of constructive alignment, you get unusually high numbers of high distinctions and distinctions, say 37% and 40% respectively, whereas your colleagues usually turn in about 10% and 15%. At the examiners' meeting your results are queried, you explain what constructive alignment is all about, your results are passed.

The same happens next semester, but mutterings about 'slack standards of assessment' are louder. The students have given your course high evaluations, which proves to your more unkind colleagues that it is indeed a soft option – although when the students see what they have to do to get the high distinction, and at what standard, they may not see it as a soft option at all.

It would have been psychologically and politically easier if you and a colleague were critical friends for each other. There would be a replication of implementing a course and if you both obtained similarly improved grade distributions, remaining colleagues at the examiners' meeting might be more easily convinced. It is a short step from there for teachers within the department to act as critical friend for each other. Maybe the whole department becomes involved, not just in improving the skills of individuals, but the offerings and working of the department itself would then become the subject of collective reflection.

Which brings us to implementation at the departmental or other institutional level.

Implementation at institutional level: Teacher and institution

We now turn to the second domain of interaction: teacher and institution. Implementing constructive alignment across the whole department, faculty or institution is obviously more complex than an individual teacher implementing one or more courses.

Leadership

The most important factor in department- or faculty-wide implementation is *leadership* (Taylor and Canfield 2007; Toohey 2002). Most of the conditions required for effective change – a felt need for change, a clear conception of an aligned teaching system, the operational decisions concerning ILOs, TLAs and assessment and grading, and providing sufficient resources – are in the hands of the departmental or school leadership, whether that is an individual or various committees on which teachers are represented.

The formal leader, be it head of department, dean or subdean, has first of all to understand constructive alignment and the demands proper implementation makes on resources, and then, once the decision to implement it has been made, to emphasize with a smile that 'We *are* going ahead with this, you know!' The matter then becomes one of expertise in implementing, a point we return to later. There will also need to be other sorts of leader. A process leader orchestrates the various phases of implementation. A political leader is necessary who understands how the committee system works, who knows whose elbows to grip in easing the implementation through various committees and whose ruffled feathers to smooth of those who feel that their babies – the forms for courses and programmes, the teacher feedback and student feedback questionnaires, the software for collating and reporting student progress – have to be redesigned.

Once the decision to implement constructive alignment has been taken, there will need to be widespread *consciousness raising*, addressing such questions as: What *is* constructive alignment, what are the advantages, how difficult is it to implement, why go to all that bother and anything else the staff may want to know. This phase may well require the services of an outside consultant who can answer any questions, correct the misapprehensions and ease the anxieties that many are likely to hold.

The second phase is the actual *implementation*, where ideally somebody can work within the department who is an expert in both the content being taught and in constructive alignment. This involves working closely with teachers on writing intended learning outcomes, which must be done correctly, as all else, the teaching/learning activities and the assessment tasks, hinge on the ILOs. In our experience, one or a few teachers in the department 'get it' fairly quickly; their ILOs are well written and they have a flair for generating aligned and inventive TLAs and ATs. Their courses will become models for others, so it is important that these pioneers get it right. These people should be identified and become internal resources persons for others in the department – with a formal status, such as 'constructive alignment facilitator' – and their teaching loads adjusted accordingly. When this happens, the external subject consultant can take a much lower profile, perhaps becoming a resource to be called on from time to time. A department needs to become self-sufficient as soon as possible, problems arising being solved by those who know and understand the workings of the department. As we emphasize later, the institution's staff developers should have an ongoing role here.

Strategies of implementation

Do you start small with one or two courses or do you go for broke and implement across the board? Is it best to do so a course at a time, seeing how it goes, what the problems are, what works and what doesn't and learning from initial mistakes, introducing constructive alignment more broadly as colleagues become convinced? Or is it better to be more top-down, to announce ultimate deadlines that *must* be met, with rewards for the early birds and penalties for the slackers? Michael Fullan (cited in Toohey 2002: 196) suggests the former strategy, which sounds very logical. Try pilot studies first and then as it becomes apparent that the change is going to work, senior management will take it up and bring about the necessary policies and directives for the whole reform to work. But does this mean every institution has to run its own pilot studies? At what point is likely success assured? What do you do about those who still have doubts but whose cooperation is needed?

There will always be doubters. There are teachers who see themselves as committed researchers and who don't want to spend what could be time doing research in designing new courses that – as far as they are concerned – are working well enough already. Other teachers, frequently the older ones, see themselves as inspirational lecturers with a wealth of teaching experience behind them and a knowledge of all the Level 2 teaching tricks; they see no reason to change their teaching. If the conservative teachers are in the minority, a sound strategy is to leave them to it; they'll come to see that they'll be left behind. When a whole department requires courses to be written in a certain format, with ILOs, TLAs and ATs spelt out, with 'official' rubrics for different assessment tasks or outcomes, the conservative teacher would find it difficult not to fall in line. Or as Toohey reports (2002), people will start to see that 'they don't have to feel bad about spending so much time on teaching because they're getting so much reward from it and enjoying their teaching time' (p. 196). Most younger teachers don't have so much baggage and self-belief in their teaching and may indeed welcome a whole-department approach.

The answer to the question of strategy – start small at first, or go for it across the board – surely depends on the balance of pro- or anti-feeling among those who have to participate in one way or another. If change is to be effected, everyone – or a large majority – needs to be positively committed. If the implementation was a collective decision by a department in which all or most cheerfully voted to implement constructive alignment, you have an excellent start as colleagues can mutually support each other in maintaining their commitment, keeping up motivation, solving problems and so on (Taylor and Canfield 2007). (We summarize this account of a successful change to constructive alignment in Chapter 13, along with examples of implementations at the course level.) But where, as often happens, the decision comes top-down, there is a danger of a culture of compliance forming and how things play out thereafter depends on many factors (Knight and Trowler 2000).

The best case scenario is both top-down and bottom-up, where both troops and managers agree to implement: they need each other if it is to work. If a department wants to go ahead and the middle managers are half-hearted, fearing perhaps the criticisms of more conservative colleagues; or if the managers are gung-ho but the teachers feel they are already doing a good a job and see the direction to change as a criticism, trouble lies ahead. When new programmes or courses are approved, it is common practice in outcomes-based institutions to require a statement of outcomes for each course, what TLAs and ATs address what outcomes – but in a compliant culture, once the paperwork is done, it is business as usual: lecture plus tutorial and the majority of the final grade by examination.

Where the majority of a department or faculty needs convincing, starting small with a few courses involving one or a few willing teachers is much more likely to bring the majority around when they see how successful it is.

Change conceptions first or actions?

We know that teachers teach in a way consistent with their conceptions of teaching (Kember 1998). So before implementing constructive alignment itself, should we address teachers' conceptions first, by getting participants to *think* about teaching in terms of a Level 3 theory? Kember thinks that we should, as teachers would then understand more clearly what Level 3 teaching meant: otherwise, they will revert to their old ways.

Guskey (1986), by way of contrast, says it is easier to change people's behaviour first, *then* to change their thinking. He sees improving teaching as like getting people to quit smoking. Education campaigns, which are aimed at what people think, are not as effective as 'No smoking' signs, or raising the tobacco tax. Then, when their behaviour is forced to change, people begin to think it might be a good idea to stop smoking anyway. Accordingly, Guskey suggests that teaching development should aim at changing teachers' behaviour first, then their beliefs will follow and the change will be maintained. According to this approach, the dean or whoever would issue a directive: 'From Semester 1, 2010, all departments will use constructive alignment. In the meantime, workshops will be run, of which all staff are required to attend at least two.'

It works both ways. Some sort of official directive is necessary to get things moving. Thinking and doing reinforce each other, as in any reflective prac-tice. Let us say you are not really convinced that constructive alignment is a good idea, but you are willing to give it a try. But you find it does work. You see that students are learning things you never anticipated; you begin to revise your ideas and conclude that good teaching is about what students do, not what teachers do. No longer sceptical, you ask: 'Why does it work?', a question that involves a transformation in thinking.

Ho (2001) created an explicit link between changing conceptions and appropriate teaching behaviour by confronting teachers with what they said they believed with what they actually did: as a result, many changed their conceptions and their practices, with positive results for the students' approaches to learning. Prosser and Trigwell (1998) also emphasize that ways of teaching are interlinked with what teachers think teaching is. They need to:

1 become aware of the way they conceive learning and teaching, within the subjects they teach
2 examine carefully the context in which they are teaching, so that they are aware of how that context affects they way they teach
3 seek to understand the way their students perceive the learning and teaching situation
4 continually revise, adjust and develop their teaching in light of this developing awareness.

To help teachers achieve this self-awareness, Prosser and Trigwell have developed the *Approaches to Teaching Inventory* (ATI), which addresses what they think and what they do. Levels 1 and 2 are combined in an information transmission/teacher-focused approach, which is contrasted with a conceptual change/student-focused approach (Level 3). This is a very useful instrument in teaching development, making teachers really think about the nature of teaching and learning.

Teachers always have some sort of theory of teaching, as we saw in connection with Figure 12.2 (p. 250), but it is usually implicit and unexamined. The possibility that there are different ways of looking at teaching does not occur to many teachers. Entwistle (1997) points out that the systemic (Level 3) view 'offers a powerful insight to many staff in higher education who have not thought about teaching and learning in this way before ... Indeed, that insight can bring about a totally new conception of teaching'(p. 129). And with that insight, the recognition that practice will need to change will follow.

Once constructive alignment is up and running successfully, conceptions will assuredly change. However, it might facilitate implementation by embarking first on conception changing using Prosser and Trigwell's *ATI* in a series of workshops, before proceeding with the actual implementation itself.

Formative evaluation

Even before courses are implemented, plans for ongoing formative evaluation need to be established. As Toohey (2002) wisely puts it: 'Evaluation will always occur whether planned or not' (p. 197). Someone, usually the sceptics, will be only too willing to watch closely for any problems and gleefully pass on the good news that this new-fangled approach isn't working. Such judgments are anecdotal and most frequently made from a different perspective from that on which the course was designed. Critics of problem-based learning point out for instance that PBL graduates don't know as much as traditional medical graduates – and can even produce evidence to prove that. Horror, PBL is a failure! Well, no, actually, because PBL graduates were *intended* to know less, and in the time they would otherwise spend knowing more, they would learn the skills to deploy what they do know more effectively and where they don't know, how to go about finding out what they need to know. On those criteria, PBL is demonstrably more effective than traditional teaching (pp. 156–7).

The answer to such ill-informed criticism is to pre-empt it by planning a departmental or institutional evaluation. As with the individual teacher, the general plan is to employ action research (see pp. 253–4), only with a whole department or institution the design of the action research would need to be more comprehensive. In addition to the evidence taken from the students' and the teacher's perspectives, we have the departmental perspective to take into account.

The department, or its teaching quality committee (if it doesn't have one it should have, see later), could submit a reflective report on the experience in implementing constructive alignment at the end of the first year of implementation. Issues to be addressed in the report may include:

1 Impact on teaching. Data from teachers' portfolios could be compiled, and course evaluations by students.
2 Impact on student learning. Much the same data as gathered by teachers for individual course evaluations (p. 253ff).
3 Comparisons across different aligned courses: What ones are working well? What ones are experiencing difficulties? What difficulties and how were they dealt with?
4 What operational structures has the department with respect to implementing and monitoring the innovation?
5 Concerns regarding continuing implementation.
6 An action plan for future improvement.

Regular sharing sessions, where staff tell each other what is working for them and what is not working, are excellent in themselves and also provide data on how well constructive alignment is working and where it is not. The experience of one teacher could easily provide the answer – or at least a point of reflection – for another who is experiencing problems.

The formative evaluation of courses is an intrinsic part of implementation. It provides formative feedback and material on what is working and what is not, with transformative reflection suggesting how solutions to problems might be tried in the action research model to achieve ongoing quality enhancement.

It also pre-empts the nasty gibes of the doubters.

Implementation at institutional level: Student and the institution

We now turn to the final interface between students and the institution. Most of these aspects have been dealt with already. Graduate attributes are student-related factors that are woven deeply into the programmes and courses and are dealt with particularly in Chapter 5. Student feedback on how graduate attributes are working from their perspective may be considered to be important, as they may not be fully represented in course ILOs.

Many universities administer a graduate survey to students at the time of graduation or shortly after graduation when the graduates have been in the workforce. Apart from asking information on career destination and development, these survey questionnaires also provide useful feedback on graduates' reflections on how well the graduate attributes have been met (see examples of graduate survey questionnaires provided in 'Further reading' at the end of the chapter). The survey data should be substantiated, if possible, by focus group interviews of senior year students or graduates asking them to reflect on the overall university learning experience with respect to achieving the graduate attributes. Feedback from these sources provides valuable food for transformative reflection by the institution at all levels.

Student input from questionnaires is very important: both from questionnaires directly related to action research in implementing and improving constructively aligned courses (p. 253ff) and from more general aspects of their learning. Apart from evaluating and providing feedback on teaching, learning evaluation questionnaires asking students to self-evaluate their own learning experience and outcomes encourages them to be reflective learners. *The Course Experience Questionnaire* (CEQ) (Ramsden 1991), used regularly in Australian universities since 1993, is an all-purpose questionnaire to gauge students' reactions to particular courses. It contains the following scales: good teaching, clear goals and standards, appropriate assessment, appropriate workload, generic skills, learning community, overall satisfaction. In the present context, it could be used to gauge the student response to a course before constructive alignment was implemented and the response by successive cohorts after implementation. Changes in scale score could be used as a basis for transformative reflection for enhancing teaching and assessment practices. The CEQ, as a general instrument, also enables both longitudinal comparisons within a course from cohort to cohort, to horizontal comparisons across courses, comparing constructive alignment with non-aligned courses or with constructively aligned courses with each other.

Student representation on committees, especially committees dealing with teaching and learning at departmental or institutional level, is important for obtaining student input on how implementation is progressing: in fact, student representation should be part of normal quality enhancement procedures.

Apart from the general induction or orientation to university that students get, should there be any special induction with reference to constructively aligned teaching and learning? Or should this be left to when students turn up to classes on day one and are given their course outlines, just like in any other course?

The answers to these questions probably depend on the stage of implementation. If students are used to traditional teaching and they are facing a large-scale changeover in the upcoming semester, it could well be good public relations, as well as saving multiple explanations, to have a meeting of students with presentations about the 'new' approach to teaching and assessment, how knowledge of outcomes will make things clearer for them, followed by a discussion panel with Q&A, with some input from senior students who have experienced constructively aligned courses. Taylor and Canfield (2007) found that with increasing exposure to constructively aligned teaching, students' ratings along 'good teaching', 'clear goals and standards' and 'appropriate assessment' scales progressively increased. It would be very helpful for first-year students to hear this sort of experience of constructively aligned teaching from older colleagues.

The reflective institution

Let us now discuss more general issues of quality assurance (QA) and quality enhancement (QE). QA is concerned with maintaining the quality of the work institutions do, and so QA procedures tend to be *retrospective*: assuring that appropriate accountability and fire-fighting mechanisms have been working, that money has been well spent.

Quality enhancement, contrariwise, is *prospective*, concerned with reviewing not only how well the whole institution works in achieving its mission, but also how it may keep improving in doing so. QE mechanisms look to the future, ensuring that through appropriate monitoring structures using transformative reflection, teaching and learning will be continually monitored and enhanced, exactly along the lines of formative evaluation for implementing constructive alignment. An effective quality enhancement system pre-empts the need for quality assurance.

Just as transformative reflection by individuals is founded on a theory of teaching, quality enhancement in institutions is founded on a generally held philosophy of teaching: the scholarship of teaching and learning.

The scholarship of teaching and learning

Boyer (1990) introduced the term 'the scholarship of teaching', but in recent years, as the concept has become more and more popular, the term 'learning' has very appropriately been added. In the current concept of 'the scholarship of teaching and learning', or SoTL, lies the recognition that teaching and learning have their own research and knowledge base, their own *scholarship*, that in most universities not so many years ago was simply unrecognized and still is in many universities. In other universities, SoTL is recognized in mission statements but not in practice, for example when it comes to promotions or appointment.

A genuine SoTL culture leads inevitably to several structures that require and support transformative reflection with regard to teaching.

Teaching and research

Possibly the single most important influence of a SoTL culture in an institution is that teaching is accorded at least the same status and the same traction in personnel decision making as does research. It may do so on paper, but it is still usually the case that the promotion goes to the individuals with most publications, even in universities where the most important function of the university in the public eye, and in its activities, is in fact teaching. This discrimination does not occur only in promotions. Many universities do not allow publications on the teaching of one's own discipline to 'count' either in an individual's CV or in the departmental publications list that is used for funding purposes.

Teaching development grants

Many universities provide teaching development grants to encourage and support innovative approaches to teaching and learning for individual or groups of teachers. The teaching development grants may come from the university's internal funding or from external sources such as the National Teaching Development Grants scheme in Australia, the Higher Education Academy in the UK, and the University Grants Committee in Hong Kong. Allocation of funding to individual projects is usually done via a peer review process of proposals submitted by individual or groups of teachers.

There are advantages and disadvantages to internal versus external funding. External funds are more lavish, but many teachers, not at all intimidated by applying for grants in their content research, are reluctant to apply for funds and go through all that form filling to research their own teaching, because they do not consider themselves educational researchers. Internal funding, with smaller amounts, is not nearly such a hassle. Many teachers, who later did significant research into their own teaching, started small. Universities should not therefore think that because external teaching development funding agencies are out there they needn't bother with an internal funding system. Indeed, many universities that are serious about their teaching take a thin slice from across the main budget and dedicate that to teaching development. It is vital that in encouraging teaching development projects, university-wide policy should be in place to ensure that scholarly publications on teaching should be recognized on the same level as publications in content area research.

Many teaching development projects are action research in nature, authentic to a real-life teaching and learning context, rather than attempts to be representative and generalizable with a tight research design. Typically, teachers or teams of teachers design projects on such topics as curriculum development, constructive alignment, PBL, peer tutoring, clinical and applied learning, independent learning by students, innovative assessment tasks, web-based learning and assessment and various teaching and learning resources. External consultants, or internal departmental resource persons could work together to identify issues and develop project proposals. Teaching and learning development centres (see following section) should also play an important role in coordinating teachers or groups of teachers in identifying and developing proposals on various teaching and assessment issues and to provide ongoing support during the implementation and dissemination of the teaching development projects.

As a general rule, teaching development projects are expected to disseminate their results to the wider teaching and learning community. Many projects have developed their own websites, and organized sharing seminars or thematic conferences to share their project results and insight both within and beyond their respective institution. For example, the following arose from projects funded by the University Grants Committee of Hong Kong:

- the first Asia-Pacific Conference on Problem-based Learning in 1995
- an international conference on Enhancing Teaching and Learning Through Assessment in 2005
- the adoption of constructive alignment throughout the Hong Kong Polytechnic University flowed from another funded project on constructive alignment.

Teaching and learning development centres

Teaching and learning development centres (a generic name covering staff development units, educational development centres and so on) have previously been the poor country cousins in the establishment of universities: they have been underfunded, understaffed and frequently with the staff classified not as academics but as part of administration. What unaligned thinking! If the advisors on academic matters such as teaching are not even classified as academics, it's inviting academics not to take staff development seriously. In the past, too, the main job of the teaching and learning development centres was to provide one-off workshops for teachers on a voluntary attendance basis and to provide service courses on educational technology.

The teachers who attended voluntary workshops were mostly the already good teachers; those who didn't attend were frequently those who most needed to. The effect was to widen the gap between good and poor teachers. The basic problem was that the centres were at best perceived through Level 2 lenses, as places for providing tips for teachers or as remedial clinics for poor or beginning teachers. At worst, they were seen as inessential luxuries and when the hard times in Australia began in the 1990s, many were simply closed down to save money, an act as sensible as throwing all the doctors off an aircraft to lighten it while the pilot is having a heart attack.

This sorry state of affairs has recently turned around. With the demands from fee-paying students for good teaching, the sudden emergence of SoTL as a Level 3 theoretical basis for teaching, and in UK especially, the provision of compulsory courses for new academics and the establishment of the Higher Education Academy, the perception and role of teaching and learning development centres have changed hugely for the better. It is also being recognized that these centres have a peripheral as well as a central locus. That is, the best work in staff development, as we have found in our experience in implementing constructive alignment, is done from within the unit that provides the teaching, usually the department, when the staff developer is also an expert in the content taught in that department. This is not such a hard call as may appear: after all, a staff developer always comes – or should always come – from a background in teaching a content area; it is simply a matter of allocating staff developers accordingly. Some faculties and schools have their own teaching and learning development centres, particularly in medicine and law.

There is also a central, generic role for these centres. It is self-evident that all central decisions that bear on teaching and learning should involve the experts in teaching, learning and assessment. The design of course and programme approval forms, the architecture of teaching areas, software and hardware requirements of the platform used for teaching, regulations on assessment procedures and the reporting of assessment results are all areas that have direct effects on the effectiveness of teaching and learning. These and related decisions should therefore receive input from the teaching and learning experts.

Teaching developers should *not* be involved as 'teaching police', in assessing individuals and supplying information about individuals on their teaching competence for personnel decisions, such as contract renewal. This utterly compromises their role. The argument is the same as that about revealing error in summative as opposed to formative assessment (p. 97–8). The teaching and learning development centres' role is formative, not summative, and teachers must feel free to expose their weaknesses in teaching and express their doubts. Additionally, there is the issue of professional ethics, that the relationship between any professional person and client is based on confidentiality and on acting in the client's interests. It is deplorable that in some universities the directors of teaching development centres are required to gather such information on individuals for use in personnel decisions.

Teaching portfolios

We came across the use of teaching portfolios in the implementation of constructive alignment, but they are a useful part of quality enhancement generally. A teaching portfolio is a collection of evidence about your teaching and your students' learning, and a self-reflection on that evidence. It is your own quality enhancement process with the intended outcomes of helping you to:

1 keep a personal record of your teaching practice
2 reflect on your teaching philosophy and practice
3 identify your strengths and areas for improvement as a teacher
4 plan your professional teaching development.

While a teaching portfolio may also be appropriately used as part of the institutional quality assurance process for summative teaching evaluation and other relevant decision making, the formative and summative use of the teaching portfolio should be clearly differentiated. If used summatively, the aims and criteria for assessment of the portfolio should be clearly stated so that the portfolio could be appropriately structured and reflected on accordingly.

Box 12.1 suggests some contents of a teaching portfolio.

Box 12.1   Contents of a teaching portfolio

There is no standard list of contents of a teaching portfolio but it should include a statement of your theory of teaching on which all your teaching decisions are (or should be) based. The following is an indication of the types of evidence you could consider including.

1 Evidence provided by yourself:

- Statement of your personal teaching philosophy underlying your own teaching.
- Teaching qualifications and experience, focusing on your current teaching and other teaching-related responsibilities.
- Achievements in teaching and other teaching scholarly activities, such as: teaching innovations, teaching materials and resources, curriculum development, postgraduate supervision, professional teaching development, action research and teaching-related publications, contributions to enhancement of teaching and learning within the institution, any official recognition of your teaching achievement, such as teaching awards or invitation to present in conferences etc.
- Administrative duties enabling you to promote teaching and learning beyond your own, such as responsibilities as course or programme leader, member of teaching and learning committees, member of teaching innovation group etc.

2 Evidence provided by colleagues, students and others:

- Feedback from peer review from colleagues who have observed your teaching (see peer review below).

- Evaluation and feedback from colleagues on your course materials and content.
- Student evaluation of and feedback to your teaching, additional to the institution's quality assurance process: formal and informal student feedback provided by students during their learning with you, unsolicited emails, correspondence, 'thank you' cards from past and present students indicating their appreciation of your teaching. Pages of raw evaluation data, no matter how positive, should not be included in the portfolio. Summary of the evaluation and your reflection on the results are more informative.
- Evaluation of and feedback on any teaching development activities you have offered.

3 An overall self-reflection on:

- The strengths of your teaching.
- Areas for further improvement.
- Action plan for further professional development.

In the context of implementing constructive alignment, your reflection should focus on the alignment between the intended learning outcomes, teaching/learning activities, assessment tasks and grading, and how the alignment could be enhanced.

All your claims should be supported by concrete examples: your teaching materials, samples of student work, teaching development workshop materials etc., and how your decision making is informed and based on your personal teaching philosophy.

There is no fixed format to a teaching portfolio, just that it should be designed and structured to effectively reflect your teaching achievements and how your students' learning has been affected by your teaching, with reference to the context in which the portfolio is to be used. The portfolio is normally presented as a written document, either in hard or soft copy format, but the electronic format is becoming more common. Appropriate multimedia presentations could be considered such as a video or audio tape of your own teaching with accompanied self-reflection. The teaching portfolio should be a succinct documentation highlighting your strengths, accomplishment and reflection on your teaching, normally no more than three or four pages long. Detailed examples should be included in the appendices and an indication that further details could be available on request. A lengthy portfolio may hide the wood with all the trees – and bore your readers.

Courses in tertiary teaching

Another way in which a university can show commitment to teaching is what many universities are already doing in the UK at least: require all new staff to attend a course on teaching. The Higher Education Academy is now accrediting all such courses. This means that new teachers, having undergone staff development or teacher education, will be entering the profession with some knowledge of the student learning approach and a Level 3 theory.

The value of such courses is anecdotally attested to by the following comment in response to an enquiry we put to a teacher in one UK university: 'Whenever we propose or update a course we need to fill in a form in which we specify up to five learning outcomes. When we list the different pieces of assessment, we have to say which learning outcome each assessment assesses. Not sure how reflective people are in filling out the form. Some take it seriously – mainly those who took a teaching course we now require for starter lecturers' (Zoltan Dienes, private communication).

Such courses thus have excellent potential for bringing about a culture change in universities, based on the scholarship of teaching and learning. It should be standard practice outside the UK. Now that in most universities teaching is the major activity for most staff, and the expectation of stakeholders in the general public, it seems strange that people should be allowed into this high-level profession who are effectively unqualified to carry out a major part of their duties.

Peer review of teaching

The primary purpose of peer review is to provide formative feedback for continuing professional development of individual teachers. A teacher invites a colleague, a critical friend, to observe his/her teaching and/or teaching materials to provide feedback for reflection and improvement: in effect a QE process through action research of your own teaching. Peer review should form a major part of the overall teaching quality enhancement process, but only peers should be involved, not those in a position to make personnel decisions. Peer review has been used for summative evaluation as part of the institutional quality assurance process to satisfy external quality audit bodies, but as always, the formative and summative use of peer review must be clearly differentiated and agreed on by individual teachers. When used for summative purpose for personnel decision making, clear aims, procedures, guidelines, and assessment criteria must be stated and agreed by all parties concerned.

Box 12.2 gives an example of some conditions for effective formative peer review.

Peer review should include the following four stages:

1 Pre-review meeting between the reviewer and you (the reviewee) to discuss purpose and intended outcomes of the review, type of feedback that would be helpful to you and to make logistic arrangements. The focus of the review should also be clear: What specific aspects of your teaching you

---

Box 12.2   Some conditions for effective peer review (PR) of teaching for quality enhancement

Following are some of the issues to be observed for effective PR:

1 The purpose and the intended outcomes of the PR exercise should be clearly defined.

2 It should involve all types of teaching staff (part time, full time, contract and tenure).

3 Participation must be voluntary.

4 The reviewee should be given the choice of:

  a his/her reviewer
  b which classes to be observed or what teaching materials to be reviewed
  c the focus of each review session
  d use of review feedback for other purposes such as an application for promotion
  e who should have access to the review report.

5 Staff development should be provided for both reviewer and reviewee.

6 All feedback should be returned to the reviewee and used for developmental purposes only.

7 Appropriate support provided to reviewee to enhance further improvement.

---

want to receive feedback on – are you trying a TLA to enhance student participation in a lecture situation and would like to have feedback from your peer as to the effect? Would you like to have peer feedback on a new e-learning package you have developed?

2 The actual review usually involves a real-time teaching session. Students should be informed why an extra person is present in the classroom. The reviewer should be non-intrusive to the teaching and learning process. It is useful for both parties together to review a videorecording of the teaching session. A checklist or feedback proforma is useful for feedback purposes (see 'Further reading'). The review can also involve reviewing teaching materials or resources.

3 Post-review meeting. Reflect on your teaching before the post-review meeting to identify any issues that you would like to discuss. During the meeting, feedback is provided for further discussion and maybe clarification. Feedback should be specific addressing the previously agreed focus

and supported by evidence. It should be constructive providing suggestions for reflection and improvement. Further review could also be arranged if appropriate.

4 Post-review reflection by yourself based on the feedback to identify areas for improvement and to develop an action plan for future changes. Keep the review report in your teaching portfolio for record and future reference.

Other structures at departmental level

Departmental teaching and learning committee

One of these, with student representation, should be established to make on-the-ground decisions relating to the setting up, design and administration of courses and programmes, to monitor teaching, define problems and benchmark with other similar departments locally and overseas. Such decisions should be made on the scholarship of teaching and learning, and to that end, a member of the university's teaching and learning development centre should be present to advise.

This committee might, for example, review deviations from expectations as to the annual grade distributions and remedies proposed. Out of this, too, can come ideas for action research at a departmental level. It is important to keep track with data that reflect change, such as student feedback, samples of student learning outcomes, staff reports, performance statistics and so on, which is kept in departmental archives. The work of this committee could give rise to action research projects within the department. Operating at the departmental level means that the problem of the reluctant under-performing teacher is drastically redefined. *Teaching* is now the focus, not the problems that *individual teachers* might have.

Regular departmental 'sharing sessions'

This is where staff can tell each other what is working for them and what is not working. Alternatives that achieve better alignment may be explored, by pooling colleagues' ideas and by consulting the teaching and learning development centre and the departmental committee. A genuine sharing of problems and solutions through the lenses of constructive alignment can lift the game of the whole department.

Student feedback on teaching

This should be organized through the department, not the faculty or central administration. Questionnaires should be worded to be supportive of constructive alignment: for example, are students clear about the ILOs, what standards they have to reach to attain the various grades, that the TLAs in their experience really help them to achieve the ILOs.

Staff–student consultative committee

Here, students and staff can share views about the quality of their learning experiences. Focus groups might be organized and students might be asked to submit what they think are their best performances, to be placed in departmental archives as exemplars of good learning.

Research and teaching

The head of department should give strong encouragement to teachers to research and publish in teaching their content area, as well as research in the content itself.

A regular departmental retreat

Held at least annually, this is where teaching-related matters are top of the agenda.

Some marginal quality assurance procedures

Some mechanisms, in place in the name of quality assurance rather than of quality enhancement, can backfire, as they discourage risk taking and innovation.

External examiners

External examiners in the British system are a time-honoured means of ensuring that similar standards operate across institutions. It is important to bring outside perspectives and contacts to bear and to feel confident that one's own standards are comparable to those elsewhere.

Frequently, the role of external examiner is restricted to examining the setting and marking of final papers and to adjudicate the summative assessment of students. The person doing this needs to be completely aware of, and in sympathy with, the department's theory of teaching. We know of cases where the examiner required the examination questions to be changed well into the teaching of the course concerned – and thereby putting alignment at risk. External examiners, selected for their content rather than for their educational expertise, may discourage innovative assessment practices and encourage decontextualized assessment. The pressure to comply with the external examiner is considerable in institutions where the examiner's comments are seen and discussed outside the department concerned. However, if the word 'examiner' is replaced with 'consultant', an outside advisor who can visit the department to advise on assessment and other matters to do with teaching and learning, the problem is solved.

External panels

External panels are often required to accredit and validate programmes and courses. This is a common quality assurance procedure that has obvious value, particularly where staff are required to deliver new courses in directions in which they may have had little experience, in which case course accreditation helps to ensure minimal standards. A similar argument applies to programmes that require approval by external professional bodies. Both procedures, however, discourage innovative teaching, although recently professional bodies increasingly require outcomes-based teaching for accreditation purposes.

External panels may well exert strong pressure to include more and more content. Each panel member thinks his or her own special interest must be given 'adequate' treatment – which is code for rather more treatment than is being proposed – a common result being an overloaded curriculum. Programme leaders and committees usually anticipate such pressures – they obviously design courses that they think are likely to be approved – and so the curriculum is overloaded from the start. Teaching subsequently becomes a frantic scramble to 'cover' all the listed topics – yet we know that coverage is 'the greatest enemy of understanding' (Gardner 1993: 24).

Panels may encourage conservatism in teaching, particularly when the panel has key figures from the profession whose knowledge of education is what they went through years ago in their own professional training. So it is easy to anticipate problems and err on the cautious side: 'Let's get the validation over first, then we will innovate as much as we like!'

Once a course has been approved, however, it tends to be set in concrete. Changing an already validated course or programme can be difficult. It may easily turn out that the curriculum is indeed overloaded; that the student intake has changed; that recent research, post-validation, suggests that the curriculum should be changed. It may be possible to make minor modifications immediately, but any major changes are either not allowed, because they were not in the validated documents, or they have to go through yet another round of committees. Administrators usually discourage any attempt to do so. In one institution, a move to PBL was vetoed by a senior administrator: 'The course may have to be revalidated. What if it doesn't succeed? What then, eh?'

Teaching evaluation

Teaching evaluation may follow one of two methods that exactly parallel the measurement model and the standards model (pp. 170–8). Evaluating teachers by a single instrument, such as a student feedback questionnaire, is operating according to the measurement model. Such instruments are worded to apply across all departments so that teachers can be compared along a quantitative scale, for promotion, awards, contract renewal and the like. This is a common approach to evaluating teaching, even in institutions that are otherwise quite innovative. It is an excellent example of misalignment. Such across-the-board measures assume that the default method of teaching is lecturing; the students rate the teacher on such items as 'speaks clearly', 'hands out clear lecture notes' and the like. This can be a serious impediment to reflective teaching. A teacher using a range of well-aligned

TLAs automatically gets a low score – and is passed over for promotion. Back to lecturing it is! We have seen it happen in several institutions; it would never happen in an institution running on the scholarship of teaching and learning. Teaching evaluation *à la* measurement model is an example of administrative convenience overriding educational sense (see Figure 12.3, p. 276).

Teaching should be evaluated using the standards model. That is, there are several criteria for good teaching and the teacher's task is to provide evidence that addresses those criteria, with evidence from a range of appropriate sources collected in a teaching portfolio (see earlier), where a teacher outlines his or her philosophy of teaching and then demonstrates how that is put into practice with samples of teaching and student evaluations specifically tuned to particular courses.

Distinguished teacher awards

Distinguished teacher awards frequently raise similar concerns if they are awarded on the basis of scores to such teaching evaluation questionnaires. But that aside, there are still worries. The message is: 'See? We reward good teaching in our institution!' – and it is indeed good to reward people for doing an outstanding job. However, it has to be done carefully, otherwise the message to the great majority of teachers – by definition the undistinguished ones – is that distinguished teachers are born, not made. The very names 'distinguished teacher' or 'outstanding teacher' suggest that here we have a bird of a rare species, whose exotic plumage ordinary teachers cannot hope to match. The sparrows and starlings therefore cannot be blamed if they follow what nature intended and teach on in their own undistinguished way. A generous distinguished teacher award system may also have the effect of absolving management from further support for teaching development.

Distinguished teacher awards encourage the perception that an outstanding teacher is one who does teacherly things better than other teachers do. Therefore, while distinguished teachers themselves tend to operate from Level 3, as reflective practitioners (Dunkin and Precians 1992), formal awards promulgate a Level 2 view of teacher as performer. Reward the excellent teachers by all means, but if we want quality teaching at an institutional level, the focus should not be on what the individual teacher does, but on the *teaching system* in the university. Recipients of awards may have nothing to do with all that crucial developmental teamwork – curriculum development, tutor mentoring, decisions as to delivery and assessment – that makes it possible for the star teacher to strut his or her stuff.

A revealing slant on this issue of individual versus collective responsibility for teaching comes from an international comparison of mathematics teaching carried out by Stigler and Hiebert (1999). They analyzed videotapes of classroom teaching in three different countries and found that each culture developed its own 'script' for teaching. Japan had a script based on a Level 3 theory of teaching, while the US script was based on learning routines at Level 1. Not surprisingly, Japanese students achieved better results than did

American students. But what determined the Japanese learning outcomes was the script, not the particular actor who delivered it. Awarding Oscars to the actors is not likely to improve their scripts. Just so in quality enhancement; we should be focusing on the script, not on the actor. Distinguished teacher awards, like quality assurance itself, are retrospective; they focus on what has been done; they do not make teaching across the board better in future: it is not quality enhancement.

By contrast, let us look briefly at awards in the Chinese school system, which might better be called distinguished teach*ing* awards:

> Good teachers may be honoured with titles (and salary bonuses). Such titles are awarded after they have been observed and have given demonstration lessons in a competitive situation, at one to three days' notice, in front of tens or hundreds of their peers ... The teachers ... act as mentors to younger teachers and their mentoring role includes giving further demonstration lessons.
>
> (Cortazzi and Jin 2001: 121)

Good teaching is seen here as a collective responsibility that works *prospectively* to enhance future teaching in the institution or district.

Now why don't we in the west do that?

Student feedback questionnaires

Many institutions have mandatory student feedback questionnaires as summative evaluations at the end of each course, using standard questions across all courses. We have already discussed the difficulties with that. Additionally, student feedback questionnaires share with distinguished teacher awards the problem that they usually focus on the actor, not on the script. They tend to measure charisma, the Dr Fox Effect, not teaching effectiveness in terms of improved student learning (see p. 108). Used formatively, however, student feedback questionnaires make eminent sense where questions are tailored to specific courses on aspects on which feedback is required as in the formative evaluation of implementing constructive alignment (pp.260–1).

In short, some common quality assurance procedures have the opposite effect to that intended, conceived as they are within a retrospective framework. While the above procedures may be well meant, if two edged, other institutional aspects are unequivocally negative.

Negative impacts on Level 3 teaching

Throughout this book, we have continually referred to counterproductive procedures and policies. The following is a brief recap.

Distorted priorities

Distorted priorities are a major source of mis- or non-alignment. Probably all institutions would put educational considerations as their top priority in their mission statements. However, there is an institution to run, which generates a set of administrative priorities. Administrators want things to run on schedule; they want to ensure that plagiarism cannot occur, that public criticism about standards or fairness should be avoided, that awkward cases are anticipated and legislated for before they arise and cause trouble, that research is promoted over teaching because the university's prestige is based on research output and so on.

For all this to happen (or not to happen), the safest working assumption is that students, and more recently teachers, are not to be trusted; the answer is to establish a Theory X climate. Unfortunately, as we saw in Chapter 4, good learning thrives in a Theory Y climate. However, as a completely Theory X climate would be unbearable and a completely Theory Y climate unmanageable, we compromise (see Figure 12.3).

Figure 12.3   Administrative and educational needs – striking the right balance

How the two sets of priorities are balanced is what separates a quality institution from a mediocre institution, in terms of teaching and learning. A quality institution is biased towards establishing the optimal conditions for learning (point Y), a mediocre one towards administrative convenience (point X). Where does your institution lie?

What sort of things distort priorities?

A quantitative mindset

Quantitative assumptions reduce complex issues to units that can be handled independently, rather than as part of the larger interactive system to which they belong. Thus, the curriculum becomes a collection of independent competencies, basic skills, facts, procedures and so on; passing becomes a matter of accruing sufficient independent correct answers.

A particular problem is the misapplication of the measurement model of assessment. Table 12.1 summarizes.

The demands of the measurement model are simply incompatible with those of good teaching.

Norm-referenced assessment

A particular example of quantitative assessment is norm-referenced assess-

Table 12.1 Demands of the measurement model and those of good teaching

Measurement model	Good teaching
Performances need to be quantified, so they are reduced to correct/incorrect units of equivalent value that can be added	Students need to learn holistic structures that cannot meaningfully be reduced to units of equal importance
A good test creates 'a good spread' between students, preferably normally distributed	Good teaching produces reduced variance
The characteristic being measured is stable over time	Good teaching produces change: it is called 'learning'
Students need to be tested under standardized conditions	Students need to be tested under conditions that best reveal an individual's learning

ment, in particular grading on the curve. We might decree that the top 15% of graduates will achieve first class honours and then boast 'See here, all our departments are teaching to the same high standard!', but that is an illusion. We have no idea of the real standards reached by any department. Worse, grading on the curve makes aligned assessment impossible.

Invigilated examinations
These are hard to justify educationally, but are useful logistically and for assuring the public that plagiarism is under control.

Who teaches the first years?
Assigning the most junior teachers, who can't argue back, to teach those enormous first-year classes that the senior teachers don't want to teach is not according to the scholarship of teaching and learning.

Emphasize research at the expense of teaching
Although many universities officially place equal emphasis on teaching and research, research is almost invariably perceived as the activity of greater prestige and in promotions is rewarded more than is teaching. Some department heads do not even recognize publications on research into teaching the very subject the department is charged to teach as 'real' research.

In sum, impediments to quality teaching and learning result from poor alignment to the purpose of the institution, just as impediments to good student learning result from poor alignment of teaching/learning activities and assessment practices to ILOs. Quality teaching means trying to enact the aims of the institution by setting up a delivery system that is aligned to those aims. In practice, however, many institutions in their policies, practices and reward systems actually downgrade teaching. Some of this is externally imposed, ironically by some aspects imposed by quality assurance procedures. Other practices fall into the category of institutional habits; it's always been that way and it does not occur to question them.

Whatever the reasons for their existence, any adverse effects they might have on teaching and learning need to be identified and minimized. Task 12.1 is designed not for teachers but for administrators: heads of department, deans, DVCs.

Task 12.1   Do your quality assurance processes encourage or discourage aligned teaching?

Reflect on current quality assurance processes: are they encouraging or discouraging the implementation of constructively aligned teaching and learning?

You as head of department/dean of faculty:

QA procedures encouraging	*QA procedures discouraging*

On reflection, what changes would you make?

_____

_____

You as senior management (e.g. DVC, chairman of quality assurance committee) of the university:

QA procedures encouraging	*QA procedures discouraging*

On reflection, what changes would you make?

_____

_____

Now some tasks for teachers. There were two tasks in Chapter 3 that we should now revisit as Tasks 12.2 and 12.3.

Task 12.2   Follow-up of Task 3.3

In Task 3.3, we asked you to reflect on a critical incident in your teaching/assessment and how you dealt with the problem then. Let us say you are faced with a similar incident now, after having read this book thus far. Consider it in terms of the following questions:

a What do you think is the problem? What has gone wrong? What is the evidence for a problem?

_____

_____

_____

b What is (are) the cause(s) of the problem?

_____

_____

_____

c How would you deal with the problem now?

_____

_____

_____

d What is the difference between your present answers here and your previous answers? Compared with Task 3.3, what change have you made in dealing with the problem? Why have you made such changes?

_____

_____

_____

Summary and conclusions

A framework for implementing constructive alignment

So far we have been discussing the framework of constructive alignment as a means of rethinking familiar decisions about curriculum, teaching and assessment. We now need a framework for implementing it. Teachers, students and the institution need to reflect on their domains of interaction: teacher and students, teacher and institution and students and institution. Although ILOs, TLAs and ATs have been put in place, arrangements must be made for feedback from all parties to gauge how implementation is proceeding and what adjustments might need to be made.

Task 12.3   Follow-up of Task 3.4

In Task 3.4, we asked you to identify the *three most worrying* problems in teaching a semester- or year-long unit; one that you would realistically hope to minimize by reading this book. What actions will you take to address these problems after reading this book so far?

1 _____
  _____
  _____

2 _____
  _____
  _____

3 _____
  _____
  _____

What is the theoretical basis for your actions?
  _____
  _____
  _____

Revisiting transformative reflection

The mechanism underlying successful implementation is transformative reflection, which is a cyclical process, using theory to analyse problems and to derive solutions and test them. This is known as reflective practice as used by individual practitioners, but exactly the same process applies to individuals on committees and in leadership roles.

Implementation in the individual classroom: Teacher and students

Once a teacher is committed to trying constructive alignment in a course, the main problem of implementation is to mould its shape so that it fits the procedural and collegial requirements of the institution: assessment regulations are likely to be the most constraining. Action research, using reflective practice, is a good paradigm for achieving the best fit. It is important to systematically collect evidence as to progress, both from the students' and from your own perspective and to use a 'critical friend' to help in transformative reflection. This friend reappears in the peer review of teaching.

Implementation at institutional level: Teacher and institution

Implementing constructive alignment over a range of courses across a department or faculty is obviously more problematic than in one course. Good leadership is essential. There are many leadership roles that may be filled by different individuals, some by committees: to make the decision to 'go ahead' without deferring to sceptics, to summon the necessary resources, to provide the necessary pedagogical expertise; to grip the right political elbows, to conduct the implementation orchestra. Equally important is to set up formative evaluation, as in the case of implementing courses.

Implementation at institutional level: Student and the institution

The third interface is between the department or institution and the students. Students need to be represented on all committees dealing with teaching and learning and to provide feedback on department-wide implementation. Students at this level are a useful source of feedback on an aspect that may not arise in course implementation: graduate attributes. Also their feedback on general courses, such as the *Course Experience Questionnaire*, is particularly useful here for comparative purposes. Students would also find it helpful to have a suitable induction into constructive alignment, with inputs from students who have been there before.

The reflective institution

The implementation of constructive alignment raises issues that apply to quality assurance and quality enhancement measures for the whole institution. Such measures should be founded in the scholarship of teaching and learning, involving staff development, continuing formative evaluation and policies and procedures for recognizing quality teaching and learning as an institutional priority. This way, teachers' conceptions will move towards Level 3 and they will teach with conviction and a sense of priority.

Further reading

On reflective practice

Brockbank, A. and McGill, I. (1998) *Facilitating Reflective Learning in Higher Education.* Buckingham: Society for Research into Higher Education/Open University Press.

Cowan, J. (1998) *On Becoming an Innovative Teacher.* Buckingham: Open University Press.

Schon, D.A. (1983) *The Reflective Practitioner: How Professionals Think in Action.* London: Temple Smith.

Schon's book deals with the whole question of improving professional practice by reflection, using examples from several professions. The other two books refer specifically to university teaching. Brockbank and McGill provide detailed help in setting up situations (based mainly on the Schon model) to promote reflection with colleagues and on one's own teaching, with respect to promoting student learning and formal action learning projects. Cowan distinguishes several kinds of reflection, how teachers can best use reflection, how teachers can encourage their students to reflect and how to structure groups and reflective learning journals in ways that best promote the appropriate kind of reflection. The book is driven by a cycle of questions, examples, strategies and generalizations from the examples.

On action research

Gibbs, G. (1992) *Improving the Quality of Student Learning.* Bristol: Technical and Educational Services.

Kember, D. (2000) *Action Learning and Action Research: Improving the Quality of Teaching and Learning,* London: Kogan Page.

Kember, D. (2001) Transforming teaching through action research, in D.A. Watkins and J.B. Biggs (eds) *Teaching the Chinese Learner: Psychological and Pedagogical Perspectives.* Hong Kong: University of Hong Kong Comparative Education Research Centre/Camberwell, Victoria: Australian Council for Educational Research.

Kember, D. and Kelly, M. (1993) *Improving Teaching through Action Research.* Green Guide No. 14. Campbelltown, NSW: Higher Education Research and Development Society of Australasia.

Gibbs's book describes several strategies for deep learning and 10 action research case studies in British tertiary institutions in which one or more of these strategies were used. Kember (2000) or Kember and Kelly (1993) describe how action research may be implemented and Kember (2001) describes a number of particular action research projects conducted in Hong Kong tertiary institutions.

On graduate surveys

Australian Graduate Survey (AGS): http://strategic.curtin.edu.au/ags.html

Examples of graduate survey questionnaires: University of Illinois: http://www.pb.uillinois.edu/dr/gs/ University of Washington: http://72.14.253.104/search?q=cache:DWc1HZI4OSwJ:www.washington.edu/oea/pdfs/reports/OEAReport9808q.pdf+%22graduate+survey%22&hl=en&ct=clnk&cd=98&gl=au

On teaching portfolios

http://ftad.osu.edu/portfolio/
www.city.londonmet.ac.uk/deliberations/portfolios/ICED_workshop/
seldin_book.html
Samples of teaching portfolios from different disciplines: http://Wings.buffalo.edu/
provost/cltr/files/teaching_portfolio.htm#portfolio_guidelines www.wsu.edu/
provost/teaching.htm
Electronic teaching portfolios: http://electronicportfolios.com/portfolios/
site2000.html http://eduscapes.com/tap/topic82.htm

On peer review of teaching

www.edna.edu.au/edna/go/highered/hot_topics/cache/offonce/pid/960   under
Teaching – Peer review of teaching.
Review proformas used in different teaching/learning situations from the University
of Tasmania: www.utas.edu.au/tl/improving/peerreview/

Other resources

www.unisanet.unisa.edu.au/learningconnection/staff/practice/
evaluationpeerreview.asp
http://www.utexas.edu/academic/cte/PeerObserve.html

On the scholarship of teaching and learning

Carnegie Academy for the Scholarship of Teaching and Learning (CASTL) Campus
Program with the American Association of Higher Education (AAHE). http://
www.sotl.ilstu.edu/
The Journal of the Scholarship of Teaching and Learning http://www.iupui.edu/~josotl/
Google 'Scholarship of teaching and learning' or 'SoTL' and you'll get all
you'll ever need to know about contacts, conferences, and journals.

13

Constructive alignment as implemented: Some examples

In this chapter, we present examples of constructive alignment in action from several institutions. First, we present a faculty-wide implementation of constructively aligned courses illustrating the principles of implementation discussed in Chapter 12. We then present courses in several different areas: veterinary science, accounting, engineering, information systems, management sciences and nursing. These courses are recent implementations of constructive alignment, designed within institutional resourcing, policies and procedures and with ongoing quality enhancement. They are produced here with the permission of each course designer. The formatting and method and extent of implementation are quite varied: some, for example, using quantitative, and others qualitative, methods of assessment and grading; some specifying quite precisely the alignment between ILOs and their associated teaching/learning activities and assessment tasks; others using a more holistic alignment. This diversity is excellent, as it shows that there is no one way of implementing constructive alignment. Transformative reflection is carried out realistically within each individual teacher's interpretation of the concept of alignment and according to his or her own zone of feasibility.

A faculty-wide implementation*

In 1997, the Faculty of Veterinary Science, University of Sydney, was in poor shape. It was suffering from a steady decline in government funding, the culture was disintegrating and lacked direction, students complained about teaching that was 'didactic and uninspiring'. There was a call for it to be amalgamated with two other small faculties.

---

* Source: Taylor and Canfield 2007.

That call for amalgamation was the wake-up – together with the internal appointment, in 1998, of a visionary dean who was determined to turn a bad situation around. He organized meetings with the then 55 (now approximately 70) academic staff members and a range of stakeholders – students, the veterinary profession, industry and key university personnel – who made clear their comments and criticisms of the faculty. It hurt, but putting all that together showed a way forward.

The first thing to be changed was the culture of the faculty. The plan was to make it more outwardly focused, receptive to the needs of students, the profession and funding/industry bodies and to place it on a growth trajectory for sustainability. The leadership became distributed, with staff being given greater responsibility for teaching decisions; teaching was to be more student-centred, a move that coincided with a university-wide initiative in 2000 to support innovation and install quality enhancement systems. Staff agreed on a new goal: 'A shared culture of excellence and scholarship in teaching and learning.' There were three interacting principles to guide implementation of the new student-centred curriculum:

1 Professionalism in education, involving the shared leadership in the newly restructured faculty, with rewards for teaching and support in staff development.
2 An innovative constructively aligned curriculum based on teaching scholarship.
3 Quality enhancement, through a culture of continuous improvement based on evidence gained in particular from action research.

Supporting professionalism

The decision was made at the start to use an across-the-board approach, rather than focus on a few innovators and work out from them. This is not the usual approach (p. 258). However, the dean's change strategy was to build and articulate a new culture with shared values and a sense of a cohesive identity as a faculty, a strategy that the staff strongly supported. The dean used the distributed leadership model to spread responsibility personally among the staff. Departmental boundaries were removed so that teaching was organized by faculty teams not from the old departments and cross-disciplinary units became easily feasible. External facilitators conducted workshops on leadership and teamwork to make the new structure work effectively and for colleagues to feel secure with collegial support yet free to think laterally and share ideas.

Professionalism was supported by rewards for good teaching, small teaching development grants to focus on innovative teaching, aligning the new curriculum to graduate attributes. Professionalism in teaching was progressively increased by staff development activities and numerous workshops and by recruitment. New staff were appointed on their interest in student-centred learning and their willingness to undertake formal training in education. By 2006, a third of the staff had qualified for the graduate certificate in educational studies (higher education).

Scholarly teaching

The curriculum was completely reconstructed. The old departmental subjects were replaced with integrated units drawing from several subject areas with a strong case-based emphasis. Timetabled teaching was reduced by 25%, the final year being a lecture-free zone, using experiential learning in professional placements. All teaching was designed to be constructively aligned, using graduate attributes to provide a framework for the whole curriculum. Large class teaching was held to a maximum of 50% of teaching time and was mostly less than this, thus allowing a greater range of TLAs including e-learning, case-based learning, placements and practical classes.

Pains were taken to create a Theory Y climate. As one student commented: 'You feel welcome and invited to contribute to all aspects of the faculty and they seem genuinely pleased about feedback.'

Quality enhancement through evidence-based teaching

Quality enhancement procedures involved action research by staff members with frequent, ongoing data collection and constructive reflection on evidence obtained that might throw light on the quality of teaching and learning and how it might be improved. Sources of evidence included: students, graduates, staff and the university. Agreed minimal levels of performance focused attention on struggling courses and additional resources used to improve performance. Staff development workshops and external consultants were used as needed. The teaching and learning quality enhancement exercise was overseen by the faculty learning and teaching committee and there were also quality enhancement initiatives in research and clinical practice.

What is the evidence for the success of the innovations? The *Student Course Experience Questionnaire* scale scores rose steadily from year 2000 and in 2005, the faculty obtained highest or second highest score in the university in five out of the seven scales. In the years 2000–2006, 25 staff had received teaching awards, while in the preceding seven years, none had. One of the spurs to this dramatic achievement was the decision to seek, and in 2005 to obtain, North American accreditation, which became a 'catalyst for transforming the local curriculum into one that had global acceptance and relevance'.

On a norm-referenced note, the faculty is today one of the leading veterinary and animal science schools in Australia, with a great increase in student demand and a correspondingly high admissions index. This was not, however, at the expense of research. On the contrary, in the warmer, task-oriented search for excellence in teaching, the indicators for research excellence also increased: publications, research monies relative to the rest of the university and numbers of successful research students while the ratings by research students for supervision, infrastructure, research climate etc. rose from worst in the university to best during the period in question.

Taylor and Canfield (2007) saw the following factors as important in helping to establish and sustain the goal of scholarly teaching:

1 inspirational leaders and effective strategic planning
2 commitment to shared leadership for student-centred learning
3 agreed faculty culture inclusive of all staff and students
4 engagement of external stakeholders in curriculum reform
5 curriculum alignment with graduate attributes
6 curriculum evaluation and accreditation for quality enhancement
7 enabling and supportive structures in faculty and university
8 innovation and research into student learning.

Comment

This astonishing success story shows what can be done with the leadership, the will and the commitment to the scholarship of teaching and learning. The overriding principle is *alignment*: every decision made has to conform to the culture established to implement constructive alignment. It is highly significant that the university as a whole was also committed to student-centred learning and was able to come up with the support structure needed in terms of staff developers, policies and procedures.

This is a textbook example, with one apparent exception, of the principles of implementation outlined in Chapter 12:

1 *Strong and committed leadership* and the thorough commitment of all staff (pp. 256–7). A few of the older academic staff did not share this commitment at first: some took early retirement, to be replaced by younger staff who did commit to the faculty goal; remaining doubters simply joined the teaching teams and were swept along with the general flow – and in due course became converts.
2 *Theoretical basis to the change* was there from the start: the scholarship of teaching in general and constructive alignment in particular when it came to course design. It was this SoTL theory that allowed the transformative reflection following the bad experience.
3 *Formative evaluation* was built in from the start and orchestrated by a teaching and learning committee. Staff contributed too with their own teaching development projects.
4 *Strategies for change.* The one apparent exception to the principles raised in Chapter 12 was Fullan's recommendation that one starts small and works outwards, based on successes (p. 258). The present decision to go full on across the whole faculty was a bold one, but given that the *status quo* was non-viable, and the faculty was totally restructured around the central

goal to establish 'sustainable, scholarly teaching', this was in the event the right decision.

5 *Change teachers' conceptions first or make them teach differently first?* Here, teachers were required to teach differently, but the reasons, the theory underlying the change, were always upfront. The general answer to this point again lies in the climate created. Teachers weren't just ordered: 'You teach differently!' A rich context was provided in which the difference in teaching from what most were used to, to what was required was fully supported by both physical resourcing and by a change in climate of thinking about teaching.

6 *The faculty climate* was thus a vital part of this context: a supportive Theory Y climate in which both staff and students felt mutual responsibility.

The fact of this transformation in the space of five years from one of the struggling to one of the best institutions for preparing veterinarians and animal scientists in Australia must allay any doubts that constructively aligned teaching is impractical.

Veterinary science

Our first example of an aligned course is from the faculty we have just examined. 'Animal Structure and Functions 3A' (ASF3A) is a second-year course of a four-year degree programme of BAnVetBioSc at the University of Sydney. The number of students in the course in 2006 was 78. The course was designed by a team, the details supplied by Dr Rosanne Taylor and Dr Melanie Collier.

Course aims

The aims of this course are that students will integrate knowledge of structure (anatomy) and function (physiology) and draw on concepts introduced in Animal Science 2 to build their understanding of key systems that are integral to the maintenance of internal homeostasis. These concepts provide a basis for investigating the effect of genes, biotechnology, nutrition and reproductive changes on animal function and production in year 3 units.

Intended learning outcomes (ILOs)

On completion of this unit students will be able to:

ILO1 *Analyse* the contribution of hormones to maintenance of internal homeostasis in animals
ILO2 *Critically analyse* applied animal physiology research articles
ILO3 *Advise* how the natural mechanisms animals use for defence from

foreign molecules and organisms can be manipulated to confer immunity

ILO4 *Advise* on animal management practices that meet the physiological needs of animals (considering the animals' sensory structures, central processing, autonomic and motor responses)

For purposes of illustration, we show alignment of the TLAs and ATs for ILOs 2 and 4 only.

Teaching and learning activities (TLAs)

TLA1: Critical review

The students undertake a critical review of two recently published research papers on pain/welfare/research in animal husbandry/slaughter. They are encouraged to make their own choice as to topic. The specific ILOs of the critical review are that students will:

1 critically evaluate scientific literature
2 relate the principles of neural processing to analysis of animals' responses to husbandry procedures
3 use the structure and characteristics of good scientific writing
4 provide constructive feedback on scientific writing of peers.

It is intended that undertaking this task will develop and demonstrate students' knowledge of central neural processing, sensory processing, pain and consciousness and provide an opportunity for students to integrate and apply these principles to assessment of humane animal husbandry and slaughter methods. As the task is completed, students will also develop key graduate attributes for animal and veterinary bioscientists in information retrieval, information management, critical analysis, written expression and animal welfare, attributes that will be further developed and assessed in their final-year honours/research project. The peer-assessment component provides an opportunity to reflect on their own scientific writing, to develop skills in editing and commenting on the work of peers and to improve on the quality of their own written work prior to final submission.

The students are prepared for the review with a tutorial on scientific writing to dissect and analyse a published paper and a class on how to critically review literature, which is supported by documents and a website showing students how to conduct their own critical review. A literature searching session with the librarians helps students learn how to find and to evaluate other sources of information that may be useful.

TLA2: Peer review

Students are required to review a critical review of their peers. The topic reviewed is completely different from the one they investigated in order to increase their appreciation of the other work in the field.

Students use grade descriptors and criteria to provide constructive feedback to their peers on a proforma by the following week. They frequently write several pages of useful suggestions and feedback on the hard copy (this is very popular with their peers) in accord with grade descriptors in the unit handbook:

1   purpose of research
2   selection and approach
3   quality of evidence
4   conclusions
5   general comments on format, word limit, grammar, spelling
6   suggested mark (/20)

One week later the students submit their revised critical review. The teacher sees the original, student comments, papers and the final submission. Only the final submission is marked; the earlier versions and comments give feedback to students on how they have improved their work to let the peer reviewers know that they have provided good constructive advice.

Assessment task (AT)

Critical review of research papers

(Addresses ILOs 2 and 4.) The critical review used in TLA1 forms part of the assessment of the course. The students are given a list of papers and are encouraged to make their own choice depending on their interest. This task encourages them to read more widely and to include some reviews and alternative perspectives. Feedback from the teachers is provided to students on how their works have improved. The critical review is worth 20% of the course, which is 6/24 credit points of one semester of the whole programme.

This assessment task is the only time where ILO2 is assessed in this unit. ILO4, as broader and encompassing several topics, is also assessed in other ways, including a written examination and project. The grading criteria are based on a combination of students' application of scientific knowledge in their evaluation of the work, as well as their ability to express their ideas effectively in the scientific critique.

Grading criteria for the critical reviews are provided to students in the handbook and are reproduced in Table 13.1.

Online resources

http://www.deakin.edu.au/studentlife/academic_skills/undergraduate/handouts/
     crit_analysis.php
http://eebweb.arizona.edu/courses/Ecol437/reading1.pdf

Table 13.1 Grading criteria for the critical review of literature in veterinary science

Grade	Introduction/literature review
High distinction or mastery 85–100%	The report represents work of an exceptional standard: • is a highly articulate and professional document • includes complex critical comments with extended justification (and appropriate referencing) in all sections that reflect an applied and transposable understanding of key issues • demonstrates initiative and originality in analysis or interpretation Comprehensive and highly professional: • shows a high level of thought, knowledge and reflection • student is able to relate material to other knowledge domains • review critiques literature well, incorporating many sources to develop an argument with little to no summarizing of previous work • may resolve theoretical and/or empirical problems and show evidence of creative or innovative conceptualization • discussion is integrated into a logical, coherent whole: 'tells a story' and leads logically into research proposed • creates a sense of mastery of literature and relevant technical issues
Distinction or high level of achievement 75–84%	The report is of a superior standard: • is well written (as in credit) and free of errors • includes coherent critical comments with substantial justification (and appropriate referencing) in all sections that reflect an integrated understanding of key issues • provides evidence of broader appreciation of the relationships between key aspects of studies in this field • demonstrates complex, deep understanding of the subject matter Effective and comprehensive: • evidence of thought and reflection • often relates material to other knowledge domains • includes critical appraisal, but may also summarize rather than evaluate some aspects of literature • review identifies and attempts to resolve theoretical puzzles • essential content within the domain is successfully integrated

(continued)

Table 13.1 (continued)

Grade	Introduction/literature review
Credit good level of achievement 65–74%	The report: • is complete, well structured and well presented • is written in a clear style that communicates points effectively on first reading • synthesizes and applies concepts appropriately to the problem • includes coherent critical comments with justification based on evidence in all sections that reflect a sound understanding of key issues • uses evidence/argument from the literature in the field in analysis Review identifies and defines major issues: • clear and strong arguments are developed within some major issues • some tendency to summarize literature rather than develop an integrative and logical argument • technical issues treated competently
Pass 50–64%	The report: • addresses all four major themes in the analysis but does not integrate or relate key ideas and issues effectively • is presented in an organized manner but may contain irregularities in style, expression that do not interfere with meaning • provides critical comments with justification in some sections that reflect a basic understanding of key issues • demonstrates that the literature in the field has been consulted Review identifies some major issues: • comments are essentially descriptive • minimal critical analysis is attempted • *or* analysis lacks depth • *or* analysis is somewhat confused • main focus is on concrete issues • lack of integrating argument • some technical expertise revealed • may have non-major factual errors
Fail > 50%	The report: • does not address the four major themes of the analysis • evidence of plagiarism or academic dishonesty • presented in a disorganized, incoherent manner • contains no/little or inappropriate critical comments • provides no/little justification for critical comments • does not show any appreciation of the literature in the field

Accounting

'Accounting 1' is a one-semester core course in the first year of a three-year bachelor of business administration (BBA) degree programme offered by the Department of Accountancy of the Faculty of Business at the City University of Hong Kong. The number of students in each class is 200. The course was designed by Dr Olivia Leung of the Department of Accountancy.

Course aims

1 Provide students with technical knowledge in processing, preparing and reporting accounting information in accordance with GAAP (generally accepted accounting principles) for external users in a modern economy.
2 Provide students with general knowledge about internal control procedures and financial ratios.
3 Encourage students to be responsible and active learners.

Intended learning outcomes (ILOs)

On completion of this course, student will be able to:

ILO1 *Record* accounting transactions related to cash, receivables, inventories, fixed assets, payables, shareholders' equity, revenues, costs of merchandise sold and expenses
Prepare financial statements (balance sheets, statements of shareholders' equity, statements of retained earnings, and income statements) for servicing and merchandising companies
ILO2 *Identify* and *explain* fundamental GAAP (generally accepted accounting principles)
Select and *apply* the appropriate GAAP to support accounting treatments in preparing financial reports
ILO3 *Identify* internal control procedures over cash, receivables, inventories and fixed assets
Calculate and *interpret* fundamental financial ratios based on information collected from balance sheets and income statements
ILO4 *Be a responsible learner: attend* classes and *submit* assignments on time and prepared, *be attentive* in classes; *follow* teaching schedule closely; be an active learner: *actively participate* in class activities; be *self-motivated.*

Teaching and learning activities (TLAs)

TLA1: Situation: Interactive lecture
Concepts and general knowledge of financial accounting are presented with PowerPoint slides:

- Personal digital assistant (PDA) questions and answers: students respond to questions in lectures using their PDAs and the lecturer provides feedbacks based on students' responses.
- Work-along exercise: students are given exercises and are encouraged to work along with the lecturer and their peers as the lecturer covers each topic. This exercise helps students follow the lecture closely and to visualize the applications of the concepts.
- Concept map: in the beginning or at the end of each lecture, the lecturer uses the concept maps to demonstrate links between various topics presented in the lecture.

Major focus: ILOs 1, 2 and 4; minor focus: ILO3.

TLA2: Situation: Tutorial

Technical procedures and practice questions are covered:

- Weekly tutorial assignments: assignments for each week are specifically assigned to give students opportunity to think through the concepts and to apply the concepts to various business transactions.
- Various in-class activities: students are given various activities such as work-along practice questions, group discussions, self-test multiple-choice questions, ideas sharing and presenting time etc.

Major focus: ILOs 1, 3 and 4; minor focus: ILO2.

TLA3: Situation: Outside classroom activities

Additional help is provided outside official class time:

- Tutor consultation: each tutor provides four consultation hours weekly to help his/her students with technical issues or issues with learning accounting in general.
- SI (Supplementary Instruction) scheme: performing second-year accounting major students are selected to be SI leaders. Each leader will head a group of FB2100 students and to meet with them weekly to provide additional help on self-learning skills in accounting.
- Helpdesk: extra help is provided to students who have difficulties when they are preparing for mid-term test and final examination. Designated helpers provide help to students throughout the week before mid-term test and final examination to answer students' technical questions.

Major focus: ILOs 3 and 4; minor focus: ILOs 1 and 2.

Assessment tasks (ATs)

AT1: Tutorial assignments and participation (15%)

Weekly tutorial assignments are given to students to assess students' understanding and knowledge on topics listed in the weekly teaching schedule.

Major focus: ILOs 1 and 4; minor focus: ILOs 2 and 3.

AT2: Group project (15%)

Students in tutorial classes are grouped into four groups (i.e. each group is made up of four to six students). Each group will be given a project on either internal control procedures or financial ratios. Groups are required to submit written reports.
   Major focus: ILO3.

AT3: Mid-term test (30%)

The test is designed to assess students' technical knowledge in analysing business transactions, journalizing and preparing financial statements for external reporting.
   Major focus: ILOs 1 and 2.

AT4: Final examination (40%)

The examination is designed to assess students' technical knowledge in analysing business transactions, applying accounting principles to support accounting treatments, journalizing preparing financial reports for external users.
   Major focus: ILOs 1 and 2.

Grading criteria

Some examples of grading criteria are shown in Table 13.2.

Engineering

'Engineering principles and design' is a one-semester course in the first year of a three-year bachelor of manufacturing engineering programme in the Faculty of Science and Engineering at the City University of Hong Kong. Usual enrolments are 180 students. The course was designed by Dr Lawrence Li of City University Hong Kong, in consultation with Mark Endean, Open University, Milton Keynes, UK.

Course aims

Engineers plan, analyse, design and build anything that may move and sustain load – products range from toys to automobiles and aircraft. They employ an energy source and convert it into mechanical motions in machines such as robots or pumps. This is the second of two closely linked courses, 'Mechanics' and 'Engineering Principles and Design'. Both courses aim to lay down the foundations of mechanical engineering principles in such a way

Table 13.2 Examples of grading criteria of different assessment tasks in accounting

Group project (AT2)

ILO	Content	Excellent A+ A A−	Good B+ B B−	Adequate C+ C C−	Marginal D
ILO3	Each group is given a case on internal control procedures Each group is required to write a report to study the case and to analyse the business's control procedures	Able to precisely identify and explain both strong and weak existing internal control procedures; able to design internal control procedures specifically for the company	Able to identify and describe both strong and weak existing internal control procedures; able to suggest some commonly used internal control procedures	Able to identify and briefly describe strong and weak existing internal control procedures	Able to identify strong and weak existing internal control procedures

Mid-term (AT3) and final examination (AT4)

ILO	Excellent A+ A A−	Good B+ B B−	Adequate C+ C C−	Marginal D
ILO1	Able to journalize accounting transactions in all areas covered with appropriate account titles and amounts; able to project the impacts of the journal entries to financial statements	Able to journalize accounting transactions in most covered areas; able to project the impacts of some journal entries to financial statements	Able to journalize some accounting transactions; able to carry some journal entries to financial statements	Able to journalize some accounting transactions
	Able to prepare all financial reports for both servicing and merchandising companies in an accurate and appropriate manner and format in reflecting a true and fair view of the financial reports	Able to prepare all financial reports for either servicing or merchandising companies in an accurate manner in reflecting a true and fair view of the financial reports	Able to prepare most financial reports for either servicing or merchandising companies	Able to prepare some financial reports for either servicing or merchandising companies

ILO2	Able to identify and clearly explain GAAP in writing; able to demonstrate application skills by selecting the appropriate GAAP in supporting various accounting treatments	Able to identify and describe GAAP in writing; able to discriminate between different principles under GAAP	Able to recall and describe some principles under GAAP	Able to recall some principles under GAAP

that the students can identify the appropriate concepts required in given engineering problems and apply them to formulate the suitable engineering solutions.

Intended learning outcomes (ILOs)

On successful completion of this course, students should be able to:

ILO1 *Apply* the principles of mechanical kinetics to single degree of freedom vibration systems
ILO2 *Outline* the fundamental theory of friction and wear and its applications in engineering
ILO3 *Describe* the basic theories of fluid mechanics and heat transfer
ILO4 *Apply* the basic engineering mechanics principles to the design and implementation of a simple engineering system (such as a projectile machine) and the evaluation of its performance
ILO5 *Work* effectively as a *team* member in a small-scale engineering project

Teaching and learning activities (TLAs)

TLA1: Situation: Large class
This is a typical lecturing setting but efforts are made to insert short questions regarding the lesson so that students have opportunities to discuss with each other. From time to time students are asked to discuss among themselves for a couple of minutes regarding a topic that has just been taught. This is to give them some space to relax between topics and provide a review of the lesson so far.
   Major focus: ILOs 1 and 2; minor focus: ILO3.

TLA2: Situation: Small group
Students interact more closely with the teacher than is possible in the large class: much use is made of think-aloud modelling in mathematical problems.

Students likewise solve problems and receive diagnostic feedback. Both large and small class teaching variously address the first three ILOs. Small class – the format is flexible and the teaching context is problem solving. The students are first asked to work among themselves to see whether a solution can come up. If not, the teacher will join one group and solve the problem. After that, the students are encouraged to teach each other regarding the problem before the class proceed to the next question.

Major focus: ILOs 1 and 2; minor focus: ILO3.

TLA3: Situation: laboratory

The lab exercises are designed to supplement the taught materials such as friction, fluid mechanics and heat transfer.

Major focus: ILOs 1 and 3.

TLA4: Student-centred activity (SCA)

SCA is a project that utilizes the subject material of the courses 'Mechanics' and 'Engineering Principles and Design' to design a simple mechanism. The students are expected to work in teams to develop the schematic design, perform the kinematics/kinetic analysis, make an analysis of loading, investigate the behaviour of the components under elastic and dynamic loading and make appropriate design decisions. The students also investigate friction and lubrication aspects of the components and finalize their design.

Major focus: ILOs 4 and 5.

Assessment tasks/activities (ATs)

There are three major assessment situations: final examination, laboratory report and the SCA (project) according to the weighting in Table 13.3.

Examination and laboratory report are numerically marked and grades awarded accordingly.

The SCA (project) is graded using the following criteria.

Group assessment

a Prototype (30%) – the working machine built to given specifications will be assessed based on its design, effectiveness, reliability and workmanship.
b Software (30%) – a simple software programme will be written to determine the control parameter(s) for the machine to perform a given task (e.g. to propel the golf ball for a specified distance). The software can be implemented in any preferred computer languages or application software such as Excel.
c Report (40%) – the typed report shall include:

  • sketches of different design and related comments
  • calculations behind the final design

Table 13.3 Weighting of the three assessment tasks in engineering with respect to the ILOs

ATs	Examination	Laboratory report	SCA	Total (%)
ILO 1	20	5	—	25
ILO 2	10	—	—	10
ILO 3	10	5	—	15
ILO 4	—	—	45	45
ILO 5	—	—	5	5
Total (%)	40	10	50	100

- drawings with clear major dimensions
- calibration data and graphs
- reconciliation between theory and practice
- software algorithm, description and also listing if available
- anything that is useful to explain and promote the project work.

Peer-assessment

Assessment of others is an important skill for a professional engineer. Near the end of the project, each student will be asked to assess different members of the group objectively. This is used to differentiate the project contribution from each group member and their effectiveness as an engineering team player. The results are used to calculate the final project mark for each student.

Information Systems

'Management Information Systems I' is a one-semester core course in the first year of a three-year bachelor of business administration (BBA) degree programme offered by the Department of Information Systems of the Faculty of Business at the City University of Hong Kong. The number of students registered in the course in 2006–2007 academic year is 810, divided into smaller classes. The course was designed by Dr Ron Chi-Wai Kwok of the Department of Information Systems.

Course aims

1 Provide students with knowledge about the technological foundation of business information systems.
2 Equip students with the essential skills to work with common computer applications in today's business world.

3 Familiarize students with business information systems relevant to their professional career and applications in Hong Kong.

Intended learning outcomes (ILOs)

On completion of this course, student will be able to:

ILO1 *Describe* the basic concepts of information systems, their composition, configuration and architecture, including the internet and web-based technologies in particular

ILO2 *Explain* the social, economic, regulatory, political and mainly ethical aspects in the development, implementation and use of information systems in international business settings

ILO3 *Apply* the general knowledge and methodologies of information systems, including the use of hardware and software, to *devise* and *evaluate* effective solutions to international business problems, given the information needs

ILO4 *Design* and *develop* particular constructs and models to support various levels of international business activities using different tools such as Microsoft FrontPage, Microsoft Access and Microsoft Excel

ILO5 *Work* productively as part of a team and, in particular, *communicate* and *present* information effectively in written and electronic formats in a collaborative environment

Teaching and learning activities (TLAs)

TLA1: Situation: Interactive lecture

Concepts and general knowledge of information systems are explained:

- Personal digital assistant (PDA) questions and answers: students respond to questions in lectures using their PDAs and the lecturer provides feedbacks based on students' response.
- Gobbets: showing videos about business cases and scenarios using the e-Organization (e-Org) cases.
- Concept map: the lecturer uses concept maps to conceptualize presented materials.
- Role play: students act as IT technicians and assemble a computer system.
- PDA one-minute note: at the end of the lecture, the lecturer reminds students to use their PDAs to write down the main topic that they find most difficult to understand in the session or the major question that they want to raise. In the next lecture, the lecturer provides feedback based on students' concerns in their one-minute notes.

Major focus: ILOs 1 and 2; minor focus: ILO3.

TLA2: Situation: Computer lab tutorial

Technical aspects of information systems design and development are covered:

- Computer lab exercises: hands-on activities on Microsoft FrontPage, Excel and Access.
- Group project discussion: discussion on various aspects of the group project (setting up a web page and a database for an online store, using Excel for decision support).

Major focus: ILO4; minor focus: ILOs 3 and 5.

TLA3: Situation: Outside classroom activities

Additional help provided outside official class time:

- e-token: a PDA system in which students earn e-tokens by completing some learning-oriented activities such as crossword puzzles that are downloadable to their PDAs. Students can complete the downloaded PDA exercises at any time and anywhere (e.g. in MTR or on a bus).
- Online helpdesk: an online system to provide extra help to students having difficulties with the course outside the classroom. During the assigned periods, students can raise their questions about mid-term test or final examination in the online system. The tutors will answer their questions within four hours during the office hour.

Major focus: ILOs 1 and 3; minor focus: ILO2.

Assessment tasks (ATs)

AT1: Tutorial assignments and participation (10%)

Two assignments (3% each) are given to assess the student's competence level working with Microsoft FrontPage, Microsoft Access and Microsoft Excel.
   Major focus: ILO4, minor focus: ILOs 3 and 5.

AT2: Group projects (35%)

The project is divided into three phases; each is designed to assess the student's ability in constructing interactive web pages, working with databases and devising decision support models in a business setting.
   Major focus: ILOs 3 and 4; minor focus: ILO5.

AT3: Mid-term test (15%)

The test is designed to gauge the student's grasp of information systems concepts and knowledge, as well as the ability to apply them to solve business problems in various situations.
   Major focus: ILOs 1 and 3; minor focus: ILO2.

AT4: Final examination (40%)

The examination is designed to gauge the student's grasp of information systems concepts and knowledge, as well as the ability to apply them to solve business problems in various situations.

Major focus: ILOs 1 and 3; minor focus: ILO2.

Grading criteria

Some examples of grading criteria are shown in Table 13.4.

Table 13.4 Some examples of grading criteria for different assessment tasks in information systems

Group project phase 1 (AT2)

ILO	Content	Excellent A+ A A–	Good B+ B B–	Adequate C+ C C–	Marginal D
ILO3 **ILO4**	Overall design (sizing, grouping, alignment, colour, look and feel, etc.)	Designed in a professional way: fonts and graphics complement each other, text is in the appropriate size, making it easy to read, appropriate use of colour, easy navigation through the pages	The ability to design a professional webpage is demonstrated in most pages with a few exceptions	The quality in most pages are average (e.g. inappropriate font size/item grouping/font colour/background colour, etc.)	A merely acceptable design in general
ILO4	Creativity	Highly creative design: novel and original, clearly superior to templates or examples covered in class	Design with some creative idea, on top of templates or examples covered in class	Average design with few creative ideas	Little creativity shown
ILO4	Practicability	Extremely practical design: can be considered a usable	Quite a practical design: lacking a few minor	Average design, but not very practical since a few major	Only satisfies a small number of

product even commercially, since it satisfies all the functional requirements set out	components to be considered complete	components are not implemented	practical needs

Mid-term (AT3) and final examination (AT4)

ILO	Excellent A+ A A−	Good B+ B B−	Adequate C+ C C−	Marginal D
ILO1	Demonstrate sound knowledge of most materials covered, able to describe all concepts of information systems and to identify relationship between difference concepts	Able to describe various major concepts of information systems with thorough comprehension of each and able to discriminate between different concepts	Able to recall and describe some important concepts of information systems and able to show some linkages between different concepts	Able to recall major concepts of information systems with simple description, with ability to grasp linkages between a small number of concepts
ILO2	Able to explain impact of information systems from various perspectives and how this determines the use of information systems in international business settings based on sound knowledge	Able to explain information systems' impacts in the various aspects, with well-rounded knowledge in international business settings	Able to explain some of the information systems' impacts in some aspects, with some knowledge in international business settings	Able to explain a few important impacts of information systems, with knowledge limited in local business settings
ILO3	Able to make critical judgments by applying sound information systems knowledge, compare and discriminate between ideas and create unique solutions to business problems	Able to apply various components of information systems to solve open-ended as well as closed-ended business problems using skills and knowledge acquired	Able to apply some components of information systems to solve simple problems using skills and knowledge acquired	Able to apply some components of information systems to form partial solution to business problems using skills and knowledge acquired

Quality enhancement

To facilitate quality enhancement both for the course teachers/programme leader and also individual students, Dr Kwok makes use of the assessment grade results for transformative reflection.

Course-level achievement

Table 13.5 shows the integrated (averaged) grades of all students in a given course, with respect to different ATs and different ILOs. It also shows the overall grades of students in each AT and each ILO, as well as the final grade of students at the course level.

Thus, students in the course are good at ILO4 and ILO5, but just okay in ILO1 and ILO2. Based on these results, the course leader may need to focus more on facilitating students achieving ILOs 1 and 2 in the next semester. The programme leader can think about the adjustment of the curriculum of the year 2 courses accordingly, in order to help students strengthen their ILOs 1 and 2. The year 2 course leaders can also have a better understanding of their incoming students and better prepare the courses on these issues.

Table 13.5 A quality-enhancement measure focusing on the mean results for a given course

The left-hand column lists the assessment tasks, the top row the ILOs. Cell entries are the mean grades obtained in the course

ATs	ILO1	ILO2	ILO3	ILO4	ILO5	Total
AT1				A–		A–
AT2				A–		A–
GP1			A	A	A–	A–
GP2			B+	A–	B+	A–
GP3			A–	A–	A–	A–
MTT	C+	C	B			B–
FEX	B–	B–	B			B–
PAT					A–	A
Total	**B–**	**B–**	**B+**	**A–**	**A–**	**B**

GP1 – group project 1
GP2 – group project 2
GP3 – group project 3
MTT – mid-term test
FEX – final examination
PAT – tutorial participation

Individual student achievement

Table 13.6 shows how the quality enhancement system works for an individual student's performance in the ATs and in each of the ILOs.

This student is weak in ILO1 and ILO2, but strong in ILO4 and ILO5; weak in mid-term test and final examination, but good in group project. This provides feedback to the student about the sort of areas represented by ILOs 1 and 2 and would help his/her decision making in years 2 and 3 to choose courses that would reinforce their learning in these areas if appropriate.

Table 13.6 A quality-enhancement measure focusing on the results obtained by an individual student

The left-hand column lists the assessment tasks, the top row the ILOs. Cell entries are the grades obtained by an individual student in the course

ATs	ILO1	ILO2	ILO3	ILO4	ILO5	Total
AT1				A–		A–
AT2				B+		B+
GP1			A+	A+	B+	A
GP2			A–	A	B	A–
GP3			A	A–	A–	A–
MTT	C+	C–	C			C
FEX	C	C+	B			C+
PAT					A	A
Total	**C**	**C+**	**B**	**A–**	**A–**	**B**

Management sciences

'SOM1: Design of Service Delivery Systems' is a one-semester course in the second year of the Service Operations Management degree programme offered by the Department of Management Sciences of the Faculty of Business at the City University of Hong Kong. It is also offered as an elective or an out-of-discipline course to other students. The number of registered students in 2006/07 is 74. The course was designed by Ms Sandy Wong of the Department of Management Sciences.

Course aims

This course provides students with the knowledge of how to address the major issues involved in the design of the service package and the service delivery system. The strategic role of the supporting service facility and the challenges of delivering exceptional service quality are emphasized in the context of service organizations.

Intended learning outcomes (ILOs)

On successful completion of this course, students should be able to:

ILO1 *Describe* the service concept and the nature of services

ILO2 *Discuss* the competitive service strategy and the role of information in services with examples

ILO3 *Critically discuss* the service delivery including the service process and service encounter

ILO4 *Identify* service quality problems and use the quality tools for *analysis* and *problem solving*

ILO5 *Recommend* the facility design features to *identify* bottleneck operation and *remove* the anxiety of disorientation

ILO6 *Evaluate* the service facility location to *minimize* total flow–distance of a service process layout and to *estimate* the expected revenues and market share

Teaching and learning activities (TLAs)

TLA1: Situation: Interactive lecture

- Lectures: concepts and general knowledge of service operations management are explained.
- PDA questions and answers: students respond to questions in lectures using their PDAs and the lecturer provides feedback based on students' response.
- Peer learning: students will be asked to work in a group of two or three to recap and answer questions of the major topics that they learned in the previous lecture. They are required to share and present their answers to the class.
- Videos: videos about business cases and scenarios are shown and followed with class discussion.
- PDA one-minute note: at the end of the lecture, the lecturer reminds students to use their PDAs to write down the main topic that they find most difficult to understand in the session or the major question that they want to raise. In the next lecture, the lecturer provides feedback based on students' concerns in their one-minute notes.
- Learning log: students have to respond to each of the ILOs addressed in each lecture. Responses and reflection can vary from how they learned

it, what activities reinforced the concepts learned, resources they used to learn the concept etc.

Major focus: ILOs 1, 2, 5 and 6; minor focus: ILOs 3 and 4.

TLA2: Situation: Tutorial

Students are required to team up with their classmates and participate in the following activities:

- Role play: students act as service providers and customers to simulate service encounters.
- Tutorial exercises and activities: students respond to and participate in in-class exercises and activities. They are required to apply real-life examples or their own service experiences to their learnt subjects.
- Group discussion and case study: discussion on various aspects of the assigned major issues or questions as well as the assigned case studies.

Major focus: ILOs 3 and 6; minor focus: ILOs 1, 2, 4 and 5.

TLA3: Situation: Outside classroom activities

Students are required to carry out some learning-oriented activities outside their classroom such as mystery shopping, walk-through audit, servicescape, process flow and layout improvement. Students present their findings and results of work to the class.

Major focus: ILOs 3, 4 and 5.

Assessment tasks/activities (ATs)

Group work (45% AT1, AT2, AT3)

The objective of group work is to equip students with the necessary knowledge, attitude and skills to become a deep learner by means of small group discussion and sharing. Students are required to form a group of 4–5 to work on the group course work, introduce themselves and exchange contact information; give a name to the group and appoint a group leader for coordination; let the teacher have the group name, student ID and names as well as the leader's contact number. Students are also asked to identify their learning expectations of the course.

AT1: Outside activities and presentation (15%)

Teams are asked to carry out some outside classroom activities to apply what they learned in lectures and to present the results of work during tutorial classes in week 9 and 10. Students may use other forms of presentation (e.g. role play, debate etc.). All team members have to show up but it's not necessary for all members to do the presentation.

Major focus: ILOs 3, 4 and 5.

AT2: Tutorial exercises and activities (20%)

Students can team up to a maximum of four to work on the assigned tutorial exercises and activities. Marks will be awarded to those students who demonstrate their familiarity with literature, their preparation and understanding of the topics and, more importantly, their contributions to the assigned activities.

Major focus: ILOs 1, 2, 3 and 5; minor focus: ILOs 4 and 6.

AT3: In-class participation and discussion (10%)

Students are required to critically discuss, share and present the assigned topics. Students can pair up or work individually to participate in the discussion topics and issues. They are expected to think and learn how to engage in an exchange of ideas to construct their understanding of knowledge and not just to memorize it. Students are expected to point out agreements or disagreements, to raise appropriate questions and to brainstorm solutions to problems. Extra marks are awarded to those who can draw relevant implications to apply their daily life examples of service experiences. PDAs are required for the Q&A session.

Major focus: ILOs 1, 3, 5 and 6; minor focus: ILOs 2 and 4.

Individual work (55% AT4, AT5, AT6)

AT4: Learning log (5%)

The purposes of the learning log are to develop students' awareness of all the ILOs and learning processes; to develop their ability to reflect on learning activities; and to encourage instructors to inform students of weekly learning outcomes. Learning logs are submitted via BlackBoard.

Major focus: all ILOs.

Self-reflection on outside activities (5%)

This is the individual work component of AT1. Each student is required to prepare and submit a one-page write-up to report their self-reflection on the assigned outside activities, focusing on (a) their reflection on the subjects/topics they learned during the activities, (b) comments on their feelings about their learning experience and (c) give recommendations for further improvement.

Major focus: all ILOs.

AT5: Mid-term test (15%)

The mid-term test is scheduled during lecture session. It addresses only the first three ILOs for revision purpose and assesses the understanding of key concepts. The format is multiple-choice and/or closed-book short essays.

Major focus: ILOs 1 and 3; minor focus: ILO2.

AT6: Final exam (30%)

The final exam is a two-hour semi-closed-book in-class exam consisting of essay-type questions (both qualitative and quantitative). Students are allowed to bring in one A4-sized study aid prepared by themselves but no additional stickers or labels can be attached. Students are required to quote examples to support their arguments if appropriate.

Major focus: ILOs 5 and 6; minor focus:ILOs1 and 3.

Grading criteria

Some examples of grading criteria are shown in Table 13.7.

Table 13.7 Some examples of grading criteria for different assessment tasks in management sciences

AT2: Tutorial exercises and activities

Excellent A+ A A− 4.3 4.0 3.7	Good B+ B B− 3.3 3.0 2.7	Adequate C+ C C− 2.3 2.0 1.7	Marginal D 1.0	Failure 0.0
Clearly and correctly state most critical points and important contributions of the assigned exercises and activities Discuss issues critically Draw significant and relevant implications to Hong Kong service sector Good presentation skills Strong evidence of familiarity with literature	Clearly and correctly state some critical points and important contributions of the assigned exercises and activities Discuss issues critically Draw some relevant implications to Hong Kong service sector Good presentation skills	Clearly and correctly state some critical points and contributions of the assigned exercises and activities	State a few critical points and contributions of the assigned exercises and activities	Little or no evidence of contributions to the assigned exercises and activities

(continued)

Table 13.7 (continued)

AT4: Learning log

Excellent A+ A A– 4.3 4.0 3.7	Good B+ B B– 3.3 3.0 2.7	Adequate C+ C C– 2.3 2.0 1.7	Marginal D 1.0	Failure 0.0
Strong evidence of developing an awareness of learning expectations and processes as well as the ability to reflect on learning progress	Evidence of developing an awareness of learning expectations and processes as well as the ability to reflect on learning progress	Some evidence of developing an awareness of learning expectations and processes as well as the ability to reflect on learning progress	Sufficient organization of their learning that marginally enables the student to progress without repeating the assignment	Little or no evidence of ability to organize the learning and overall understanding of what the class is all about

AT6: Final examination

Excellent A+ A A– 4.3 4.0 3.7	Good B+ B B– 3.3 3.0 2.7	Adequate C+ C C– 2.3 2.0 1.7	Marginal D 1.0	Failure 0.0
Strong evidence of original thinking Good organization, capacity to analyse and synthesize Superior grasp of subject matter Evidence of extensive knowledge base	Evidence of grasp of subject, some evidence of critical capacity and analytic ability Reasonable understanding of issues Evidence of familiarity with literature	Student who is profiting from the university experience Understanding of the subject Ability to develop solutions to simple problems in the material	Sufficient familiarity with the subject matter to enable the student to progress without repeating the course	Little evidence of familiarity with the subject matter Weakness in critical and analytic skills Limited or irrelevant use of literature

Nursing

'Philosophy and Science of Nursing' is a one-semester core course of a two-year part-time master of nursing degree programme in the Department of Nursing Studies of the Li Ka Shing Faculty of Medicine at the University of Hong Kong. The students are practising nurses, 33 in number. The course was designed by Dr Agnes Tiwari of the Department of Nursing Studies.

Course aims

Although nursing is a practice discipline, it cannot solely rely on the accepted theories of practice. For nursing to evolve, it must continually expand its knowledge base, which should be disseminated and applied to practice. As the development of science entails the interpretation of phenomena and events, the context within which nursing science is located must be taken into account. Furthermore, the advancement of nursing science requires its practitioners to have the skills and inclination to reflect on the quality of one's thinking and to use one's critical thinking skills to engage in more thoughtful thinking and problem solving in work situations.

In this course, students will be able to develop and practice metacognitive self-correction (using one's own thinking to improve one's own thinking) while they interpret, analyse, explain and evaluate the philosophy and science of nursing within the western and Chinese context.

Intended learning outcomes (ILOs)

At the end of this module, students should be able to:

ILO1 *Explain* the nature of the philosophy of nursing and *relate* it to the western and Chinese philosophical context
ILO2 *Describe* and *reflect* on the development of nursing knowledge
ILO3 *Explain* the historical evolution of nursing science
ILO4 *Analyse* the metaparadigm of nursing in terms of nursing, health, client and environment
ILO5 *Reflect* on and *evaluate* the contemporary perspectives of nursing
ILO6 *Analyse* and *theorize* the interrelationships among nursing theory, research, practice and education

Teaching and learning activities (TLAs)

TLA1: Mini-lecture
A teacher-led mini-lecture precedes students' discussion activity. The purpose of the mini-lecture is to deliver key concepts and principles pertaining to the ensuing discussion.

TLA2: Small group discussion
Divided into small groups during the discussion activity, students develop and practise higher order cognitive skills as they *explain, analyse, reflect, evaluate* and *theorize* the philosophy and science underpinning nursing, with an aim to advance nursing practice and science from the past and present. Guidelines, framed in a series of critical thinking questions based on the ILOs of the particular class, are provided to help students conduct critical,

interactive and dialectical discussion. Through the process of discussion, not only do students acquire disciplined-based knowledge, they also practise the habit of using their own thinking to improve their own thinking (metacognitive self-correction), which is an important nursing skill as nurses must be able to form good judgment in their professional work based on their own critical thinking. The teachers act as facilitators during student-led discussion by promoting meaningful discussion but not providing answers or solutions. In addition, one of the teachers records the thought processes demonstrated by the students in a selected group using the Holistic Critical Thinking Scoring Rubric (HCTSR) (Facione and Facione 1994) as an assessment of the students' ability to think critically about an authentic issue.

TLA3: Teacher-led think-aloud

After the discussion, a teacher-led think-aloud is used to provide feedback on students' responses to the critical thinking questions in the group selected. The teacher talks through the thought processes as demonstrated by the students during their discussion based on the HCTSR measures. Given the concentrated effort of using the HCTSR in the measurement of critical thinking, only one group can be assessed in each discussion session. The other groups of students are encouraged to listen to the feedback and learn from others' experience.

Assessment tasks (ATs)

Assessment is entirely by portfolio. The student:

1 submits two items of work, each item of which may cover one or more (whole or part) of the ILOs and is limited to 2000–2500 words
2 justifies the selection of each of the items in relation to the ILOs
3 ensures that the two portfolio items jointly cover *all five* of the ILOs specified for this module.

Students are given examples of items that may be submitted but are encouraged to go beyond the list. Examples include: an action plan, book or article review, a case study, a concept map, critical incidents, learning diaries, letter-to-a-friend, reflective diary, reflective report of a group discussion and the like.

Grading criteria

The criteria used to assess the quality of students' portfolio items are given in Table 13.8. Each item is graded holistically, but as the university requires a numerical grade, the grade for each item is converted to a percentage, as in Table 13.8, and the average of the two computed – which is then converted back to a letter grade.

Table 13.8 Holistic grading for the assessment portfolio in nursing

Grade	Description	Understanding demonstrated	Evidence provided (examples)
A ≥ 70	Excellent	Understanding at an extended abstract level	Theorize about a topic Generalize to new applications Reflect on experience
B 60–69	Good	Understanding at a relational and application level	Apply theory to practice Recognize good and bad applications
C 53–59	Fair	Understanding at a multistructural declarative level	Describe nursing knowledge Explain nursing philosophy Comprehend selected nursing theories
D 50–52	Pass	Understanding at the lowest nominal level	Name the concepts or theories Focus on one conceptual issue
F ≤ 49	Fail	Fail to achieve the stated learning objectives	Miss key issues Demonstrate erroneous understanding

Comments and conclusions

The examples in this chapter illustrate possible ways of implementing constructively aligned teaching, learning and assessment under differing conditions of class size, level of teaching, disciplinary areas, various contextual conditions such as faculty regulations as to assessment and personal philosophy of the teacher. Class sizes ranged from large (over 200 students), medium (70–80 students) to small (around 30 students); mode from full-time to part-time and levels from first-year undergraduate to postgraduate. Most courses were conceived in a qualitative framework for assessment, others in a quantitative; some assessed the ILO, others the assessment task.

What all examples have in common is that the TLAs and ATs were aligned to the clearly stated ILOs on the basis of the learning verbs in each ILO.

Intended learning outcomes

All the course ILOs are derived from the course aims and are articulated in a way that identifies what students are intended to achieve through attending the course. Verbs such as *identify, describe, explain, analyse, evaluate, apply, design, reflect* and *theorize* are used to indicate the levels of understanding or performance students are expected to achieve with respect to the content areas. These ILOs include both declarative and functioning knowledge, ranging from multistructural to extended abstract in terms of their SOLO levels. In several courses, relative importance of the ILOs is reflected in the amount of teaching and learning support in the TLAs and by the weighting of the assessment tasks in deriving the final grade.

Most of these courses also include the more generic ILOs on team work and communication to address appropriate graduate attributes.

Teaching and learning activities

Several different situations were used as contexts for TLAs:

1 *Large classes of hundreds of students in traditional lecture theatres.* Examples from accounting, engineering and information systems show that even this unpromising situation can be made interactive by engaging students in student-centred learning activities such as peer discussion and learning, role play, developing concept maps, using PDA for Q&A and one-minute notes and working on work-along exercises.
2 *Small group situations.* TLAs such as small group discussions on case study and problem solving, working on tutorial exercises, while role play and think-aloud modelling were used in accounting, information systems, management sciences and nursing.
3 *Laboratory.* The laboratory context, supporting discipline-specific learning activities for functioning knowledge ILOs were used in engineering and information systems.
4 *Individual and group projects.* Individual projects were used as TLAs in engineering and group projects in information systems: in both cases, the TLA became the assessment task.
5 *Outside the classroom.* Accounting, information systems and management sciences all required students to engage in TLAs outside the classroom such as peer teaching, helpdesk, tutor consultation, individual work with PDAs, peer tutoring and field trips.
6 *Peer-assessment,* authentic to much professional practice, is used formatively as a TLA in veterinary science.

Assessment tasks

A variety of assessment tasks are used. Where departments had regulations requiring examinations, the latter were used strategically, as in point 1:

1 *Written tests and examinations.* These are used in many of these courses, but mainly to assess declarative knowledge as in such verbs as 'identify', 'describe', 'explain' and 'evaluate'. The danger, mostly avoided here, is that where regulations stipulate that x% of the final grade must be by examination, the functioning knowledge ILOs might be under-assessed.

2 *Project work* is used to assess functioning knowledge in accounting (group), engineering (individual) and information systems (group).

3 *TLA as assessment task.* Alignment is maximized when the TLA becomes the AT: critical review of research papers in the veterinary science; tutorial exercises and assignments in accounting, information systems and management sciences; and the student-centred activities (SCA) project in engineering.

4 *Portfolio assessment.* Nursing used a portfolio of two items that students chose and that had to address all ILOs.

5 *Peer-assessment* was used formatively and summatively in engineering.

Grading

Constructive alignment itself is achieved once TLAs and ATs are aligned to the ILOs. There are two remaining tasks: to turn the student's performance on a task into a grade or mark; and, after assessing individual ATs, to combine the results into a final grade. This may be done in various ways, according to the content area, the context including institutional policies and personal decision:

1 *Assessing individual performances.* Grades can be allocated by judging a students' performance top-down against established grading criteria or rubrics; or by quantitatively accruing marks bottom-up. Most courses here used judgment against grading criteria, so that the difference between grades reflected qualitative differences in performance.

2 *Deriving the final grade.* However an individual performance is assessed, it needs to be combined with other assessments to form a final grade for the student. Where marking the individual task has been done, combining results presents no problem: it is a matter of averaging the obtained results. Where the initial assessments have been made qualitatively, top-down, they can be converted into a number scale which can then be dealt with arithmetically, as in veterinary science, management sciences and nursing (see Tables 13.1, 13.7 and 13.8). Holistic assessment was not used in these examples, but an example appears in Box 11.2 (p. 224).

3 *Assessing the ILO or assessing the task.* We saw examples of both here. Assessing the task occurs in veterinary science (critical review of literature), in engineering (SCA project, examinations) and management science (tutorial tasks and participation, learning log and examination). Assessing the ILO on the basis of a variety of sources occurs in accounting, information systems and nursing. It is interesting to note that this issue is independent of the task. The same task, such as tests and examinations, can be assessed in itself, or as a source of evidence in an ILO.

We are extremely grateful to the designers of the faculty implementation of constructive alignment, and of the courses we have just visited, for allowing their inspirational work to be included here. They nicely demonstrate that, although so different in content and detail, constructively aligned teaching and learning can be implemented in so many different areas and institutional contexts: constructive alignment is a robust animal that can adapt to a variety of conditions. These courses are not here as models to be emulated in detail. Undoubtedly, they will change as a result of ongoing quality enhancement, as all good teaching does. Transformative reflection is by definition transforming. Our intention in presenting these examples is rather that they will provide ideas to fertilize your own transformative reflection about your teaching and assessment.

A final task (Task 13.1) asks you to revisit the intended outcomes that we have identified at the beginning of this edition (p. xx) and reflect on how well they have been achieved as far as you are concerned.

In the last paragraph of the previous edition of this book, the quality enhancement systems in place in the UK, Hong Kong and Australia were compared. The most staggering difference between the systems lay in the amount of money spent on teaching development. The hope was expressed that 'by the third edition of this book, these figures will have equalized: upward' (p. 289). Sad to relate, this has not been the case in purely monetary terms. There is no doubt, however, that the focus on the quality of teaching and learning has certainly been adjusted upwards in all these countries and elsewhere, as outlined in Chapter 1 of the present edition.

We hope that this trend, for institutions and systems to concern themselves about the quality of their teaching, will continue. We would further hope that the concepts and practice of outcomes-based teaching and learning, and its implementation through the reflective use of constructive alignment, will continue to play its role in this ongoing process of enhancing the quality of teaching and learning at university.

Task 13.1   Your achievement of the intended outcomes of this book

We have identified five intended outcomes for readers of this book (see page xx). We have discussed the theory and practice of designing and implementing constructively aligned teaching and learning and provided task activities for the different stages of designing and implementing constructive alignment. Now that you have finished reading the book, and hopefully have done the tasks, we would like to ask you to undergo some self-reflection and self-assessment of your achievement of these intended outcomes.

Your evaluation on achievement of intended outcome:

1 _____
_____

2 _____
_____

3 _____
_____

4 _____
_____

5 _____
_____

Your overall reflection:

1 Some of the most important things that you have gained from the book:
_____
_____
_____

2 Questions that you still have regarding designing and implementing constructive alignment:
_____
_____

3 Actions that you will take to try answer these questions:
_____
_____
_____

4 What is your intention to implement constructive alignment in your future teaching? Put a cross on the continuum to indicate your position:

_____

No intention   Definitely
to implement   intend to implement

References

Abercrombie, M.L.J. (1969) *The Anatomy of Judgment*. Harmondsworth: Penguin.

Abercrombie, M.L.J. (1980) *Aims and Techniques of Group Teaching*. London: Society for Research into Higher Education.

Airasian, P. and Madaus, G. (1972) Criterion-referenced testing in the classroom, *Measurement in Education*. Special Reports of the National Council on Measurement in Education 3, No. 4, East Lansing, MI.

Albanese, M. and Mitchell, S. (1993) Problem-based learning: a review of literature on its outcomes and implementation issues, *Academic Medicine*, 68: 52–81.

Anderson, L.W. and Krathwohl, D.R. (2001) *A Taxonomy for Learning, Teaching, and Assessing: A Revision of Bloom's Taxonomy of Educational Objectives*. New York: Addison Wesley Longman.

Ashworth, P., Bannister, P. and Thorne, P. (1997) Guilty in whose eyes? University students' perceptions of cheating and plagiarism, *Studies in Higher Education*, 22: 187–203.

Ausubel, D.P. (1968) *Educational Psychology: A Cognitive View*. New York: Holt, Rinehart & Winston.

Baillie, C. and Toohey, S. (1997) The 'power test': its impact on student learning in a materials science course for engineering students, *Assessment and Evaluation in Higher Education*, 22: 33–48.

Balchin, T. (2006) Evaluating creativity through consensual assessment, in N. Jackson, M. Oliver, M. Shaw and J. Wisdom (eds) *Developing Creativity in Higher Education: An Imaginative Curriculum*. Abingdon: Routledge.

Ballard, B. and Clanchy, J. (1997) *Teaching International Students*. Deakin, ACT: IDP Education Australia.

Barrie, S. (2004) A research-based approach to generic graduate attributes policy, *Higher Education Research and Development*, 23: 261–76.

Barrows, H.S. (1986) A taxonomy of problem-based learning methods, *Medical Education*, 20: 481–6.

Bath, D., Smith, C., Stein, S. and Swann, R. (2004) Beyond mapping and embedding graduate attributes: bringing together quality assurance and action learning to create a validated and living curriculum, *Higher Education Research and Development*, 23: 313–28.

Beach, C., Broadway, R. and McInnes, M. (2005) Higher education in Canada. www.jdi.econ.queensu.ca/

Bereiter, C. and Scardamalia, M. (1987) *The Psychology of Written Composition*. Hillsdale, NJ: Lawrence Erlbaum.

Biggs, J.B. (1973) Study behaviour and performance in objective and essay formats, *Australian Journal of Education*, 17: 157–67.

Biggs, J.B. (1979) Individual differences in study processes and the quality of learning outcomes, *Higher Education*, 8: 381–94.

Biggs, J.B. (1987a) *Student Approaches to Learning and Studying*. Hawthorn, Victoria: Australian Council for Educational Research.

Biggs, J.B. (1987b) Process and outcome in essay writing, *Research and Development in Higher Education*, 9: 114–25.

Biggs, J.B. (1993a) What do inventories of students' learning processes really measure? A theoretical review and clarification, *British Journal of Educational Psychology*, 63: 1–17.

Biggs, J.B. (1993b) From theory to practice: a cognitive systems approach, *Higher Education Research and Development*, 12: 73–86.

Biggs, J.B. (1996) Enhancing teaching through constructive alignment, *Higher Education*, 32: 1–18.

Biggs, J.B. and Collis, K.F. (1982) *Evaluating the Quality of Learning: The SOLO Taxonomy*. New York: Academic Press.

Biggs, J. and Davis, R. (eds) (2001) The subversion of Australian universities. http://www.uow.edu.au/arts/sts/bmartin/dissent/documents/sau/

Biggs, J.B., Kember, D. and Leung, D.Y.P. (2001) The Revised Two Factor Study Process Questionnaire: R-SPQ-2F, *British Journal of Educational Psychology*, 71: 133–49.

Biggs, J.B. and Moore, P.J. (1993) *The Process of Learning*. Sydney: Prentice-Hall Australia.

Billet, S. (2004) Workplace participatory practices – conceptualizing workplace as learning environments, *The Journal of Workplace Learning*, 16, 4: 312–24.

Black, P. and Wiliam, D. (1998) Assessment and classroom learning, *Assessment in Education: Principles, Policies & Practice*, 5: 5–74.

Bligh, D.A. (1972) *What's the Use of Lectures?* Harmondsworth: Penguin.

Bloom, B.S., Hastings, J.T. and Madaus, G.F. (1971) *Handbook of Formative and Summative Education of Student Learning*. New York: McGraw-Hill.

Bok, D. (2006) *Our Underachieving Colleges: A Candid Look at How Much Students Learn and Why They Should be Learning More*. Princeton, NJ: Princeton University Press.

Boud, D. (1985) *Problem-based Learning in Education for the Professions*. Sydney: Higher Education Research and Development Society of Australasia.

Boud, D. (1986) *Implementing Student Self-assessment*. Green Guide No. 5. Sydney: Higher Education Research and Development Society of Australasia.

Boud, D. (1995) *Enhancing Learning through Self-assessment*. London: Kogan Page.

Boud, D. and Feletti, G. (eds) (1997) *The Challenge of Problem-based Learning*. London: Kogan Page.

Boulton-Lewis, G.M. (1998) Applying the SOLO taxonomy to learning in higher education, in B. Dart and G. Boulton-Lewis (eds) *Teaching and Learning in Higher Education*. Camberwell, Victoria: Australian Council for Educational Research.

Boyer, E.L. (1990) *Scholarship Reconsidered: Priorities for the Professoriate*. Princeton, NJ: Carnegie Foundation for the Advancement of Teaching.

Brandenburg, D. and Ellinger, A. (2003) The future: just-in-time learning expectations and potential implications for human resource development, *Advances in Developing Human Resources*, 5, 3: 308–20.

Brew, A. (1999) Towards autonomous assessment: using self-assessment and peer-assessment, in S. Brown and A. Glasner (eds) *Assessment Matters in Higher Education*. Buckingham: Society for Research into Higher Education/Open University Press.

Brockbank, A. and McGill, I. (1998) *Facilitating Reflective Learning in Higher Education*. Buckingham: Society for Research into Higher Education/Open University Press.

Brown, S. and Glasner, A. (eds) (1999) *Assessment Matters in Higher Education*. Buckingham: Society for Research into Higher Education/Open University Press.

Brown, S. and Knight, P. (1994) *Assessing Learners in Higher Education*. London: Kogan Page.

Burns, G. and Chisholm, C. (2003) The role of work-based learning methodologies in the development of life-long engineering education in the 21st century, *Global Journal of Engineering Education*, 7, 2: 179–90.

Carless, D., Joughin, G., Liu, N.-F. and associates (2006) *How Assessment Supports Learning*. Hong Kong: Hong Kong University Press.

Chalmers, D. and Fuller, R. (1996) *Teaching for Learning at University*. London: Kogan Page.

Chalmers, D. and Kelly, B. (1997) *Peer Assisted Study Sessions (PASS)*. University of Queensland: Teaching and Educational Development Institute.

Chan, C.K.K. (2001) Promoting learning and understanding through constructivist approaches for Chinese learners, in D.A. Watkins and J. Biggs (eds) *Teaching the Chinese learner: Psychological and Pedagogical Perspectives*. Hong Kong: Comparative Education Research Centre, University of Hong Kong/Camberwell, Victoria: Australian Council for Educational Research.

Cho, P. (2007) Enhancing teaching and learning in group projects through poster assessment, in S. Frankland (ed) *Enhancing Teaching and Learning through Assessment: Deriving an Appropriate Model*. The Assessment Resource Centre, the Hong Kong Polytechnic University/the Netherlands: Springer.

Cho, P. and Tang, C. (2007) Implementation and feedback on the use of reflective writing as a component of a clinical assessment, in S. Frankland (ed) *Enhancing Teaching and Learning through Assessment: Deriving an Appropriate Model*. The Assessment Resource Centre, the Hong Kong Polytechnic University/the Netherlands: Springer.

Cohen, S.A. (1987) Instructional alignment: searching for a magic bullet, *Educational Researcher*, 16, 8: 16–20.

Cole, N.S. (1990) Conceptions of educational achievement, *Educational Researcher*, 18, 3: 2–7.

Collier, K.G. (1983) *The Management of Peer-group Learning: Syndicate Methods in Higher Education*. Guildford: Society for Research into Higher Education.

Cortazzi, M. and Jin, L. (2001) Large classes in China: 'good' teachers and interaction, in D. Watkins and J. Biggs (eds) *Teaching the Chinese Learner: Psychological and Pedagogical Perspectives*. Hong Kong: Comparative Education Research Centre, University of Hong Kong/Camberwell, Victoria: Australian Council for Educational Research.

Cowan, J. (1998) *On Becoming an Innovative Teacher*. Buckingham: Open University Press.

Cowan, J. (2002) *On Becoming an Innovative University Teacher*. Buckingham: Society for Research into Higher Education/Open University Press.

Cowan, J. (2006) How should I assess creativity?, in N. Jackson, M. Oliver, M. Shaw and J. Wisdom (eds) *Developing Creativity in Higher Education: An Imaginative Curriculum*. Abingdon: Routledge.

Crooks, T.J. (1988) The impact of classroom evaluation practices on students, *Review of Educational Research*, 58: 438–81.

D'Andrea, V. and Gosling, D. (2005) *Improving Teaching and Learning in Higher Education: A Whole Institution Approach*. Maidenhead: Open University Press/ McGraw-Hill Educational.

Dart, B. and Boulton-Lewis, G. (eds) (1998) *Teaching and Learning in Higher Education*. Camberwell, Victoria: Australian Council for Educational Research.

Davis, B.G. (1993) *Tools for Teaching*. San Francisco: Jossey-Bass.

Dearing, R. (1997) *National Committee of Inquiry into Higher Education (Dearing Report)*. Higher Education in the Learning Society, Report of the National Committee. Norwich: HMSO.

Diederich, P.B. (1974) *Measuring Growth in English*. Urbana, IL: National Council of Teachers of English.

Dienes, Z. (1997) *Student-led Tutorials: A Discussion Paper*. Falmer: School of Experimental Psychology, University of Sussex.

Donnelly, K. (2004) *Why Our Schools are Failing*. Canberra: Menzies Research Centre.

Dunkin, M. and Precians, R. (1992) Award-winning university teachers' concepts of teaching, *Higher Education*, 24: 483–502.

Ellsworth, R., Duell, O.K. and Velotta, C. (1991) Length of wait-times used by college students given unlimited wait-time intervals, *Contemporary Educational Psychology*, 16: 265–71.

Elton, L. (1987) *Teaching in Higher Education: Appraisal and Training*. London: Kogan Page.

Elton, L. (2005) Designing assessment for creativity: an imaginative curriculum guide. http://www.heacademy.ac.uk/2841.htm (click 'Lewis Elton').

Elton, L. and Cryer, P. (1992) *Teaching Large Classes*. Sheffield: University of Sheffield Teaching Development Unit.

Entwistle, N. (1997) Introduction: phenomenography in higher education, *Higher Education Research and Development*, 16: 127–34.

Entwistle, N. and Entwistle, A. (1997) Revision and the experience of understanding, in F. Marton, D. Hounsell and N. Entwistle (eds) *The Experience of Learning*. Edinburgh: Scottish Universities Press.

Entwistle, N., Kozeki, B. and Tait, H. (1989) Pupils' perceptions of school and teachers – II: relationships with motivation and approaches to learning, *British Journal of Educational Psychology*, 59: 340–50.

Entwistle, N. and Ramsden, P. (1983) *Understanding Student Learning*. London: Croom Helm.

Ewell, P.T. (1984) *The Self-regarding Institution: Information for Excellence*. Boulder, CO: National Center for Higher Education Management Systems.

Facione, P.A. and Facione, N.C. (1994) Holistic Critical Thinking Scoring Rubric (HCTSR). http://www.insightassessment.com/HCTSR.html

Falchikov, N. and Boud, D. (1989) Student self-assessment in higher education: a meta-analysis, *Review of Educational Research*, 59: 395–400.

Feather, N. (ed) (1982) *Expectations and Actions*. Hillsdale, NJ: Lawrence Erlbaum.

Feletti, G. (1997) The triple jump exercise: a case study in assessing problem solving, in G. Ryan (ed) *Learner Assessment and Program Evaluation in Problem-based Learning*. Newcastle, NSW: Australian Problem Based Learning Network.

Fox, D. (1989) Peer assessment of an essay assignment, *HERDSA News*, 11, 2: 6–7.

Frederiksen, J.R. and Collins, A. (1989) A systems approach to educational testing, *Educational Researcher*, 18, 9: 27–32.

Fullan, M. (1993) *Change Forces: Probing the Depth of Educational Reform.* London: Falmer Press.

Fuller, R. (1998) Encouraging active learning at university, *HERDSA News,* 20, 3: 1–5.

Gabrenya, W.K., Wang, Y.E. and Latane, B. (1985) Cross-cultural differences in social loafing on an optimizing task: Chinese and Americans, *Journal of Cross-cultural Psychology,* 16: 223–64.

Galton. F. (1889) *Natural Inheritance.* New York: Macmillan.

Gardner, H.W. (1993) Educating for understanding, *The American School Board Journal,* July, 20–24.

Gibbs, G. (1981a) *Teaching Students to Learn.* Milton Keynes: Open University Press.

Gibbs, G. (1981b) *Twenty Terrible Reasons for Lecturing.* Oxford: Oxford Polytechnic.

Gibbs, G. (1992) *Improving the Quality of Student Learning.* Bristol: Technical and Educational Services.

Gibbs, G. (1999) Using assessment strategically to change the way students learn, in S. Brown and A. Glasner, *Assessment Matters in Higher Education: Choosing and Using Diverse Approaches.* Buckingham: Society for Research into Higher Education/Open University Press.

Gibbs, G. (2006) On giving feedback to students. http://www.brookes.ac.uk/services/ocsd/firstwords/fw21.html

Gibbs, G., Habeshaw, S. and Habeshaw, T. (1984) *53 Interesting Ways to Teach Large Classes.* Bristol: Technical and Educational Services.

Gibbs, G. and Jenkins, A. (eds) (1992) *Teaching Large Classes in Higher Education.* London: Kogan Page.

Gibbs, G., Jenkins, A. and Wisker, G. (1992) *Assessing More Students.* Oxford: PCFC/Rewley Press.

Goodlad, S. and Hirst, B. (eds) (1990) *Explorations in Peer Tutoring.* Oxford: Blackwell.

Goodnow, J.J. (1991) Cognitive values and educational practice, in J. Biggs (ed.) *Teaching for Learning: The View from Cognitive Psychology.* Hawthorn, Victoria: Australian Council for Educational Research.

Gow, L. and Kember, D. (1990) Does higher education promote independent learning?, *Higher Education,* 19: 307–22.

Gow, L. and Kember, D. (1993) Conceptions of teaching and their relation to student learning, *British Journal of Educational Psychology,* 63: 20–33.

Guilford, J.P. (1967) *The Nature of Human Intelligence.* New York: McGraw-Hill.

Gunstone, R. and White, R. (1981) Understanding of gravity, *Science Education,* 65: 291–99.

Guskey, T. (1986) Staff development and the process of teacher change, *Educational Researcher,* 15, 5: 5–12.

Guttman, L. (1941) The quantification of a class of attributes: a theory and a method of scale construction, in P. Horst (ed) *The Prediction of Personal Adjustment.* New York: Social Science Research Council.

Hales, L.W. and Tokar, E. (1975) The effects of quality of preceding responses on the grades assigned to subsequent responses to an essay question, *Journal of Educational Measurement,* 12: 115–17.

Harris, D. and Bell, C. (1986) *Evaluating and Assessing for Learning.* London: Kogan Page.

Hattie, J.A. (2003) Teachers make a difference. http://www.arts.auckland.ac.nz/faculty/index.cfm?P=8650

Hattie, J., Biggs, J. and Purdie, N. (1996) Effects of learning skills interventions on student learning: a meta-analysis, *Review of Educational Research,* 66: 99–136.

Hattie, J. and Purdie, N. (1998) The SOLO model: addressing fundamental measurement issues, in B. Dart and G. Boulton-Lewis (eds) *Teaching and Learning in Higher Education*. Camberwell, Victoria: Australian Council for Educational Research.

Hattie, J. and Watkins, D. (1988) Preferred classroom environment and approach to learning, *British Journal of Educational Psychology*, 58: 345–9.

Hess, R.D. and Azuma, M. (1991) Cultural support for schooling: contrasts between Japan and the United States, *Educational Researcher*, 20, 9: 2–8.

Higher Education Council (1992) *Higher Education: Achieving Quality*. Canberra: Australian Government Publishing Service.

Hmelo, C.E., Gotterer, G.S. and Bransford, J.D. (1997) A theory-driven approach to assessing the cognitive effects of PBL, *Instructional Science*, 25: 387–408.

Ho, A. (2001) A conceptual change approach to university staff development, in D.A. Watkins and J.B. Biggs (eds) *Teaching the Chinese Learner: Psychological and Pedagogical Perspectives*. Hong Kong: Comparative Education Research Centre, University of Hong Kong/Camberwell, Victoria: Australian Council for Educational Research.

Holbrook, J. (1996) Using ordered-outcome items in chemistry, in J. Biggs, *Testing: To Educate or to Select?* Hong Kong: Hong Kong Educational Publishing Co.

Hudson, L. (1966) *Contrary Imaginations*. London: Methuen.

Hussey, T. and Smith, P. (2002) The trouble with learning outcomes, *Active Learning in Higher Education*, 3, 3: 220–33.

Jackson, N. (2003) Nurturing creativity through an imaginative curriculum, *Imaginative Curriculum Project*, Learning and Teaching Support Network, Higher Education Academy.

Jackson, N. (2005) Our creative enterprise, *Imaginative Curriculum Network*, Newsletter, December.

Jackson, N., Oliver, M., Shaw, M. and Wisdom, J. (eds) (2006) *Developing Creativity in Higher Education: An Imaginative Curriculum*. Abingdon: Routledge.

Johnson, D.W. and Johnson, R.T. (1990) *Learning Together and Alone: Cooperation, Competition and Individualization*. Englewood Cliffs, NJ: Prentice-Hall.

Johnston, D. (2002) Private communication.

Jones, J., Jones, A. and Ker, P. (1994) Peer tutoring for academic credit, *HERDSA News*, 16, 3: 3–5.

Jones, R.M. (1968) *Fantasy and Feeling in Education*. New York: New York University Press.

Keller, F. (1968) 'Goodbye teacher . . .', *Journal of Applied Behavior Analysis*, 1: 79–89.

Kember, D. (1998) Teaching beliefs and their impact on students' approach to learning, in B. Dart and G. Boulton-Lewis (eds) *Teaching and Learning in Higher Education*. Camberwell, Victoria: Australian Council for Educational Research.

Kember, D. (2000) *Action Learning and Action Research: Improving the Quality of Teaching and Learning*. London: Kogan Page.

Kember, D. (2001) Transforming teaching through action research, in D.A. Watkins and J.B. Biggs (eds) *Teaching the Chinese Learner: Psychological and Pedagogical Perspectives*. Hong Kong: Comparative Education Research Centre, University of Hong Kong/Camberwell, Victoria: Australian Council for Educational Research.

Kember, D. and Kelly, M. (1993) *Improving Teaching through Action Research*. Green Guide No. 14. Campbelltown, NSW: Higher Education Research and Development Society of Australasia.

Kember, D. and McKay, J. (1996) Action research into the quality of student learning: a paradigm for faculty development, *Journal of Higher Education*, 67: 528–54.

King, A. (1990) Enhancing peer interaction and learning in the classroom through reciprocal questioning, *American Educational Research Journal*, 27: 664–87.

Kingsland, A. (1995) Integrated assessment: the rhetoric and the students' view, in P. Little, M. Ostwald and G. Ryan (eds) *Research and Development in Problem-based Learning. Volume 3: Assessment and Evaluation*. Newcastle, NSW: Australian Problem Based Learning Network.

Kjos, B. (no date) Brave new schools. http://www.crossroad.to/text/articles/tnmfobe1196.html

Knapper, C. and Cropley, A. (2000) *Lifelong Learning in Higher Education*. London: Kogan Page.

Knight, P. (2006) The assessment of 'wicked' competences. http://kn.open.ac.uk/public/getfile.cfm?documentfileid=10242

Knight, P. and Trowler, P.R. (2000) Departmental level cultures and the improvement of teaching and learning, *Studies in Higher Education*, 25: 69–83.

Knight, P. and Yorke, M. (2004) *Assessment, Learning and Employability*. Buckingham: SRHE/Open University Press.

Lai, P. and Biggs, J.B. (1994) Who benefits from mastery learning?, *Contemporary Educational Psychology*, 19: 13–23.

Lai, P. and Tang, C. (1999) Constraints affecting the implementation of a problem-based learning strategy in university courses. Implementing problem-based learning. *Proceedings from the 1st Asia-Pacific Conference on Problem-Based Learning*, Hong Kong: The Problem-based Learning Project.

Lake, D. (1999) Helping students to go SOLO: teaching critical numeracy in the biological sciences, *Journal of Biological Education*, 33: 191–8.

Lane, B. (2006) Cheating study dismays dons, *The Australian: Higher Education*, 22 February.

Laurillard, D. (2002) *Rethinking University Teaching*. London: Routledge Falmer.

Leach, L., Neutze, G. and Zepke, N. (2001) Assessment and empowerment: some critical questions, *Assessment and Evaluation in Higher Education*, 26: 293–305.

Leinhardt, G., McCarthy Young, K. and Merriman, J. (1995) Integrating professional knowledge: the theory of practice and the practice of theory, *Learning and Instruction*, 5: 401–8.

Lejk, M. and Wyvill, M. (2001a) Peer assessment of contributions to a group project: a comparison of holistic and category based approaches, *Assessment and Evaluation in Higher Education*, 26: 61–72.

Lejk, M. and Wyvill, M. (2001b) The effect of inclusion of self-assessment with peer-assessment of contributions to a group project: a quantitative study of secret and agreed assessments, *Assessment and Evaluation in Higher Education*, 26: 551–62.

Lohman, D.F. (1993) Teaching and testing to develop fluid abilities, *Educational Researcher*, 22, 7: 12–23.

Lynn, L.E. (1996) *What is the Case Method? A Guide and Casebook*. Tokyo: The Foundation for Advanced Studies on International Development.

McGregor, D. (1960) *The Human Side of Enterprise*. New York: McGraw-Hill.

MacKenzie, A. and White, R. (1982) Fieldwork in geography and long-term memory structures, *American Educational Research Journal*, 19, 4: 623–32.

McKay, J. and Kember, D. (1997) Spoon feeding leads to regurgitation: a better diet can result in more digestible learning outcomes, *Higher Education Research and Development*, 16: 55–68.

McKeachie, W., Pintrich, P., Lin, Y.-G. and Smith, D. (1986) *Teaching and Learning in the College Classroom.* Lansing, MI: University of Michigan, Office of Educational Research and Improvement.

Magin, D. (2001) A novel technique for comparing the reliability of multiple peer-assessments with that of single teacher assessments of group process work, *Assessment and Evaluation in Higher Education,* 26: 139–52.

Maier, P., Barnett, L., Warren, A. and Brunner, D. (1998) *Using Technology in Teaching and Learning.* London: Kogan Page.

Maier, P. and Warren, A. (2000) *Integrating Technology in Learning and Teaching.* London: Kogan Page.

Marton, F. (1981) Phenomenography – describing conceptions of the world around us, *Instructional Science,* 10: 177–200.

Marton, F. and Booth, S.A. (1997) *Learning and Awareness.* Hillsdale, NJ: Lawrence Erlbaum.

Marton, F. and Säljö, R. (1976a) On qualitative differences in learning – I: outcome and process, *British Journal of Educational Psychology,* 46: 4–11.

Marton, F. and Säljö, R. (1976b) On qualitative differences in learning – II: outcome as a function of the learner's conception of the task, *British Journal of Educational Psychology,* 46: 115–27.

Masters, G. (1987) *New Views of Student Learning: Implications for Educational Measurement.* Research working paper 87.11. Melbourne, Victoria: University of Melbourne, Centre for the Study of Higher Education.

Masters, G.N. (1988) Partial credit model, in J.P. Keeves (ed) *Handbook of Educational Research Methodology, Measurement and Evaluation.* London: Pergamon Press.

Mazur, E. (1998) *Peer Instruction: A User's Manual.* Englewood Cliffs, NJ: Prentice-Hall.

Messick, S.J. (1989) Meaning and values in test validation: the science and ethics of assessment, *Educational Researcher,* 18, 2: 5–11.

Miller, M.A. and Ewell, P.T. (2005) *Measuring Upon College Level Learning.* San Jose, CA: National Center for Public Policy in Higher Education.

Morris, S. (2001) Too many minds miss the mark, *The Australian,* 5 September.

Moss, P.A. (1992) Shifting conceptions of validity in educational measurement: implications for performance assessment, *Review of Educational Research,* 62: 229–58.

Moss, P.A. (1994) Can there be validity without reliability? *Educational Researcher,* 23, 2: 5–12.

National Center for Supplemental Instruction (1994) *Review of Research Concerning the Effectiveness of SI.* Kansas City, MO: NCSI, University of Missouri at Kansas City.

Newble, D. and Clarke, R. (1986) The approaches to learning of students in a traditional and in an innovative problem-based medical school, *Medical Education,* 20: 267–73.

Nightingale, P., Te Wiata, I., Toohey, S., Ryan, G., Hughes, C. and Magin, D. (eds) (1996) *Assessing Learning in Universities.* Kensington, NSW: Committee for the Advancement of University Teaching/Professional Development Centre, UNSW.

Novak, J.D. (1979) Applying psychology and philosophy to the improvement of laboratory teaching, *The American Biology Teacher,* 41: 466–70.

Oliver, R. and Herrington, J. (2001) *Teaching and Learning Online: A Beginner's Guide to E-learning and E-teaching in Higher Education.* Mt Lawley, WA: Centre for Research in Information Technology and Communications, Edith Cowan University.

Petty, G. (2006) *Evidence-based Teaching.* Cheltenham: Nelson Thomas.

Piaget, J. (1950) *The Psychology of Intelligence.* London: Routledge & Kegan Paul.

Pope, N. (2001) An examination of the use of peer rating for formative assessment in the context of the theory of consumption values, *Assessment and Evaluation in Higher Education*, 26: 235–46.

Prosser, M. and Trigwell, K. (1998) *Teaching for Learning in Higher Education*. Buckingham: Open University Press.

Race, P. and Brown, S. (1993) *500 Tips for Tutors*. London: Kogan Page.

Ramsden, P. (1984) The context of learning, in F. Marton, D. Hounsell and N. Entwistle (eds) *The Experience of Learning*. Edinburgh: Scottish Academic Press.

Ramsden, P. (1991) A performance indicator for quality in higher education: the Course Experience Questionnaire, *Studies in Higher Education*, 16: 129–49.

Ramsden, P. (1992) *Learning to Teach in Higher Education*. London: Routledge.

Ramsden, P. (2003) *Learning to Teach in Higher Education*. London: Routledge.

Ramsden, P., Beswick, D. and Bowden, J. (1986) Effects of learning skills interventions on first year university students' learning, *Human Learning*, 5: 151–64.

Rangan, K. (1995) Choreographing a case class. http://www.hbsp.harvard.edu/products/cases/casemethod/rangan.pdf

Ryan, G. (1997) Promoting educational integrity in PBL programs – choosing carefully and implementing wisely, in J. Conway, R. Fisher, L. Sheridan- Burns and G. Ryan (eds) *Research and Development in Problem-based Learning. Volume 4: Integrity, Innovation, Integration*. Newcastle, NSW: Australian Problem Based Learning Network.

Saberton, S. (1985) Learning partnerships, *HERDSA News*, 7, 1: 3–5.

Salmon, G. (2003) *E-moderating: The Key to Online Teaching and Learning*. London: Kogan Page.

Santhanam, E., Leach, C. and Dawson, C. (1998) Concept mapping: how should it be introduced, and is there a long term benefit?, *Higher Education*, 35: 317–28.

Savin-Baden, M. (2000) *Problem-based Learning in Higher Education: Untold Stories*. Buckingham: Society for Research into Higher Education/Open University Press.

Scardamalia, M. and Bereiter, C. (1999) Schools as knowledge-building organizations, in D. Keating and C. Hertzman (eds) *Today's Children, Tomorrow's Society: The Developmental Health and Wealth of Nations*. New York: Guilford.

Scardamalia, M., Bereiter, C. and Lamon, M. (1994) The CSILE Project: trying to bring the classroom into World 3, in K. McGilley (ed) *Classroom Lessons: Integrating Cognitive Theory and Classroom Practice*. Cambridge, MA: MIT Press.

Schmeck, R. (ed.) (1988) *Learning Strategies and Learning Styles*. New York: Plenum.

Schon, D.A. (1983) *The Reflective Practitioner: How Professionals Think in Action*. London: Temple Smith.

Scouller, K.M. (1996) Influence of assessment methods on students' learning approaches, perceptions, and preferences: assignment essay versus short answer questions, *Research and Development in Higher Education*, 19, 3: 776–81.

Scouller, K. (1997) Students' perceptions of three assessment methods: assignment essay, multiple choice question examination, short answer examination. Paper presented to the Higher Education Research and Development Society of Australasia, Adelaide, 9–12 July.

Scouller, K. (1998) The influence of assessment method on students' learning approaches: multiple choice question examination vs. essay assignment, *Higher Education*, 35: 453–72.

Shepard, L.A. (1993) Evaluating test validity, *Review of Research in Education*, 19: 405–50.

Shuell, T.J. (1986) Cognitive conceptions of learning, *Review of Educational Research*, 56: 411–36.

Smythe, D. (2006) Research paper assignments that prevent plagiarism, in D. Carless, G. Joughin, N.-F. Liu and associates (eds) *How Assessment Supports Learning.* Hong Kong: Hong Kong University Press.

Sonnemann, U. (1954) *Existence and Therapy.* New York: Grune & Stratton.

Spady, W. (1994) *Outcome-based Education (OBE): Critical Issues and Answers.* Arlington, VA: American Association of School Administrators.

Starch, D. (1913a) Reliability of grading work in mathematics, *School Review,* 21: 254–9.

Starch, D. (1913b) Reliability of grading work in history, *School Review,* 21: 676–81.

Starch, D. and Elliott, E.C. (1912) Reliability of the grading of high school work in English, *School Review,* 20: 442–57.

Stedman, L.C. (1997) International achievement differences: an assessment of a new perspective, *Educational Researcher,* 26, 3: 4–15.

Steffe, L. and Gale, J. (eds) (1995) *Constructivism in Education.* Hillsdale, NJ: Lawrence Erlbaum.

Stenhouse, L. (1975) *Introduction to Curriculum Research and Development.* London: Heinemann Educational.

Stephenson, J. and Laycock, M. (1993) *Using Contracts in Higher Education.* London: Kogan Page.

Sternberg, R.J. and Zhang, L.F. (eds) (2001) *Perspectives on Thinking, Learning, and Cognitive Styles.* Mahwah, NJ: Lawrence Erlbaum.

Stigler, J. and Hiebert, J. (1999) *The Teaching Gap.* New York: Free Press.

Sumsion, J. and Goodfellow, J. (2004) Identifying generic skills through curriculum mapping: a critical evaluation, *Higher Education Research and Development,* 23: 329–46.

Susskind, A. (2006) Cheat wave, *The Bulletin,* Wednesday 18 October.

Tait, H., Entwistle, N.J. and McCune, V. (1998) ASSIST: a reconceptualisation of the Approaches to Study Inventory, in C. Rust (ed) *Improving Students as Learners.* Oxford: Oxford Brookes University/Oxford Centre for Staff and Learning Development.

Tang, C. (1991) Effects of two different assessment procedures on tertiary students' approaches to learning. Doctoral dissertation, University of Hong Kong. http://sunzi1.lib.hku.hk/hkuto/record/B31232413

Tang, C. (1993) Spontaneous collaborative learning: a new dimension in student learning experience?, *Higher Education Research and Development,* 12: 115–30.

Tang, C. (1996) Collaborative learning: the latent dimension in Chinese students' learning, in D. Watkins and J. Biggs (eds) *The Chinese Learner: Cultural, Psychological and Contextual Influences.* Hong Kong: Centre for Comparative Research in Education/Camberwell, Victoria: Australian Council for Educational Research.

Tang, C. (1998) Effects of collaborative learning on the quality of assessments, in B. Dart and G. Boulton-Lewis, (eds) (1998) *Teaching and Learning in Higher Education.* Camberwell, Victoria: Australian Council for Educational Research.

Tang, C. (2000) Reflective diaries as a means of facilitating and assessing reflection. Paper presented to the Pacific Rim Conference on Higher Education Planning and Assessment, Hilo, Hawaii, 3–7 June. www.ecu.edu.au/conferences/herdsa/main/papers/nonref/pdf/CatherineTang

Tang, C., Lai, P., Tang, W. et al. (1997) Developing a context-based PBL model, in J. Conway, R. Fisher, L. Sheridan-Burns and G. Ryan (eds) *Research and Development in Problem-based Learning. Volume 4: Integrity, Innovation, Integration.* Newcastle, NSW: Australian Problem Based Learning Network.

Taylor, C. (1994) Assessment for measurement or standards: the peril and promise of large-scale assessment reform, *American Educational Research Journal*, 31: 231–62.

Taylor, R. and Canfield, P. (2007) Learning to be a scholarly teaching faculty: cultural change through shared leadership, in A. Brew and J. Sachs (eds) *The Transformed University: Scholarship of Teaching and Learning in Action*. Sydney: Sydney University Press.

Thomas, E.L. and Robinson, H.A. (1982) *Improving Reading in Every Class: A Source Book for Teachers*. Boston, MA: Allyn & Bacon.

Tiwari, A., Chan, S., Sullivan, P.L., Dixon, A.S. and Tang, C. (1999) Enhancing students' critical thinking through problem-based learning. Paper presented to the 1st Asia-Pacific Conference on Problem-Based Learning, Hong Kong, 9–11 December.

Tomporowski, P.D. and Ellis, N.R. (1986) Effects of exercise on cognitive processes: a review, *Psychological Bulletin*, 99: 338–46.

Toohey, S. (2002) *Designing Courses for Universities*. Buckingham: Open University Press.

Topping, K.J. (1996) The effectiveness of peer tutoring in further and higher education: a typology and review of the literature, *Higher Education*, 32: 321–45.

Torrance, H. (ed) (1994) *Evaluating Authentic Assessment: Problems and Possibilities in New Approaches to Assessment*. Buckingham: Open University Press.

Trigwell, K. and Prosser, M. (1990) Using student learning outcome measures in the evaluation of teaching, *Research and Development in Higher Education*, 13: 390–97.

Trigwell, K. and Prosser, M. (1991) Changing approaches to teaching: a relational perspective, *Studies in Higher Education*, 22: 251–66.

Trueman, M. and Hartley, J. (1996) A comparison between the time-management skills and academic performance of mature and traditional-entry university students, *Higher Education*, 32: 199–215.

Tulving, E. (1985) How many memory systems are there?, *American Psychologist*, 40: 385–98.

Tyler, R.W. (1949) *Basic Principles of Curriculum and Instruction*. Chicago: University of Chicago Press.

Tyler, S. (2001) The perfect teaching tool? Paper presented to Learning Matters Symposium 2001, Victoria University, Melbourne, 6–7 December.

Tynjala, P. (1998) Writing as a tool for constructive learning – students' learning experiences during an experiment, *Higher Education*, 36: 209–30.

Walker, J. (1998) Student plagiarism in universities: what are we doing about it?, *Higher Education Research and Development*, 17: 89–106.

Ware, J. and Williams, R.G. (1975) The Dr Fox effect: a study of lecturer effectiveness and ratings of instruction, *Journal of Medical Education*, 50: 149–56.

Waters, L. and Johnston, C. (2004) Web-delivered, problem-based learning in organisation behaviour: a new form of CAOS, *Higher Education Research & Development*, 23, 4: 413–31.

Watkins, D. and Biggs, J. (eds) (1996) *The Chinese Learner: Cultural, Psychological and Contextual Influences*. Hong Kong: Centre for Comparative Research in Education/Camberwell, Victoria: Australian Council for Educational Research.

Watkins, D. and Hattie, J. (1985) A longitudinal study of the approach to learning of Australian tertiary students, *Human Learning*, 4: 127–42.

Watson, J. (1996) Peer assisted learning in economics at the University of NSW. Paper presented to the 4th Annual Teaching Economics Conference, Northern Territory University, Darwin, 28 June.

Watson, J. (1997) A peer support scheme in quantitative methods. Paper presented to the Biennial Conference, Professional Development Centre, University of NSW, 20 November.

Webb, G. (1997) Deconstructing deep and surface: towards a critique of phenomenography, *Higher Education*, 33: 195–212.

Weller, M. (2002) Assessment issues in a web-based course, *Assessment and Evaluation in Higher Education*, 27: 109–16.

Wiggins, G. (1989) Teaching to the (authentic) test, *Educational Leadership*, 46: 41–7.

Wilson, K. (1997) Wording it up: plagiarism and the interdiscourse of international students. Paper presented to the Annual Conference, Higher Education Research and Development Society of Australasia, Adelaide, 8–11 July.

Wiske, M.S. (ed) (1998) *Teaching for Understanding: Linking Research and Practice*. San Francisco: Jossey-Bass.

Wittenberg, H. (2006) *Current and Future Trends in Higher Education*. Commissioned by the Austrian Federal Ministry for Education, Science and Culture.

Wittrock, M.C. (1977) The generative processes of memory, in M.C. Wittrock (ed) *The Human Brain*. Englewood Cliffs, NJ: Prentice-Hall.

Wong, C.S. (1994) Using a cognitive approach to assess achievement in secondary school mathematics. Unpublished MEd dissertation, University of Hong Kong.

Yamane, D. (2006) Concept preparation assignments: a strategy for creating discussion-based courses, *Teaching Sociology*, 34: 236–48.

Yuen-Heung, J., To, D. and Ney, C. (2005) Measuring qualitative attributes: using a multidimensional approach to measure university learning goals. The 1st International Conference on Enhancing Teaching and Learning through Assessment, Hong Kong Polytechnic University, 13–15 June.

Zeng, K. (1999) *Dragon Gate: Competitive Examinations and Their Consequences*. London: Cassell.

Index

Note: Only the first author of multi-authored work is listed. Authors are not listed when only a passing reference is made to their work. *References* are not included in this Index. Terms that recur constantly, such as ILO, TLA, assessment, outcomes and so on, are indexed only when the reference is significant.

The Society for Research into Higher Education

The Society for Research into Higher Education (SRHE), an international body, exists to stimulate and coordinate research into all aspects of higher education. It aims to improve the quality of higher education through the encouragement of debate and publication on issues of policy, on the organization and management of higher education institutions, and on the curriculum, teaching and learning methods.

The Society is entirely independent and receives no subsidies, although individual events often receive sponsorship from business or industry. The Society is financed through corporate and individual subscriptions and has members from many parts of the world. It is an NGO of UNESCO.

Under the imprint *SRHE & Open University Press*, the Society is a specialist publisher of research, having over 80 titles in print. In addition to *SRHE News*, the Society's newsletter, the Society publishes three journals: *Studies in Higher Education* (three issues a year), *Higher Education Quarterly* and *Research into Higher Education Abstracts* (three issues a year).

The Society runs frequent conferences, consultations, seminars and other events. The annual conference in December is organized at and with a higher education institution. There are a growing number of networks which focus on particular areas of interest, including:

Access	FE/HE
Assessment	Graduate Employment
Consultants	New Technology for Learning
Curriculum Development	Postgraduate Issues
Eastern European	Quantitative Studies
Educational Development Research	Student Development

Benefits to members

Individual

- The opportunity to participate in the Society's networks
- Reduced rates for the annual conferences
- Free copies of *Research into Higher Education Abstracts*
- Reduced rates for *Studies in Higher Education*

- Reduced rates for *Higher Education Quarterly*
- Free online access to *Register of Members' Research Interests* – includes valuable reference material on research being pursued by the Society's members
- Free copy of occasional in-house publications, e.g. *The Thirtieth Anniversary Seminars Presented by the Vice-Presidents*
- Free copies of *SRHE News* and *International News* which inform members of the Society's activities and provides a calendar of events, with additional material provided in regular mailings
- A 35 per cent discount on all SRHE/Open University Press books
- The opportunity for you to apply for the annual research grants
- Inclusion of your research in the *Register of Members' Research Interests*

Corporate

- Reduced rates for the annual conference
- The opportunity for members of the Institution to attend SRHE's network events at reduced rates
- Free copies of *Research into Higher Education Abstracts*
- Free copies of *Studies in Higher Education*
- Free online access to *Register of Members' Research Interests* – includes valuable reference material on research being pursued by the Society's members
- Free copy of occasional in-house publications
- Free copies of *SRHE News* and *International News*
- A 35 per cent discount on all SRHE/Open University Press books
- The opportunity for members of the Institution to submit applications for the Society's research grants
- The opportunity to work with the Society and co-host conferences
- The opportunity to include in the *Register of Members' Research Interests* your Institution's research into aspects of higher education

Membership details: SRHE, 76 Portland Place, London
W1B 1NT, UK Tel: 020 7637 2766. Fax: 020 7637 2781.
email: srheoffice@srhe.ac.uk
world wide web: http://www.srhe.ac.uk./srhe/
Catalogue: SRHE & Open University Press, McGraw-Hill
Education, McGraw-Hill House, Shoppenhangers Road,
Maidenhead, Berkshire SL6 2QL. Tel: 01628 502500.
Fax: 01628 770224. email: enquiries@openup.co.uk –
web: www.openup.co.uk

Related books from Open University Press
Purchase from www.openup.co.uk or order through your local bookseller

ON BECOMING AN INNOVATIVE UNIVERSITY TEACHER
REFLECTION IN ACTION
Second Edition

John Cowan

This innovative and readable book is not something to be cherry-picked for quick hints and tips. It is a work to be read and re-read and savoured for its humanity, sagacity, practicality and reflection upon the all-important relationships between teaching and learning and the teacher and the learner.

British Journal of Educational Technology

... a delightful and unusual reflective journey ... the whole book is driven by a cycle of questions, examples, strategies and generalizations from the examples. In all, it is the clearest example of practise-what-you-preach that I have seen.

John Biggs, Honorary Professor of Psychology, University of Hong Kong

This is a unique book, written by a well-known figure in HE who has broad experience and a long track record as an exemplary and caring teacher ... The book is unique because it is written in a very personal manner, with a sharing of the author's varied experiences and great enthusiasm for the processes of teaching and communication.

Jenny Moon, Bournemouth Media Centre and Independent Consultant

[Cowan's] innovative approach to the authorship of a well researched and practical book is worthy of particular mention ... Practitioners that are keen to allow spaces for innovative approaches to professional development in learners will find this text readable and thought provoking.

Teaching in Higher Education

On Becoming an Innovative University Teacher shows readers how to plan and run innovative activities to engage their students in effective reflective learning. The book uses an unusual and accessible method: each chapter begins by posing a question with which university and college teachers can be expected to identify; then answers the question by presenting a series of examples, thereafter the writer frankly airs his own second thoughts on what he has offered.

In the second edition of this popular book, Cowan maintains his relaxed and readable style, and the book features revised coverage to make it even more accessible and useful. The examples have been updated throughout and a new chapter looks at innovation and reflection in the context of contemporary higher education.

This is key reading for all university teachers, whether new or experienced, who want to revitalise their teaching.

Contents
Preface: Why did I write this book? – Introduction – What is meant in education by 'reflecting'? – What does reflection have to offer in higher education? – On what models can we base reflective learning and teaching? – How does analytical reflection affect learning? – How does evaluative reflection affect learning? – What can we do to encourage students to reflect effectively? – How can you adapt ideas from my teaching, for yours? – Why and how should we start innovating nowadays? – How can such innovations be evaluated? – Where should you read about other work in this field? – Postscript – References – Index.

2006   240pp
978–0–335–21992–6 (Paperback)

FACILITATING REFLECTIVE LEARNING
SECOND EDITION

Anne Brockbank and Ian McGill

Praise for the previous edition:

This is a passionate and practical book

Teaching in Higher Education

This book offers valuable insights into a process for becoming a reflective learner and for developing students into reflective learners as well.

Studies in Higher Education

This significantly revised edition includes the most current thinking on reflective learning as well as stories from academics and students that bring to life the practical impact of reflection in action. Based on sound theoretical concepts, the authors offer a range of solutions for different teaching situations, taking into account factors such as group size, physical space, and technology. They also offer facilitation rather than traditional teaching methods as a productive and useful skill that helps teachers and encourages students to interact and develop reflexive skills that can be used beyond their student years.

Based on rigorous theories, *Facilitating Reflective Learning in Higher Education* offers new insights for university and college teachers seeking to enhance or diversify their practices and allows them to effectively facilitate their students' reflective learning.

Contents
*Acknowledgements to second edition – Acknowledgements to first edition – **Part I Learning and reflection** – Our themes – Learning philosophies and principles – What is learning? A review of learning theories – Requirements for reflection – Reflection and reflective practice – **Part II Facilitating learning and reflective practice** – Academic practice and learning – Methods of reflection for tutors – Methods and assessment of reflective learning – Becoming a facilitator: Enabling reflective learning – Facilitation in practice: Basic skills – Facilitation in practice: Further skills – **Part III Exemplars** – Action learning (learning sets) – Academic supervision – Mentoring – Conclusion.*

2007   192pp
978–0–335–22091–5 (Paperback)   978–0–335–22092–2 (Hardback)